D1499030

Liberalizing Foreign Trade

Volume 1

Liberalizing Foreign Trade

Edited by
Demetris Papageorgiou, Michael Michaely, and
Armeane M. Choksi

Volume 1

The Experience of Argentina, Chile, and Uruguay

ARGENTINA *Domingo Cavallo and Joaquín Cottani*
CHILE *Sergio de la Cuadra and Dominique Hachette*
URUGUAY *Edgardo Favaro and Pablo T. Spiller*

Basil Blackwell

First published 1991

Basil Blackwell, Inc.
3 Cambridge Center
Cambridge, Massachusetts 02142, USA

Basil Blackwell Ltd
108 Cowley Road, Oxford, OX4 1JF, UK

Library of Congress Cataloging in Publication Data

Liberalizing foreign trade/edited Demetris Papageorgiou, Michael Michaely, and Armeane M. Choksi.
p. cm.
Includes index.
Contents: v. 1. Liberalizing Foreign Trade. The Experience of Argentina, Chile, and Uruguay – v. 2. Liberalizing Foreign Trade. The Experience of Korea, the Philippines, and Singapore – v. 3. Liberalizing Foreign Trade. The Experience of Israel and Yugoslavia – v. 4. Liberalizing Foreign Trade. The Experience of Brazil, Colombia, and Perú – v. 5. Liberalizing Foreign Trade. The Experience of Indonesia, Pakistan, and Sri Lanka – v. 6. Liberalizing Foreign Trade. The Experience of New Zealand, Spain, and Turkey – v. 7. Liberalizing Foreign Trade. Lessons of Experience in the Developing World
ISBN 0–631–16666–1 (v. 1). ISBN 0–631–17595–4 (7-vol. set).
1. Commercial policy. 2. Free trade. 3. International trade.
I. Papageorgiou, Demetris, 1938–. II Michaely, Michael, 1928–.III. Choksi, Armeane M., 1944–.
HF 1411.L497 1989 v. 1
382′.3–dc19

88–37455
CIP

British Library Cataloguing in Publication Data

A CIP catalogue record for this book is available from the British Library.

Typeset in 10 on 12pt Times
by TecSet Ltd
Printed in Great Britain by T. J. Press Ltd., Padstow

Contents

About the Editors

Demetris Papageorgiou is the Chief of the Country Operations Division in the Brazil Department of the World Bank. He has served as a senior economist in the Country Policy Department and as an economist at the Industry Division of the Development Economics Department.

Michael Michaely is the Lead Economist in the Brazil Department of the World Bank. Previously he was the Aron and Michael Chilewich Professor of International Trade and Dean of the Faculty of Social Sciences at the Hebrew University of Jerusalem. He has published numerous books and articles on international economics.

Armeane M. Choksi is Director of the Brazil Department in the Latin American and Caribbean Region of the World Bank. He is co-editor with Demetris Papageorgiou of *Economic Liberalization in Developing Countries*, and has written on industrial and trade policy.

Editors' Preface

The General Objective

"Protection," said the British statesman Benjamin Disraeli in 1845, "is not a principle, but an expedient," and this pronouncement can serve very well as the text for our study of *trade liberalization*. The benefits of open trading have by now been sufficiently demonstrated and described by economic historians and analysts. In this study, we take them for granted and turn our minds from the "whether" to the "how."

The Delectable Mountains of open trading confront the pilgrim with formidable obstacles and there are many paths to the top. The direct route seldom turns out to be the best in practice. It may bring on rapid exhaustion and early collapse, while a more devious approach, skirting areas of excessive transition costs, may offer the best prospects of long-term survival.

Given the sharp diversity of economic background and experience between different countries, and indeed, between different periods in the same country, we should not expect the most favorable route to turn out the same for each country, except perhaps by accident. There are, however, fundamental principles underlying the diversities and it is our thesis that a survey and analysis of a sufficiently broad spectrum of countries over sufficiently long development periods may serve to uncover them.

With this object in view, we set out to study as many liberalization experiences as possible and aimed at including all liberalizations in developing countries in the post-world war period. However, the actual scope of this study had three limitations. First, we restricted the study to market-based economies. Second, experiences with highly inadequate data had to be excluded. Third, to be an appropriate object of study, an experience had to be of some minimum duration. Applying these criteria, we were left with the study of liberalization experiences in the 19 countries listed at the end of this preface. This volume deals with three of these countries (Argentina, Chile, and Uruguay). Five other volumes contain the rest of the country studies, and the seventh volume presents the synthesis of the country analyses.

Definitions

"Trade liberalization" implies any change which leads a country's trade system toward neutrality in the sense of bringing its economy closer to the situation which would prevail if there were no governmental interference in the trade system. Put in words, the new trade system confers no discernible incentives to either the importable or the exportable activities of the economy.

By "episode" we mean a period long enough to accommodate a significant run of liberalization acts terminating either in a swing away from liberalization or in a period where policy changes one way or another cease to be apparent.

The "episode of liberalization" thus defined is the unit of observation and analysis employed in each of our country studies.

Identification of Liberalization Episodes

There are three main indicators of a move in the direction of neutrality: (a) a change in the price system; (b) a change in the form of intervention; (c) changes in the foreign exchange rate.

Price system

The prices in question are nominal protection rates determining consumption patterns and, more importantly, effective protection rates affecting production activities. Any change which lowered the average level and distribution of rates of protection would count as a move toward neutrality. Typically, such a change would arise from a general reduction in tariffs, but it might also be indicated by the introduction, rather than the removal, of instruments of government intervention, or even, indeed, by the raising rather than the lowering of the incidence of government intervention. An instance of this might be the introduction of export subsidies in a protective regime previously biased against exports and favoring import substitution. Another instance might be the introduction or increase of tariffs on imported raw materials and capital goods in a regime where tariffs have previously escalated over the whole field, with the zero and lower rates applying on these imports.

Form of Intervention

The form of intervention may be affected by a change in the quantitative restriction (QR) system itself or by replacing QRs with tariffs. Although the actual changes might be assigned price *equivalents*, it is not feasible to assign price equivalents to their comprehensive effects. Moreover, the reactions they induce are so different from responses to price signals that they are better treated as a separate category.

The Exchange Rate

A change in the level of a *uniform* rate of exchange, since it does not discriminate between one tradeable activity and another, is not of itself an instrument of intervention. A move from a *multiple* to a uniform rate would, however, be equivalent to a change in intervention through commercial policy instruments; changes in the rate would modify the effect of commercial policy instruments already in being, for example, where QR systems are operated through the exchange control mechanism itself or where tariffs effective at an existing rate become redundant at a higher rate. Failing detailed studies of the impact of exchange rate changes on QRs or tariffs we take as a general rule that a formal and real *devaluation* constitutes a step towards liberalization.

Policies and Results

We do not take the actual degree of openness of the economy as an indicator in itself of a liberalization episode. Liberalization policies may commonly be expected to lead to an increase in the share of external trade but this is not an inevitable result. For instance, if, starting from a state of disequilibrium, liberalization is associated with a formal devaluation imports may actually fall. Therefore attempts to detect liberalization by reference to trade ratios rather than to policy *intentions* would be misleading. Exceptionally, however, the authors of the country studies have used trade performance as an indication of liberalization, particularly where actual changes in imports can be used to measure the degree of relaxation, or otherwise, of QRs.

Measurement of Degrees of Liberalization

In each country study we have attempted to indicate the degree of liberalization progressively attained by assigning to each year a mark for performance on a scale ranging from 1 to 20. A mark of 20 would indicate virtually free trade, or perfect neutrality, a mark of 1 would indicate the highest possible degree of intervention. These indices are subjective and peculiar to each country studied and in no way comparable between countries. They are a rough and ready measure of the progress, or otherwise, of liberalization as perceived by the authors of the country study in question. They reflect, for instance, assessments of nominal and effective rates of protection, the restrictiveness of QRs, and the gap between the formal exchange rate and its equilibrium level.

Analysis of Successful Liberalization Exercises

To arrive at criteria of what makes for success in applying liberalization policies, the following questions might be asked in our studies.

1 What is the appropriate speed and intensity of liberalization?
2 Is it desirable to have a separate policy stage of replacement of nonprice forms of trade restrictions by price measures?
3 Is it desirable to treat productive activities during the process of trade liberalization uniformly or differentially?
4 If uniform treatment is indicated, how should it be formulated?
5 On what pattern of performance of the economy is the fate of liberalization likely to hinge?
6 Is it desirable to have a stage of export promotion? If so, what should its timing be in relationship to import liberalization?
7 What are the appropriate circumstances for the introduction of a liberalization policy?
8 How important are exogenous developments in deciding the sustainability of liberalization?
9 Finally, what *other* policy measures are important, either in their existence or absence, for a successful policy of trade liberalization?

Lurking behind many of these issues are the (potential) probable costs of adjustment of a liberalization policy and, in particular, its possible impact on the employment of labor.

Scope and Intention of our Study

The general purpose of our analysis is to throw up some practical guidance for policymakers and, in particular, for policymakers in developing countries where the economic (and political) climate tends to present the greatest obstacles to successful reform. It is for this reason that (as already explained) we have based our studies on the experience of a wide spread of countries throughout the developing world. All country studies have followed a common pattern of inquiry, with the particular analytical techniques left to the discretion of the individual authors. This approach should yield inferences on the questions raised above in two different ways; via the conclusions reached in the country studies themselves, and via the synthesis of the comparative experience of trade liberalization in these countries.

The presence of a common pattern of inquiry in no way implies that all country studies cover the same questions in a uniform manner. Not all questions are of equal importance in each country and the same quantity and quality of data were not available in all countries. Naturally, the country studies differ on the issues they cover, in the form of the analysis, and in the structure of their presentation.

The country studies are self-contained. Beyond addressing the questions of the project, each study contains sufficient background material on the country's attributes and history of trade policy to be of interest to the general reader.

The 19 countries studied, classified within three major regions, are as follows.

Latin America

Argentina	by Domingo Cavallo and Joaquín Cottani
Brazil	by Donald V. Coes
Chile	by Sergio de la Cuadra and Dominique Hachette
Colombia	by Jorge García García
Peru	by Julio J. Nogués
Uruguay	by Edgardo Favaro and Pablo T. Spiller

Asia and the Pacific

Indonesia	by Mark M. Pitt
Korea	by Kwang Suk Kim
New Zealand	by Anthony C. Rayner and Ralph Lattimore
Pakistan	by Stephen Guisinger and Gerald Scully
Philippines	by Florian Alburo and Geoffrey Shepherd
Singapore	by Bee-Yan Aw
Sri Lanka	by Andrew G. Cuthbertson and Premachandra Athukorala

The Mediterranean

Greece	by George C. Kottis
Israel	by Nadav Halevi and Joseph Baruh

Portugal	by Jorge B. de Macedo, Cristina Corado, and Manuel L. Porto
Spain	by Guillermo de la Dehesa, José Juan Ruiz, and Angel Torres
Turkey	by Tercan Baysan and Charles Blitzer
Yugoslavia	by Oli Havrylyshyn

Coordination of the Project

Armeane M. Choksi, Michael Michaely, and Demetris Papageorgiou, of the World Bank's Latin American and Caribbean Region, are the directors of this research project. Participants in the project met frequently to exchange views. Before the country studies were launched, the common framework of the study was discussed extensively at a plenary conference. Another plenary conference was held to discuss early versions of the completed country studies, as well as some emerging general inferences. In between, three regional meetings were held to review phases of the work under way. An external Review Board consisting of Robert Baldwin (University of Wisconsin), Mario Blejer (International Monetary Fund), Jacob Frenkel (University of Chicago and Director of Research, International Monetary Fund), Arnold Harberger (University of Chicago and University of California – Los Angeles), Richard Snape (Monash University), and Martin Wolf (Chief Economic Leader Writer, Financial Times) contributed to the reviewing process of the country studies and of the synthesis volume.

Argentina, Chile, and Uruguay are presented in this volume. The series' other publications are the following:

Volume 2: Liberalizing Foreign Trade. The Experience of Korea, the Philippines, and Singapore;
Volume 3: Liberalizing Foreign Trade. The Experience of Israel and Yugoslavia;
Volume 4: Liberalizing Foreign Trade. The Experience of Brazil, Colombia, and Perú;
Volume 5: Liberalizing Foreign Trade. The Experience of Indonesia, Pakistan, and Sri Lanka;
Volume 6: Liberalizing Foreign Trade. The Experience of New Zealand, Spain, and Turkey;
Volume 7: Liberalizing Foreign Trade. Lessons of Experience in the Developing World

Demetris Papageorgiou, Michael Michaely, Armeane Choksi

Part I

Argentina

Domingo Cavallo
Director,
Fundación Mediterranea, Argentina
and
Minister of Foreign Relations, Argentina

Joaquín Cottani
Fundación Mediterranea, Argentina
and
The World Bank, Washington, D.C.

Contents

List of Figures

List of Tables

Acknowledgments

Several people deserve our deepest gratitude. Our colleagues at Instituto de Estudios Económicos sobre la Realidad Argentina y Latinoamericana (IEERAL), Carlos Sánchez and José Luis Arrufat (labor markets) and Raúl García (econometric methods), contributed their expertise at several stages of this work. Jorge Ingaramo was an excellent research assistant, who also provided invaluable suggestions for improving the first three chapters. Adolfo Sturzenegger, Carlos Givogri, Aldo Arnaudo, Aldo Dadone, and Wylian Otrera also read the manuscript and made useful comments.

Special thanks are, of course, due to the World Bank specialists who participated in the four meetings where preliminary drafts were presented. The feedback we received from project co-directors Michael Michaely, Armeane Choksi, and Demetris Papageorgiou substantially improved these drafts, while the enlightening comments of Arnold Harberger, Deepak Lal, Ian Little, Mario Blejer, Donald Coes, Dominique Hachette, and Nadav Halevi helped us to refine the analysis and to clarify certain complex sections of the text. Any remaining errors are our sole responsibility.

The organization of the manuscript would have been much more difficult had it not been for the extraordinary efficiency of the IEERAL word processor operators Mabel Juárez, Ana María Vitale, and Silvia Ochoa. In addition, our visits to Washington and to World Bank meetings at Buenos Aires, Santiago, Salvador, and Lisbon would have been less valuable had it not been for the assistance of Isabelle Kim and Maria Lozos.

Introduction

Argentina's economic performance from 1860 to 1929, while it followed an export-led growth strategy, was impressive. In contrast, stagnation and high inflation became endemic under the import substitution model followed after the Great Depression. In 1976 a strong government decided to transform the country into a market economy fully integrated in world trade and finance. The plan, however, failed completely. Within less than five years the reversal of liberalization policies had begun. This study focuses on this major liberalization attempt and the reasons for its failure, paying particular attention to the timing and sequencing of trade liberalization and the role of accompanying policies.

Our investigation begins with a long-term overview of trade policies and growth; an index of liberalization for the period 1950–83 is constructed against this backdrop (chapter 1). Chapters 2 and 3 contain detailed descriptions of the two principal liberalization episodes: the Krieger-Vasena episode (1967–70) and the Martínez de Hoz episode (1976–81). In each case we look at the joint effects of structural reforms and stabilization on macroeconomic performance and resource allocation. In chapter 4 we examine the critical role of economic policy in the later episode's reversal after 1981, with particular emphasis on the causes of the real appreciation of the domestic currency as the major determinant of this reversal. Finally, in chapter 5 we summarize the inferences or conclusions that can be drawn from the Argentine experience. Three aspects of policy implementation emerge from the analysis as fundamental to understanding the Argentine experience: the sequencing of export and import liberalization, the timing of financial liberalization, and the synchronization between liberalization and stabilization.

The study includes three appendices. The method used for estimating real effective exchange rates for exports and imports is described in appendix 1. The behavior of output, employment, and imports in various agricultural and manufacturing activities is examined in a more disaggregated fashion in appendix 2. A formal econometric model and some simulations used to estimate the effect of different determinants of real exchange rate behavior on real appreciation between 1976 and 1981, as reported in chapter 4, are presented in appendix 3.

1

Long-term Overview of Trade Policies and Growth

Argentina, located in South America's southern cone, has a territorial area of 2.8 million km^2 and a population of 30 million. More than one third of the population live in Greater Buenos Aires.

The pampas produce most of the cereals and beef destined for domestic consumption and export. Some of the main industrial cities are concentrated there, spread along the industrial belt of the Paraná river.

Argentina is a developing country. Per capita income is slightly above US$2,000 and has grown at an annual rate of only 2 percent on average between 1960 and 1980. Although almost 80 percent of all exports are either primary agricultural products or manufactures of agricultural origin, by the 1970s agriculture contributed only 13 percent of gross domestic product (GDP). Moreover, its share has eroded steadily since 1950. The participation of manufacturing in GDP increased from 28 percent during 1950–4 to 34 percent during 1965–9. Since that time it has decreased to 27 percent. The sectors producing primary and manufactured goods (potentially tradeables) have become less important during the 1970s in favor of construction and services (which produce nontradeable goods). This change in structure has arisen not from a normal process of growth and development but, on the contrary, from the failure of tradeable sectors to achieve sustained expansion.

From Export-led Growth to Import Substitution

From around 1860, Argentina's economy grew rapidly, led by burgeoning agricultural exports. Until 1880, production of traditional commodities such as hides, tallow, and wood expanded considerably. During 1880–1900 domestic production increased in variety, substituting for imports of foodstuffs and building materials, but the most remarkable feature of the period was the huge increase in grain exports as the frontier of marginal lands was expanded. Sheep and cattle raising grew considerably as well, and the country exported livestock until technological improvements made it possible to sell frozen and chilled beef abroad after 1900.

Exports expanded at an annual rate of about 5 percent between 1875 and 1914, and somewhat more slowly between 1914 and 1929. The reasons for this boom are to be found in an efficient allocation of resources. Land was abundantly available and its shadow price was small, making intensive land use profitable. Labor immigrated from other countries, and foreign capital inflows financed railroad construction, infrastructure and other investments associated with exports. The country adopted an almost free-trade strategy with full integration into world markets. Such taxes on imports and exports as existed were levied mainly to collect revenue.

The characteristics of export-led growth in Argentina – intensive use of natural resources, changes in export structure to achieve permanence in external stimuli, and influx of capital and labor from abroad – are common to the "staples" model of trade and growth. In this sense, Argentina resembles other countries of recent settlement, like Canada and Australia, which grew considerably before the Great Depression under the influence of primary exports ("staples" in growth theory jargon). Historical evidence does not support the thesis that rural interests inhibited industrial surge. it seem unquestionable that trade specialization was the natural response to comparative advantages in the rural sector.

Before 1930, manufacturing was limited to export-related branches. International conditions changed in 1929: according to Economic Commission for Latin America (ECLA) estimates, terms of trade deteriorated by 33 percent between 1925–9 and 1930–4 and the volume of exports fell by about 6 percent. As a result, imports decreased by 40 percent, providing an incentive to substitute domestic production for imports. Fiscal policy acted countercyclically, especially after 1935, and both exchange rate and commercial policies which tended to improve the internal terms of trade of manufacturing with respect to agriculture were adopted. These measures proved to be a powerful stimulus to local manufacturing, which achieved an annual expansion rate of 3.4 percent in 1929–43. The external terms of trade improved after 1934 and the volume of exports was maintained, thanks to the efforts of the government to preserve traditional markets.

Import substitution proceeded in stages; 1929–48 is generally regarded as the first stage. The light or "easy" branches, that is, foodstuffs, textiles, clothing, and leather products, were industrialized mostly in the second half of the 1930s when the authorities combined exchange rate devaluation with import duties to protect infant industries. World War II slowed down manufacturing growth, because of restrictions on imports of capital goods, but conditions were favorable for exports, which expanded.

Changes in political orientation after 1945 brought neglect of exports: import substitution had to take over the burden of achieving a reasonable rate of growth consistent with external balance. The poor performance of the export sector was rooted in domestic policy conditions: while external terms of trade improved by 24 percent between 1935–9 and 1947–9, the internal terms of trade fell by 20 percent as a result of high tariffs.

Import substitution lacked the dynamism required to avoid foreign exchange shortages; recurrent balance-of-payments disequilibria were the result. The Perón years (1946–55) were not characterized, as is commonly believed, by a significant industrial surge; most of the emphasis was on improving the production of nontradeable services at the expense of tradeable goods. Moreover, economic policies failed to facilitate the transition from light branches of manufacturing to those that required more capital intensive technologies.

The new government that came to power in 1955 improved internal terms of trade to promote agricultural exports. The economy adopted a trade system less closed than under Perón but not as open as before the Great Depression. Unfortunately, Argentine history since 1955 has been marked by political instability, frequent changes in relative prices, and balance-of-payments disequilibria. Despite the efforts of the authorities to eliminate foreign exchange bottlenecks, import capacity has continuously constrained industrial output, giving rise to classic stop–go cycles. Domestic industrialization increased the demand for imports of capital goods and inputs at the expense of consumer goods. As a consequence, imports became less elastic with respect to relative prices and more elastic with respect to income, thereby aggravating the external bottleneck. For many years, recurrent external crises, bringing in their wake substantial recessions, have limited internal growth.

The shift to import substitution changed the trends of several economic indicators. The reduced openness is clear from figure 1.1; figure 1.2 depicts the development of exports, agricultural value added and government services, and total GDP. Up to the 1940s, total exports and agricultural value added had long-term rates of growth similar to that of the overall GDP. The same was true for government services. Between 1940 and the early 1950s, agriculture stagnated, exports declined sharply, and government services expanded very rapidly. Agricultural performance improved after the early 1950s, although somewhat more slowly than in earlier decades. Exports expanded again, while government value added grew less quickly than in the preceding period. These trends are related to the behavior of relative prices. The real agriculture and nonagriculture prices reported in figure 1.3 help to explain the sector stagnation which started during the 1930s.

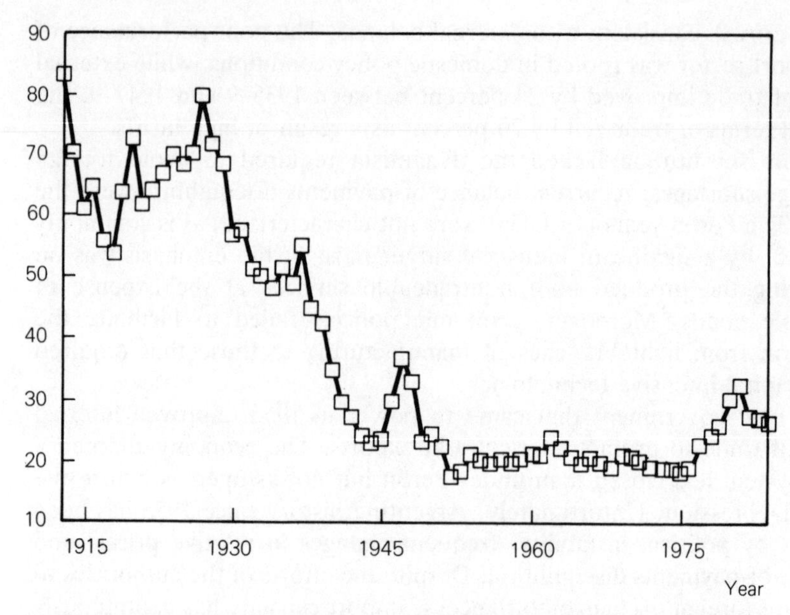

Figure 1.1 Degree of openness: imports plus exports over GDP, constant prices, 1913–1984

Source: IEERAL (Instituto de Estudios Económicos sobre la Realidad Argentina y Latinoamericana) (1986)

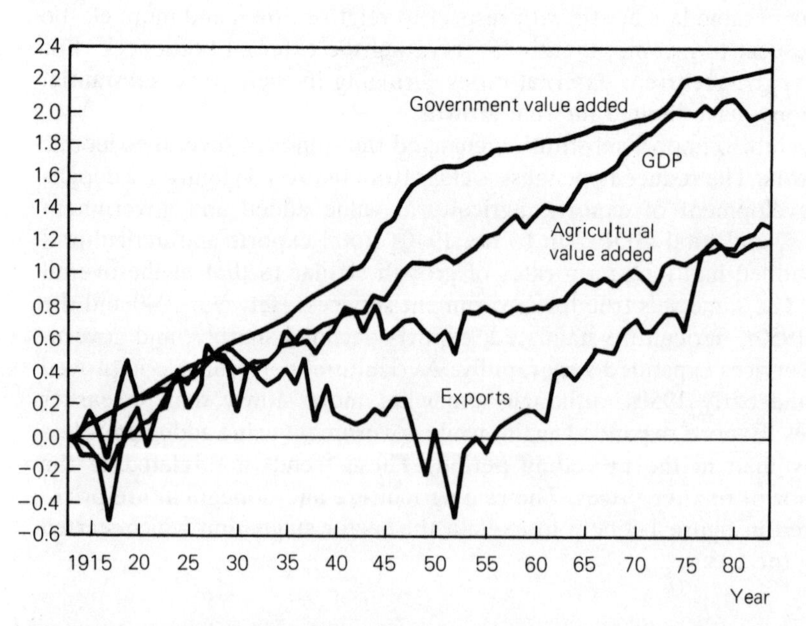

Figure 1.2 Indices of GDP, value added by government, agriculture, and exports, 1913–1984 (logarithmic scale 1913=0)

Source: Cavallo (1985b)

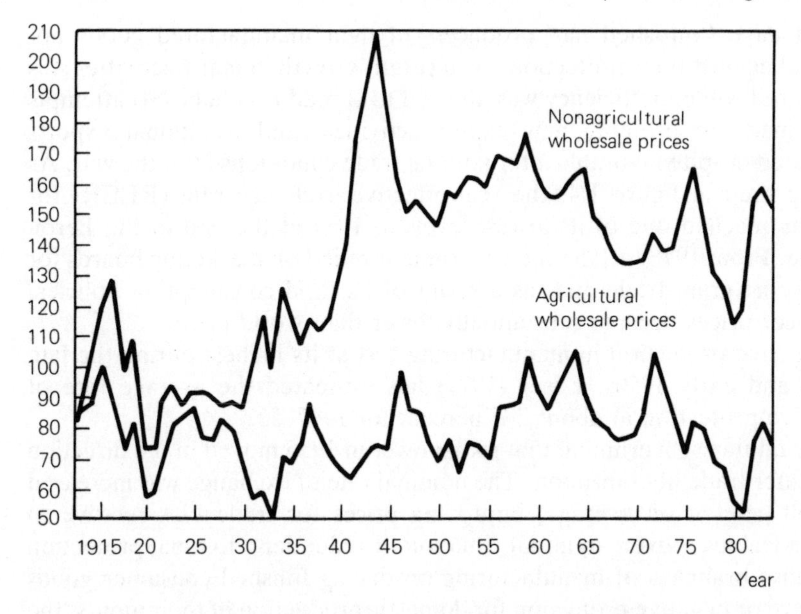

Figure 1.3 Relative prices of agricultural and nonagricultural tradeable goods with respect to the price of domestic goods, 1913–1984. The consumer price index is used as deflator
Consumer price index used as deflator.
Source: Cavallo (1985b)

Changes in Commercial Policies, 1950–1975

The protectionist system gained momentum in 1948–53 during the Peronist regime. Students of Argentine history have long questioned the commercial policy of those years (see for example Díaz-Alejandro, 1970; Mallon and Sourrouille, 1975). The policy, they say, overprotected existing branches of manufacturing that had practically exhausted their import substitution potential by 1945. Prohibitive tariffs, often accompanied by import restrictions or outright prohibitions, virtually isolated finished consumer good industries from foreign competition; their effective protection was further increased by subsidized inputs. The principal instruments of the policy were import licenses, exchange permits, and overvalued exchange rates.

The multiple exchange rate system discriminated against exports of both traditional agricultural and nontraditional manufactured goods, while favoring so-called "essential" imports including basic metals, fuel, intermediate inputs, and spare parts, as well as capital goods required by the industries that had grown and consolidated during the war. Many of these inputs could have been produced at home, and industries producing them would have flourished had producers of light manufactured goods not lobbied against their protection. As a result, growth in many activities was hampered while inefficiency was allowed to spread in others. No attempts were made to promote new export activities, and traditional exports stagnated despite favorable international trade conditions after the war. As can be seen in figure 1.4, the real effective exchange rate (REER) for exports reached one of its lowest levels in 1954 at the end of the Perón regime. From 1946 to 1955 the government relied on marketing boards for the export grain trade and, as a result of its food consumption policies, producer prices became substantially lower than world prices.

Effective protection in manufacturing was at its highest during the late 1940s and early 1950s. Loser (1971) has estimated the average rate of effective protection at about 295 percent for 1947–52.

The military government that took power in 1955 moved in the direction of greater trade liberalization. The nominal rate of exchange was increased by 150 percent on average, improving prices for tradeables relative to nontradeables. Given an initial situation of redundant nominal protection for those branches of manufacturing producing finished consumer goods and zero or negative protection for domestic production of their inputs, the impact of devaluation perhaps reduced effective protection in well-established activities. Other measures helped to create a more liberal

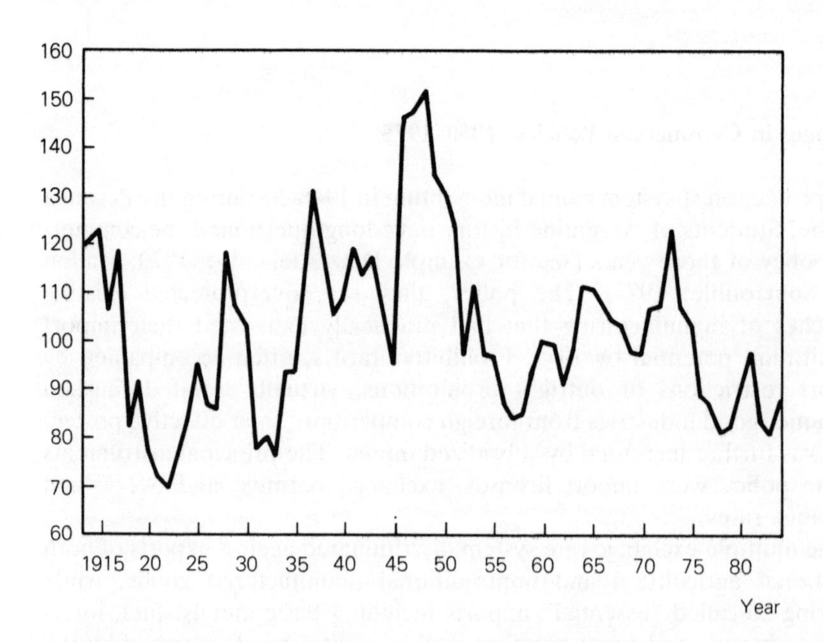

Figure 1.4 Real effective exchange rate of exports, 1913–1984
Source: Cavallo (1985b)

atmosphere than that of the Peronist period: bilateralism was replaced by multilateral arrangements, foreign investment was encouraged, and the state monopoly of the grain trade was discontinued.

By 1959, Argentine import tariffs were higher not only than those of industrialized countries but also than those of other protectionist Latin American nations such as Brazil and Chile. Macario (1964) has found the weighted average of nominal duties to be as high as 151 percent. However, as pointed out by Díaz-Alejandro (1970, p. 272), more than half the imports entered duty free owing to exemptions and special regimes.

The government of Arturo Frondizi, elected in 1958, launched an industrialization plan based on the development of "basic" industries and high-technology branches of manufacturing (oil refining, steel, cars, chemicals, paper, and so on) and on the intensive exploitation of mineral resources. Direct foreign investment was explicitly encouraged to stimulate these activities. The new industries not only were protected from foreign competitors by tariffs and import restrictions, but were also allowed to import capital goods and inputs at very low or zero tariffs in virtually unlimited quantities. As a result, the import coefficient rose for the economy as a whole and the aggregate capital-to-labor ratio increased.

The surge in imports during the period 1958–62 did not indicate significant trade liberalization. The protectionist system simply extended the use of trade-restrictive instruments to promote new activities. Up to then, commercial policies had simply responded to the demands of established pressure groups. From 1958 to 1962, however, commercial policies were tailored to the needs of an official strategy designed to attract foreign capital and expand heavier manufacturing branches. Once these branches were established, new pressure groups were created which fought to defend the new status quo, thus further confusing an already haphazard set of commercial policies. In Díaz-Alejandro's words, "new industrialization policies induced fresh resource misallocations" (Díaz-Alejandro, 1970, p. 271).

Massive devaluations were needed in 1959 and 1962 to cope with external crises. Since devaluations were accompanied by monetary restraint, they enormously contracted real output, especially in 1959 when the GDP fell by 6.5 percent.

The trade balance yielded surpluses from 1963 to 1966 under the Presidency of Arturo Illia of the Radical Party. However, this improvement in external conditions was achieved mainly by keeping import restrictions high and, to a lesser extent, by promoting some exports. In fact, the introduction of compensatory tax incentives to industrial exports dates from this period.

By 1966 the protectionist system was less restrictive than that which had existed during the late 1940s and early 1950s, mainly because quantitative restrictions (QRs) decreased. However, both the level and the variance of

Table 1.1 Legal tariffs for a sample of industries in 1966

Sectors	*Tariffs*
Fuel and electricity	91
Foodstuffs and beverages	139
Tobacco	175
Textiles	71
Clothing	306
Paper	206
Chemical products	197
Rubber	190
Leather	239
Glass, stones, and ceramics	209
Metals	212
Iron and steel	173
Vehicles and nonelectrical machinery	186
Automobiles and tractors	521
Electrical machinery	207
Average	181

Source: CONADE (Consejo Nacional de Desarrollo, 1967); cited in FIEL (Fundación de Investigaciones Económicas Latinoamericanas), 1980

tariffs were still very high, as is shown in table 1.1. Several nontariff regulations complicated the picture: official customs prices, advance deposits on imports, and profuse use of tariff exemptions. The first noticeable reduction in tariffs since the war took place in 1967 under the *de facto* government of General Onganía and the economic administration of Adalbert Krieger-Vasena. To compensate partially for the effect of a 40 percent devaluation on domestic prices, *ad valorem* import duties were reduced to about half their previous level.[1] Although it is unlikely that tariff reductions really exposed domestic producers of manufactures to increased foreign competition (the levels of most tariffs were just too high), the reform did mean a movement towards rationalization of the tariff structure which was reflected in a lower variance of tariffs among sectors. Along with the devaluation, the government imposed taxes on traditional exports of 25 percent, 20 percent, and 16 percent, depending on the product. These taxes were gradually reduced later. In addition, subsidies to nontraditional exports were eliminated, along with deposit requirements on imports. Bans were lifted on all but a specific list of commodities.

1 Taking a simple average, tariffs decreased from 119 percent to 61 percent (see FIEL, 1980, p. 68).

The structure of nominal and effective protection which resulted from the 1967 tariff reform has been well documented in a detailed study by Berlinsky and Schydlowsky (1977). According to the data presented by these authors (see chapter 2, table 2.10), the Argentine economy was far from liberalized by 1969, even though average protection had decreased significantly in relation to previous years. The effective protection rate (EPR) was 97 percent for manufacturing and −13 percent for agriculture. Import-competing manufacturing activities were protected with a rate of about 130 percent. Two main characteristics emerge from the study:

1. EPRs to value added were, in general, higher than nominal protection rates (NPRs);
2. export incentives were (highly) negative.

The first characteristic simply reflects the fact that nominal tariffs on finished goods are higher than tariffs on inputs. The second feature of the system is clear evidence of the anti-export bias found by many authors commenting on the Argentine case (see, for example, Berlinsky and Schydlowsky, 1977; Nogués, 1983). In addition to tariffs, the protective system still included import prohibitions on some goods (notably automobiles, tractors, and car engines) along with import quotas and licenses, special tariff exemptions, and prior deposit requirements.

To produce any lasting effect, the process of trade liberalization initiated in 1967 needed to be intensified; in fact, however, there is evidence that protectionism increased between 1969 and 1976. QRs were extensively used during this period. By 1976, there were import prohibitions on 734 different commodities and import licenses protecting the production of many commodities. More than 3,800 items were subject to a previous six-month deposit of some 40 percent of the cost, insurance, and freight (c.i.f.) value of imports. Under conditions of rising inflation, this meant a significant increase in import costs. Multiple exchange rates were instituted again in 1971. The higher effective rates were for imports and nontraditional exports, and the lower were for traditional exports. Real exchange rates (RERs) appreciated during 1971–5, thereby depressing the relative price of tradeables. In sum, the anti-export bias became stronger as a result of exchange and commercial policies.

A Frustrated Move toward Liberalization

In March 1976, a new military government took power and the appointed economic team, led by José Martínez de Hoz, started what can be considered as the first and only significant attempt at trade liberalization in Argentina's history.

By that time, Argentina was a repressed economy, both commercially and financially. This condition, far from being new, was almost chronic, as can be inferred from figure 1.5. The data reveal that domestic terms of trade have been systematically lower than external terms of trade – the outcome of implicit or explicit taxes on trade arising from import and export restrictions. Trade was not, however, the only activity to suffer economic repression; financial policy was similarly repressive. Domestic interest rates were subject to low ceilings and exchange controls were imposed to prevent capital from migrating abroad. High inflation made for negative real interest rates, with a consequent decline in money demand, as illustrated in figure 1.6. Inflation, in turn, was high because of very large and persistent fiscal deficits financed by domestic credit creation (figure 1.7).

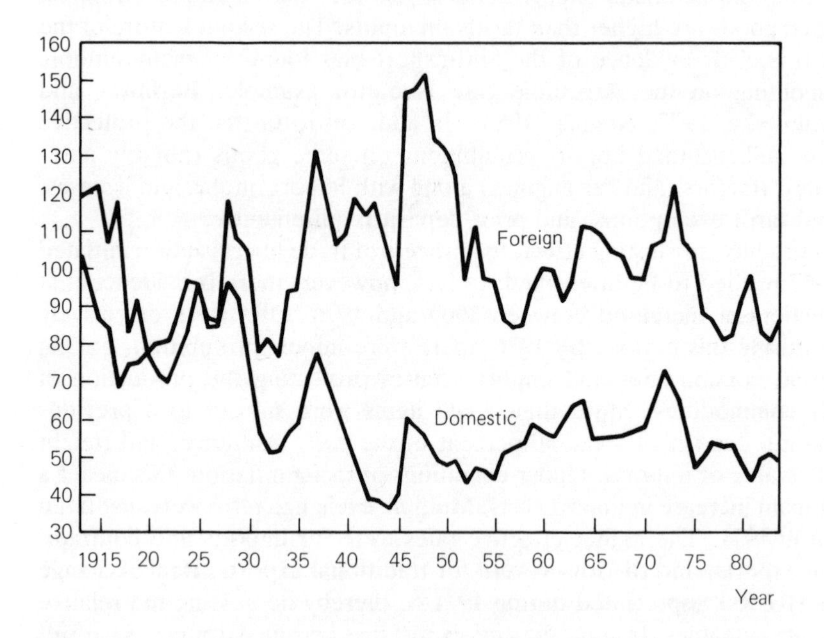

Figure 1.5 Foreign and domestic terms of trade, 1913–1984
Source: Cavallo (1985b)

The Martínez de Hoz administration (1976–81) was firmly committed to economic liberalization, with the particular goal of reversing the excessive government intervention that had characterized the Peronist regime. In April 1976, immediately following the military coup, controls on domestic prices were eliminated. Exchange rate unification was achieved by the end of 1976, at which time the black market disappeared. The financial

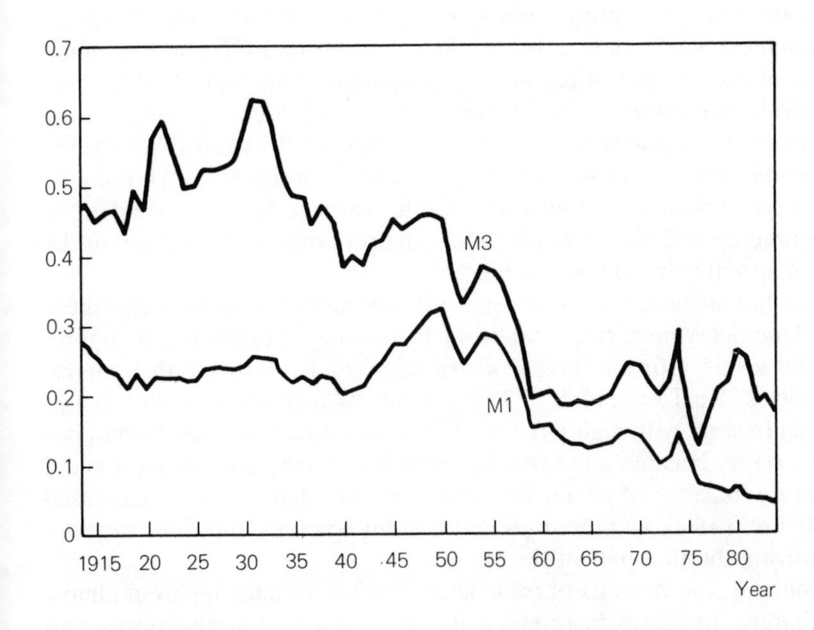

Figure 1.6 M1 and M3 as proportions of gross domestic product in current prices, 1913–1984
Source: Cavallo (1985b)

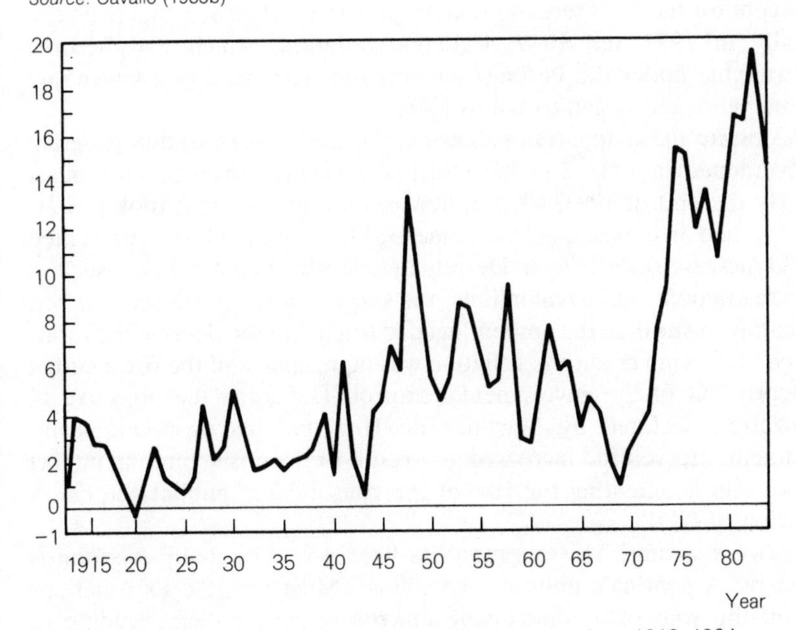

Figure 1.7 Ratio of the fiscal deficit to gross domestic product, 1913–1984
Source: Cavallo (1985b)

reform of June 1977 lifted ceilings on domestic interest rates. Taxes on traditional exports were practically eliminated during 1977, and the capital account of the balance of payments was opened at the end of 1978.

Import liberalization was much more gradual and discriminatory, but the trade account reached record levels of openness in 1979 and 1980. During those years, most QRs had been eliminated and, for most sectors, nominal tariffs were at their lowest historical levels. Tariff reduction was intended to continue up to 1984, at which time some proportional escalation in the nominal structure would be retained.

Trade liberalization in Argentina did not incur the usual adjustment costs. Unemployment rates, far from increasing, actually fell to unprecedented levels. Nor did income distribution goals conflict with commercial policies. Real wages fell in 1976, mainly as a result of wage controls designed to cope with high inflation, but increased again in 1979 and after as wage policy became more flexible. Initially, the increase in imports did not create balance-of-payments problems. Foreign reserves increased steadily up to 1980, and the trade and current accounts improved substantially during the first part of the episode.

In contrast, the benefits of trade liberalization became apparent almost immediately. Increases in productivity were observed in agriculture and manufacturing, while consumer gains were evident in the case of many tradeable products. Investment rates were relatively high during the period and, except for the 1978 recession, GDP growth reached acceptable levels, especially in 1977 and 1979. Endemic inflation, which had become uncontrollable under the Peronist government, stabilized at a lower rate for some years and began to fall in 1980.

Yet, despite these apparent successes, the trade liberalization program was abandoned in 1981–2 in the midst of a severe balance-of-payments crisis. By the end of 1983, when a new civilian government took power, Argentina had an external debt of some US$45 billion,[2] which represented a sixfold increase since 1975–6. Despite drastic adjustment policies, such as import restrictions and devaluations, the surplus in the trade account was significantly lower than the amount needed to service the debt on the terms required by foreign creditors. Inflation was high again and the fiscal deficit was clearly out of the government's control. Defeating the objective of liberalization declared by Martínez de Hoz and his economic team, government intervention increased as a result of the crisis, limiting import activities and augmenting the size of the consolidated public sector as a proportion of GDP.

What went wrong? This question has been posed by many economists puzzled by Argentina's unusual experience. Most sensible explanations focus on the role of accompanying macroeconomic policies leading to

2 Billion, thousand million throughout; dollars, US dollars throughout.

excessive real appreciation of the peso. During the trade liberalization episode, several attempts were made to reduce inflation gradually. Domestic macro policies were thus geared to this objective rather than to the needs of the trade liberalization program. Real appreciation was the direct consequence of the lack of coordination among the fiscal, monetary, and exchange rate policies used to disinflate; however, as we argue in chapter 4, the timing and sequencing of liberalization reforms may also have been a source of undesired fluctuations in the real exchange rate.

Index of Trade Liberalization, 1950–1983

The long-term pattern of commercial policies since 1950 is summarized in figure 1.8 through the construction of an index of trade liberalization. This index is ordinal and has been drawn on a scale ranging from 1 to 20, with 1 representing the most highly controlled trade regime and 20 indicating a free-trade scenario. Thus an increase in export or import taxes, QRs and direct government intervention in foreign trade reduces the index, and vice versa. The indicator is, of course, highly subjective and does not correspond to any well-defined economic variable but to a combination of qualitative and quantitative aspects of trade.

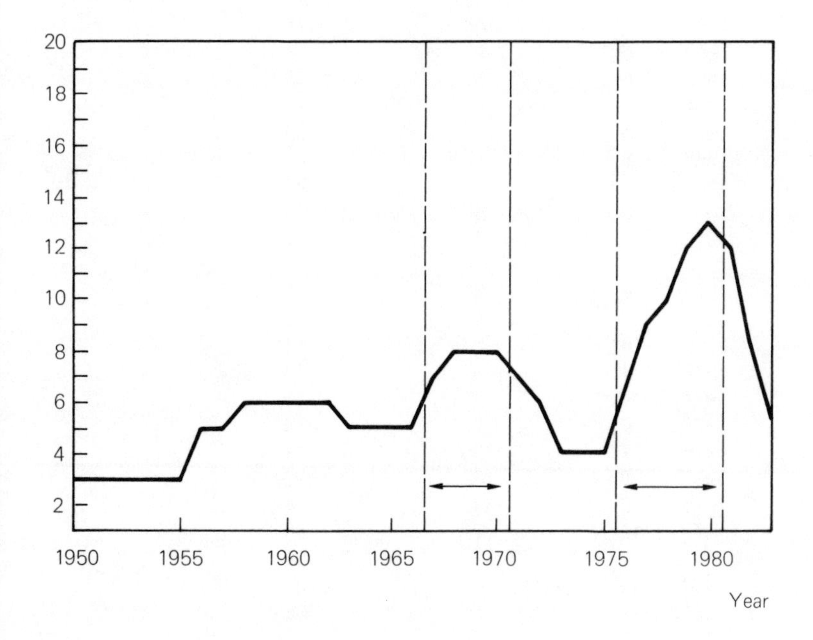

Figure 1.8 Index of liberalization, 1950–1983
Source: Own elaboration (as explained in text)

One of the quantitative indicators used in the construction of the index is the gap between the external and the internal terms of trade shown in figure 1.5 and table 1.2. When this gap increases, either implicit tariffs on imports or implicit taxes on exports are higher, accounting for a rise in the antitrade bias (a fall in the index of liberalization). During the early 1950s, this bias was high but decreasing (a peak had been observed by the late

Table 1.2 Index of liberalization, terms-of-trade gap, and degree of openness, 1950–1983

Year	*Index of liberalization*	*Terms-of-trade gap (%)*	*Degree of openness (%)*
1950	3	84	24
1951	3	76	23
1952	3	55	18
1953	3	64	18
1954	3	51	21
1955	3	53	20
1956	5	36	20
1957	5	32	21
1958	6	32	20
1959	6	36	21
1960	6	43	21
1961	6	44	21
1962	6	32	24
1963	5	34	22
1964	5	47	21
1965	5	56	20
1966	5	53	21
1967	7	49	20
1968	8	47	20
1969	8	40	21
1970	8	39	21
1971	7	43	20
1972	6	34	19
1973	4	55	19
1974	4	47	19
1975	4	57	19
1976	7	38	19
1977	9	32	23
1978	10	28	24
1979	12	29	26
1980	13	44	30
1981	12	55	33
1982	8	34	27
1983	5	29	28

Source: Cavallo, 1988; IEERAL, 1986; own data

1940s when commercial policy restrictions reached record levels). The gap narrowed significantly in 1955–8 after Perón was overthrown. It then remained more stable until 1963–6, when it widened again under the civilian government of Arturo Illia. Illia was overthrown by the military, and the difference between domestic and external terms of trade decreased again in 1967–70, after which it rose, reaching a new peak in 1975 under the presidency of Isabel Perón. Once again, the return to power of the armed forces was associated with a closure of the gap between 1976 and 1979. An external crisis then led to a reversal in policy, and the gap reopened after 1981.

Another quantitative indicator of changes in commercial policy regimes is the degree of openness, which is measured by the ratio of exports plus imports to the GDP in constant prices. Data shown in table 1.2 and figure 1.9 allow us to distinguish three different periods from a long-term perspective: an improvement in the openness ratio from 1952 to 1962, a downward trend to 1975 (briefly reversed in 1968–70), and a significant increase from that time to 1981.

Neither the degree of openness nor the difference between the domestic and foreign terms of trade can be regarded as adequate indicators of commercial policy changes on a yearly basis. The ratio of imports plus exports to the GDP is affected by exogenous shocks and RER fluctuations

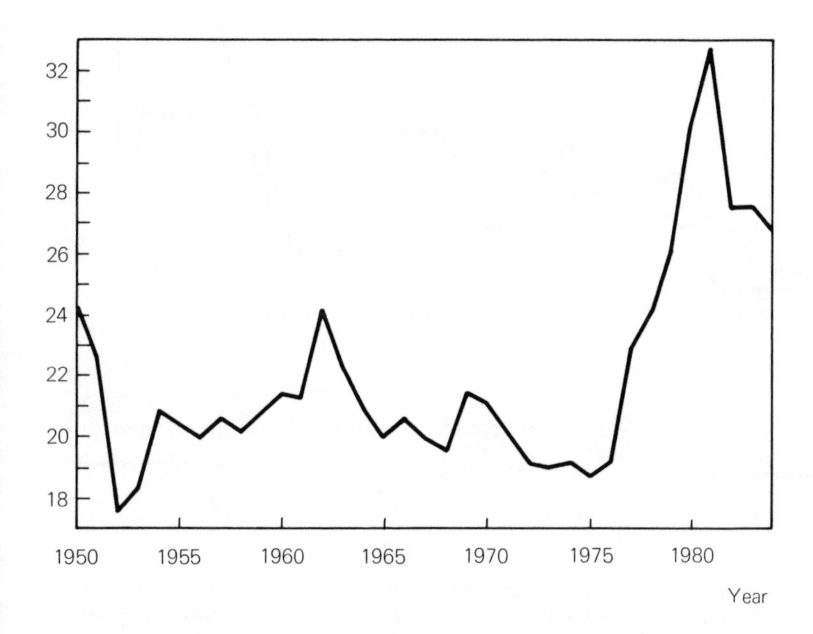

Figure 1.9 Degree of openness, 1950–1984 (exports plus imports over gross domestic product)
Source: IEERAL (1986)

which are not necessarily associated with changes in trade regimes, while real devaluations generally close the terms-of-trade gap when QRs are present. Moreover, shifts in aggregate demand produced by expansionary fiscal or monetary policies increase the domestic price of importables when quotas exist, thereby raising the antitrade bias implicit in the terms-of-trade differential.

The dotted line in figure 1.10 shows a scaled variation of the average of the degree of openness and the gap between foreign and domestic terms of trade (AVG).[3] To emphasize structural changes in commercial policies rather than events associated with short-run macroeconomic management, the index of liberalization was constructed so as to reflect the incidence of institutional changes in trade policy conditions while smoothing out the differences within each trade regime. Thus weight has been given to such events as (a) the elimination of export marketing boards in 1955, (b) the shifts from QRs to tariffs in 1956, 1967, and 1977, (c) the rationalization in tariffs occurring in 1958, 1967, and 1976 and (d) the return to QRs and multiple exchange rates in 1963, 1973, and 1982. The relative importance

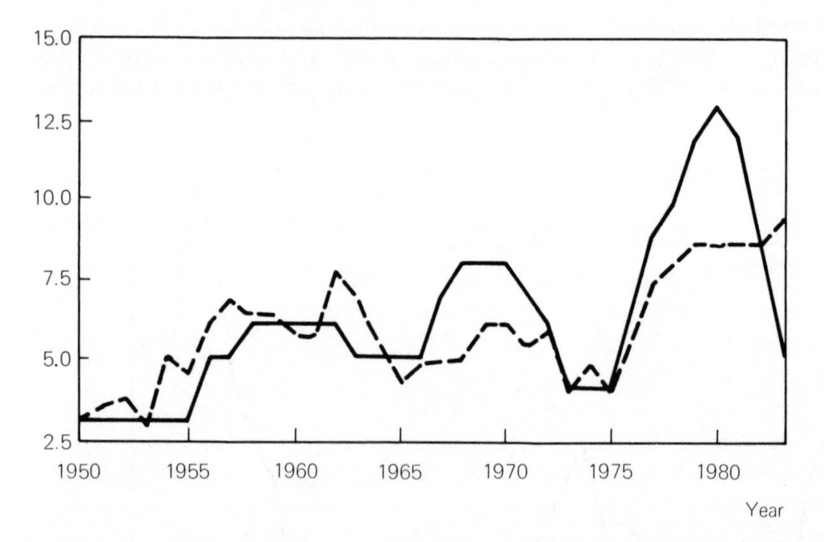

Figure 1.10 Index of liberalization and average of quantitative indicators of trade policies, 1950–1983: ——, index; – – –, AVG, the average of the terms-of-trade gap and the degree of openness
Source: Own elaboration (as explained in text)

3 To construct AVG, the following procedure was followed: (a) the degree of openness and the terms-of-trade gap shown in table 1.2 were recalculated using a common proportional scale (3–13) whereby the lowest (highest) terms-of-trade gap was given the highest (lowest) scale value; (b) the two variables were averaged using equal weights, and a correction of two index points was needed in all years so that the initial value of AVG was equal to 3.

of quantitative and qualitative information in the construction of the index can be inferred from figure 1.10 where the index of liberalization and AVG are plotted together. It should be noted that the correction for "institutional" factors is especially important from 1960 to 1972 and after 1979.

Trade liberalization, as reflected by the index, took place in 1976–81 (the Martínez de Hoz episode) and, to a lesser extent, in 1967–70 (the Krieger-Vasena episode). However, only the 1976–81 episode is truly relevant in terms of the magnitude of the changes in policy involved and the favorable expectations it created. In contrast, the Krieger-Vasena tariff reform was only perceived as a pragmatic move designed to cope with stabilization problems (that is, compensating for the price effect of a maxi-devaluation) and not as reflecting a profound ideological shift towards free trade. Nevertheless, the rationalization in tariffs it produced was very important in simplifying trade negotiations with other countries, and could have been a successful first stage of a trade liberalization process had a firmer political commitment existed. Chapters 2 and 3 contain full descriptions of the Krieger-Vasena and the Martínez de Hoz episodes respectively. The main features and events are summarized here in tables 1.3 and 1.4.

Formal Exchange Rate System

Since 1930, Argentina has experienced several exchange rate systems, including fixed rates, adjustable pegs, and crawling pegs, with single, dual, or multiple rates. Occasionally, the exchange rate was allowed to float temporarily in order to attain instant market equilibrium. A system of pre-announced crawl (*tablita*) was in effect in 1979–80.

Multiple rates existed from 1930 to 1957, a period also characterized by strict exchange controls. These instruments were used to foster import substitution up to World War II and were continued thereafter. In 1949, for example, there were three official rates: the "basic" rate for primary exports, the "preferential" rate for essential imports, and the "free" rate (actually controlled). In practice, however, even more effective exchange rates were available because the government also decided on the mix of rates applicable to each transaction. In 1958 the exchange rate was unified and devalued as a result of a standby agreement with the International Monetary Fund (IMF). The system worked as a "dirty float" during 1959, after which government intervention in the foreign exchange market became increasingly active. The nominal exchange rate was finally pegged at a fixed level between 1960 and 1962 but, as a result of an external crisis, it was devalued again in 1962 and most exchange controls were eliminated. This situation lasted until November 1963, when temporary controls on financial transactions were imposed again to halt capital outflows.

Table 1.3 Summary table of liberalization episodes

	1967–70 episode	*1976–81 episode*
Broad nature	Unannounced tariff cut, partially compensated devaluation, less reliance on QRs	Two-stage reform: first stage (1976–8) characterized by across-the-board tariff cut and QR elimination; second stage (1979–81) characterized by a program of pre-announced quarterly tariff reductions
Size, duration	Small, short	Larger, longer
Economic circumstances before		
Balance of payments	Good current account performance but low reserves owing to capital outflows	Large current account deficits, low level of reserves
Terms of trade	High relative to historical levels but falling	Falling after the commodity boom of the early 1970s
Rate of inflation	Stable, above 20%	Very high and accelerating, above 300%
Growth rate	Near zero in 1966	Negative in 1975
Degree of openness to foreign trade	Low	Very low
External shocks	No	No
Political circumstances		
New government	Yes	Yes
Type of government	Military, strong	Military, strong
Ideological shift	Not much	Yes
Public perception and debate	None	Not much during first stage, some after
International influence	Stand-by agreement with IMF, some increase in foreign investment	Short-term capital inflows, little direct investment
Accompanying policies		
Exchange rate	Large devaluation, then fixed unified exchange rate	Unified decision-variant crawling peg, then pre-announced crawl
Export promotion	Through higher real exchange rate, fiscal incentives were reduced	Lower fiscal incentives, higher financial incentives
Export taxes	Increased, then reduced gradually	Reduced sharply
Monetary policy	Relaxed, passive	Tight first, then passive and accommodating
Fiscal policy	Decrease in budget deficit	Deficit is reduced in 1976–7 but then is kept high as interests on public debt accumulate
Capital controls	Relaxed slightly	Totally eliminated in 1979
Implementation		
Departures from pre-announced scheme	No pre-announcement of stages, hence no departures	Pre-announcement of tariff reductions during second stage, destabilizing departures
Economic performance		
Employment	Increased	Increased
Inflation	Fell quickly	Decreased, but slowly
Growth performance	Improved, sustained expansion	Low for the period 1976–81, unstable output behavior
Real wages	Fell	Fell, then improved
Degree of openness	Relatively unchanged	Increased (imports more than exports; hence trade account worsened)

Table 1.4 Trade and exchange rate policies and their reversals

1967–71 episode	
Mar 1967	40% devaluation
	Adoption of a fixed and uniform exchange rate
	Reduction in import tariffs
	Elimination of some QRs
	Increase in export taxes (traditional exports)
	Elimination of tax incentives (nontraditional exports)
1968	Gradual reduction in export taxes
	Reestablishment of fiscal incentives
Jun 1970	Another compensated devaluation
1971	Implementation of a multiple exchange rate system
	Balance-of-trade deficit and introduction of trade restrictions (episode's reversal)
1976–81 episode	
1976	Unification of exchange rate system
	Implementation of decision-variant crawling peg
	Across-the-board tariff cut (Decree 3008)
	Elimination of QRs except for cars and basic metals
	Further tariff reductions (with emphasis in the second semester)
	Elimination of export taxes
1978	Elimination of remaining QRs
	Elimination of controls on capital mobility (Dec)
	Exchange rate pre-announcement starts (Dec)
1979	Pre-announced tariff reduction program starts (Res.1634/78)
	First deviation from plan takes place (Res. 6/79)
	Second deviation from plan takes place (Res. 493/79)
1981	First discrete (10%) devaluation takes place, implying abandonment of active crawling peg regime
	Import restrictions start to be increased, implying reversal in trade policies

The first experience with a crawling peg system began in 1964–6 when nine "mini-devaluations" gradually adjusted the level of the nominal exchange rate to account for the excess of domestic over foreign inflation. A period of fixed exchange rates followed between 1967 and 1971, during which time there were two large compensated devaluations (in March 1967 and June 1970). A short interval described by Martirena-Mantel (1981) as the "timid crawling peg" episode began in April 1971. This episode lasted until August 1971 and was characterized by four mini-devaluations which raised the price of the dollar by 25 percent.

A dual exchange rate system was created in September 1971. The commercial rate was fixed, and the financial rate, although initially floating, soon became pegged also. The premium between the two markets was higher than 80 percent and encouraged a system of disguised mini-devaluations which, in essence, converted the system into a crawling peg from 1971 to 1973. The method consisted of "gradually moving the negotiation of commercial transactions from the market with the lower rate to the market with the higher rate" (Martirena-Mantel, 1981).

A return to fixed exchange rates took place in 1973. In a context of high inflation, the RER was allowed to appreciate significantly, thus encouraging expectations of devaluation until March 1975, when the commercial exchange rate was devalued by 100 percent and the financial rate by 50 percent, and again in June 1975, when nominal devaluations were 160 percent and 100 percent respectively.

After these strong devaluations, the exchange rates were adjusted every two months until November 1976, when the exchange rate system was unified. The government then adopted the practice of depreciating the peso daily. Between 1976 and 1978, the adjustments followed a decision-variant unannounced rule. In December 1978, the crawl started to be pre-announced and was used as a disinflation instrument. The result was a significant real appreciation of the peso because domestic inflation failed to keep in step with the decreasing crawl rates. As devaluation expectations began to build up, the exchange rate was discretely adjusted on three occasions between March and June 1981. At that time, the authorities introduced a system of exchange rate insurance to borrowers. Despite the devaluations, one-sided expectations against the peso were still high. The Banco Central therefore introduced a dual exchange rate system whereby the commercial rate was indexed and the financial rate was allowed to float. This system lasted until December 1981 when the exchange rate was again unified and exchange rate insurance was eliminated.

2

The Krieger-Vasena Episode

The trade liberalization policy implemented in 1967 can be characterized as a once-and-for-all tariff cut. Along with the general reduction in tariffs, the reform also eliminated import prohibitions on many commodities and prior deposit requirements for all imports except consumer goods.

Political Circumstances

In June 1966 a coup d'état put an end to the government of Arturo Illia who had been elected President in 1963. His administration lacked much of the support required from the military and trade union leaders. Unions were largely controlled by the Peronist Party which had been banned at the time of the 1963 election. The military government that took power immediately after the coup was committed to eliminating the causes that had led the country to stagnation and to establishing the conditions for economic expansion and sustained development.[1]

However, it was not until March 1967 that the government launched an economic plan designed to meet these objectives. This occurred shortly after Adalbert Krieger-Vasena was appointed Minister of Finance. According to de Pablo (1970), the new economic team pursued a strategy of achieving monetary and price stability as a pre-condition for sustained growth. Thus immediate measures were aimed at reducing inflation and achieving fiscal discipline in a relatively short time (approximately a year). The opportunity for engaging in tariff reform was given by the sharp devaluation of March 1967. Tariff reductions were directed to compensate partially for the effect of the devaluation on the domestic prices of imported inputs. Hence trade liberalization was mainly conceived of as a part of a stabilization package, although some structural effects associated with the policy were expected as well.[2]

1 Official declaration, July 1966.

2 According to Decree 1410/67, the legal instrument of the reform, lower tariffs would correct distortions which, in the past, had led to resource misallocations and lower efficiency in manufacturing (see Alemann, 1969).

From a more institutional point of view, the reform was necessary to facilitate trade negotiations both at the world (General Agreement on Tariffs and Trade (GATT)) and regional (Latin American Free Trade Association (LAFTA)) levels. In this sense, the move to a more rational tariff structure was another step taken by Argentina toward greater integration in world markets and international trade institutions. The trend was initiated in 1965 with the adoption of the Brussels Tariff Nomenclature (BTN), and this was followed by the decision to join GATT.

Economic Circumstances when the Policy was Introduced

At the beginning of 1967, the Argentine economy was relatively active. As shown in table 2.1, the GDP was at the upper part of the cycle in 1965 when the economy was on the way to recovery from the 1962–3 crisis. However, the process came to a halt by 1966, a year in which real output stagnated. The average unemployment rate was 5.6 percent in 1965 and about the same in 1966. Although this rate was above the "natural rate of unemployment," the level was relatively low in comparison with previous years. Although the rate of inflation had enjoyed five years of stability, it was considered high by international standards. Thus the immediate concern of policymakers was to reduce it.

Another problem was that the stock of international reserves was low and had not increased much since the external crisis of 1962. It appears from table 2.1 that, although the trade and current accounts improved very significantly in 1963–6, capital flight continued, accounting for the low level of reserves in 1966 when the latter represented only 22 percent of imports. Capital outflows responded to expectations of devaluation built during a period of small adjustments in the nominal exchange rate (crawling peg) which resulted in real appreciation of the domestic currency.

Table 2.1 Economic performance before the 1967 trade reform

Aggregates	*1960*	*1961*	*1962*	*1963*	*1964*	*1965*	*1966*
1 GDP, constant prices (index)	100	107	105	103	113	124	124
2 Inflation (GDP deflator) (%)	22	11	25	28	26	28	24
3 Trade account balance (million US$)	− 170	− 496	− 140	384	333	293	469
4 Current account surplus (million US$)	− 204	− 585	− 273	234	33	182	252
5 Net capital inflows (million US$)	515	392	620	− 57	− 202	− 167	− 210
6 Reserves (million US$)	698	496	192	322	192	265	251

Source: Banco Central

The Stabilization Plan, 1967–1969

Trade liberalization took place at a time when the government had embarked on a stabilization plan aimed at reducing inflation, increasing foreign reserves, and expanding output capacity. Argentine officials signed a standby agreement with the IMF in 1967. Unlike previous stabilization efforts (most notably in 1959 and 1962), IMF conditionality was not as strong this time. Traditionally, the economy had been exposed to shock treatments of devaluation and sharp monetary contraction with tremendous stagflationary results. The new strategy was to attack the cost–push elements embedded in inflation by means of wage and price controls (income policy), while relying on fiscal discipline, rather than domestic credit contraction, to reduce aggregate demand.

The plan successfully curbed inflation. In addition, the effect of the devaluation was to reverse the direction of capital movements. Soon, capital started to flow into the country and the reserves position of the Banco Central improved. At the same time, the government sought to increase capacity by raising public investment which, in turn, was expected to stimulate private investment through some sort of "acceleration" mechanism.

A more detailed description of the different policies pursued by the Krieger-Vasena administration is given below.

Exchange Rate Policy

The government introduced new exchange market rules in March 1967, of which the principal were as follows:

1. discrete devaluation of the peso from 255 to 350 pesos to the dollar;
2. adoption of a fixed uniform exchange rate;
3. elimination of exchange controls on capital flows (which dated back to 1963).

In order to absorb part of the capital gain made by holders of foreign assets (basically, commercial banks), a once-and-for-all tax was imposed on these holdings at the rate of 80 pesos per dollar. The exchange rate was kept fixed at 350 pesos until a second devaluation in June 1970. Multiple rates were not adopted until September 1971, when a dual system was created. The evolution of the RER which accompanied this trade liberalization episode is presented in table 2.2. The pattern shows that the RER overshot its new equilibrium level when the devaluation took place in March 1967. To avoid a sharp inflationary effect, the devaluation was partly offset by tariff cuts and export tax increases.

Table 2.2 Real exchange rate index, 1967–1968 (1966 = 100)[a]

1967								1968			
Jan	*Feb*	*Mar*	*Apr*	*May*	*Jun*	*III*	*IV*	*I*	*II*	*III*	*IV*
106	106	136	143	139	134	129	125	125	124	122	122

[a] Nominal exchange rate deflated by wholesale price index.

Sources: nominal exchange rate, Banco Central (daily averages); wholesale price index, Instituto Nacional de Estadísticas y Censos (INDEC)

According to the Instituto de Desarrollo Económico y Social (IDES), the combination of tariff cuts and the devaluation in 1967 accounted for a net 30 percent increase in the domestic price of imported raw materials and intermediate products (IDES, 1967). The effect on the domestic price of imported capital goods was 16 percent, as calculated by Ribas et al. (1967). In turn, the Cámara Argentina de la Industria Electrónica (CADIE) estimated the impact effect of the compensated devaluation for a representative sample of import goods and found a 25 percent price increase (CADIE, 1967). All these studies indicate that the tariff reduction only partially compensated for the devaluation.

Export Taxes

In a country like Argentina, in which grain and beef make up a large part of the export bill, a sharp devaluation reduces real wages, giving rise to increased salary demands. Thus any attempt to raise the RER by simply resorting to a devaluation is either inflationary (if there is wage and monetary accommodation) or achievable only at a high social cost. Trying to control the real price of tradeables by means of nominal adjustments in the exchange rate is an empty gesture in the presence of strong trade unions and an accommodating monetary policy. However, most governments are reluctant to accept the recessive effects created by tight monetary policy and wage controls following devaluation as well as the changes in income distribution that usually accompany them, even assuming that they have the political power to enforce these controls.

The way that the authorities solved this policy dilemma in 1967 was to raise export taxes in order to dampen the domestic prices increased by the devaluation. Again, the compensation was partial: export taxes were imposed on traditional exports at rates of 25, 20, and 16 percent depending on the product. The average rate increased from 7.6 to 21.7 percent, yielding a net increase in the effective exchange rate of about 18 percent for traditional export commodities. Unlike tariffs, export taxes were not expected to change permanently. The idea was to keep export taxes high while the undervaluation of the peso lasted, and to reduce them gradually as the RER fell on account of domestic price increases. This happened in 1968, markedly during the second semester. By 1969, the average export tax was back to 10 percent.

Export Promotion Policies

The impact effect of the devaluation on the real exchange rate for nontraditional exports was higher than for traditional goods since the former group was not subject to export taxes. In contrast, these exports were granted a subsidy in the form of a 12 percent tax rebate (*reintegro*) which was temporarily suspended in March 1967. Later, exporters of nontraditional goods were allowed to deduct 10 percent of the free on board (f.o.b.) value of exports from their income tax bill (the corporate income tax rate was 33 percent) and tax reimbursements were reestablished in 1968. Table 2.3 shows the change in the nominal effective exchange rate of nontraditional exports during 1967.

Table 2.3 Evolution of the effective exchange rate of nontraditional exports in 1967

Month	*Exchange rate (pesos per US$)*	*Sales tax rebate (%)*	*Income tax deduction (%)*	*Total*	*Index (Feb 67 = 100)*
Feb 1967	255	12	0	285	100.0
Mar 1967	350	0	0	350	122.5
Nov 1967	350	0	3.3	361	126.6

Source: de Pablo, 1970

Income Policy

The cost–push elements built into inflation were successfully attenuated by wage controls. Law 17224 substituted a system of administered wage increases for private negotiations between trade union leaders and firm representatives. A general increase was decreed in April 1967 before nominal wages were frozen. The raise established rates of increase varying from 8 to 24 percent depending on the date that the last contract had been signed (most salary agreements were negotiated annually). Thus all wages were set at real equivalent levels without altering their structure.

Noncompulsory price controls were instituted among industrial producers. Firms were invited to participate in an agreement with the government by which they committed themselves not to increase prices during a certain period of time in return for some special benefits.[3] Most

3 The benefits were of two kinds: (a) the public sector would only purchase goods from participating firms; (b) a special credit line was created, offering loans to consumers in the form of purchase certificates redeemable only for goods produced by those firms.

large firms joined the agreement, which was a success in terms of the observance of the commitments while it lasted. Inflation started to fall in September 1967 and was kept low during 1968 and 1969.

Fiscal Policy

The consolidated deficit of the public sector was 4 percent of GDP in 1966. This was reduced to 1.2 percent in 1967, 1.4 percent in 1968, and 1.1 percent in 1969. This impressive fiscal achievement was the result of increased taxes and an improvement in the operations of public enterprises, as can be inferred from table 2.4. Current spending decreased only slightly and public investment rose.

In 1967 the government introduced some reforms of the tax system. The sales tax rate was increased for some durable consumption goods, new taxes were created (on real estate and bank loans), and penalties on tax payment delays were made more severe. However, the main source of increase in revenue collection was export taxes.

Expansionary fiscal policy was pursued in 1968 when the government planned to increase investment by 30 percent, through their Public Works Program, to help manufacturing to recover after a period of relative stagnation. The increase in supply rapidly spread from the construction sector to the rest of the economy, thereby raising fiscal revenue. As a result, the deficit increased only slightly in real terms. In 1969 the deficit reached its lowest point thanks to a reduction in current spending of about 0.5 percent of GDP.

Table 2.4 Government budget (consolidated public sector), 1965–1971 (percentage of gross domestic product)

Year	*Current expenditure*	*Public investment*	*Current revenue*	*Capital revenue*	*Government deficit*	*Public enterprise saving*	*Public sector deficit*
1965	16.0	6.5	18.8	0.3	2.3	0.0	3.2
1966	18.4	6.4	20.1	0.4	4.4	0.3	4.1
1967	18.3	7.6	23.3	0.5	2.2	1.0	1.2
1968	18.0	8.3	22.7	0.5	3.0	1.6	1.4
1969	17.5	8.2	22.5	0.5	2.8	1.7	1.1
1970	17.4	8.5	22.8	0.4	2.6	1.5	1.1
1971	16.9	8.2	20.3	0.3	4.5	0.7	3.8

Source: Economic Commission for Latin America (ECLA)

Monetary Policy

As mentioned earlier, the Argentine government signed a standby agreement with the IMF in 1967. Policy objectives with respect to the growth of real money supply during 1967 and 1968 can be inferred from the letters of intent sent by Argentine officials to IMF authorities. We know, for example, that the maximum rates of expansion allowed for domestic credit (money base minus net foreign assets) were 25 percent in 1967 and 16 percent in 1968. However, since no taxes were to be levied on capital inflows and no attempts were to be made to "sterilize" them, the permitted changes in the money base stock were actually greater. Domestic prices, in contrast, were not expected to rise as much on account of direct wage and price controls.

A second source of monetary expansion was introduced in June 1968, when minimum reserve coefficients were reduced as a way of supplying new credit to consumers. (Personal credit lines had been authorized by the Banco Central in August 1967.) The change in reserve ratios was very significant and implied a potential increase in M1 of an additional 40 percent. This was later considered excessive and credit expansion margins were in practice reduced. Plainly, the government sought a significant increase in liquidity in 1968 to promote the recovery of the manufacturing sector and also to match the increased demand for real money balances that would follow the expected fall in inflation. Policy was less expansionary in 1969, a year in which officials simply tried to keep the real stock of money more or less constant. The actual evolution of monetary aggregates is shown in table 2.5. The supply of means of payments (M1) deflated by wholesale prices grew by 7.6 percent in 1967, 21.9 percent in 1968, and 3.2 percent in 1969.

Table 2.5 Evolution of monetary aggregates in real terms, 1966–1969

Year	*Quarter*	*M0/P*	*M1/P*	*M3/P*
1966	I	13.69	16.28	24.81
	II	13.26	16.15	24.55
	III	13.45	16.54	25.15
	IV	13.84	17.75	26.35
1967	I	14.58	17.34	26.32
	II	15.03	17.35	26.43
	III	14.34	16.29	25.41
	IV	16.22	19.10	29.04
1968	I	16.55	19.34	30.32
	II	16.66	20.46	32.01
	III	16.43	20.88	33.13
	IV	17.64	23.29	36.70
1969	I	19.34	23.70	38.51
	II	20.46	23.06	38.03
	III	20.88	22.47	37.65
	IV	23.29	24.03	39.90

Source: Banco Central

The Capital Account

Direct controls on capital mobility were eliminated in 1967. Restrictions on outflows were not necessary after the peso became undervalued. In fact, capital movements reversed and short-term credit started to flow into the country, attracted by the positive differential between domestic and foreign interest rates. The authorities did little to restrict these inflows since, as noted before, they were not concerned about tightening monetary variables.

There was also direct foreign investment during this period. Table 2.6 contains the relevant information: increases in foreign debt and direct foreign investment represented about 12 percent of average of gross private investment between 1967 and 1972.

Table 2.6 Capital movements and direct foreign investment, 1967–1972 (annual averages in millions of pesos at constant 1970 prices)

	Foreign debt increment				
Period	*Exchange insurance*	*No exchange insurance*	*Direct foreign investment*	*Total*	*Gross private investment*
1967–9	111.6	373.8	534.5	1,019.9	10,150.5
1969–72	446.7	986.8	395.1	1,828.6	13,056.0

Source: Cavallo and Petrei, 1983

Implementation of the Liberalization Policy

The tariff reform was neither gradual nor pre-announced. There was one significant step – a generalized tariff cut – in March 1967. The government, however, left the door open for further revisions in the tariff structure, and a special commission was created to take care of individual requests. Some changes were introduced in June and September of the same year.

The reform simplified the Argentine tariff system considerably. Under the previous import regime, there had been 60 different tariff levels starting from zero and reaching a maximum of 605 percent, with the higher levels being 20, 25, 45, 50, 55, 75, 95, 120, 140, 155, 175, 185, 190, 195, 220, 320, and 325 percent.

The new system reduced the number of tariff levels to 16 and the maximum tariff to 140 percent; the difference between each pair of levels was 10 percentage points. In fact, the larger cuts were at the very high levels, whereas duties below 100 percent were reduced less. The reform introduced a classification of tariffs based on the following: (a) the economic nature of goods – consumption, investment, and intermediate; (b) the degree of elaboration, ranging from 1 to 10; (c) the existence (or lack) of a domestically produced substitute. The levels of duties for each category are presented in table 2.7. Tariffs were lower for intermediate and capital goods than for consumption goods; for noncompeting imports, tariffs were lower than if domestic production had existed.

Although the reform undoubtedly approached a more rational tariff structure, in many cases (most notably consumer goods) it did little more than eliminate "water." In other cases the effect on domestic prices was more than offset by the devaluation, so that relative prices increased.

Other duties with tariff-like effects, such as *Arancel Consular* and *Servicio de Estadísticas*, were not eliminated at all. However, the Banco Central did eliminate the prior-deposit requirement to importers of intermediate and capital goods in September 1967. The deposit (40 percent of the value of imports) accrued no interest, and its effect on import costs was equivalent to a 3.6 percent tariff surcharge across the board (Berlinsky and Schydlowsky, 1977).

Some import prohibitions were eliminated but others were maintained. Especially among the latter were the limitations on cars, tractors, and motors which had existed for about a decade.

Table 2.7 Economic classification of tariffs under the 1967 reform

Type of goods		*1*	*2*	*3*	*4*	*5*	*6*	*7*	*8*	*9*	*10*
I Intermediate											
	(a)	40	50	60	70	80	90	100	110	120	130
	(b)	5	5	10	20	20	20	30	30	40	40
II Consumption											
	(a)	110	110	120	120	130	130	130	130	140	140
	(b)	30	40	50	60	70	80	90	100	110	120
III Capital											
	(a)	40	50	60	70	70	80	80	90	90	100
	(b)	30	30	30	40	40	40	40	50	50	50

(a) Applicable when there is a domestically produced substitute available; (b) otherwise.

Source: Alemann, 1969

Another important feature of the protection regime that remained unchanged in 1967 was the extent of import duty exemptions under special promotion regimes. These allowed beneficiaries to import certain goods duty free that other buyers usually had to purchase from domestic producers at higher prices. These permits produced segmentation in some markets.

Effective Rates of Protection

The protection regime in force in 1965 was the result of the consolidation of existing customs duties and exchange surcharges into tariffs, classified according to the BTN into 99 chapters and about 6,800 positions. CONADE (1967) has estimated the protection structure existing in 1965.[4] Two sets of EPRs were calculated, each covering 19 activities in agriculture, manufacturing, and mining (table 2.8). EPR_1 represents the "implicit" effective protection rate, obtained by comparing domestic and border prices of final goods and inputs; EPR_2 is the "potential" rate, calculated on the basis of legal tariffs.

High levels of tariff redundancy are immediately apparent: while the unweighted mean of EPR_2 is 422 percent, the implicit EPR, or EPR_1, is

Table 2.8 Sectoral effective protection rates in 1965

Sector	*EPR_1*	*EPR_2*
1 Crops	−18.2	−41.8
2 Livestock	−11.5	−29.6
3 Forestry	−39.4	−76.5
4 Mining	−64.7	−4.0
5 Fuel and electricity	11.1	88.9
6 Foodstuffs and beverages	29.0	588.9
7 Meat packing	−24.0	−56.0
8 Tobacco	186.7	269.1
9 Clothing	76.2	1,051.6
10 Lumber	172.1	602.7
11 Paper and paperboard	298.8	1,370.7
12 Printing and publishing	−11.0	−69.9
13 Chemical products	198.2	763.2
14 Rubber products	−9.1	351.6
15 Leather	18.0	711.1
16 Stone, glass, and ceramics	−9.3	308.6
17 Metals	272.6	726.9
18 Machinery	242.0	720.0
19 Other industries	179.6	741.1

	Unweighted mean	*Standard deviation*	*Coefficient of variation*
EPR_1 (implicit effective tariff)	78.9	115.7	1.47
EPR_2 (potential effective tariff)	422.3	1,210.9	2.87
NPR_1 (implicit nominal tariff)	28.5	34.2	1.20
NPR_2 (potential nominal tariff)	145.1	148.8	1.02

Source: CONADE, 1967

4 CONADE stands for Consejo Nacional de Desarrollo, an official agency in charge of economic planning and technical advice to the government. The results of their research on effective protection are documented in two papers by Wainer (1970) and Cuervo (1972).

just 79 percent on average. However, the unweighted mean of the *nominal* tariffs yielded 145 percent according to the same CONADE study. A comparison of this figure with 422 percent (the average EPR_2) yields an estimate of the degree of *escalation* built into the legal protection scheme, since it reflects the fact that inputs were less protected than final goods on average, thereby yielding $EPR_2 > NPR_2$. Note that the escalation coefficient of 2.9 is much higher than those found in other countries by authors investigating protection levels at about the same time.[5] The protection bias granted to consumer goods over intermediate and capital goods was particularly important.

Another remarkable aspect of the 1965 protection structure was the extent to which legal exemptions and special import regimes reduced actual revenue collection from tariffs:

> In 1964, 44.6 percent of imports, measured in dollars, were introduced duty-free and, of the remaining 55.4 percent, subject to surcharges, 28.6 percent paid 20 percent and 35.6 percent paid 40 percent. In 1965, 50.4 percent was imported duty-free and, of the rest, 31.5 percent paid a 20 percent surcharge and 32 percent paid 40 percent. There follows that more than $\frac{3}{4}$ of imports either paid no tariffs or were charged very low duties. (Alemann, 1969)

As a result, collected tariffs represented a very low proportion of imports compared with legal tariff rates.

More general characteristics of the protection system in 1965 were first that it created an obvious anti-export bias, where primary activities such as crops had negative EPRs while import substitution industries such as metals had excessively high EPRs and second that it generated a bias against foreign investment since the US dollar became undervalued for financial transactions while the effective exchange rate for imports of industrial equipment and materials was kept high.

The impact of Krieger-Vasena's reforms on EPRs is shown in table 2.9. Six sectors exhibited negative EPRs: crops, livestock, meat packing, forestry, mining, and printing and publishing. All the others had positive and high degrees of protection which fell significantly after the reform.[6]

5 See Cuervo (1972, p. 109) for a comparison of escalation coefficients in a sample of countries during the 1960s.

6 The EPR for leather products must be interpreted with care. Since Argentina has a comparative advantage in the production of these goods, the legal protection rates to domestic market sales, as they appear in table 2.9, are irrelevant. They simply reflect the fact that import tariffs on final leather goods were redundantly high and, at the same time, raw material purchases were heavily subsidized. By the same token, the 1967 EPR (reflecting negative value added at world prices) should not mislead us into believing that the leather industry was turned into an inefficient activity.

Table 2.9 Impact of the 1967 tariff reform on effective protection rates

Sector	*1965*	*1967*
1 Crops	−41.8	−44.2
2 Livestock	−29.6	−41.5
3 Forestry	−76.5	−37.9
4 Mining	−4.0	−59.5
5 Fuel and electricity	88.9	49.0
6 Foodstuffs and beverages	588.9	263.5
7 Meat packing	−56.0	−65.0
8 Tobacco	269.1	263.0
9 Clothing	1,051.6	498.1
10 Lumber	602.7	320.2
11 Paper and paperboard	1,370.7	601.4
12 Printing and publishing	−69.9	−30.0
13 Chemical products	763.2	293.6
14 Rubber products	351.6	213.4
15 Leather	711.7	−259.7
16 Stone, glass, and ceramics	308.6	119.0
17 Metals	726.9	346.8
18 Machinery	720.0	392.8
19 Other industries	741.1	378.0

	Unweighted mean	*Standard deviation*	*Coefficient of variation*
Potential effective tariff (1965)	422.3	1,210.9	2.87
Potential effective tariff (1967)	181.4	65.0	0.36
Potential nominal tariff (1965)	145.1	148.4	1.02
Potential nominal tariff (1967)	66.7	30.9	0.46

Source: CONADE, 1967

The unweighted mean decreased from 422 to 181 percent and the coefficient of variation plummeted from 2.87 to 0.36. For nominal tariffs, the effect was similar: the mean fell from 145 to 66 percent and the coefficient of variation dropped from 1.02 to 0.46. Notice that the escalation coefficient, measured by the EPR/NPR ratio did not change significantly (2.7 in 1967 compared with 2.9 in 1965). Neither did the ranking of EPRs: the Spearman rank-order correlation coefficient between the two columns is 0.80.

The 1969 situation as documented by Berlinsky and Schydlowsky (1977) is summarized in table 2.10. One of the main differences between this work and the CONADE (1967) study is that Berlinsky and Schydlowsky adjusted the EPRs for water in the tariff in cases where legal tariffs were prohibitive. For example, in comparing group II (processed foods) in table 2.10 with row 6 in table 2.9, it would be misleading to conclude that effective protection to the domestic market fell from 263 to 44 percent between 1967 and 1969, since no further significant changes in the tariff

Table 2.10 Nominal and effective protection in 1969 (percent)

Industry group	*Nominal protection*			*Effective protection to value added*		
	Export	*Domestic*	*Av.*	*Export*	*Domestic*	*Av.*
1 Agriculture, forestry, fishing	−10.0	−10.0	−10.0	−12.8	−12.8	−12.8
2 Mining and energy	0.0	29.9	29.3	−11.6	33.0	32.1
Primary production, total	−9.9	−5.8	−6.4	−12.8	−8.4	−9.1
3 Processed foods	−8.9	6.8	2.4	−29.5	44.0	23.6
4 Tobacco and beverages	−10.0	50.8	49.9	−447.5	94.5	87.0
5 Construction materials	−12.0	29.1	29.1	3.6	31.4	31.3
6(a) Intermediate products I	−7.5	55.9	50.7	−25.8	146.0	131.8
6(b) Intermediate products II	−0.8	69.3	67.2	−118.1	9.3	122.0
7 Nondurable consumer goods	11.8	57.4	56.2	−10.0	49.8	48.2
8 Durable consumer goods	12.0	88.7	88.4	−113.0	144.5	143.7
9 Machinery	14.0	89.7	87.6	−2.4	120.3	116.5
10 Transport equipment	0.0	108.7	108.7	0.0	207.0	207.0
Manufacturing, total	−6.8	57.1	51.1	−39.7	111.0	97.4
Manufacturing, less beverages and tobacco	−6.7	57.5	51.1	−35.5	112.5	97.9
All industries	−7.9	40.9	35.5	−20.1	55.3	46.9
(a) Export industries						
Primary activities	−10.0	−10.0	−10.0	−12.8	−12.8	−12.8
Manufacturing	−8.6	−4.7	−1.7	−31.2	44.4	8.3
Total	−9.3	−7.0	−7.6	−16.0	−9.6	−11.2
(b) Import-competing industries						
Primary activities	0.0	37.2	37.2	0.0	33.8	33.8
Manufacturing	6.3	76.0	73.9	−73.6	132.7	126.4
Total	6.3	75.8	73.7	−73.6	131.3	125.2

Source: Berlinsky and Schydlowsky, 1977

took place during that period. In fact, most of the legal 263 percent protection rate was redundant in 1967. The adjustment for water in this and other sectors explains the relatively low average EPR of 55 percent found by these authors for all sectors including primary activities compared with CONADE's value of 181 percent.

Another interesting aspect of the study by Berlinsky and Schydlowsky is that it permits measurement of the anti-export bias implicit in each manufacturing branch by comparing the NPRs and EPRs for domestic sales and exports. Thus, whereas the average nominal tariff on imports was 75.8 percent for import-competing industries, the average tax on export industries was 9.3 percent. The gap is even wider when EPRs are considered (131.3 percent versus 16 percent). It goes without saying that, whatever the initial level, the anti-export bias in 1969 was still very high for every manufacturing branch.

Economic Performance Following the Plan

Inflation

The rate of inflation diminished considerably in 1968, 1969, and 1970, as shown in table 2.11. Measured by the GDP deflator, inflation was only 10 percent on average during those three years compared with 27 percent for the preceding period 1962–7. The falling rate, which was mainly a result of the reduction in the fiscal deficit, also reflects the government's ability to break inflation inertia through direct wage and price controls. In addition, external prices fell for a number of agricultural commodities, accounting for the negative rates of inflation observed for some months (table 2.12).

Other external shocks that influenced inflation performance were the reduction in beef demand by the European Economic Community and the restrictions on beef imports imposed by the United Kingdom at the end of 1967. These shocks affected internal prices by generating an excess supply of beef in the domestic market. As a very important item in the consumption basket of most Argentine families, beef has a decisive weight in the consumer price index. Table 2.13 shows the evolution of (wholesale and consumer) beef prices compared with the cost of living index. It turns out that the domestic relative price of beef fell dramatically between 1966 and 1969 despite an improvement in the REER for beef exports (see table 2.17). Because of the external restrictions, the law of one price failed to hold automatically in this case. In fact, situations like this are not uncommon, even for typically tradeable commodities: producers in the small economy may not always sell "all they want at the given price." Critics of the Krieger-Vasena plan claimed that the administration took advantage of the fall in beef prices for short-run stabilization purposes and, in so doing, exacerbated changes in supply conditions that created prob-

Table 2.11 Major price indices and annual inflation rates, 1960–1973

	Price indices			*Inflation rates*		
Year	*GDP deflator*	*Wholesale price*	*Consumer price*	*GDP deflator*	*Wholesale price*	*Consumer price*
1960	100.0	100.0	100.0	—	—	—
1961	111.3	108.8	113.5	11.3	8.2	13.5
1962	139.9	141.1	145.3	25.7	30.4	28.1
1963	179.2	181.7	180.3	28.1	28.7	24.0
1964	226.5	229.5	220.2	26.4	26.3	22.2
1965	290.1	284.2	283.2	28.1	23.8	28.6
1966	359.7	340.8	373.5	24.0	19.9	31.9
1967	459.9	428.6	482.7	27.9	25.7	29.2
1968	508.5	469.0	561.0	10.6	9.4	16.2
1969	552.1	497.5	579.2	8.6	6.0	3.2
1970	613.2	567.5	679.4	11.1	14.0	17.3
1971	843.2	792.2	923.5	37.5	39.5	35.9
1972	1,374.8	1,398.9	1,464.4	63.0	76.5	58.5
1973	2,262.1	2,103.5	2,346.0	64.5	50.3	60.3

—, not applicable.

Sources: Banco Central and INDEC

Table 2.12 Monthly rates of inflation measured by the wholesale price index, 1966–1969

Month	*1966*	*1967*	*1968*	*1969*
Jan	1.1	1.1	1.7	0.4
Feb	1.1	1.3	− 0.2	0.0
Mar	0.1	1.9	− 0.7	− 0.3
Apr	2.0	2.1	− 0.2	0.2
May	2.8	3.2	2.1	3.6
Jun	2.2	3.3	0.2	1.6
Jul	1.2	2.4	0.3	0.8
Aug	1.4	2.3	0.8	2.0
Sep	1.6	1.1	0.6	1.3
Oct	3.0	2.2	− 0.3	− 1.7
Nov	2.6	− 0.2	− 1.1	− 0.1
Dec	1.5	− 1.7	0.7	− 0.6

Source: INDEC

Table 2.13 Evolution of domestic beef prices, 1966–1972 (1960 = 100)

Year	Cost of living index	Beef price index: Consumer	Beef price index: Producer
1966	374	376	330
1967	483	439	401
1968	561	480	424
1969	579	477	441
1970	679	651	645
1971	923	1,151	1,176
1972	1,463	1,806	1,884

Source: INDEC

lems later on.[7] In this sense, a more aggressive export policy, officially promoted to find new markets for beef, may have been necessary to avoid further complications.

In 1969 a series of events brought social and political instability to the country. Labor conflicts were intensified by an uprising of workers and students which took place in Córdoba in May – an incident marked by riots and street revolts known as the *Cordobazo*. The government sought to calm social unrest by changing the Minister of Economics. Thus, Krieger-Vasena resigned in June, to be replaced by José M. Dagnino Pastore. A year later, it was the President himself who had to resign.

The resultant uneasy sociopolitical environment forced the governments that followed until 1973 (still under military rule) to adopt wage control policies less strict than those of their predecessor. This pliancy together with the surge in beef prices after 1970 caused the authorities to lose control of inflation rates, and in 1971 fiscal discipline was abandoned as well (see table 2.4).

One of the main limitations of Krieger-Vasena's anti-inflationary strategy was that its insistence on price controls kept the relative price structure of industrial goods unchanged for too long. Pressures for price increases accumulated and resulted in higher inflation rates when controls were lifted.

Real Wages

The combination of administered salary increases and the devaluation provoked a reduction in real wages in 1967. Having frozen nominal wages,

7 The reduction in cattle stock induced by the low relative prices of beef caused a shortage of beef by 1970 and hence a reversal in the price trend.

Table 2.14 Evolution of real wages by sector, 1966–1973 (index 1960 = 100 deflated by cost of living)

Year	*Total*	*Agriculture, forestry, and fishing*	*Mining*	*Manufacturing*	*Electricity, gas, and water*	*Construction*	*Commerce*	*Transportation*	*Finance*	*Other services*
1966	100.0	100.0	100.0	100.0	100.0	100.0	100.0	100.0	100.0	100.0
1967	97.8	90.9	96.1	100.0	105.8	101.1	101.4	94.9	100.1	97.7
1968	92.9	89.2	82.4	92.8	103.4	92.9	96.7	91.8	96.0	93.6
1969	97.5	93.0	89.1	95.5	117.2	94.5	103.4	94.1	97.9	101.8
1970	101.1	99.7	85.8	98.9	118.3	97.4	106.2	97.4	100.9	106.2
1971	106.3	113.4	84.0	102.5	133.3	102.8	109.4	102.5	106.2	107.9
1972	100.1	110.8	75.9	95.3	124.6	95.3	105.4	95.9	99.4	101.1
1973	108.4	116.8	84.6	101.7	143.7	105.7	120.1	103.2	111.1	110.0

Source: Llach and Sánchez, 1984

the government tried to improve workers' incomes by cutting social security taxes and increasing family compensations. Despite this effort, real wages fell again in 1968 (table 2.14).

The situation changed in 1969 when two nominal adjustments were made, one in January and the other in September, immediately after the *Cordobazo*. Since inflation was very low during that year (3.6 percent, measured by the cost of living index) real wages improved, starting an upward trend that was only interrupted in 1972. The overall increase during this period was higher for wages in the nontradeable sectors (see table 2.15). For instance, real wages increased by 33 percent between 1966 and 1971 for electricity, gas, and water, and by only 2.5 percent for manufacturing.

Table 2.15 Relative wages of tradeable and nontradeable sectors, 1960–1972

Year	W_T/W_{NT}
1960	0.8856
1961	0.8794
1962	0.8652
1963	0.8733
1964	0.9248
1965	0.9390
1966	0.9535
1967	0.9512
1968	0.9375
1969	0.9164
1970	0.9154
1971	0.9488
1972	0.9551

Source: Llach and Sánchez, 1984

Social distress, as expressed by the events of May 1969, was probably more a reaction to political authoritarianism than a reflection of workers' impoverishment. In fact, by resorting to export tax increases on food, the government attained stabilization with a much lower impact on real wages than previous plans had achieved.

Real Effective Exchange Rates

The nominal exchange rate was kept fixed from March 1967 to June 1970 (when it was devalued by 12.5 percent). This stability was possible because, initially, the exchange rate was overvalued and inflation was cut to relatively low levels.

In tables 2.16 and 2.17 we have arranged information on REERs at different aggregation levels. Our basic figures correspond to a sample of 46 manufacturing activities (Standard Industrial Classification (SIC) five-digit aggregation), five crops, and livestock. The nominal exchange rate has been inflated by foreign prices and deflated by the domestic wholesale price index. This was then multiplied by one plus the tariff on imports in the case of importables, one plus the subsidy on exports in the case of nontraditional exports, and one minus export taxes in the case of traditional exports. Details of these calculations are given in appendix 1.

REERs for manufacturing were then converted to three- and two-digit averages by using relative production levels as weights. The results are presented in table 2.16. The second and third columns (1965 and 1967) are useful for analyzing the impact of the exchange rate cum tariff shock (the

Table 2.16 Real effective exchange rates for selected manufacturing activities, 1965, 1967, 1969 (m$n per US dollar at constant 1960 prices)

Sector		*1965 import*	*1967 import*	*1969 import*	*1969 export*
3	Total manufacturing	190.8	168.5	120.0	83.2
31	Foodstuffs, beverages, and tobacco	152.9	124.2	n.a.	82.5
311	Foodstuff products	152.9	124.2	n.a.	82.5
32	Textiles, clothing, and leather products	214.2	141.4	122.5	76.0
321	Textile products	192.6	120.2	125.3	71.7
322	Clothing and apparel	254.0	180.5	117.3	84.0
34	Paper, paperboard, and printing	171.1	142.8	116.0	83.5
341	Paper and paperboard	171.1	142.8	116.0	83.5
35	Chemical products	159.7	143.2	116.5	70.6
351	Basic industrial chemical products	166.9	140.4	124.9	66.5
352	Other chemical products	165.2	135.5	120.8	77.3
355	Rubber products	132.0	157.6	125.9	80.4
36	Stone, glass, and ceramics	178.3	142.5	108.1	87.3
362	Glass products	191.2	161.4	127.2	87.3
369	Nonmetal mineral products	165.7	124.0	89.6	87.3
37	Metals	157.9	164.2	130.0	102.4
371	Basic industries of iron and steel	149.5	155.0	127.9	104.1
372	Other basic metal industries	206.8	217.4	142.2	92.6
38	Metallic products, machinery, and equipment	224.8	249.2	146.2	88.1
381	Metallic products	186.7	164.4	140.0	91.0
382	Nonelectrical machinery	169.4	173.4	150.7	92.2
383	Electrical machinery	185.1	176.1	149.2	90.0
384	Transport equipment	320.9	407.3	140.6	81.3
385	Professional equipment	216.4	167.6	153.8	92.4

m$n, peso moneda nacional, an old monetary unit equivalent to one billionth of an austral (i.e. 1 A = 10^9 m$n).

Table 2.17 Real effective exchange rates for selected traditional exports, 1965, 1967, 1969 (m$n per US dollar at constant 1960 prices)

Product	*1965 export*	*1967 export*	*1969 export*
Cereals	51.6	57.2	n.a.
Oil seeds	54.1	63.9	n.a.
Fruits	56.2	62.9	n.a.
Wool	53.5	53.9	n.a.
Livestock	54.5	61.8	n.a.
Industrial crops	59.3	64.8	n.a.
Total agriculture	54.6	60.9	71.0
Meat packing	59.0	65.3	76.8
Vegetable oils	61.0	71.7	70.8
Total traditional exports	59.5	63.4	73.3

m$n, see footnote to table 2.16.
n.a., not available.

1967 data correspond to the end of that year). Since no further significant changes took place in the tariffs and in the nominal exchange rate between 1967 and 1969, some of the differences observed between the third and fourth columns of the table must be interpreted as being due to (a) the use of different methods in the estimation of nominal protection rates and (b) real appreciation produced by a domestic rate of inflation higher than foreign inflation between the two years. As commented earlier, 1969 tariff rates were adjusted for "water" in the cases where tariff redundancy was too evident. The comparison between the fourth and fifth columns of table 2.16 gives an eloquent idea of the magnitude of the anti-export bias still existing after the reform: the RER for manufacturing imports was 44 percent higher than that for manufacturing exports.

The REER was even lower for traditional exports owing, of course, to export taxes. These increased in 1967 but were reduced afterwards. In any case, the initial jump in taxes was more than offset by the devaluation, so that the whole period showed a favorable trend in REERs for traditional exports, as documented in table 2.17. Unfortunately, we do not have information about REERs for nontraditional exports in 1965 and 1967, but we know that they were increased by the devaluation and by export promotion policies. The main commercial incentive was given by tax rebates or *reintegros* in 1968, the rate being 12 percent of the f.o.b. value. This was increased to 15 percent during the first semester of 1970. In addition, credit incentives became more important after the second semester of 1969.

The movement of REERs permits the inference that some of the biases implicit in the protection structure of 1965 were reduced, though by no means eliminated, after March 1967.

1 The anti-export bias decreased because the REER for traditional and nontraditional exports increased while the effective rate on import-competing activities fell substantially.
2 The bias favoring protection to consumer good industries was reduced because the cut in tariffs was more pronounced than in the case of intermediate and capital goods.
3 The bias against foreign investment decreased after the compensated devaluation because foreign investors received more pesos for their dollars and had to pay lower prices for imported inputs and capital goods. As shown earlier (see table 2.6), direct investment from abroad was encouraged by these measures.

External Transactions

The trade reform did not noticeably open up the economy, as table 2.18 makes clear. In fact, the degree of openness, measured by the ratio of imports plus exports to GDP, was lower during the 1967–71 period than during 1961–6. This was especially true for imports, indicating that the tariff cut did not in fact expose the economy to the pressure of increased foreign competition. However, RER depreciation may have actually contributed to the reduction in import demand.

Changes in import composition reflect the changes in the structure of REERs during this period. Thus the participation of consumer goods rose

Table 2.18 Aggregate imports and exports, 1966–1971

	Imports		*Exports*		
Year	*Real terms (million pesos at constant 1960 prices)*	*Ratio to GDP*	*Real terms (million pesos at constant 1960 prices)*	*Ratio to GDP*	*Openness ratio*
1961–5	1,189.4	10.4	1,262.1	11.0	21.4
1966	1,122.1	8.9	1,474.2	12.0	20.9
1967	1,125.2	8.7	1,456.7	11.5	20.2
1968	1,195.9	8.8	1,436.9	10.8	19.6
1969	1,476.0	10.1	1,677.6	11.5	21.6
1970	1,472.0	9.5	1,788.4	11.8	21.3
1971	1,595.2	9.8	1,577.9	9.7	19.5

Source: Banco Central

Table 2.19 Import structure, 1966–1971 (percent)

Year	Consumer goods	Intermediate goods	Investment goods	Total
1961–5	13.1	60.8	26.1	100.0
1966	13.5	70.2	16.3	100.0
1967	16.1	66.5	17.4	100.0
1968	24.5	58.2	17.3	100.0
1969	21.0	61.6	17.4	100.0
1970	21.3	60.8	17.9	100.0
1971	18.0	62.9	19.1	100.0

Source: based on INDEC data

as a result of the tariff cuts (see table 2.19). The structure of exports also moved in the direction signaled by REER changes. These changes were more marked in the case of nontraditional exports, the participation of which rose accordingly (see table 2.20).

Exports of primary products and manufactures of agricultural origin (taken as a proxy for traditional goods) fell in 1967 and 1968 despite an increase in REERs. We have already explained that the decline in beef exports (19 percent) was mainly due to restrictions in foreign markets. What is more difficult to explain is the substantial drop in other agricultural exports between 1966 and 1968 (cereal exports alone were reduced by 39 percent). Here, we have to take into consideration the fall in foreign prices (see table 2.21) and the fact that, although temporary and compensated for by the real depreciation, the increase in export taxes in 1967 may have discouraged domestic producers. This is relevant when we compare export performances during the Krieger-Vasena and Martínez de Hoz episodes. Nontraditional exports, however, more than doubled between 1965 and

Table 2.20 Export structure, 1966–1971 (percent)

Year	Traditional	Nontraditional	Total
1961–5	91.8	8.2	100.0
1966	91.6	8.4	100.0
1967	89.8	10.2	100.0
1968	84.9	15.1	100.0
1969	85.1	14.9	100.0
1970	88.4	11.6	100.0
1971	87.5	12.5	100.0

Source: based on INDEC data

Table 2.21 External terms of trade, 1960–1973 (1963 = 100)

Year	*Export price / Import price × 100*
1960	93
1961	93
1962	86
1963	100
1964	103
1965	97
1966	95
1967	94
1968	91
1969	93
1970	86
1971	96
1972	105
1973	123

Source: ECLA

1969, reflecting a high response to both real depreciation and export subsidies. On average, the export-to-income ratio for the economy as a whole was barely maintained from 1961–6 to 1967–71.

Income and Product

The period 1966–72 was one of sustained GDP growth, little of which can be directly attributed to trade liberalization. The sectors that expanded most were construction, electricity, gas and water, mining, and manufacturing (see tables 2.22–2.24). Agriculture, however, stagnated. We have already commented on the policies that led to this relatively good performance of the economy. Briefly, these can be characterized as a combination of expansionary monetary and fiscal policies, with the latter being implemented through public investment in a sort of balanced-budget fashion. Public investment increased significantly and produced a quick recovery which started in the construction sector and spread to manufacturing and other activities. The strategy was, for the most part, inward looking: industry grew mainly as a result of larger sales to the domestic market, although industrial exports also increased. These exports, however, were too small when the plan started for a strong impact on growth to be expected.

Table 2.22 Gross domestic product by sector, 1965–1972 (millions of pesos at 1960 prices)

Year	Agriculture, forestry, and fishing	Mining	Manufacturing	Electricity, gas, and water	Construction	Commerce	Transportation	Finance	Other services	GDP at factor costs	GDP at market prices	Effect of the variation in terms of trade	Net retribution to factors abroad	Gross national income
1965	1,834.9	159.3	3,882.1	210.8	365.9	2,069.6	884.5	415.1	1,635.8	11,457.8	12,543.6	54.3	− 48.9	12,549.0
1966	1,766.3	168.1	3,907.7	227.2	388.5	2,058.4	884.5	427.4	1,701.4	11,529.6	12,624.6	49.5	− 159.9	12,514.2
1967	1,842.1	188.4	3,966.9	244.2	438.5	2,079.4	893.3	438.8	1,749.2	11,840.7	12,958.7	− 12.9	− 185.6	12,760.2
1968	1,742.1	211.7	4,224.7	263.9	517.9	2,189.7	940.8	458.1	1,796.2	12,345.1	13,515.5	− 57.9	− 189.7	13,267.9
1969	1,837.6	232.5	4,682.4	287.5	616.9	2,416.7	1,006.0	481.9	1,842.2	13,403.7	14,669.6	− 142.4	− 186.5	14,340.7
1970	1,940.6	248.3	4,977.9	319.8	674.8	2,516.2	1,055.6	489.6	1,898.5	14,121.3	15,459.3	− 222.9	− 177.3	15,059.1
1971	1,842.8	257.3	5,458.5	348.6	651.9	2,681.4	1,096.8	512.7	1,950.2	14,800.3	16,198.4	− 19.3	− 240.5	15,938.5
1972	1,697.8	263.2	5,738.9	385.5	683.6	2,765.9	1,115.0	538.9	2,028.6	15,262.5	16,704.6	133.9	− 206.9	16,631.5

Source: Banco Central

Table 2.23 Annual rates of growth in gross domestic product by sector, 1965–1972 (percent)

Year	Agriculture, forestry, and fishing	Mining	Manufacturing	Electricity, gas, and water	Construction	Commerce	Transportation	Finance	Other services	Total
1965	5.9	3.8	13.8	15.3	3.8	10.3	9.2	3.7	3.6	9.1
1966	− 3.7	5.5	0.7	7.8	6.2	− 0.5	–	3.0	4.0	0.6
1967	4.3	12.1	1.5	7.5	12.9	1.0	1.0	2.7	2.8	2.7
1968	− 5.4	12.4	6.5	8.1	18.1	5.3	5.3	4.4	2.7	4.3
1969	5.5	9.8	10.8	8.9	19.1	10.4	6.9	5.2	2.6	8.6
1970	5.6	6.8	6.3	11.2	9.4	4.1	4.9	1.6	3.1	5.4
1971	− 5.0	3.6	93.7	9.0	− 3.4	6.6	3.9	4.7	2.7	4.8
1972	− 7.9	2.3	6.0	10.6	4.9	3.2	1.7	5.1	4.0	3.1

–, negligible.

Source: Banco Central

Table 2.24 Gross domestic product participation by sector, 1965–1972 (percent)

Year	*Agriculture, forestry, and fishing*	*Mining*	*Manufacturing*	*Electricity, gas, and water*	*Construction*	*Commerce*	*Transportation*	*Finance*	*Other services*	*Total*
1965	16.0	1.4	33.9	1.8	3.2	18.1	7.7	3.6	14.3	100.0
1966	15.3	1.5	33.9	2.0	3.4	17.8	7.7	3.7	14.7	100.0
1967	15.5	1.6	33.5	2.1	3.7	17.6	7.5	3.7	14.8	100.0
1968	14.1	1.7	34.3	2.1	4.2	17.7	7.6	3.7	14.6	100.0
1969	13.7	1.7	35.0	2.1	4.6	18.1	7.5	3.6	13.7	100.0
1970	13.7	1.8	35.2	2.3	4.8	17.8	7.5	3.5	13.4	100.0
1971	12.5	1.7	36.8	2.4	4.4	18.1	7.4	3.5	13.2	100.0
1972	11.1	1.7	37.9	2.5	4.5	18.2	7.3	3.5	13.3	100.0

Source: Banco Central

In general, most manufacturing activities expanded in real terms but, since little of this was the result of trade liberalization, a more specific analysis by categories does not seem necessary.

Employment

Tables 2.25 and 2.26 give information on employment by sector during the period under analysis. The following conclusions emerge:

1 aggregate employment increased during the episode at an annual rate of 2.4 percent between 1966 and 1969;
2 the increase was higher for wage earners than for other occupied persons (owners and self-employed workers);
3 participation in overall employment fell in the case of tradeable sectors (agriculture, manufacturing, and mining).

In addition, tables 2.27–2.30 indicate the following:

1 labor productivity grew noticeably in all sectors except agriculture, finance, and other services (that is, personal services and government);
2 unemployment rates increased in 1967 but then fell, reaching their lowest mark in 1969.

Again, we do not believe that a more disaggregated analysis of employment by sectors would yield more significant results.

Income Distribution

The success of the Krieger-Vasena administration in avoiding a sharp reduction in real wages and the sustained increase in employment over the 1966–72 period improved income distribution as measured by the share of wages in national income. This is true even if the indicator is corrected by the ratio of the number of wage earners to total employment (see table 2.31) which increased throughout the period. As argued by Llach and Sánchez (1984), this correction is needed when there are changes in the composition of employment between wage earners and self-employed workers. The corrected estimate accounts for the share of average wages in the per capita income of employed individuals, whether they are wage earners or not.

Table 2.25 Occupation by sector, 1960–1972 (thousands of workers)

	Agriculture, forestry, and fishing		*Mining*		*Manufacturing*		*Electricity, gas, and water*		*Construction*		*Commerce*		*Transportation*		*Finance*		*Other services*		*Total*	
Year	*Wage earners*	*Other*	*Wage earners*	*Other*	*Wage earners*	*Other*	*Wage earners*	*Other*	*Wage earners*	*Other*	*Wage earners*	*Other*	*Wage earners*	*Other*	*Wage earners*	*Other*	*Wage earners*	*Other*	*Wage earners*	*Other*
1960	809.4	785.5	39.6	2.7	1,506.1	448.1	77.7	1.0	388.1	126.7	579.7	535.1	474.7	82.5	102.3	16.0	1,489.7	202.0	5,467.3	2,199.6
1961	765.4	762.4	41.4	2.6	1,516.0	431.2	78.4	1.1	412.0	124.8	587.4	542.2	470.8	85.4	108.2	16.5	1,544.4	211.3	5,524.6	2,177.5
1962	755.7	740.0	43.7	2.4	1,408.9	415.0	78.3	1.1	372.2	123.0	594.3	549.4	449.5	88.4	113.9	17.1	1,597.5	221.0	5,415.3	2,157.4
1963	753.1	718.3	43.0	2.2	1,322.4	399.4	79.3	1.2	355.9	121.2	602.5	556.6	428.8	91.6	116.4	17.8	1,630.0	231.2	5,333.3	2,139.4
1964	748.2	697.2	41.1	2.1	1,437.1	384.3	89.5	1.2	352.3	119.4	611.0	564.0	440.6	94.9	118.9	18.4	1,691.9	241.8	5.533.6	2,123.3
1965	747.6	676.7	45.1	1.9	1,499.1	369.9	96.6	1.2	365.0	117.7	607.3	571.5	463.5	98.3	122.3	19.1	1,757.4	252.9	5,707.4	2,109.1
1966	690.9	669.1	45.4	1.7	1,477.4	358.2	100.2	1.2	372.8	128.2	611.5	581.4	469.9	103.8	125.4	19.8	1,839.1	264.5	5,736.2	2,128.0
1967	733.1	661.6	44.1	1.6	1,506.5	346.9	101.6	1.2	408.0	139.6	618.1	591.5	473.7	109.7	127.8	20.7	1,898.9	276.6	5,917.2	2,149.0
1968	717.2	654.1	47.2	1.4	1,473.7	336.0	101.4	1.2	465.7	152.0	625.7	601.8	469.6	115.9	133.8	21.5	1,953.0	289.2	5,993.8	2,173.2
1969	749.2	646.8	45.4	1.3	1,537.6	325.4	100.6	1.2	541.5	165.6	633.5	612.3	475.2	122.5	141.5	22.4	2,012.9	302.4	6.244.6	2,199.8
1970	756.5	639.5	45.8	1.1	1,546.2	315.1	100.5	1.2	566.1	180.3	649.2	623.0	496.0	129.4	149.2	23.3	2,070.7	316.8	6,380.5	2,299.3
1971	749.5	635.7	52.4	1.2	1,583.3	331.0	108.2	1.3	579.5	193.8	667.8	630.2	504.9	133.3	150.4	23.9	2,113.5	328.9	6,509.5	2,279.3
1972	742.6	631.8	54.9	1.4	1,626.6	347.8	116.3	1.4	576.7	208.2	673.6	637.5	504.9	137.4	150.4	24.5	2,161.6	342.0	6,607.6	2,331.9

Source: Llach and Sánchez, 1984

Table 2.26 Sectoral participation of workers in 1965 and 1970 (percent)

Year	Agriculture, forestry, and fishing	Mining	Manufacturing	Electricity, gas, and water	Construction	Commerce	Transportation	Finance	Other services	Total
Wage earners										
1965	13.1	0.8	26.3	1.7	6.5	10.6	8.1	2.1	30.8	100.0
1970	11.9	0.7	24.2	1.6	8.8	10.2	7.8	2.3	32.5	100.0
Other										
1965	32.1	0.1	17.5	0.1	5.6	27.1	4.6	0.9	12.0	100.0
1970	28.7	0.1	14.1	0.1	8.1	27.9	5.8	1.0	14.2	100.0

Source: Llach and Sánchez, 1984

Table 2.27 Labor productivity, 1965–1972 (thousands of pesos per worker at constant 1960 prices)

Year	Agriculture, forestry, and fishing	Mining	Manufacturing	Electricity, gas, and water	Construction	Commerce	Transportation	Finance	Other services	Total
1965	1.29	4.03	2.08	2.14	0.76	1.75	1.57	2.92	0.81	1.47
1966	1.30	3.57	2.13	2.24	0.77	1.73	1.54	2.95	0.81	1.42
1967	1.32	4.09	2.14	2.37	0.80	1.72	1.53	2.95	0.80	1.47
1968	1.27	4.33	2.33	2.56	0.84	1.78	1.61	2.95	0.80	1.51
1969	1.32	4.96	2.51	2.56	0.87	1.94	1.68	2.94	0.80	1.59
1970	1.39	5.28	2.67	3.14	0.90	1.98	1.69	2.85	0.80	1.65
1971	1.33	4.76	2.85	3.18	0.84	2.06	1.72	2.95	0.80	1.68
1972	1.23	4.70	2.93	3.27	0.87	2.11	1.74	3.08	0.81	1.71

Table 2.28 Unemployment rates, Greater Buenos Aires, 1966–1970 (October figures)

Sector	*1966*	*1967*	*1968*	*1969*	*1970*
Manufacturing	4.0	5.7	4.0	3.1	4.4
Electricity, gas, and water	0.0	2.0	0.0	0.0	1.2
Construction	5.9	6.1	4.6	2.9	3.7
Commerce and banking	3.4	4.4	2.7	3.0	3.2
Transport	3.5	3.9	2.6	2.3	4.0
Services	3.0	4.1	3.4	3.8	3.7
Total	5.0	6.2	4.7	4.0	5.0

Source: extracted from INDEC data

Table 2.29 Unemployment rates, Córdoba, 1966–1970 (October figures)

Sector	*1966*	*1967*	*1968*	*1969*	*1970*
Manufacturing	4.6	4.8	3.1	2.2	3.8
Electricity, gas, and water	0.0	7.0	0.0	0.0	0.0
Construction	7.6	7.9	3.8	3.2	5.3
Commerce and banking	3.9	3.6	2.1	0.0	2.7
Transport	4.1	2.3	1.7	1.5	1.2
Services	3.6	4.5	3.2	0.0	13.7
Total	6.0	7.2	4.3	3.2	4.7

Source: extracted from INDEC data

Table 2.30 Unemployment rates, Rosario, 1966–1970 (October figures)

Sector	*1966*	*1967*	*1968*	*1969*	*1970*
Manufacturing	4.2	4.8	2.7	3.6	3.0
Electricity, gas, and water	0.0	0.0	5.6	0.0	0.0
Construction	2.8	6.9	6.8	2.7	2.1
Commerce and banking	3.1	4.8	2.5	4.6	2.6
Transport	2.8	5.1	2.2	1.3	3.7
Services	4.3	1.0	3.6	1.7	2.7
Total	5.8	6.1	5.9	5.5	4.9

Source: extracted from INDEC data

Table 2.31 Income distribution, 1960–1972 (percent)

Year	W/Y	w/y
1960	33	48
1961	35	51
1962	36	51
1963	34	50
1964	34	50
1965	36	52
1966	40	57
1967	41	58
1968	41	57
1969	41	57
1970	42	59
1971	43	60
1972	39	54

W/Y, share of wages in national income (× 100).
$w/y = (W/Y)/(L_w/L)$ where L_w is the number of wage earners and L is the total employment (wage earners plus self-employed workers).

Source: Llach and Sánchez, 1984

Summary and Conclusions

The following general aspects of the 1967 tariff cum stabilization reform in Argentina are germane to the questions addressed by the trade liberalization study as a whole (see the preface to the volume).

1 The policy was, for all practical purposes, an unannounced once-and-for-all tariff cut completed by the elimination of some, but not all, quantitative restrictions.
2 It was undertaken under rather favorable initial conditions: relatively high levels of activity and employment, good export performance in the preceding three years, absence of serious external shocks, and a government which was regarded as strong and credible.
3 The compensated devaluation scheme was highly successful in avoiding dramatic changes in the status quo of income distribution while improving the external balance. In addition, the devaluation and the new structure of effective exchange rates simultaneously reduced three existing biases in the economy: the anti-export bias, the bias

favoring consumer goods production, and the bias against foreign investment.

4 Despite official declarations, there are reasons for believing that the tariff reform was more pragmatic (compensating for the devaluation, easing trade negotiations with other countries, and so forth) than a reflection of a profound ideological shift toward free trade.

5 Compared with the situation in 1965, the reform undoubtedly approached a more rational tariff structure. This and the elimination of some import prohibitions were necessary steps for the first stage of a trade liberalization program. Additional steps would have been required to secure long-term effects on resource allocation and industrial efficiency.

6 Unfortunately, no intensification of the reform occurred, perhaps reflecting the reluctance of policymakers to engage in major liberalization efforts.

The reversal in trade liberalization policies after 1970 may come as a surprise to a reader unfamiliar with Argentina's sociopolitical environment between 1969 and 1976. However, as noted before, social reactions against the military government spread after 1969, mostly motivated by uneasy feelings about political authoritarianism.

A thorough analysis of this complex period in Argentina's history remains to be written. Political scientists and sociologists are still puzzled as to the leading causes of social distress during these years, in which Argentines witnessed a wave of radicalism marked by frequent street riots, student revolts, and the emergence of terrorism. At any rate, the unrest cannot be satisfactorily accounted for by an economic situation which, if anything, had improved.

Wage demands, arising from mounting labor conflicts, increased to a point where the government lost control of inflation. From 1971 to 1973 the reversal in trade policies was linked to the increase in inflation, since failure to devalue promptly forced the authorities to restrict imports in order to avoid external imbalances. Moreover, a surge in nationalistic sentiments shared by many sectors of society sustained the reversal and paved the way for the return of Juan and Isabel Perón, under whose government (1973–6) economic policies became firmly biased against free trade.

3

The Martínez de Hoz Liberalization Episode

In the late 1970s Argentina made a move to liberalize an economy suffering from a highly distorted trade regime and a repressed financial sector. Unfortunately, the mismanagement of the transition to an open economy created new problems for the producers of tradeable goods and led to an external crisis. The inconsistent use of policy instruments is evidenced by the excessive overvaluation of the peso and the high real interest rates that prevailed during the period, phenomena which cannot be blamed on trade liberalization itself but must be ascribed to inconsistent accompanying policies. In this chapter we look at the joint effects of liberalization and stabilization on macroeconomic performance. The various trade and accompanying policy measures are described in the first four sections of the chapter while their effects on aggregate (macroeconomic) variables are dealt with in the fifth section. A more detailed analysis by sector is given in appendix 2.

Broad Nature and General Targets

The trade liberalization policy of 1976–81 encompassed a two-stage reform. The first stage (1976–8) was characterized by the following measures: (a) a tariff cut along all BTN positions; (b) the elimination of export taxes on most traditional products; (c) a change from QRs to tariffs for all commodities except steel and aluminum. The second stage (1979–81) consisted of a pre-announced schedule of quarterly tariff reductions to be applied from January 1979 to January 1984. Trade policies were reversed in 1981 as a consequence of an external crisis.

The first important tariff cut took place in November 1976. Decree 3008/76 set the levels of most tariffs to be maintained until January 1979. This first reduction was basically intended to eliminate "water" or redundancy in protection. Simultaneously, the government appointed a special commission to design a new tariff structure "compatible with the objective of sustained economic growth." The result of the commission's work was Resolution 1634/78 which established a five-year program of tariff reduction. The general features of the program were as follows: (a) it established numerical end targets; (b) the process was intended to accelerate; (c) industries were not treated uniformly. With respect to the last point, the reform did not choose a uniform tariff for all sectors as its goal, but maintained the escalated system contained in the previous structure, although reducing its intensity. In addition, the automobile industry was excluded from Resolution 1634 and given special treatment.

The general aims of the policy were to eliminate distortions in the allocation of resources, to increase the competitiveness of Argentine exports, and to introduce the beneficial effects of foreign competition into the domestic production of importables.

Implementation of the First Stage, 1976–1978

The first stage was implemented in three steps: a tariff cut, the elimination of export taxes, and a change from QRs to tariffs.

Tariffs

In November 1976 tariffs were reduced along most BTN positions. The legal instrument of the reform, Decree 3008/76, established the new tariff levels shown in table 3.1. The criteria for the classification of goods were the same as those followed in the 1967 tariff reform (Decree 1410/67; see

Table 3.1 Import tariff levels in November 1976 (percent)

	Degree of elaboration									
Economic classification	*1*	*2*	*3*	*4*	*5*	*6*	*7*	*8*	*9*	*10*
Consumption goods										
1 Produced domestically	80	80	80	85	85	95	95	95	100	100
2 Not produced domestically	25	30	35	45	50	60	65	70	80	95
Intermediate goods										
1 Produced domestically	30	35	45	50	60	65	70	80	85	95
2 Not produced domestically	5	5	10	10	15	15	25	25	30	30
Capital goods										
1 Produced domestically	30	35	45	50	50	60	60	65	65	70
2 Not produced domestically	25	25	25	30	30	30	30	35	35	35

Source: Berlinsky, 1975

Table 3.2 Economic classification of tariffs under the 1967 reform (percent)

	Degree of elaboration									
Economic classification	*1*	*2*	*3*	*4*	*5*	*6*	*7*	*8*	*9*	*10*
Consumption goods										
1 Produced domestically	110	110	120	120	130	130	130	130	140	140
2 Not produced domestically	30	40	50	60	70	80	90	100	110	120
Intermediate goods										
1 Produced domestically	40	50	60	70	80	90	100	110	120	130
2 Not produced domestically	5	5	10	20	20	20	30	30	40	40
Capital goods										
1 Produced domestically	40	50	60	70	70	80	80	90	90	100
2 Not produced domestically	30	30	30	40	40	40	40	50	50	50

Source: Alemann, 1969

table 3.2). However, a comparison of the two tables does not reflect the total extent of the 1976 changes since some tariffs had actually increased between 1967 and 1976. For example, in 1976 protection rates for some consumption goods had reached 200 percent, and were lowered to 85 and 95 percent (Berlinsky, 1978).

Tariff reduction continued in 1977, with emphasis during the second semester, and was implemented without previous announcements.[1] The effect of these regulations and Decree 3008 on the import tariff structure between October 1976 and November 1978 is illustrated in table 3.3. According to the data presented in the table, 51 percent of all positions had a tariff lower than or equal to 20 percent in 1978, whereas the same proportion had tariffs of up to 70 percent in 1976. The maximum duty fell from 210 to 100 percent. However, to raise revenue, all positions at the 5 percent tariff level were moved to 10 percent.

The effects on the protection structure by sector were studied by Nogués (1978); his results are presented in table 3.4 at the SIC three-digit level of aggregation. Along with legal tariffs, the Nogués figures include other specific taxes on imports, such as *Contribución Siderúrgica*, *Fondo de Fomento Minero*, and *Fondo Forestal*. The results, based on a sample of 40

1 Nogués (1978) has listed the main legal resolutions issued during that year: Resolutions M.E. 507/77 (cigarettes), 520/77 (electrical appliances, electronic parts, and equipment), 539/77 (pesticides), 754/77 (paper and paperboard, which also eliminated the import suspension on tractors), 967/77 (machinery for use in agriculture and industry), 983/77 (inputs for the textile industry), 990/77 (inputs for the steel industry), and 1020/77 (chemical products).

Table 3.3 Import tariff structure in October 1976 and November 1978

	Number of BTN positions		*Cumulative frequency (%)*	
Tariff (%)	*Oct 76*	*Nov 78*	*Oct 76*	*Nov 78*
0	87	89	1.1	1.1
5	2,615	0	34.0	1.1
10	51	3,609	34.7	44.8
15	299	364	38.4	49.2
20	154	168	40.4	51.3
25	67	137	41.2	52.9
30	23	100	41.5	56.4
35	0	188	41.5	54.2
40	19	625	41.7	64.0
45	1	273	41.7	67.3
50	311	2,066	45.7	92.4
55	2	191	45.7	94.7
60	219	272	48.5	98.0
65	0	78	48.5	98.9
70	399	7	53.5	99.0
75	0	40	53.5	99.5
80	1,749	0	75.7	99.5
85	0	0	75.5	99.5
90	910	11	87.0	99.6
95	0	29	87.0	100.0
100	304	2	90.8	100.0
110	229	0	93.7	100.0
120	106	0	95.0	100.0
130	149	0	96.9	100.0
140	88	0	98.0	100.0
150	3	0	98.0	100.0
200	154	0	100.0	100.0
210	2	0	100.0	100.0
Total	7,941	8,249	100%	100%

Source: FIEL, 1980

five-digit sectors (SIC), show a reduction of 41 percentage points in average nominal protection (from 94 to 53 percent) between October 1976 and December 1977, and an increase in dispersion, as measured by the coefficient of variation. To understand these results better, we have included a column of "implicit" tariff rates calculated for the same sample of goods by Berlinsky (1978) on the basis of domestic versus international price differentials. The first point of interest that emerges from the comparison of the Nogués and Berlinsky figures is the excessive water in the 1976 tariff structure: domestic value added in the selected activities was only 37 percent above value added calculated at international prices.[2] Also, the coefficient of variation was higher when implicit, instead of explicit, tariff rates were used.[3] Tariff redundancy decreased after the cuts, and the structure of protection by sector became more closely linked to implicit tariffs. This outcome is confirmed by the values of the rank-order correlation coefficients between the second and third columns (−6 percent) and the third and fourth columns (56 percent) in table 3.4.

Table 3.4 Nominal protection rates by sector, October 1976, February and December 1977 (percent)

Sector	*Official protection*		*Implicit protection*
	Oct 76	*Dec 77*	*Feb 77*
321 Textile products	108	57	41
322 Clothing and apparel	200	95	79
341 Paper and paperboard	29	29	31
351 Basic industrial chemical products	79	35	37
352 Other chemical products	99	17	0
355 Rubber products	110	45	30
362 Glass products	94	42	12
369 Nonmetallic mineral products	66	11	0
371 Basic iron and steel industries	89	48	61
372 Other basic metal industries	69	45	47
381 Metal products, except machinery and equipment	133	46	10
382 Nonelectrical machinery	98	66	20
383 Electrical machinery	89	61	56
384 Transport equipment	127	87	30
385 Professional equipment	80	50	73
Weighted average	94	53	37
Simple mean	98	49	35
Coefficient of variation	0.39	0.46	0.71
Economic classification			
Consumer nondurables	200	95	46
Consumer durables	134	74	29
Machinery	132	94	33
Intermediate goods	84	43	41

Sources: Nogués, 1978; Berlinsky, 1978

2 There are reasons to believe that differentials between domestic producer prices and c.i.f. import prices overestimated redundancy at the time Berlinsky surveyed them. On the one hand, the RER was above its long-run equilibrium mark in February 1977 (Rodríguez and Sjaastad, 1979). On the other hand, real wages and interest rates, two important variables affecting domestic costs, were abnormally low.

3 This makes perfect sense when legal tariffs are redundant. An extreme case would be a uniform legal protective rate which becomes prohibitive for all sectors. Differences in market structure, domestic costs, etc., across sectors would then determine unequal implicit tariffs even when no dispersion exists among legal tariffs.

Hence we should not be surprised that legal protective rates also became more dispersed in 1977.

Finally, table 3.4 reports average nominal protection rates for goods categorized by their economic classification. Tariff reductions did not alter "escalation" in nominal protection. Thus consumer goods continued to be more protected than capital goods and these, in turn, were more protected than intermediate products. However, this official protective structure contrasts with the structure of implicit tariffs shown in the fourth column. Notably, intermediate goods appear to be the most protected group after consumer durables. The rates are particularly high for sectors 371 and 372 (steel and other basic metals), probably because of nontariff barriers (that is, QRs). Note also that the implicit tariffs on machinery are lower than the tariffs on metals, thereby reducing implicit effective protection in the former sector (which, of course, uses metals intensively as inputs).

Export Taxes

Multiple exchange rates between 1971 and 1976 favored nontraditional over traditional exports. The gap is even wider if effective rates are considered, since both export subsidies and taxes on each class of commodities reached peak levels during that period. As a result of exchange rate unification, the real rate for traditional exports increased by 20 percent. However, since export taxes were lowered and in some cases almost totally eliminated by 1977, the rise in effective exchange rates was much more significant. Table 3.5 shows the changes made in export taxes during the liberalization episode. This policy contributed to reducing the discrimination to which traditional exports were subject.

Quantitative Restrictions

Two kinds of QRs were present in 1976: import prohibitions, affecting 100 BTN positions at the eight-digit level (Berlinsky, 1978), and import

Table 3.5 Export taxes on traditional exports (percent)

Traditional exports	*1973*	*1976*	*1977*	*1979*	*1980*
Cereals	32	50	0	0	0
Oil seeds	46	59	0	3	0
Fruits	10	10	0	0	0
Wool	11	25	5	5	0
Livestock	28	50	12	1	1
Beef	12	12	1	0	0
Vegetable oils	35	47	3	0	0

Source: Guía Práctica del Exportador e Importador, several issues

licenses. Among the commodities included in the former group, we find automobiles, tractors, transport equipment, and motor engines. Some prohibitions were eliminated in 1977, but they remained for the automobile industry until the end of 1978. The industries that were afforded protection through import licenses included some textiles, wood, chemicals, and notably capital goods and metals. Import licenses for all other sectors were eliminated with the exception of those affecting imports of steel and aluminum. For capital goods, the process was complete by the end of 1978.

As a rule, import licenses on capital goods have been granted whenever the required goods were not produced at home. This afforded protection to the domestic capital goods industry but also stimulated the adoption of capital intensive technologies using foreign equipment for which there were no domestically produced substitutes. Licenses on steel and other metals, in turn, were used to protect the state companies that produced them and were authorized in case of supply shortages. In 1980, steel importers paid a 10 percent tariff with a license and 37 percent without it. The difference (27 percent above the c.i.f. price) gives an estimate of the implicit cost of obtaining the permit.

The Second Stage, 1979–1981

The foregoing description shows a rather disorganized process of tariff reductions and elimination of QRs taking place between 1976 and 1978 without a clear announcement of the rules of the game. However, the principal purpose of this reform – the elimination of redundant protection – does appear to have been fulfilled.

The government was extremely cautious about subsequent measures. In 1978, a special commission was created (*Comisión* 50) to devise a program of further tariff reductions to be implemented from January 1979. This program was intended to intensify the process of liberalization started in 1976 and, since the new tariff cuts were expected to increase the competitiveness of imports from a situation in which water had already been eliminated, tariff reductions were gradual and pre-announced.

After months of debate among officials from the Ministry of Economics and the Banco Central, the commission came out with a five-year plan which established quarterly reductions in tariffs until January 1984 (Resolution M.E. 1634/78). The starting levels of the tariff and the final targets are reported in table 3.6. The plan maintained the criterion of grouping goods according to economic category, except that in this case case seven groups (instead of three) were defined. Each group had three aggregates to which increasing tariff levels were applicable, but this feature of the plan was obscure since there was no precise definition of the items to be

Table 3.6 Tariff program under resolution 1634/78

Economic classification	*Aggregate*	*Tariff (%)* *Jan 1979*	*Jan 1984*	*Variation (%)*
1 Consumption goods	1	65	30	59
	2	45	35	53
	3	85	40	53
2 Foodstuffs, beverages, and tobacco	1	39	12	69
	2	45	14	69
	3	52	16	69
3 Intermediate goods	1	44	18	59
	2	46	21	54
	3	348	24	50
4 Basic raw materials except those classified in groups	1	36	15	58
	2	39	17	56
	3	42	20	52
5 Basic raw materials of agricultural origin	1	21	10	52
	2	25	12	52
	3	329	14	52
6 Goods not produced domestically	1	10	10	0
	2	10	10	0
	3	10	10	0
7 Investment goods	1	46	20	56
	2	48	23	52
	3	50	27	46

Source: Nogués, 1983

included in each aggregate. Moreover, the requirement left room for much discretion in tariff allocation, which led to transfers of commodities from one aggregate to another in response to private requests.

Another characteristic of the program was that it was too gradual. In a country where protected entrepreneurs and workers fearing unemployment resist liberalization, a slow reduction in tariffs gives those pressure groups an opportunity to organize themselves more quickly and effectively than the sectors that benefit from liberalization such as consumers and exports (Medina, 1980 and Nogués, 1983). It is evident from table 3.6 that the program was not intended to change the structure of tariffs but only to reduce levels of nominal protection. According to Medina (1980), gradualism would have been justified if the end target had been a uniform tariff, but this was not so. Some changes in tariff structure did take place, however, as a consequence of departures from the pre-announced plan in 1979 and 1980.

The first deviation from the planned schedule occurred just four days after it began. Resolution M.E. 6/79 gave the economic authority power to use discretionary tariff reductions as a way of disciplining domestic producers of goods whose prices had risen more than the pre-announced devaluation rate during predefined intervals. The importance of this legal norm was not measured by its direct impact (only 2 percent of imports from January 1979 to June 1980 were affected by its application) but by the uncertainty it created among producers (FIEL, 1980; Nogués, 1983). A second source of uncertainty was introduced by Resolution M.E. 493/79 which, in April 1979, reduced the tariffs on capital goods to the levels set initially for 1984. Furthermore, duty-free imports of some investment goods not produced at home had been allowed since January 1979 by virtue of Resolution 1834/78. Lastly, imports of steel and other basic metal inputs are still heavily protected, accounting for a large reduction in the EPR in the capital goods sector.

Although the 1979–84 tariff reform covered most BTN positions, there were some exceptions. Basically, these included the commodities subject to QRs (for example, steel and aluminum) and the automobile industry. The latter was subject to a special regime that established a tariff of 95 percent for 1979 which was to fall in January of each year until it reached a final level of 45 percent.

In addition to tariffs, importers paid other taxes on imports which were not eliminated by the tariff reform. Three of them are specific to some goods: *Fondo de Fomento Minero*, *Contribución Siderúrgica*, and *Gravamen para Productos Forestales*. The rates in each case vary from 1 to 10 percent of the c.i.f. value of the imports to which they apply. Three additional taxes are general to all imports: *Arancel Consular*, *Gravamen sobre Fletes*, and *Servicio de Estadísticas*. The sum of these represents about 7 percent. These fees are not paid in return for any specific service received during the import process but are used to create funds which finance or promote other activities. In this sense, they have the same distortionary effects as tariffs. By the same token, some regulations on domestic indirect taxes which discriminate against imports are, in effect, tariff surcharges, which were found by Wisecarver (1979) to be very important for alcoholic beverages, tobacco, automobile tires, and cosmetics. An interesting example of extra protection afforded by nontariff taxes on imports is the automobile industry, in which the combined effect of all legal protection instruments added up to from 132 to 192 percent for a 95 percent tariff in 1979 and from 121 to 175 percent for an 85 percent tariff in 1980 (FIEL, 1980).

Results for overall nominal protection, including tariff and nontariff barriers, are presented in table 3.7. The figures, based on FIEL calculations, correspond to 1979 and 1980 and also include nominal export incentives.

Table 3.7 Nominal rates of protection, 1979–1980 (percent)

Sector	1979		1980	
	Imports	*Exports*	*Imports*	*Exports*
3 Total manufacturing	56.7	34.4	53.4	33.8
31 Foodstuffs, beverages, and tobacco	23.7	18.2	23.5	14.7
311 Foodstuffs	23.7	18.2	23.5	14.7
32 Textiles, clothing, and leather products	58.7	38.2	54.6	37.9
321 Textiles	51.7	33.3	47.5	30.1
322 Clothing and apparel	71.7	47.3	67.7	52.3
34 Paper, paperboard, and printing	55.3	31.2	52.4	34.9
341 Paper and paperboard	55.3	31.2	52.4	34.9
35 Chemical products	50.6	38.0	47.1	33.8
351 Basic industrial chemical products	44.1	39.0	40.8	33.2
352 Other chemical products	43.3	39.1	39.6	36.4
355 Rubber products	77.1	34.0	73.1	34.2
36 Stone, glass, and ceramics	37.8	30.1	36.0	28.0
362 Glass products	52.4	34.3	48.6	36.2
369 Nonmetal mineral products	23.7	26.0	23.7	20.0
37 Metals	49.2	30.9	47.7	27.8
371 Basic iron and steel industries	48.7	36.6	47.4	33.2
372 Other basic metal industries	52.3	− 2.4	49.5	− 3.7
38 Metallic products, machinery, and equipment	81.6	41.6	75.9	45.2
381 Metallic products	52.5	36.1	51.6	40.4
382 Nonelectrical machinery	57.8	42.1	54.2	46.4
383 Electrical machinery	55.3	40.8	51.7	45.5
384 Transport equipment	134.9	40.1	124.0	44.8
385 Professional equipment	47.6	44.0	47.3	48.5
Unweighted mean	51.9		49.2	
Standard deviation	28.6		39.3	
Coefficient of variation	0.55		0.88	

Source: based on FIEL, 1980

Accompanying Policies

Exchange Rate Policy

From 1971 to 1976, a system of multiple exchange rates existed, set by the Banco Central. Each rate was a linear combination of two basic official rates, the commercial and the financial. Thus, if the exchange rate received by exporters of a particular commodity was too low, the government could increase it by authorizing a higher proportion of the foreign exchange to be converted into pesos at the higher financial market rate. As is well known, multiple exchange rates create an implicit structure of export and import taxes and subsidies. In the case of Argentina, they also provided a basis for what Martirena-Mantel (1981) has called the "disguised crawling peg." This was a system by which the nominal exchange rate implicit in commercial transactions was adjusted in response to domestic price increases by altering the proportions of foreign exchange, accrued to exporters or required by importers, channeled through the commercial and financial markets. These implicit mini-devaluations, however, did not prevent the domestic currency from appreciating in real terms, and so maxi-devaluations became appropriate, as for instance in 1972 and 1975.

The new government moved quickly toward exchange rate unification, which was achieved by the end of 1976 when the premium between black-market and official rates also disappeared (see table 3.8). Thereafter, the government adopted the policy of depreciating the peso daily following a decision-variant unannounced crawling peg rule until the end of 1978.

Since it was unannounced, the decision-variant rule was a source of exchange rate uncertainty which, although good from the point of view of restricting destabilizing capital inflows, was not reassuring enough to encourage expectations of lower inflation. By 1978, the government was already committed to using the crawl as an active anti-inflationary instrument. Taking advantage of a sharp increase in reserves during previous years, the authorities let the nominal exchange rate grow more slowly than past inflation. However, in order to force expectations down, a clearer and more credible effort was needed. This led Banco Central officials to choose an active crawl-reduction scheme based on the pre-announcement of future rates of depreciation.

Table 3.8 Nominal exchange rates, 1971–1978 (pesos per US dollar)

	Implicit commercial[a]			
Year	*Exports*	*Imports*	*Financial*	*Black market*
1971	4.5	4.5	5.4	6.1
1972	7.9	8.2	9.8	11.5
1973	9.0	9.3	9.9	11.2
1974	9.1	8.9	9.9	16.2
1975	25.9	21.3	31.9	72.1
1976	189.4	149.7	196.3	257.8
1977	402.3	410.4	422.6	423.1
1978	790.6	805.6	814.6	808.3

[a] Calculated as exports (imports) in current pesos divided by exports (imports) in current dollars.

Source: *Index Económico* and INDEC

Forthcoming changes in exchange rates were pre-announced on five occasions: (a) from December 31, 1978 to February 28, 1979; (b) extended to December 31, 1979; (c) on January 20, 1980; (d) on December 10, 1980; (e) from February to August 1981. On the third and fourth occasions, depreciation rates, rather than exchange rate levels, were announced and the duration was not stated. In February 1981, there was a 10 percent devaluation not included in the program. This was followed by a second devaluation in March (30 percent), and after that the plan was abandoned.

Export Promotion Policy

The government maintained several instruments of promotion for nontraditional exports. The most important were the following.

1. Domestic tax refunds or *reembolsos*, amounting to up to 40 percent of the f.o.b. value of exports. Tax refunds accounted for more than 90 percent of all fiscal benefits granted to nontraditional exports in 1976–80. A plan to reduce this subsidy gradually, with a view to eventual elimination, was under way in 1980.
2. An income tax deduction of 10 percent, equivalent to 2.2 percent of exports.
3. Credit incentives of two kinds: (a) production financing or *prefinanciación* and (b) export financing or *financiación*. These are described below.

Prefinanciación is a credit system for financing production of nontraditional export goods. Between 1977 and 1981 the maximum proportion to be financed varied from 40 to 90 percent of the f.o.b. value of exports, depending on the commodity. Capital goods exports were favored by this policy, which also established differentials in interest rates and loan maturity. The size of the subsidy was determined by the proportion of exports actually financed times the difference between the market cost of credit and the preferential rate charged by the Banco Central. Loans have been denominated in US dollars since 1978, and an annual rate of 1 percent was charged as against the much higher rate prevailing in international markets.

Financiación was a system whereby exporters could discount letters of exchange at domestic banks at rates set by the monetary authority. The interest rate was 7.5 percent (for dollar-denominated loans), a value lower than the US prime rate during the late 1970s. Differences among lists of export goods were determined on the basis of loan maturity, percentage of the f.o.b. value to be financed, and periodicity of loan payments. As with *prefinanciación*, the terms favored capital goods exports significantly. The maturity period of loans was eight and a half years.

Nogués (1983) has estimated the size of financial subsidies under the assumption that exporters had full access to available credit lines with this system. The results, reported in table 3.9, show that the total subsidy granted to exporters amounted to over 60 percent for capital goods and 20 percent for consumer durables.

A third financial incentive to nontraditional exports was provided in the form of credit to foreign importers of Argentine goods. These credits could finance up to 80 percent of exports and the term of repayment were eight and a half years for capital goods and three years for consumer durables.

Income Policy

In 1976, the government liberalized all prices that had been subject to direct controls under Peronist rule. However, in order to affect the cost–push determinants of inflation, the authorities first decreed a freeze on nominal wages and then resorted to direct controls on wage increases. The failure to reduce inflation rates below the 7 percent monthly level led officials to try a temporary freeze on prices, called *tregua de precios*, between March and June 1977. The idea was to reduce inflationary expectations by forcing leading firms to avoid generalized price increases during a four-month period, but the attempt failed. Wages were made more flexible in 1977, and salaries were fully liberalized in 1979.

Financial Liberalization

In June 1977 a financial reform changed the *modus operandi* of the Argentine financial system. At that time, ceilings on interest rates on bank loans and deposits were lifted, leaving their determination exclusively to market forces. The Banco Central imposed a uniform minimum reserve rate (45 percent) on all kinds of deposits and paid interest on reserves created from time deposits. Thus the reform was clearly intended to eliminate "financial repression" in the McKinnon sense (McKinnon, 1973). This well-established characteristic of the Argentine financial system had reached an extreme in 1973–6 under the Peronist government's Regime of Nationalization of Deposits: a 100 percent reserve requirement on all deposits held by commercial banks accompanied by a complex system of direct credit allocation by the monetary authority through rediscounting. Under this regime, the role of private financial institutions had been reduced to channeling public funds and distributing them among preferred claimants. The 1977 reform thus drastically changed the rules of this particular game.

Nominal interest rates on domestic loans rose from 6 percent in May 1977 (monthly rate, subject to a ceiling) to 13.5 percent in November 1977, after which they fell to 7–8 percent. The temporary jump in interest rates

Table 3.9 Credit subsidy per US dollar of exports, 1977–1980

	Capital goods			*Consumer durables*			*Other*		
Year	*Prefinanciación*	*Financiación*	*Total*	*Prefinanciación*	*Financiación*	*Total*	*Prefinanciación*	*Financiación*	*Total*
1977	0.64	0.01	0.65	0.18	0.01	0.19	0.17	0.00	0.17
1978	0.54	0.10	0.64	0.15	0.04	0.19	0.14	0.02	0.16
1979	0.48	0.19	0.67	0.15	0.09	0.24	0.14	0.03	0.17
1980	0.36	0.25	0.61	0.12	0.12	0.24	0.11	0.05	0.16

Source: Nogués, 1983

was not entirely due to the financial reform, however, since monetary contraction was applied during the second semester of 1977 (see the next subsection). Nor was the change in regime a sudden unexpected shock. The ceiling on nominal interest rates had risen from 2 to 4 percent in 1975 and from 4 to 6 percent in 1976. As inflation went down during the months that followed the change in the government, real interest rates became positive for the first time in several years. However, segments of uncontrolled interest rates authorized by the Banco Central had existed since 1975, when the rates charged and paid by nonbank intermediaries (*financieras*) had been free and large numbers of marketable index bonds had been issued to finance government deficits.

In addition to domestic financial liberalization, the capital account became more open. A new regime of direct foreign investment, approved in 1976, pruned the superfluity of regulations that had characterized the previous one. Under the new liberalization, domestic and foreign investors were treated equally, and the subsidiaries of foreign firms were regarded as legally independent from the main branches. Restrictions on the way foreign firms could operate became minimal and investment approval was not required from the government except where security was involved or when the activities included public and financial services. Another piece of legislation (*Ley de Transferencia de Tecnología*) abolished regulations on the use of foreign technology, established lower limitations on royalty payments, and permitted the use of foreign trademarks. This also helped ease the relationships between foreign firms and domestic subsidiaries.

Capital flows other than direct foreign investment were also liberalized.[4] Regulations on external borrowing were loosened while, at the same time, controls on capital outflows became superfluous since the effect of the 1977 reform was to lower the demand for foreign assets. The first step toward liberalizing the capital account was taken in July 1976, before the unification of the exchange rate system, when private borrowers were authorized to sell foreign exchange in the free market at the going exchange rate. Loans were subject to approval by the Banco Central and had to exceed a six-month maturity period. Later on, in January 1977, the need for approval was eliminated (only registration of the debt was required) but the minimum-term condition was maintained.

The increase in interest rates after the 1977 reform and the elimination of exchange controls attracted short-run capital inflow. To prevent volatile capital outflows from eroding the monetary controls and creating future instability, the government increased the minimum term at which the private sector could borrow abroad, first to one year in August 1977 and then to two years in November 1977. Since the rate of devaluation was not pre-announced, the extension of the loan term was expected to increase

4 The discussion here draws on Frenkel (1980).

the exchange rate risk associated with external borrowing. In March 1978 it was also decided that the maturity of commercial loans for export financing could not go beyond the date at which export payments were received. A maximum six-month term was established to prevent exporters from resorting to short-term financing of nonexport activities through the extension of commercial loan terms. Similar measures were adopted for import financing.

An implicit tax on external credit was introduced in May 1978 when the Banco Central made it necessary to deposit 20 percent of the amount received through foreign loans in a non-interest-bearing account denominated in pesos. The effect of this measure was to increase the cost of foreign credit by about 1.5 percent per month (Frenkel, 1980).

Neither the deposit requirement nor the minimum-term restriction described earlier applied to public sector loans. In December 1979 the government eliminated all restrictions on private capital movements, except the requirement of a one-year grace period before borrowers could start servicing the principal. The rate of devaluation was pre-announced but, since the period covered by the announcement was less than one year, exchange rate uncertainty was not completely eliminated. In July 1980 the minimum-term condition was lifted, but by that time exchange rate announcements had become less credible.

Monetary Policy

Before the reform, monetary policy was not an active instrument of stabilization but simply followed price increases. Only the sources for expanding the monetary base changed, as domestic sources (government deficit financing, rediscounting, and so on) became less important relative to foreign sources (that is, changes in international reserves) as a result of current account surpluses that had begun to accumulate beginning in 1976. Immediately after the reform the money supply was contracted in order to deflate. As a consequence, loan interest rates nearly doubled in nominal terms, leading to a fall in investment and less activity during the last quarter of 1977 and the first half of 1978. Meanwhile, high interest rates attracted capital inflows which undermined monetary control.

Table 3.10 shows the evolution of monetary aggregates in 1976–8. Between April 1976 and May 1977, M1 and M3 grew at average monthly rates of 9.7 percent and 12.6 percent, respectively, while average inflation was 6.6 percent. Hence, money supply was passive during this period. The situation changed in June 1977. Between this month and September, the rate of expansion of M1 dropped to 4.2 percent in nominal terms (– 3.6 percent in real terms). However, since the demand for time and savings deposits increased substantially, M3 still grew at a positive real rate. In October, however, all monetary aggregates fell rather severely in

Table 3.10 Money aggregates, 1976–1978 (average monthly rate, percent)

Years	*M1*	*Time and savings deposits*	*M3*	*Loans to the private sector*
May 76–May 77				
Nominal	9.7	17.4	12.6	15.7
Real	2.9	10.1	5.6	8.5
Jun 77–Sep 77				
Nominal	4.2	15.5	10.2	14.5
Real	−3.6	6.9	1.9	5.9
Oct 77				
Nominal	1.1	8.5	5.5	6.7
Real	−10.9	−4.3	−7.1	−6.0
Oct 77–Feb 78				
Nominal	7.4	11.3	9.8	6.4
Real	−0.7	2.9	1.5	−1.6
Mar 78–Dec 78				
Nominal	9.7	9.2	9.4	10.5
Real	1.9	1.5	1.6	2.6

Source: Frenkel, 1980

real terms, and the contraction of credit persisted until February 1978. From then on, monetary policy became passive again, mainly because the government was unable to control money supply and the exchange rate at the same time. As indicated earlier, restrictions on capital mobility were eliminated in 1979. Once the government started to pre-fix nominal exchange rates with free capital mobility, money supply became endogenous, with the stock of reserves being the adjusting variable. The Banco Central set a target of 70 percent for domestic credit expansion in 1979 which was more or less consistent with the pre-announced rate of devaluation (65 percent). The actual growth of domestic credit, however, was 130 percent (see table 3.11), mainly because of a significant reduction in the minimum reserves ratio required on all kinds of deposits from an initial level of 45 percent in December 1977. Reserves fell most steeply during the last quarter of 1978 and throughout the second semester of 1979; in December of that year, the ratio was 16.5 percent.[5]

5 Although the fall in bank reserves increases the availability of domestic credit, part of the monetary effect was offset because less money had to be printed in order to pay interest on those reserves.

Table 3.11 Domestic credit expansion and devaluation rates, 1979–1980 (percent)

Year/quarter	*Rate of domestic credit expansion*	*Rate of devaluation*	*Difference*
1979			
I	21.7	16.8	4.9
II	20.8	14.5	6.3
III	22.9	11.9	11.0
IV	25.9	11.3	14.6
1980			
I	21.7	9.0	12.7
II	15.3	6.8	8.5
III	14.8	5.3	9.5
IV	18.2	3.4	14.8

Domestic credit is defined as M3 minus the stock of reserves held by the Central Bank, denominated in pesos. Both credit expansion and devaluation were calculated from average quarterly figures as opposed to end-of-period figures.

Source: Banco Central

Lack of monetary discipline remained a keynote of policy in 1980, when domestic credit grew by 90 percent while the exchange rate was devalued by only 25 percent. This time, however, the source of monetary expansion was a large fiscal deficit, part of which was financed by the Banco Central and by foreign creditors.

Fiscal Policy

According to official publications (see table 3.12), the primary public sector deficit fell from 14 percent of GDP in 1975 to 9.8 percent in 1976 and to 3.2 percent in 1977. This was achieved mainly through increased tax collection. On the expenditure side, current spending fell but this was matched by a rise in public investment. Between 1977 and 1981, current spending increased again and, despite a fall in public investment and a further increase in tax collection, the deficit doubled as a proportion of GDP.

This measure of the deficit does not include interest payments on domestic and foreign public debt, either real or nominal. However, the inclusion of real interest rate payments does not alter the picture substantially.

An alternative measurement of the deficit is derived by summing the various sources of financing. This is shown in table 3.13 using an unofficial estimation by Cavallo and Peña (1983). Note that the higher values of the

Table 3.12 Operational (ex-interest) budgetary deficit, 1975–1982 (percentage of gross domestic product)

Year	Current spending	Public investment	Current revenue	Capital revenue	Net operating result of public enterprises	Operational
1975	20.5	8.7	15.3	0.2	− 0.3	14.0
1976	15.7	13.1	18.1	0.1	0.9	9.8
1977	15.4	13.5	22.7	0.4	2.6	3.2
1978	19.6	13.0	25.4	0.6	2.7	3.8
1979	19.7	10.7	25.4	0.3	1.1	3.6
1980	22.8	9.6	26.9	0.3	0.8	4.3
1981	23.4	9.8	24.6	0.2	1.7	6.6
1982	20.0	8.4	22.2	0.3	2.5	3.4

Source: Secretaría de Hacienda

Table 3.13 Total government deficit (budgetary and nonbudgetary components) and sources of financing (percentage of gross domestic product)

Year	Total Deficit	Monetary financing		Domestic debt financing	Foreign debt financing
		Budget	Nonbudget		
1975	14.1	8.1	− 0.6	6.2	0.4
1976	12.9	3.6	0.8	7.6	0.9
1977	11.9	2.7	3.0	4.3	1.9
1978	10.1	0.2	2.2	5.6	2.1
1979	9.0	0.0	1.0	6.4	1.6
1980	11.3	3.9	2.2	2.8	2.4
1981	16.4	6.4	− 0.6	6.5	4.1
1982	17.2	6.1	0.8	7.2	3.1

Source: Cavallo and Peña, 1983

total deficit are due to (a) the influence on domestic public debt of nominal interest rate payments, which are elevated in a world of high inflation, (b) the inclusion of the extra-budgetary or Banco Central deficit as a component of the total deficit, and (c) the use of different methodologies to calculate the deficit (the Secretaría de Hacienda uses data on public revenues and expenditures while Cavallo and Peña look at the overall increase in public debt). The nonbudgetary or Banco Central deficit results from a wide range of transactions in which the monetary authority engages, such as foreign exchange operations, credit subsidies through rediscounting facilities, interest payments on bank reserves, and financial assistance to rescue private firms from bankruptcy, which are also a part of the consolidated government deficit but are not included as such in official statistics.

The deficit reported in table 3.13 is more relevant in determining the impact that asset accumulation, induced by fiscal imbalances, has on the domestic rate of inflation. It follows from the figures that, although the government emphasized the reduction of monetary financing, the overall fiscal deficit as a proportion of GDP remained very high. To finance budget imbalances, fiscal authorities started to rely heavily upon domestic borrowing (treasury bills, indexed bonds, and commercial bank loans), thereby pushing market interest rates up. Moreover, in 1980 and 1981, the public sector significantly increased its debt to foreign markets. The cost of credit soon became an important source of fiscal expansion, increasing inflation and feeding back to interest rates. By 1981, it was perfectly clear that substituting expensive debt for monetary sources of financing without reducing the deficit does not impose any fiscal discipline and may actually worsen budgetary conditions.

Economic Performance Following Liberalization

Major Prices and Inflation

The various strategies for curtailing inflation followed during the Martínez de Hoz episode produced unimpressive results. After the initial expectational shock associated with the change in government, inflation proved stubborn in resisting the changes in anti-inflationary instruments. To begin with, wage controls in 1976 and 1977 depressed real wages without significantly reducing inflation. Price controls in the second quarter of 1977 were only effective while they lasted: inflation rose again during the following quarter once prices were liberalized. The experience of monetary contraction from the fourth quarter of 1977 to the second quarter of 1978 led to high real interest rates, some destabilizing capital inflows, and a major shift from foreign to domestic assets which increased reserves and appreciated the peso. Higher rates of inflation were observed after the 1977 financial reform and in 1978, even though devaluation rates were reduced. Finally, active crawl reductions in 1979–81, unmatched by fiscal discipline, generated further reductions in the RER and a "squeeze" on tradeables. For example, in 1980, the year of lowest inflation, domestic prices doubled while the exchange rate depreciated by only 25 percent in nominal terms (see tables 3.14 and 3.15).

Real Exchange Rates and Effective Protection

The RER fell steadily from 1977 to 1981 as shown in table 3.16. Rodríguez and Sjaastad (1979) have argued that the 1978 level was around equilib-

Table 3.14 Annual inflation rates, 1976–1981

	Inflation rates (%)		
Year	*GDP deflator*	*Wholesale prices*	*Consumer prices*
1976	423	499	441
1977	160	150	176
1978	158	146	175
1979	150	149	159
1980	100	75	101
1981	n.a.	110	104

n.a., not available.
Sources: Banco Central and INDEC

rium and that the fall between 1976 and 1978 reflected the structural changes in commercial policy which had been introduced thus far. As noted previously, export taxes had been virtually eliminated by 1978 while import tariffs had become less prohibitive. Hence the RER consistent with a balanced current account was lower in 1978 than in 1976. In addition, information surveyed by FIEL (*Indicadores de Coyuntura*) revealed that international inflation measured by, for example, US wholesale price indices underestimated "true" foreign inflation measured in terms of the basket of commodities traded by Argentina. However, the fall in the RER observed in those years, especially in 1978, seems too large to be explained only by changes in commercial policy and foreign prices. Capital inflows and wealth effects induced by domestic financial policies were also an important source of real appreciation, as noted by several authors (for example, Calvo, 1985).[6] Moreover, real appreciation continued in 1979–81 despite the intensified liberalization of imports arising from the tariff program, a process which, to be sustainable in the long run, required a higher RER. The main cause of misalignment during those years was the lack of coordination between exchange rate and fiscal policies, a problem which will receive further attention in chapter 4.

Tables 3.17 and 3.18 show how real *effective* exchange rates evolved from 1976 to 1980. The changes between 1976 and 1977 reflect the combination of exchange rate unification and the cuts in import and export taxes described earlier in this chapter. Consequently, import effective rates tended to fall while REERs increased for traditional exports except fruits, meat, and industrial crops.[7] The most significant rises were for cereals, oil

6 Of course, there is also the fact that the dollar had been depreciating with respect to European currencies and the yen during the late 1970s.

7 These were the goods which experienced the lowest reductions in export taxes (the tax on industrial crops actually increased from zero to 6 percent; see table 2.5).

Table 3.15 Quarterly rates of inflation and devaluation, 1976–1981 (percent)

Year/quarter	*Inflation rate (CPI)*	*Devaluation rate*
1976		
I	59.9	62.8
II	87.5	62.6
III	18.2	12.0
IV	30.1	44.1
1977		
I	30.7	32.4
II	22.1	19.2
III	27.2	17.7
IV	33.2	25.1
1978		
I	31.2	23.3
II	29.9	15.9
III	22.7	73.9
IV	27.8	13.5
1979		
I	32.1	15.8
II	24.3	14.4
III	28.1	12.8
IV	18.4	10.8
1980		
I	18.5	8.8
II	18.6	7.0
III	14.7	5.2
IV	17.0	3.2
1981		
I	14.4	11.8
II	23.1	70.0
III	29.0	90.5
IV	22.5	38.0

CPI, consumer price index.

Sources: INDEC and Banco Central

seeds, and vegetable oils (all above 50 percent). For manufacturing imports, REERs decreased for consumer goods[8] and rose for most investment and intermediate goods.

8 This was strongly influenced by the tariff cut in sector 311 (foodstuffs) which was redundantly protected in 1976.

Table 3.16 Real exchange rate, 1976–1981 (1970 = 100)[a]

Year/quarter	*RER*
1976	
I	117.3
II	128.2
III	132.4
IV	118.0
1977	
I	114.0
II	114.4
III	105.6
IV	101.9
1978	
I	97.9
II	89.6
III	79.4
IV	72.0
1979	
I	66.0
II	63.0
III	56.7
IV	35.2
1980	
I	53.2
II	48.8
III	46.3
IV	41.8
1981	
I	42.3
II	57.5
III	63.6
IV	67.5

[a] Real exchange rate (RER) is the nominal bilateral exchange rate (US dollars) multiplied by WPI(USA)/CPI(Argentina), where WPI and CPI are respectively the wholesale and consumer price indices.

Sources: IMF, *International Financial Statistics*

Table 3.17 Real effective exchange rates for selected traditional exports, 1976–1980 (m$n per US dollar at constant 1960 prices)

Product	*1976*	*1977*	*1979*	*1980*
1 Cereals	37.1	68.0	46.8	38.9
2 Oil seeds	46.8	74.6	47.1	40.6
3 Fruits	73.6	71.8	47.0	39.7
4 Wool	54.9	68.8	44.6	39.1
5 Livestock	48.3	64.0	47.6	38.4
6 Industrial crops	107.4	80.8	50.3	40.9
Total agriculture	48.2	17.0	47.7	39.4
7 Meat packing	77.2	76.4	78.8	41.9
8 Vegetable oils	46.8	75.0	49.3	42.4
Total traditional exports	54.7	72.5	48.2	40.2

m$n, peso moneda nacional, an old monetary unit equivalent to one billionth of an austral (that is) 1 A = 10^9 m$n).
Methodology: see appendix 1.

The tariff program of Resolution 1634/78 led to further reductions in REERs which, together with the appreciation of the peso, produced the figures presented in table 3.18 for 1979 and 1980. Along with import rates, we report the REERs relevant for manufacturing exports. The comparison shows that, in 1979–80, export rates became much closer to import rates than in 1969 because of the reduction in import tariffs and the increase in export subsidies. Actually, the greater protection in 1979–80 of sales in the domestic market than of sales abroad arose from nontariff taxes on imports (whose importance has been emphasized earlier) rather than from the tariffs themselves. Recognizing this, in July 1980 the Minister of Economics announced a reduction in nontariff duties to be implemented during the following year.

Resolution 1634/78 also worked in the direction of reversing another existing bias, namely the higher protection of final consumption goods than of investment and intermediate goods. Thus we see from the figures in table 3.18 that consumption goods became the least protected in 1979–80.

These figures, however, fail to include the effect of Resolution 493/76 which accelerated liberalization in the capital goods sector. In addition, no conclusions can be drawn about relative protection levels without taking input protection into account. These shortcomings are tackled by looking at effective rates of protection. Table 3.19 shows the results of an estimation of effective protection rates by FIEL which takes into account the effects of Resolutions 1634/78, 6/79, and 493/79 described above. The

Table 3.18 Real effective exchange rates in selected manufacturing activities, 1969–1980 (m$n per US dollar at constant 1960 prices)

Sector		1969 IMP	1969 EXP	1976 IMP	1977 IMP	1979 IMP	1979 EXP	1980 IMP	1980 EXP
3	Total manufacturing	120.0	83.2	117.2	108.5	70.0	59.5	59.1	51.7
31	Foodstuffs, beverages, and tobacco	n.a.	82.5	142.9	92.2	62.4	57.7	52.0	48.0
311	Foodstuffs	n.a.	82.5	142.9	92.2	62.4	57.7	52.0	48.0
32	Textiles, clothing, and leather products	122.5	76.0	123.9	108.5	55.4	48.5	44.1	39.0
321	Textiles	125.3	71.7	106.2	95.8	51.7	48.0	41.6	36.6
322	Clothing and apparel	117.3	84.0	156.6	132.0	62.2	49.6	48.8	43.4
34	Paper, paperboard, and printing	116.0	83.5	79.7	93.0	69.1	56.8	60.4	53.2
341	Paper and paperboard	116.0	83.5	79.7	93.0	69.1	56.8	60.4	53.2
35	Chemical products	116.5	70.6	102.1	93.8	63.6	59.0	56.0	53.2
351	Basic industrial chemical products	124.9	66.5	93.0	97.1	62.8	59.2	55.9	53.1
352	Other chemical products	120.8	77.3	128.0	83.9	62.5	73.2	55.5	54.2
355	Rubber products	125.9	80.4	116.9	88.8	66.8	49.5	56.7	43.5
36	Stone, glass, and ceramics	108.1	87.3	121.2	100.5	71.0	64.2	61.7	57.9
362	Glass products	127.2	87.3	119.4	112.6	79.2	68.2	67.5	61.3
369	Nonmetal mineral products	89.6	87.3	122.9	88.7	63.1	60.3	56.0	54.5
37	Metals	130.0	102.4	116.1	124.6	84.7	71.2	71.2	61.8
371	Basic iron and steel industries	127.9	104.1	115.8	124.5	84.6	73.9	71.0	64.6
372	Other basic metal industries	142.2	92.6	117.9	124.8	85.2	55.3	72.0	45.3
38	Metallic products, machinery, and equipment	146.2	88.1	112.1	112.7	74.6	58.6	63.7	53.1
381	Metallic products	140.0	91.0	103.3	109.9	74.4	65.9	63.8	58.0
382	Nonelectrical machinery	150.7	92.2	120.7	117.3	69.8	61.8	59.5	56.4
383	Electrical machinery	149.2	90.0	99.5	112.3	63.9	59.6	56.8	53.0
384	Transport equipment	140.6	81.3	113.8	108.8	87.0	51.8	72.6	47.3
385	Professional equipment	153.8	92.4	117.4	116.1	73.1	70.4	66.5	66.5

m$n, see footnote to table 3.17; IMP, import; EXP, export.
Methodology: see appendix 1

figures are particularly interesting in connection with sectors 381 (metal products), 382 (nonelectrical machinery), and 383 (electrical machinery) because they measure the impact of unscheduled tariff reductions and increases in the price of basic inputs. As noted before, these sectors had their EPRs lowered because of both the acceleration in tariff cuts in 1979 and the maintenance of quantitative restrictions on steel imports.

Real Wages, Relative Wages, and Income Distribution

Data on the movements of aggregate wages from 1975 to 1981 are given in table 3.20. Two main results emerge: (a) real wages and the share of wages in income fell significantly after 1975, to recover only after 1978; (b) the pattern of relative wage movements is less clear but, if anything, the ratio of wages paid by tradeable activities to wages paid by nontradeable activities tended to fall between 1977 and 1981.

Table 3.19 Effective rates of protection by sector in 1980 (percent)

Sector	*1980* Res. 1634 alone	Res. 1634,6 and 493	Variation
3 Total manufacturing	88.8	85.3	−3.5
31 Foodstuffs, beverages, and tobacco	25.0	23.8	−1.2
311 Foodstuffs	25.0	23.8	−1.2
32 Textiles, clothing, and leather products	83.1	85.0	1.9
321 Textiles	87.2	84.6	−2.6
322 Clothing and apparel	75.3	85.8	10.5
34 Paper, paperboard, and printing	117.5	152.4	−25.1
341 Paper and paperboard	117.5	152.4	−25.1
35 Chemical products	60.0	58.8	−1.2
351 Basic industrial chemical products	45.0	46.4	1.4
352 Other chemical products	43.6	43.7	0.1
355 Rubber products	121.6	110.3	−11.3
36 Stone, glass, and ceramics	35.1	28.7	−6.4
362 Glass products	51.2	51.4	0.2
369 Nonmetal mineral products	20.0	6.7	13.3
37 Metals	53.1	49.8	−3.3
371 Basic iron and steel industries	42.2	42.2	0.0
372 Other basic metal industries	116.8	93.0	−13.3
38 Metallic products, machinery, and equipment	160.1	148.7	−11.4
381 Metallic products	63.6	46.5	−17.1
382 Nonelectrical machinery	62.0	31.0	−31.0
383 Electrical machinery	73.2	67.9	−5.3
384 Transport equipment	407.8	433.3	25.5
385 Professional equipment	48.7	48.9	0.2

Source: based on FIEL, 1980

The early 1970s had been characterized by income distribution policies favoring wage earners. (During those years trade unions were strong, as they were also under Perón.) Real wage increases did not necessarily follow rises in productivity and were therefore a source of inflationary pressure. In contrast, the Martínez de Hoz administration used strict wage controls to reduce inflation in 1976–7 and, as a consequence, real wages fell rather dramatically. The squeeze on wages was facilitated by a ban on trade union activity after the military coup. Wage flexibility was introduced in 1978, a recession year, and by 1979 wages were fully liberalized. From then on, real salaries increased as a result of full employment, higher labor productivity, and a falling real exchange rate. However, real appreciation made wage increases less affordable by the sectors producing tradeables, that is, agriculture, manufacturing, and mining. Accordingly, relative wages tended to decrease in these sectors.

Table 3.20 Evolution of real wages, relative wages, and income distribution, 1975–1981

Year	Real wages[a] (1970 = 100)	Relative wages[b]	Income distribution[c] (%)
1975	1.24	0.92	43
1976	0.83	0.97	28
1977	0.79	0.99	27
1978	0.77	0.89	30
1979	0.89	0.94	32
1980	0.98	0.89	37
1981	0.90	0.90	n.a.[d]

n.a., not available.
[a] Deflated by the consumer price index.
[b] $W_T W_{NT}$ where W_T represents the wages paid by tradeable sectors and W_{NT} represents the wages paid by nontradeable sectors.
[c] Average participation of wages for income.
Source: Llach and Sánchez, 1984

Commercial policies did not conflict with income distribution. The fall in real wages in 1975–8 was the result of wage controls and not of trade liberalization. Moreover, when wages were liberalized, they increased in real terms, and so did employment. Part of this effect can be explained by the fact that labor intensive nontradeable activities expanded while capital intensive importable activities contracted. The elimination of export taxes on traditional commodities did not increase the price of food significantly since it was offset by RER appreciation. However, tariff reductions and the removal of prohibitions on consumer goods imports, together with real appreciation, allowed cheaper consumption of imported items.

Real Interest Rates

Financial policies during the Martínez de Hoz period resulted in high and volatile real interest rates. The monetary reform of June 1977 put an end to persistently negative real interest rates. Moreover, the increase in the ratio of the claims of commercial banks on government to the claims of the Banco Central on government (which went from about 0.50 in 1976 to 2.3 in 1979) resulted in a rather steep increase in the real cost of credit. As a result, the ratio of time and savings deposits to demand deposits held by the public rose from about 0.70 in 1976 to about 3.00 in 1980 and the share of public debt service payments on GDP went up from 0.6 percent in 1976 to 6.5 percent in 1982 (Cavallo and Peña, 1983; Calvo, 1985).

Nominal and real interest rates for each month from January 1977 to March 1981 are reported in table 3.21. In addition, the implicit risk premium (spread between domestic and foreign cost of credit) is shown in table 3.22. Monetary contraction during the last quarter of 1977 and the first quarter of 1978 sent interest rates to record levels. However, since the

Table 3.21 Loan interest rates, 1977–1981 (percent)

	Nominal					*Real*[a]				
Month	*1977*	*1978*	*1979*	*1980*	*1981*	*1977*	*1978*	*1979*	*1980*	*1981*
Jan	6.00	13.42	7.59	6.70	6.60	− 7.80	3.18	− 2.45	2.39	4.11
Feb	6.00	11.14	7.06	6.00	8.30	− 1.00	5.86	− 0.90	1.85	3.13
Mar	6.00	9.30	7.03	5.60	11.10	2.10	0.23	− 1.03	1.70	6.24
Apr	6.00	8.34	7.06	5.20	—	0.30	− 0.74	0.61	1.34	—
May	6.00	8.17	7.14	5.40	—	− 0.30	0.81	− 1.87	0.00	—
Jun	7.45	8.90	7.26	6.40	—	0.81	4.11	− 3.22	− 0.97	—
Jul	7.94	8.02	7.60	7.00	—	2.23	3.11	0.09	4.07	—
Aug	8.34	7.79	7.94	6.00	—	− 4.23	− 0.85	− 6.71	3.03	—
Sep	9.17	7.35	8.13	5.50	—	1.89	0.68	2.78	2.61	—
Oct	12.33	7.38	7.90	5.20	—	− 1.20	− 2.55	6.85	− 0.21	—
Nov	13.66	7.58	6.98	5.40	—	5.76	− 0.93	3.56	2.76	—
Dec	13.58	7.87	6.78	6.30	—	9.39	1.50	4.26	5.48	—

—, not applicable.

[a] *Ex post* real rate, that is, nominal rate minus actual inflation.

Source: FIEL, *Indicadores de Coyuntura* (several issues), and INDEC

Table 3.22 Spread between domestic and foreign cost of credit, 1977–1981[a]

Month	*1977*	*1978*	*1979*	*1980*	*1981*
Jan	—	4.9	0.8	2.3	3.1
Feb	—	3.2	1.0	1.7	− 5.5
Mar	—	1.9	1.3	1.3	3.4
Apr	—	1.4	1.2	1.2	—
May	—	1.4	1.1	1.7	—
Jun	1.2	4.0	1.3	3.2	—
Jul	1.1	3.5	2.3	4.2	—
Aug	1.0	2.5	2.9	3.3	—
Sep	0.8	0.8	3.0	2.8	—
Oct	1.8	0.5	3.1	2.7	—
Nov	3.8	1.0	2.1	2.7	—
Dec	4.4	0.2	2.3	3.3	—

—, not applicable.

[a] Nominal interest rate on domestic bank loans minus the sum of foreign interest rate (London interbank offering rate (LIBOR)) plus the actual rate of devaluation plus transaction costs. From May to December 1978, the effect on the spread of the 20 percent deposit requirement is also taken into account.

Source: Frenkel, 1980; Calvo, 1985

attempt to control money supply was not accompanied by a floating exchange rate, asset swaps and foreign borrowing brought capital inflows which significantly boosted Banco Central reserves. Consequently, interest rates went down but the spread remained positive.

The policy of pre-announcing the rates of devaluation started in January 1979 and was accompanied by the elimination of most restrictions on capital mobility. While credibility lasted, low domestic interest rates were maintained but, as uncertainty increased, the risk premium became higher. Uncertainty increased in 1980 as the current account deficit of the balance of payments widened. This was paralleled by a large fiscal deficit which made attempts to control credit expansion very costly in terms of interest rates.

External Transactions

The opening of the Argentine economy to foreign trade is illustrated in table 3.23. The ratio of exports plus imports to GDP increased steadily from 18.3 percent in 1976 to 29.3 percent in 1980. Exports, as a percentage of GDP, increased up to 1978 despite the fall in external terms of trade (see table 3.24). They were led by traditional exports, the taxes on which fell in 1976 and 1977. The export-to-GDP ratio decreased after 1978 as the RER became overvalued. Domestic policies alone are responsible for this reduction since external terms of trade improved between 1978 and 1981. The fall in exports was lower for nontraditional products, the subsidies on which became more important after 1978. Changes in the export structure are shown in table 3.25.

The demand for imports, however, increased from 7.3 percent of GDP in 1976 to 13.7 percent in 1980, the most noticeable increase taking place during 1979 and 1980, the years of *atraso cambiario* (peso overvaluation).

Table 3.23 Aggregate imports and exports, 1971–1980

	Imports		*Exports*		
Year	*Real terms (millions of pesos at constant 1960 prices)*	*Ratio to GDP*	*Real terms (millions of pesos at constant 1960 prices)*	*Ratio to GDP*	*Openness ratio*
1971–5	1,488.5	9.3	1,498.9	9.3	18.6
1976	1,206.0	7.3	1,820.6	11.0	18.3
1977	1,529.4	8.8	2,743.5	15.7	24.5
1978	1,335.8	7.9	2,894.3	17.2	25.1
1979	1,906.6	10.4	3,059.3	16.8	27.2
1980	2,503.7	13.7	2,844.6	15.6	29.3

Source: Banco Central

Table 3.24 External terms of trade, 1970–1981 (1970 = 100)

Year	*Ratio of export price to import price*
1970	100.0
1971	109.9
1972	118.0
1973	128.0
1974	110.8
1975	106.1
1976	90.9
1977	89.5
1978	80.1
1979	83.7
1980	94.2
1981	98.6

Source: ECLA

Table 3.25 Export structure, 1971–1981 (percent)

Year	*Traditional*	*Nontraditional*	*Total*
1971–5	82.6	17.4	100.0
1976	79.2	20.8	100.0
1977	79.9	20.1	100.0
1978	77.9	22.1	100.0
1979	81.5	18.5	100.0
1980	77.7	22.3	100.0
1981	77.1	22.9	100.0

Source: based on INDEC data

As for the structure of imports (see table 3.26), its most remarkable aspect was the increase in the share of consumption goods, which seem to have a high elasticity of demand with respect to REERs. The share of investment goods also rose. Consequently, intermediate imports (which presumably had a relatively lower price elasticity) reduced their share.

Table 3.27 shows the trends in the balance of payments. The current account improved in 1976 and yielded surpluses until 1979 when the situation reversed. Developments in the capital account were favorable until 1980. External debt accumulated during all these years but especially during 1979–81 when it nearly tripled (see table 3.28). As a result, debt services increased substantially. However, the increase in public and private foreign debt net of reserves is not fully explained by current account imbalances. The magnitude of external transactions not properly

Table 3.26 Import structure, 1971–1981 (percent)

Year	*Consumption goods*	*Intermediate goods*	*Investment goods*	*Total*
1971–5	3.6	78.5	17.5	100.0
1976	1.4	87.2	11.4	100.0
1977	2.8	76.7	20.5	100.0
1978	4.7	71.6	23.7	100.0
1979	10.2	69.8	20.0	100.0
1980	18.0	60.5	21.5	100.0
1981	12.6	64.9	22.5	100.0

Source: based on INDEC data

Table 3.27 Balance of payments, 1975–1982 (million US dollars)

Year	*Exports*	*Imports*	*Trade account*	*Services*	*Current account*	*Capital account*	*Official settlements*[a]
1975	2,961	3,946	−985	−300	−1,285	191	−1,094
1976	3,916	3,033	883	−233	650	−516	134
1977	5,652	4,161	4,490	−183	1,290	1,286	2,576
1978	6,399	3,834	2,566	−732	1,834	1,334	3,168
1979	7,810	6,711	1,098	−1,648	−550	−4,726	4,176
1980	8,021	10,541	−2,519	−2,248	−4,768	2,552	−2,216
1981	9,143	9,430	−287	−4,427	−4,714	1,490	−3,224
1982	7,624	5,337	2,287	−4,645	−2,358	−2,323	−4,681

[a] Includes errors and omissions.

Source: Banco Central

Table 3.28 External debt, 1975–1981 (million US dollars)

Year	*Foreign debt*		*Reserves*	*Debt net of reserves*
	Private	*Public*		
1975	3,853.8	4,021.0	620.0	7,254.8
1976	3,090.5	5,189.0	1,812.3	6,467.2
1977	3,634.5	6,043.7	4,038.0	5,639.4
1978	4,139.1	8,357.0	6,037.2	6,458.9
1979	9,074.4	9,960.3	10,479.6	8,555.1
1980	12,703.0	14,459.0	7,683.5	19,478.5
1981	15,647.0	20,024.0	3,877.0	31,793.8

Source: Banco Central

registered, such as capital flight, direct investment abroad, unregistered travel and tourism spending, and some imports omitted for political reasons (for instance, arms imports), must also be considered.

The Capital Inflow Problem

The capital account has been disaggregated in tables 3.29 and 3.30. For 1976 and 1977 we were able to distinguish only between private and public sector flows, whereas for 1978–81 available information allowed us to separate public enterprises from the rest of the public sector. Private capital inflows surfaced at two different times during the episode: from the third quarter of 1977 to the second quarter of 1978 and from the second quarter of 1979 to the first quarter of 1980. In contrast, the public sector was a net borrower during almost every quarter in the 1976–81 period, but especially so in the last two years.

Table 3.29 Capital flows, 1976–1977 (million US dollars)

Year/quarter	*Private sector*	*Public sector*	*Total*
1976			
I	−54.1	−37.1	−91.2
II	116.7	−26.1	90.6
III	−59.2	10.0	−49.2
IV	−450.6	167.7	−282.9
1977			
I	−243.4	224.4	−19.0
II	−131.6	68.7	−62.9
III	77.5	352.0	429.5
IV	597.7	341.2	938.9

Source: Banco Central

Private capital movements are explained by the macroeconomic policies pursued by the government. The elimination of export taxes in 1976–7 generated a quick export response and the expectation of a fall in the equilibrium RER. The government reacted to the increase in reserves by letting the crawl rate fall below the gap between domestic and foreign inflation rates and, as a consequence, assets denominated in foreign currency became less desirable. In addition, deregulation in domestic financial markets increased the returns of peso-denominated assets, provoking an important reshuffling of portfolios.

As indicated earlier, monetary contraction was used to deflate from the third quarter of 1977 to the first quarter of 1978, but the experiment was short lived. Interest rates increased dramatically in nominal and real terms, attracting larger capital inflows. The government reacted by imposing restrictions on international capital mobility. The zero-interest-rate deposit required from those who borrowed in foreign markets explains the reversal

Table 3.30 Capital flows, 1978–1981 (million US dollars)

Year/quarter	*Private enterprises and banks*	*Public enterprises*	*Government and central bank*	*Total*
1978				
I	819.5	185.2	71.7	1,076.2
II	351.9	120.4	−11.6	460.7
III	−410.7	261.5	149.6	0.4
IV	−828.5	286.1	304.3	−238.1
1979				
I	−58.5	169.4	−5.2	105.8
II	717.0	103.4	151.5	971.9
III	917.5	209.0	157.3	1,283.8
IV	986.6	275.0	153.6	1,415.2
1980				
I	539.3	383.0	310.1	1,232.4
II	−1,413.8	427.0	259.3	−727.4
III	1,212.9	346.0	5.9	1,564.8
IV	−767.9	866.0	383.9	482.0
1981				
I	−3,232.4	1,070.0	1,414.1	−748.2
II	−68.9	437.0	669.6	1,037.7
III	−51.2	167.0	133.8	249.6
IV	456.4	322.0	172.3	950.7

Source: Banco Central

in private capital flows observed in the second half of 1978 (see table 3.30). However, the minimum-term condition established earlier does not seem to have been effective.[9]

A new wave of capital inflows occurred in 1979 after the government began to pre-announce depreciation rates below the current rate of inflation. The change in regime reduced exchange rate risks considerably while the announcements remained credible. At the same time, the government eliminated most controls on capital mobility to allow for a full integration of domestic and foreign financial markets. A change in exchange rate expectations around 1980 led to an increase in the risk premium and negative private capital flows. These, however, are under-estimated in table 3.30 since asset transfers are not well documented by

9 The reasons are easy to understand. Borrowers in need of short-term loans can always make longer-term commitments and hedge against the risk of devaluation by holding foreign assets until repayment is due. This poses no problems when expectations of real depreciation are low and access to the domestic exchange market is unrestricted.

balance-of-payments statistics. Despite capital outflows, the government delayed the necessary adjustment in the exchange rate. The fall in reserves was compensated for by an increase in external borrowing to finance the fiscal deficit. As a result, the process of currency appreciation continued until it became politically and economically unsustainable.

Real Output and Investment

Real output, which had stagnated in 1975, fell in 1976, particularly in the first two quarters. It recovered in 1977 but fell again in 1978 as a consequence of high real interest rates induced by monetary contraction. During 1979, real interest rates decreased because of foreign capital inflows, permitting a significant expansion in GDP. However, as real appreciation reduced the relative price of tradeable goods, output growth decelerated in 1980 and the economy moved into a new recession in 1981. At that time, real interest rates were high despite exchange rate policy announcements because of an increase in the risk premium.

In terms of their share of GDP, the sectors that suffered most were those producing tradeable goods because the changes in relative prices operated against them. For example, the share of manufacturing fell from 27 to 22 percent of GDP while that of financial services went up from 6.8 to 9.1 percent (table 3.31).

Despite high real interest rates, the share of gross domestic investment in GDP increased throughout the period (table 3.32). The components of investment that explain the rise in the investment-to-output ratio are public construction and imported equipment. The increase in the latter is, of course, explained by the significant fall in the REER for capital equipment.

Deindustrialization

One of the most striking effects associated with the Martínez de Hoz episode is the process of deindustrialization that it provoked. This is clear from table 3.31. Overvaluation of the peso affected nearly every branch of manufacturing. Additionally, high and volatile real interest rates exerted contractionary effects on both supply and demand. In fact, the behavior of both real interest rates and RERs has much to do with expansionary fiscal policy, which worked as a two-edged sword: it prevented the spread of unemployment, but it also squeezed tradeables even harder and pushed interest rates upwards. The combination of high real interest rates and exchange rate appreciation led to bankruptcies in manufacturing. Compared with previous years, the number of failures was lower under Martínez de Hoz, but the firms going bankrupt were significantly larger (see table 3.33).

Table 3.31 Gross domestic product and gross domestic product participation by sector, 1976–1981 (percent)

Year	*GDP*[a]	*Agriculture, forestry, and fishing*	*Mining*	*Manufacturing*	*Electricity, gas, and water*	*Construction*	*Commerce*	*Transportation*	*Finance*	*Other services*
1976	10,066	13.8	2.2	27.1	3.1	6.7	14.3	10.6	6.8	15.5
1977	10,703	13.3	2.3	27.4	3.0	7.1	14.4	19.6	7.3	14.7
1978	10,343	14.1	2.4	25.3	3.2	7.3	13.7	10.7	8.0	15.3
1979	11,022	13.6	2.4	26.1	3.3	7.0	14.2	10.7	8.1	14.6
1980	11,148	12.6	2.4	24.8	3.5	7.4	14.9	10.7	8.0	14.7
1981	10,423	13.7	2.6	22.2	3.7	7.2	14.7	10.9	9.1	15.9

[a] In australes at 1970 constant prices.

Source: Banco Central

Table 3.32 Investment rate, 1975–1981 (percentage of gross domestic product)

Year	Gross domestic investment (percentage of GDP)	Construction investment		Equipment	
		Public	Private	National	Imported
1975	19.4	4.1	8.1	5.6	1.7
1976	21.4	5.9	7.9	6.1	1.5
1977	24.1	7.4	6.9	7.1	2.7
1978	21.9	6.9	7.2	5.5	2.3
1979	23.2	5.7	7.5	5.6	2.7
1980	22.0	5.4	7.7	5.1	3.8
1981	19.5	4.8	7.4	3.5	3.8

Source: Banco Central

Table 3.33 Business failures in manufacturing activities, 1966–1981

Year	No. of firms	Mean of liabilities (constant prices, index 1966 = 100)
1966	332	100
1967	356	142
1968	387	230
1969	482	318
1970	650	403
1971	501	149
1976	26	9
1977	48	964
1978	126	542
1979	121	1,442
1980	174	2,379
1981	279	994

Source: García Pareja and De Marchi, 1984

Employment

In assessing employment during the Martínez de Hoz episode, three facts are important: (a) open rates of unemployment were low over the period; (b) real appreciation encouraged the shift of labor from manufacturing to service activities; (c) some expanding services included informal activities.

Developments in the labor market are illustrated in tables 3.34–3.37. Several conclusions emerge from the data. Aggregate employment increased during the episode at an annual rate of 0.6 percent between 1976

Table 3.34 Occupation by sector, 1975–1980 (thousands of workers)

Year	*Agriculture, forestry, and fishing*		*Mining*		*Manufacturing*		*Electricity, gas, and water*		*Construction*		*Commerce*		*Transportation*		*Finance*		*Other services*		*Total*	
	Wage earners	*Other*	*Wage earners*	*Other*	*Wage earners*	*Other*	*Wage earners*	*Other*	*Wage earners*	*Other*	*Wage earners*	*Other*	*Wage earners*	*Other*	*Wage earners*	*Other*	*Wage earners*	*Other*	*Wage earners*	*Other*
1975	722.3	620.5	56.9	1.8	1,841.5	403.1	132.2	1.7	570.2	258.3	732.4	660.0	552.0	150.3	169.0	26.4	2,421.8	384.5	7,198.2	2,506.6
1976	715.6	616.7	54.6	1.8	1,831.8	403.8	127.5	1.6	596.8	286.5	732.4	676.7	513.7	141.1	169.0	27.6	2,427.2	390.9	7,168.6	2,546.6
1977	709.0	612.8	53.9	1.9	1,805.9	404.4	122.9	1.6	625.6	317.7	776.5	693.8	471.1	132.5	183.5	28.8	2,441.5	397.4	7,196.9	2,591.0
1978	702.5	609.0	51.0	1.9	1,768.0	405.0	118.6	1.5	623.9	352.4	776.5	711.3	445.0	124.4	190.5	30.2	2,497.5	404.1	7,133.5	2,639.8
1979	696.0	605.3	50.1	2.0	1,753.7	405.6	114.3	1.5	629.7	390.9	846.9	729.3	414.1	116.8	198.9	31.6	2,493.1	410.8	7.196.8	2,693.6
1980	684.0	601.5	48.7	2.0	1,726.2	406.2	109.5	1.5	643.4	433.4	882.7	647.7	385.4	109.7	211.9	33.0	3,532.2	417.7	7,229.0	2,752.7

Source: Llach and Sánchez, 1984

Table 3.35 Sectoral participation of workers, 1975–1980 (percent)

Year	*Agriculture, forestry, and fishing*	*Mining*	*Manufacturing*	*Electricity, gas, and water*	*Construction*	*Commerce*	*Transportation*	*Finance*	*Other services*	*Total*
Wage earners										
1975	10.0	0.8	25.5	1.8	7.9	10.3	7.8	2.3	33.6	100.0
1976	10.0	0.8	25.5	1.8	8.3	10.2	7.2	2.3	33.9	100.0
1977	9.9	0.7	25.1	1.8	8.7	10.8	6.6	2.5	33.9	100.0
1978	9.8	0.7	24.8	1.7	8.7	10.9	6.2	2.7	34.5	100.0
1979	9.7	0.7	24.4	1.6	8.7	11.8	5.7	2.8	34.6	100.0
1980	9.5	0.7	23.9	1.6	8.9	12.2	5.3	2.9	35.0	100.0
Other										
1975	24.7	0.1	16.1	0.1	10.3	26.3	6.0	1.1	15.3	100.0
1976	24.2	0.1	15.9	0.1	11.3	26.6	5.5	1.0	15.3	100.0
1977	23.6	0.1	15.6	0.1	12.3	26.8	5.1	1.1	15.3	100.0
1978	23.1	0.1	15.4	0.1	13.3	26.9	4.7	1.1	15.3	100.0
1979	22.5	0.1	15.0	0.1	14.5	27.1	4.3	1.2	15.2	100.0
1980	21.8	0.1	14.7	0.1	15.7	27.2	4.0	1.2	15.2	100.0

Source: Llach and Sánchez, 1984

Table 3.36 Average labor productivity, 1975–1980 (thousands of pesos per worker at constant 1960 prices)

Year	*Agriculture, forestry, and fishing*	*Mining*	*Manufacturing*	*Electricity, gas, and water*	*Construction*	*Commerce*	*Transportation*	*Finance*	*Other services*	*Total*
1975	1.47	4.23	2.83	3.48	0.93	2.19	1.71	2.78	0.82	1.74
1976	1.54	4.48	2.71	3.73	0.98	2.04	1.78	2.58	0.84	1.71
1977	1.57	4.96	2.86	4.06	1.05	2.07	2.04	2.74	0.85	1.78
1978	1.61	5.27	2.67	4.34	1.02	1.90	2.11	2.87	0.85	1.72
1979	1.69	5.63	2.99	5.00	1.04	2.01	2.41	3.04	0.87	1.85
1980	1.61	6.06	2.91	5.61	1.06	1.93	2.59	3.37	0.88	1.83

Source: based on Banco Central data and Llach and Sánchez, 1984

Table 3.37 Unemployment rates, Greater Buenos Aires, 1976–1980 (percent)

Sector	*1976*	*1977*	*1978*	*1979*	*1980*
Manufacturing	4.2	1.5	1.9	2.8	3.1
Electricity, gas, and water	0.0	0.0	2.9	0.0	0.0
Construction	2.1	1.7	1.2	1.5	1.7
Commerce and banking	3.5	3.0	1.6	1.3	1.8
Transport	2.8	1.4	1.0	1.3	1.5
Services	4.2	1.7	1.6	1.9	1.6
Total	4.4	2.3	2.0	2.2	2.4

Source: extracted from INDEC data

and 1980, the increase being much lower for wage earners than for other occupied persons (owners and self-employed workers). In addition, participation in overall employment fell in tradeable sectors (agriculture, manufacturing, and mining). Most remarkably, the rates of open unemployment decreased after 1976 and labor productivity grew moderately in all sectors except commerce.

Total unemployment rates were significantly low relative to normal or historic levels. As an example, the highest and lowest rates during 1966–70, the Krieger-Vasena years, were 6.2 percent and 4.0 percent respectively. The corresponding figures for the period 1976–80 were 4.4 percent in 1976 and 2.0 percent in 1978. The fact that unemployment rates did not increase and even fell during the Martínez de Hoz episode implies that the transitory effects on production of changes in unemployment arising from trade liberalization would have been gains rather than losses. However, some qualifications are necessary.

The share of the labor force as a percentage of total population decreased, as discouraged workers withdrew after the drop in real wages between 1975 and 1978 (Sánchez et al., 1979). Some people remained at home, voluntarily unemployed, while others emigrated. The first group basically consisted of so-called secondary workers (teenagers, house persons, and retired individuals) whose participation in the labor market is strongly determined by wage conditions. The loss in employment explained by labor force withdrawals, though probably very important, was common to all sectors, and not just to those negatively affected by trade liberalization.

Some labor reallocation from industry to services may have incurred excessive adjustment costs given the fact that the relative price structure (affected by domestic currency overvaluation) was not sustainable in the long run and was to be reversed in the future. The product wage rose for manufacturing activities, especially tradeable goods, and fell in services as the RER dropped below sustainable equilibrium levels. As a result, labor contracted in most manufacturing branches while it expanded in services. Tables 3.38 and 3.39 report the changes in employment during the period. Clearly, with the exception of transportation, service activities absorbed labor expelled from contracting industrial branches along with new additions to the labor force.[10]

Table 3.38 Annual changes in manufacturing employment, 1977–1981 (thousands of workers)

Branch	*1977*	*1978*	*1979*	*1980*	*1981*
311/312	−11.7	−27.1	−0.6	−11.3	−12.4
313	−0.8	−3.5	1.5	1.0	−3.7
314	−1.7	−0.5	0.2	−0.3	−0.8
321	−10.7	−15.3	−11.5	−19.5	−18.8
322	−6.9	−6.2	−2.8	−9.6	−4.1
323	0.7	0.3	−1.6	−2.8	−1.8
324	−4.7	−3.6	0.6	−2.3	−0.7
331	−2.9	−7.6	−5.0	−5.1	−4.4
332	−3.6	−1.3	−0.1	2.2	0.3
341	−1.4	0.8	−0.5	−4.0	−1.8
342	−4.9	−1.6	−0.6	2.5	−1.0
351	−2.4	−2.3	−1.1	−1.6	−3.3
352	−3.1	−5.9	−2.3	−1.5	−4.8
353	−1.3	−0.7	1.2	−1.0	−0.5
354	0.0	−0.3	0.0	−0.1	−0.1
355	−0.2	−2.5	1.4	−1.5	−3.1
356	−3.1	−2.3	0.9	0.7	−1.9
361	−1.3	−1.2	0.8	0.0	−2.8
362	0.8	0.0	−1.4	−1.7	−2.8
369	−5.8	−2.4	−0.6	−4.1	−4.1
371	−1.6	−4.3	−0.1	−2.3	−7.5
372	−0.4	−1.2	0.2	−0.3	−0.8
381	−5.6	−8.3	2.2	−8.7	−14.7
382	−2.4	−8.2	−5.0	−13.7	−17.4
383	−1.9	−4.2	−1.6	−4.0	−8.7
384	−18.3	−24.1	3.7	−3.6	−20.8
385	−0.7	−0.2	−0.6	−2.1	−1.0
390	−1.0	−1.4	−0.3	−0.9	−1.5
Total	−96.9	−135.1	−25.4	−95.6	−145.0

Sources: INDEC; *Censo Nacional Económico*, 1974; *Evolución de la Industria Manufacturera*, 1970–81

10 Transportation services were a special case. A large number of the people working in this sector were employed by the public railroad company, Ferrocarriles Argentinos, which underwent budget cuts.

Table 3.39 Annual changes in employment in the services, 1977–1981 (thousands of workers)

Branch	*1977*	*1978*	*1979*	*1980*	*1981*
Total	106.5	87.4	106.3	135.0	135.0
Construction	60.0	33.0	44.3	56.2	56.2
Commerce	61.2	17.5	88.4	54.2	54.2
Transport	– 51.2	– 34.2	– 38.5	– 35.8	– 35.8
Finances	15.7	8.4	9.8	14.4	14.4
Government	20.8	62.7	2.3	46.0	46.0

Source: Llach and Sánchez, 1984

The high mobility of labor during this period has to be explained. Argentine labor legislation has always tried to ensure job stability. Consequently, when workers are dismissed for reasons beyond their control, they are entitled to compensation paid by the employer. This compensation amounts to the equivalent of a month's salary for each year (or fraction longer than three months) the employee has worked. The remuneration on which the compensation is based cannot be greater than three times the value of the monthly minimum wage prevailing at the time when the employment contract is terminated. However, during the period 1976–81 the minimum wage was so low that readjustments of the labor force were not seriously affected by the compensation system.

When services include informal activities, losses in productivity are likely. The situation is one of disguised, rather than open, unemployment. No country-wide data are available about the size of the informal sector in the economy. A clear-cut definition of the informal sector is not possible, but examples of informal occupations abound in developing countries (for instance, housekeepers, street vendors, and so on). However, some figures related to the size of informal employment in Córdoba, Argentina's second largest city, exist in a paper by Sánchez et al. (1976) which can serve as a proxy for the rest of the country. Working on the basis of Permanent Household Surveys (PHSs), these authors found that the informal sector represented around 15 percent of total employment in 1976 (25 percent of service activities). Using unprocessed information from more recent PHSs, we have estimated the shares for 1977–81 (table 3.40). It is apparent from the figures that the size of the informal sector has increased over the period. Although the increase is an important qualification of the data on open rates of unemployment, it has little to do with trade liberalization. Once again, stabilization policies bear most of the responsibility.

Table 3.40 Informal sector, 1976–1981 (percent)

	Informal / *Total occupation*	*Services* / *Total occupation*	*Informal services*
1976	15.0	61.0	24.6
1977	15.5	62.0	25.0
1978	16.0	63.0	25.4
1979	16.5	64.0	25.8
1980	17.0	64.0	26.6
1981	17.0	64.0	26.6

Sources: second column, Sánchez et al., 1976, and own calculations based on PHSs; third column, Banco Central, *Cuentas Nacionales*

Government Budget

Trade liberalization may affect public spending, tax collection, or both. As noted earlier, total spending remained practically unchanged from 1975 to 1977 but increased from that year to 1981. The share of public investment rose up to 1977 and declined thereafter, while the sector's wage bill behaved in the opposite way. Unfortunately, it is impossible to distinguish which part of increased government spending was assigned to offset the contraction in import-competing activities expected from trade liberalization, and which part sought to avoid higher adjustment costs due to stabilization. However, to the extent that most of the increased spending was simply used to generate government employment, it did not facilitate the allocation of more resources to exportable sectors.

The other side of the relationship between trade liberalization and the budget – the impact of fiscal revenue – is easier to assess. Despite the contraction in manufacturing output, there is no evidence of a corresponding fall in domestic tax collection. Current public sector revenues increased from 15 percent of GDP in 1975 to 27 percent in 1980. This was due to the expansion of other activities and more effective control of tax evasion. Revenue from taxes on foreign trade increased significantly. Data in table 3.41 on export and import duty collection for all the years from 1970 to 1981 clearly show that tariff reductions were followed by increases in fiscal revenues in 1977–80. The evidence is not adequate to postulate a "Laffer-type curve" in import duty collection, since imports were also affected by changes in QRs and by other influences such as real appreciation. However, an inverse relation between tariff rates and revenue would not be surprising. Export tax revenues, however, varied in the same direction as export tax rates. Hence they decreased under Martínez de Hoz, but this effect was more than offset by the increase in import tax collection.

Table 3.41 Government collection of import and export duties, 1970–1981 (million US dollars)

Year	*Import duties*	*Export duties*
1970	284	176
1971	234	192
1972	187	318
1973	209	557
1974	284	465
1975	196	361
1976	276	599
1977	617	342
1978	729	203
1979	1,449	241
1980	2,661	281
1981	1,288	219

Source: Secretaría de Hacienda

4

The Determinants of Real Appreciation in 1976–1981

The critical role of economic policy in the reversal of trade liberalization after 1981 is discussed in this chapter. The sources of real appreciation, as a major determinant of this reversal, are particularly scrutinized. Three aspects of policy implementation emerge as fundamental: the inappropriate sequencing of export and import liberalization, the improper timing of financial liberalization, and the lack of synchronization between liberalization and stabilization.

Liberalization with Stabilization: the Stylized Facts

Economic policy reforms during 1976–1981 sought to liberalize trade and financial markets. At the same time, stabilization policies were used to reduce inflation. Crucial features of the Martínez de Hoz liberalization episode were the following.

1. Export liberalization came before and was more extensive than import liberalization.
2. Financial liberalization preceded trade liberalization.
3. Stabilization policies were based first on monetary contraction and then on the use of the nominal exchange rate as an active anti-inflationary instrument, with virtually no fiscal discipline whatsoever.

The trade liberalization program was a two-stage reform. During the first stage (1976–8) commercial policies relied more heavily on export liberalization and export promotion than on competitive tariff reductions. The fluctuations in export taxation are illustrated in figure 4.1. It was only during the second stage (1979–81) that tariffs were allowed to fall competitively, albeit in a gradual and discriminatory fashion.

The principal measure taken by the new authorities was to eliminate taxes on traditional exports. These were of two kinds: (a) explicit taxes, or

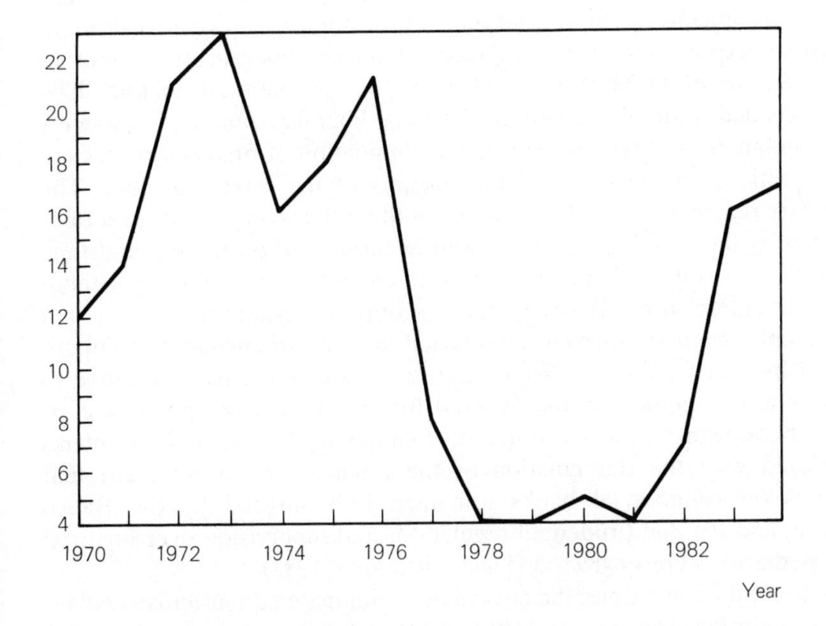

Figure 4.1 Collected export taxes as a percentage of exports
Source: Secretaría de Hacienda and INDEC (Instituto Nacional de Estadísticas y Censos)

retenciones, set at levels as high as 50 percent for cereals and 59 percent for oil seeds; (b) implicit taxes levied through the multiple exchange rate system, which was highly biased against traditional exports. Both taxes disappeared in 1977, the first gradually as *retenciones* were reduced and the second soon after the unification of the exchange rate. Nontraditional exports, however, received subsidies which rose significantly under the new regime, especially in the case of financial incentives for export promotion (*prefinanciación* and *financiación*). These incentives increased between 1977 and 1981.

The administration decreed the first tariff cut in November 1976. The tariff reduction policy continued in 1977, intensifying during the second semester, and was implemented without pre-announcement. The general consensus is that these tariff cuts merely reduced the redundancy in existing protection. Nevertheless, the first stage of the trade liberalization program also eradicated most of the import licenses and prohibitions which had proliferated under the previous regime.

The second stage consisted of a five-year program of pre-announced quarterly tariff reductions beginning in January 1979. The program was too gradual and did not treat industries uniformly; in addition, departures from the pre-announced schedule created uncertainty. Whereas the first stage fulfilled its objectives, the second stage of trade liberalization was aborted.

Just as export liberalization preceded import liberalization, another salient feature of the Martínez de Hoz episode was that financial liberalization preceded trade liberalization. Financial liberalization generally refers to a combination of two measures: the elimination of financial repression in domestic asset markets and the opening of the capital account. The monetary reform of June 1977 eliminated the ceilings on loan interest rates charged by the banking system as well as those paid on savings and time deposits. In addition, banks were free to choose their customers without the intervention of the Banco Central or other government agencies, and liberal entry regulations were established in order to encourage competition in the financial sector. Real interest rates climbed from negative to positive levels, helped by the demand for credit from the public sector, which became a strong customer of commercial banks. Two problems associated with the deregulation of the financial sector were (a) that deposits on commercial banks remained fully insured by the Banco Central, and (b) that prudential regulations and supervision over financial intermediaries were neglected (Díaz-Alejandro, 1983).

At about the same time, the government eliminated quantitative ceilings and prohibitions on external borrowing affecting commercial banks, private firms, and public enterprises, many of which were thus able to borrow in foreign markets at a time when international liquidity was high. Capital flow restrictions in the form of implicit taxes on foreign borrowing remained up to the end of 1978, but even they were subsequently eliminated. In addition, exchange rate uncertainty was significantly reduced in 1979, when the Banco Central began to pre-announce future crawl rates. Trade liberalization, however, proceeded much more slowly during the same period. By 1980, the level and variance of tariffs and other taxes on imports were still high, as our description of trade policies in chapter 3 has shown.

The final feature of the Martínez de Hoz episode – stabilization policies – was characterized by the use of monetary contraction in 1977–8 and by active crawl reductions in 1979–81. Fiscal deficits, in contrast, remained high (as shown in figure 4.2). The government emphasized reducing monetary financing of the budget deficit while relying more heavily upon domestic and foreign borrowing. However, the share of public sector expenditure in GDP increased significantly between 1977 and 1981, as shown in figure 4.3, as did the share of wages paid to public employees (figure 4.4).

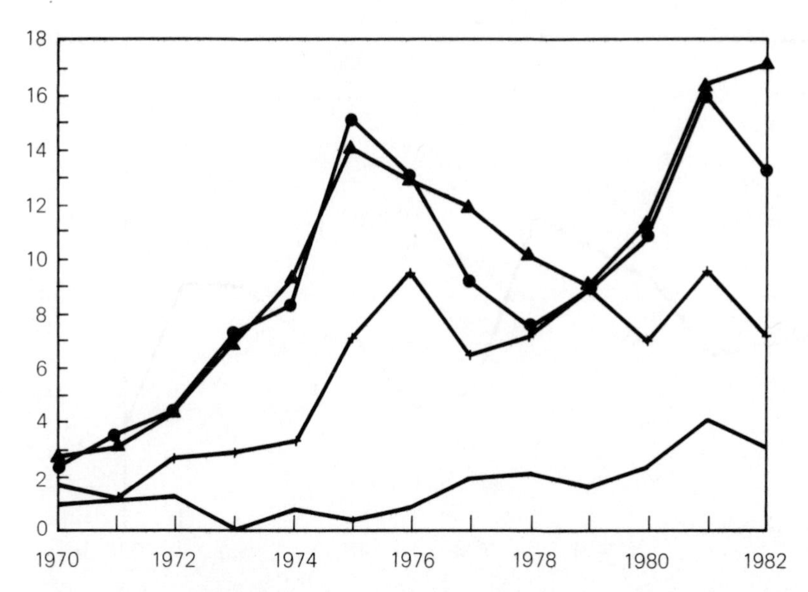

Figure 4.2 Fiscal deficit and source of financing (percentage of gross domestic product): ——, external findings; +, domestic borrowing plus external financing; •, budget deficit; Δ, total deficit (budgetary and extra-budgetary)
Source: Cavallo and Peña (1983)

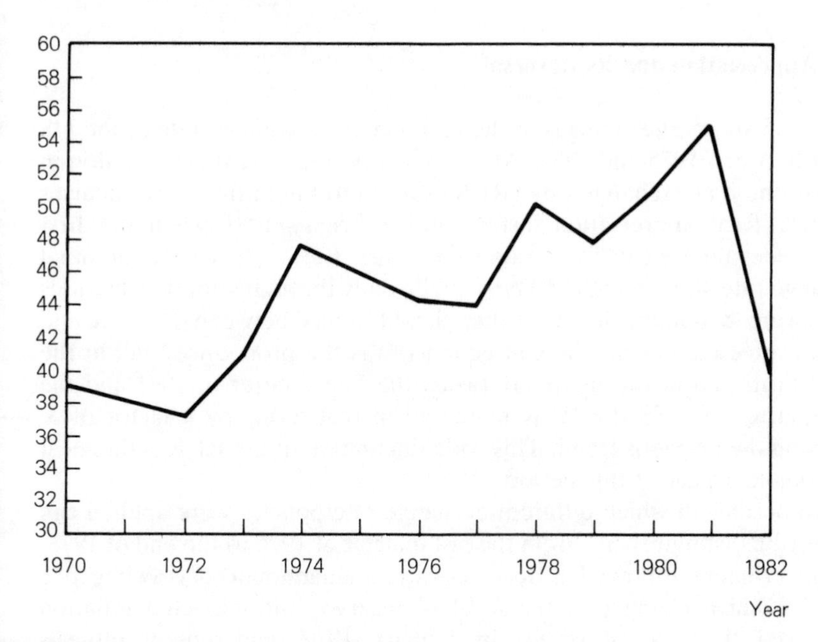

Figure 4.3 Public sector expenditure (percentage of gross domestic product)
Source: FIEL (1985)

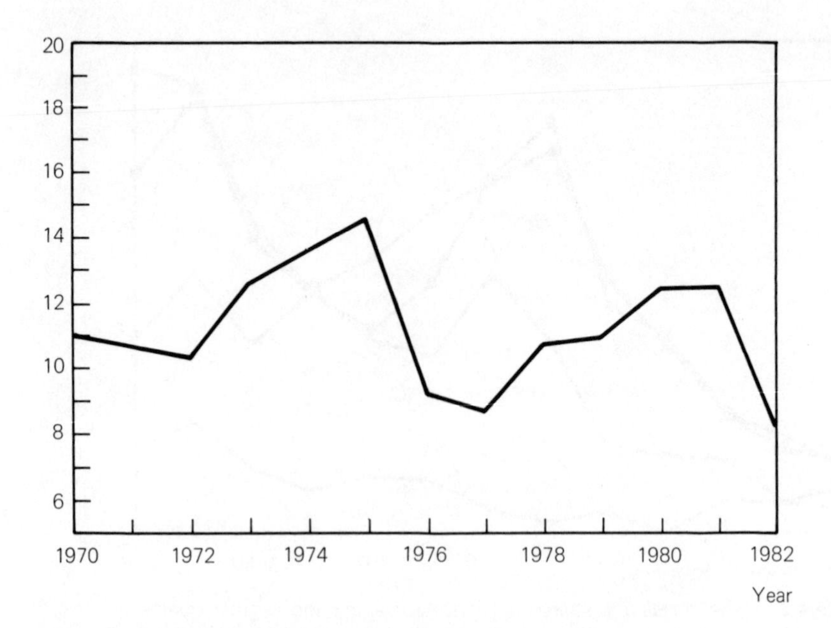

Figure 4.4 Wages paid by the public sector (percentage of gross domestic product)
Source: FIEL (1985)

Real Appreciation and its Reversal

Figure 4.5 shows the changes in the real bilateral exchange rate of the US dollar between 1975 and 1984. After a short period of real depreciation in 1975–6, the real exchange rate (RER) started to fall in the fourth quarter of 1976. Real appreciation lasted until February 1981 when the first discrete devaluation in five years took place. Before that date, nominal exchange rate adjustments had been made daily through mini-devaluations which were systematically lower than the difference between domestic and foreign price increases. The consequence was the pronounced fall in the RER illustrated in the figure. Between the first quarter of 1981 and the first quarter of 1983 the RER increased in real terms by a factor of 3, reversing the previous trend. This wide fluctuation in the RER is the most remarkable aspect of this period.

Two periods in which different exchange rate policies were applied can usefully be distinguished. From the last quarter of 1976 to the end of 1978, the government followed a decision-variant unannounced crawling peg rule, by which changes in the level of reserves and expected inflation influenced the rate of crawl. In January 1979, government officials introduced an active-downward crawling peg based on the pre-

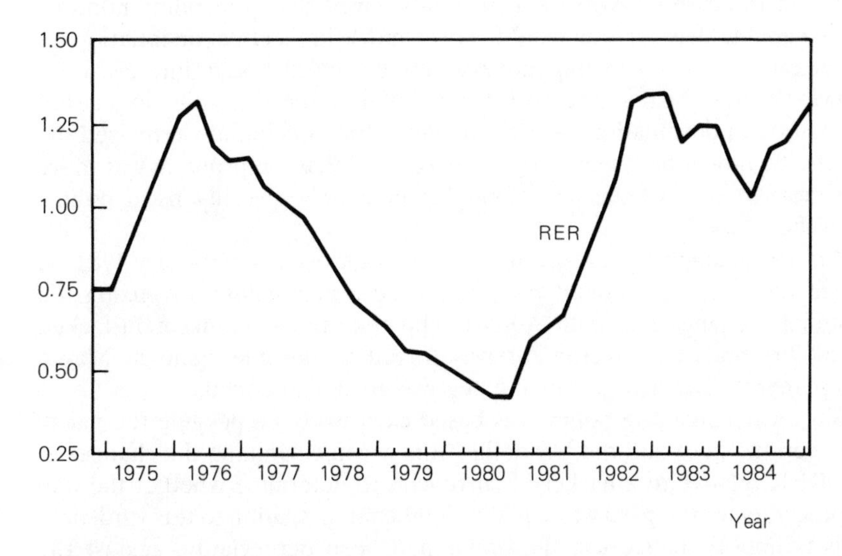

Figure 4.5 Real bilateral exchange rate of the US dollar: the index of the nominal exchange rate for exports multiplied by the US wholesale price index divided by the domestic consumer price index (quarterly averages, index 1970=1.0)
Source: IMF (International Financial Statistics), Banco Central and INDEC

announcement of future rates of depreciation. In order to induce a fall in inflationary expectations, the crawl decreased gradually. Forthcoming changes in exchange rates, called *tablita*, were pre-announced daily: the government pegged the nominal exchange rate at different points in time into the future, while committing itself to adhere to pre-announced values. In this sense, the policy used to disinflate was one of two opposed extremes – the other being to control monetary expansion while letting the exchange rate float freely. By choosing the first scheme, the government adopted the monetary approach to the balance of payments, which suggests that exchange rates can be used to control prices in small open economies while domestic credit expansion determines the level of foreign reserves.

The choice of this type of strategy is understandable in a country like Argentina. The alternative of reducing the rate of monetary growth in combination with a floating exchange rate does not necessarily avoid real appreciation, especially in the presence of a rate of inflation that is initially rigid. Countries that resorted to a real monetary contraction accompanied by a regime of flexible exchange rates saw their currencies appreciate. This occurred in the United Kingdom at the end of the 1970s, and in the United States in the early 1980s owing to capital inflows caused by rising interest rates. In the case of Argentina, it was believed that controlling nominal exchange rate depreciation would allow a more direct effect on inflationary expectations, thus avoiding adverse effects on the real interest rate. However, both the real interest rate and inflation remained high in relation to the rate of devaluation. Although many observers initially criticized the *tablita*, by now it has been fairly well accepted that the problem was more the inconsistency of the accompanying policies, especially fiscal policy, than the *tablita* itself.

An unscheduled 10 percent devaluation took place in February 1981, at which time the government pre-announced a new *tablita*, pre-fixing the nominal exchange rate until August. This time the announcement lacked credibility and the government was forced to devalue again in March (30 percent). The active crawling peg was then abandoned.

Since exchange rate policy was based exclusively on pegging the parity between the peso and the US dollar, it is worth examining the changes in the RER relative to a basket of currencies to determine whether the real appreciation of the peso was equally significant in relation to this yardstick. This is important because the dollar had been depreciating against the deutsche mark, the pound, the yen, and other hard currencies until the end of the 1970s.

The real bilateral (RER) and multilateral (RERM) exchange rates are plotted in figure 4.6. The multilateral exchange rate includes the currencies

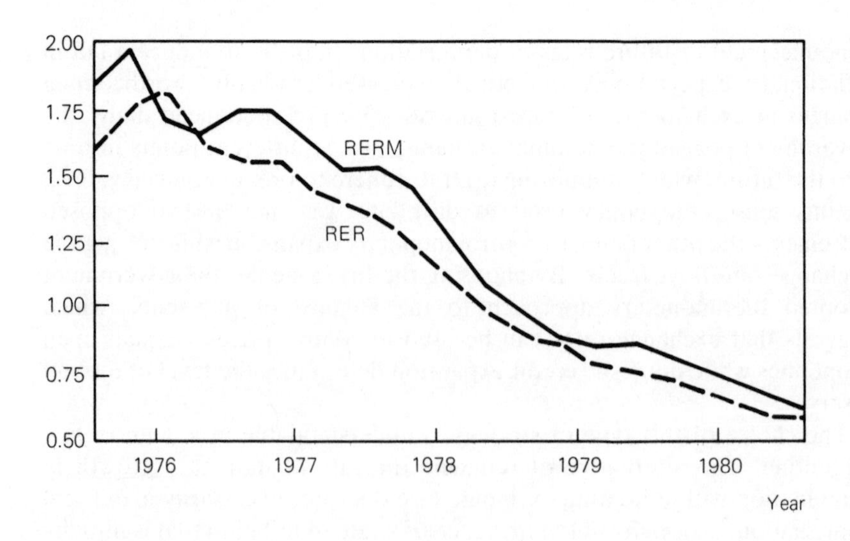

Figure 4.6 Real multilateral exchange rate (index 1970 = 1.0): RERM, real multilateral exchange rate; RER, real bilateral exchange rate
Source: IEERAL, Novedades Economicas

of countries with which Argentina has maintained significant trade flows. As expected, RERM is higher than RER after 1976. However, the difference between the two rates narrows from the middle of 1978 until it practically disappears at the point of maximum real appreciation in the first quarter of 1981. In consequence, the total appreciation of the RER between the fourth quarter of 1976 and the first quarter of 1981 is roughly the same in both cases.

Also, in our previous definitions of the RER, wholesale price indices were used to measure the variation in the foreign price of tradeable goods. However, these indices may not adequately reflect the foreign inflation implicit in the basket of goods exported and imported by Argentina. Referring to this problem, Rodríguez and Sjaastad (1979) noted that measuring inflation through the use of the US price index led to an underestimation of the true external inflation contained in the goods traded by Argentina, thus exaggerating the fall in the RER between 1976 and 1979.

In figure 4.7 we account for this effect. The full line represents the real multilateral exchange rate obtained when the ratio of the nominal exchange rate to the domestic price index is multiplied by the index of

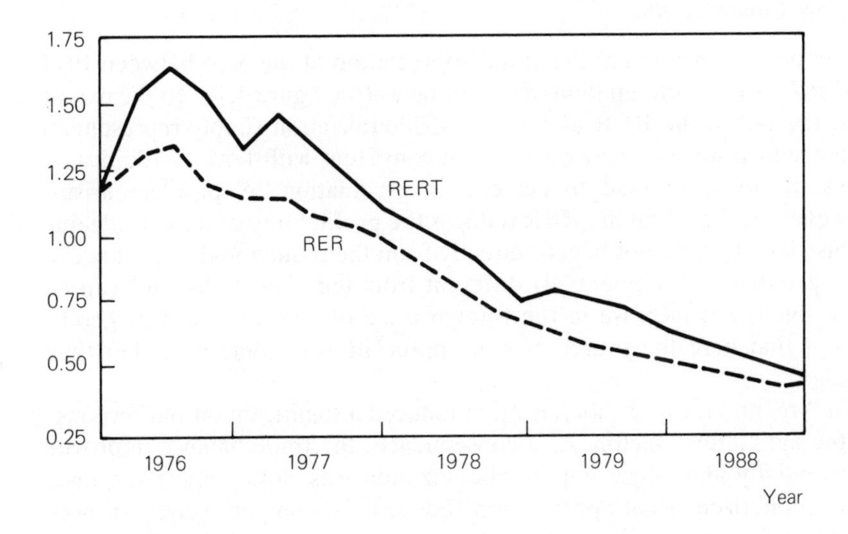

Figure 4.7 Real bilateral exchange rate calculated using an index of foreign prices of traded goods (index 1975 = 1.0): RER, real bilateral exchange rate as in figure 4.5; RERT, calculated as described in the text

foreign prices contained in Argentina's exports and imports.[1] Again, it is noted that, despite the existence of a significant difference in the direction pointed out by Rodríguez and Sjaastad, this difference also tends to disappear until the beginning of 1981.

In conclusion, the degree of real appreciation accumulated between the fourth quarter of 1976 and the first quarter of 1981 is more or less the same regardless of the means chosen to measure the RER.

The Determinants of Real Exchange Rate Behavior

Exchange rate policies are not sufficient to explain why the domestic currency appreciated so much during this period. The indices in figures 4.5–4.7 represent a real variable, the value of which cannot be determined entirely by movements in the nominal exchange rate. In fact, changes in the RER are closely related to changes in commercial policies, capital inflow or outflow, and fiscal or monetary disturbances. As we show here, the stylized facts described in the first section are crucial in explaining the phenomenon of real appreciation between 1977 and 1981.

Export Liberalization

An important element in the initial appreciation of the peso between 1977 and 1978 was the elimination of export taxes (see figure 4.1). To the extent that the fall in the RER as a result of liberalization simply represents a movement towards a new equilibrium consistent with fewer trade distortions, it does not lead to currency overvaluation. A problem arises, however, as the fall in the RER reduces the profitability of those tradeable industries which do not benefit directly from the reduction in export taxes. This problem is not essentially different from the "Dutch disease" caused by a significant increase in the foreign price of "enclave" export goods, except that here the source of real appreciation is domestic rather than foreign.

In Argentina, export liberalization induced a significant output response in the agricultural sector. As a consequence, the trade balance improved substantially and, since import liberalization was slow, export surpluses were monetized. Real appreciation reduced the competitiveness of non-traditional exports, inducing fresh distortions as export subsidies were used to keep effective rates high.

1 The foreign price index is calculated as the ratio of exports plus imports in current dollars to exports plus imports at constant prices. Thus, in addition to world inflation, this index also captures the depreciation or appreciation of the US dollar relative to the other hard currencies in which Argentine tradeable goods are quoted in foreign markets.

In the next chapter we discuss the problems that can result from a unilateral liberalization of traditional exports accompanied by measures promoting nontraditional exports when they are used as an early stage in a program of generalized liberalization. In effect, the fall in the RER damages the profitability of the nontraditional export sector which will demand compensatory subsidies in order to compete internationally. At the same time, the low RER creates a disincentive for foreign investment because foreign investors will receive fewer pesos per dollar in real terms. Additionally, the real appreciation favors activities such as tourism outside the country and contraband (smuggled) imports, further complicating the process of opening the economy and stabilizing the balance of payments. These problems can only be avoided if imports and exports are simultaneously liberalized in whatever type of gradualist program is chosen.

Capital Inflow

During the late 1970s Argentina, like other South American countries, received an influx of foreign capital which was fostered by domestic policies and international financial conditions. The oil price booms of the 1970s created buoyant conditions in international financial markets. On the one hand, oil exporters accumulated large surpluses which were channeled to capital-starved nations. On the other hand, real interest rates were negative, providing an incentive to borrow abroad to which many developing nations responded. Argentina was no exception but, as in other countries, domestic policies helped to transform an otherwise healthy opportunity into an overborrowing crisis.

Net capital inflow (see figure 4.8) became especially significant in 1979 and 1980 when controls on capital mobility were lifted. However, when restrictions were imposed (as in 1978), capital inflow was effectively reduced (see chapter 3 for a full discussion of this problem).

As capital flowed into the domestic economy, the volume of deposits at commercial banks increased and the loanable capacity of financial intermediaries became correspondingly higher. The prices of land, houses, and stocks went up, generating an important wealth effect which helped to exacerbate the appreciation of the domestic currency. Foreign reserves piled up, making it possible to sustain current account imbalances while appreciation lasted.

Inconsistency between Exchange Rate and Monetary Policy

The lack of coordination between exchange rate and monetary policy was the main source of instability during the 1979–81 period. Indeed, the expansion of domestic credit implicit in the consolidated Treasury–Banco Central deficit was inconsistent with the exchange rate rule, as shown in

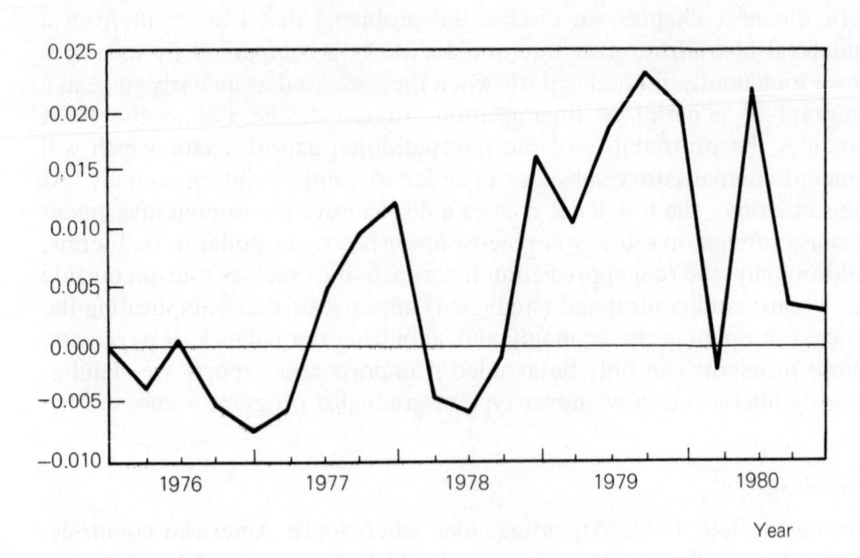

Figure 4.8 Net capital inflow as a proportion of gross domestic product (Capital inflow minus debt service payments over gross domestic product)
Source: Banco Central

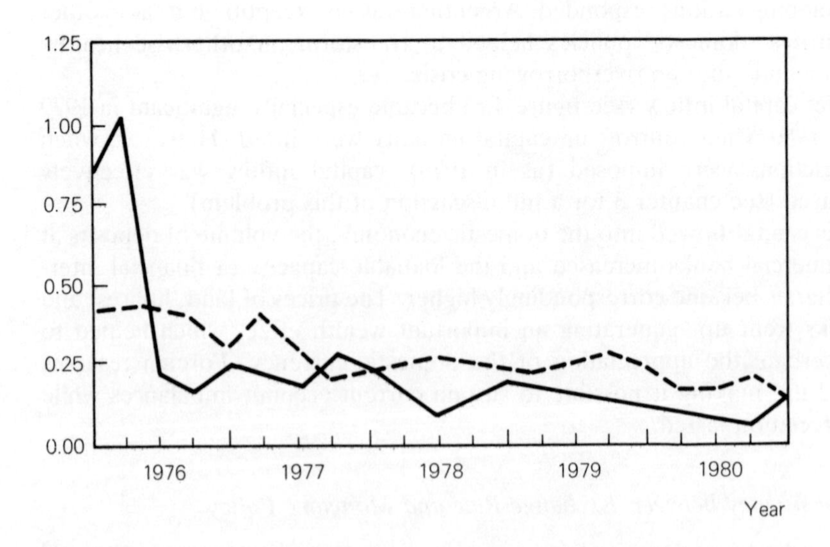

Figure 4.9 Rates of domestic credit expansion and exchange rate devaluation (percent): ——, devaluation rate; – – –, domestic credit expansion rate
Source: Banco Central

figure 4.9, thereby leading to a gradual depletion of reserves and subsequent speculation against the peso in 1981.

Government Spending

Another aspect of macroeconomic policy which helps to explain real appreciation during the Martínez de Hoz episode has to do with increased government spending as a proportion of GDP (see figure 4.3). Government spending can affect the level of the RER in different ways: one has to do with demand composition between tradeables and nontradeables. It has been argued (Rodríguez, 1980) that, if the government spends more than the private sector on nontradeables, their relative price will increase (the RER will fall) as government expenditure rises and vice versa. That spending patterns may vary between the government and the private sector is clear from the fact that both the level and the composition of public expenditure are basically exogenous variables, while private demand depends on relative prices, wealth, and disposable income. In this case the significant factor is the different composition of public and private demand for goods and services. The idea is that, by increasing its expenditure, the government crowds out the private sector and changes the composition of demand between tradeables and nontradeables. This is true regardless of how the increase in spending by the government is financed. For example, if domestic borrowing is used instead of direct or indirect taxes, domestic real interest rates will rise, reducing private absorption. However, if the deficit is financed by printing money, disposable income will fall as households and entrepreneurs internalize the effect of the inflation tax in their budgetary constraints. The only possible exception to a nearly complete crowding out of the private sector is foreign borrowing, which usually affects the balance between domestic income and absorption, leading to increased demand for both tradeables and nontradeables.

Other important links between government spending and the RER are the role of government spending in determining wages and the intersectoral effects of indirect taxation. These supply-side effects on relative prices should be distinguished from the demand-side effects just discussed. Suppose that the government raises the salaries paid to public servants above the equilibrium level prevailing in the economy, or that labor demand increases as the administration creates new public posts. Either way, the share of wages paid by the government will increase as a proportion of GDP, as occurred in Argentina under Martínez de Hoz (see figure 4.4). The general level of wages in the economy is driven up, assuming that unemployment is not too high. Since the prices of tradeables are exogenous and constant, as long as nominal exchange rates and commercial policies are not adjusted, an increase in wages will squeeze profitability in the tradeables sector. Conversely, the price of nontradeables will rise as wage costs increase. Substitution effects on demand and supply will decide the size of the ultimate effect on the RER, but it is clear that the latter will fall under these conditions. If, in addition, the increased public spending is financed by collecting more indirect taxes, these will further depress the RER as they are passed on to the prices of nontradeables. Even if the law of one price does not hold strongly for tradeables, their demand would still be more elastic than in the case of nontradeables, with a consequent higher incidence of indirect taxes on the profitability of tradeables.

Empirical Evidence

To assess the relative importance of trade and accompanying policies in explaining real appreciation, a simple dynamic model of RER determination was estimated using quarterly data and was then simulated under alternative policy scenarios. Details of the model and its estimation are given in appendix 3, where we also show the various simulations used to derive our main conclusions. Unfortunately, owing to a lack of appropriate quarterly data for government spending, the effect of this variable could not be properly captured in our results. Export taxes, capital inflow, and the mix of monetary and exchange rate policies account for about 65 percent of real appreciation between the last quarter of 1976 and the first quarter of 1981, with each factor having almost equal weight in explaining the total variation.

While export taxes and the monetary–exchange rate policy mix were controlled domestically, the same was not true for capital inflow which was affected, in part, by external conditions. The increase in international liquidity between the years of the sample certainly affected the size of capital inflow in Argentina but, as argued before, the decision to remove controls on private capital mobility early in the liberalization process, together with the use of foreign loans to finance the fiscal deficit, also determined a significant proportion of overborrowing. Our estimates show that about half the fall in the RER directly attributable to capital inflow could have been avoided had the government pursued prudent fiscal and financial measures. Other external factors, such as foreign terms of trade, do not seem to account for a significant effect on the RER, although these terms did tend to improve between 1976 and 1981.

It is concluded that if trade, fiscal, and financial policies had been implemented more consistently, the RER would have stabilized near its 1970 level (appendix 3, figure A3.2). This would have avoided the sharp U-shaped fluctuation experienced during the last decade. Under these conditions, the anti-inflationary program would have been successful and the trade and financial reforms would have transformed the previously repressed economy into a more competitive free economy without experiencing exaggerated costs during the transition.

A more consistent trade policy would have allowed a greater increase in imports during the period 1977–8. This would have avoided the accumulation of surpluses in the current account that resulted from the combination of export liberalization and promotion. To achieve this, the tariff program should have been implemented earlier and more rapidly. However, the expansion of domestic credit should have been more in accordance with the rate of pre-announced devaluation in 1979 and 1980. This would have required a reduction in the fiscal and quasi-fiscal deficits. Finally, the opening of the capital account should have taken place only after fiscal equilibrium was reached and inflation was brought under control (figure 4.10).

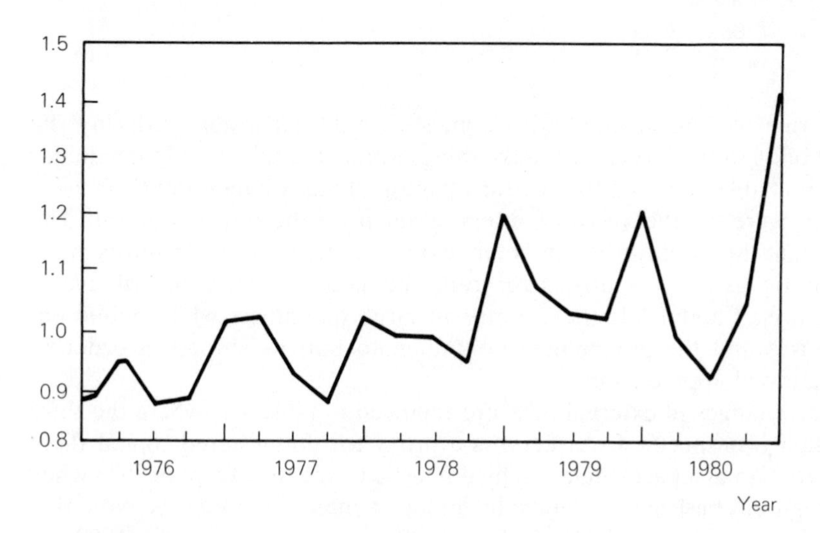

Figure 4.10 Foreign terms of trade, 1976–1981 (index 1970 = 1.0)
Source: Cavallo (1985b)

The Genesis of the External Crisis

Real appreciation had two main adverse effects on the balance of payments. It produced a squeeze on tradeables, leading to a huge trade account deficit in 1980, and it raised foreign debt, both private and public, engendering higher interest payments, especially as foreign interest rates increased in 1982.

By 1980, most private agents thought that the low level of the RER was not sustainable and expected a devaluation. To begin with, the exchange

Table 4.1 Changes in external debt and reserves, 1976–1981 (million US dollars)

	Private sector		*Public sector*	
Year	*Increase in foreign private debt*	*Nonspecified transfers*	*Increase in foreign public debt*	*Increase in reserves*
1976	– 763.3	n.a.	1,168.0	1,192.3
1977	544.0	n.a.	854.7	2,226.5
1978	504.6	883.0	2,313.3	1,998.4
1979	4,935.3	2,311.0	1,603.3	4,442.4
1980	3,628.6	6,641.0	4,498.7	– 2,849.0
1981	2,944.0	5,233.0	5,565.0	– 3,569.0

n.a., not available.

Source: Banco Central

rate rule was inconsistent with domestic credit expansion, reducing the credibility of the former. To make things worse, the collapse of three major private banks revealed the critical situation of many banks and *financieras* which were on the verge of intervention from the Banco Central. The resultant threat of further monetary expansion to bail out depositors made domestic assets less attractive from the point of view of risk-averse investors. Capital left the country in large quantities, while public enterprises and the government continued to borrow abroad in order to sustain real appreciation.

The changes in external debt are reported in table 4.1, where the third column (nonspecified transfers) is a proxy for unregistered capital flight and foreign asset accumulation by domestic residents, except in 1978 when the figure is basically explained by undocumented arms imports. Note that the change in private debt net of capital flight became negative in 1980 and 1981, years in which exchange rate expectations reversed and private agents began to expect large devaluations. In contrast, increases in public debt net of foreign reserves became high and positive in those years, indicating that public borrowing, intended to sustain real appreciation, in fact financed the accumulation of foreign assets by private agents.

Political criticism intensified as the strong real appreciation increased the competitiveness of import goods *vis-à-vis* domestic manufacturing. Unfortunately, the target of most critics was the tariff program and not the accompanying macropolicies which had been directly responsible for the overvaluation of the peso. Thus, when the external crisis arose, a reversal in trade policies followed. In 1982 financial lending to Argentina was drastically cut and the government was forced to devalue. Real depreciation of the domestic currency was accompanied by import restrictions in the form of quotas, licenses, and import prohibitions in order to generate trade account surpluses to service the debt. Despite these measures, the government was not able to equilibrate the current account and a substantial deficit persisted.

The Tourism Problem

In addition to capital flight, the Martínez de Hoz episode was afflicted by a strong bias favoring tourism abroad. Figures on travel and tourism spending are plotted in figure 4.11. Values are expressed in US dollars at constant 1960 prices, shown along with the RER relevant to tourism. Two main conclusions follow from the table. Firstly, tourism spending is highly elastic with respect to the RER: an estimation of the elasticity for the sample period used in the table yields −2.0. Secondly, tourism spending in foreign countries increased in 1968–70, the Krieger-Vasena years, and again in 1978–81, the Martínez de Hoz years. Both periods were characterized by a unified exchange rate system, lack of exchange controls, and the absence of a black market for foreign exchange. During every other year in the sample, the existence of exchange controls and black markets imposed an implicit tax on tourism and, most probably led to an underestimate of the size of tourism spending. Exchange rate unification eliminates this

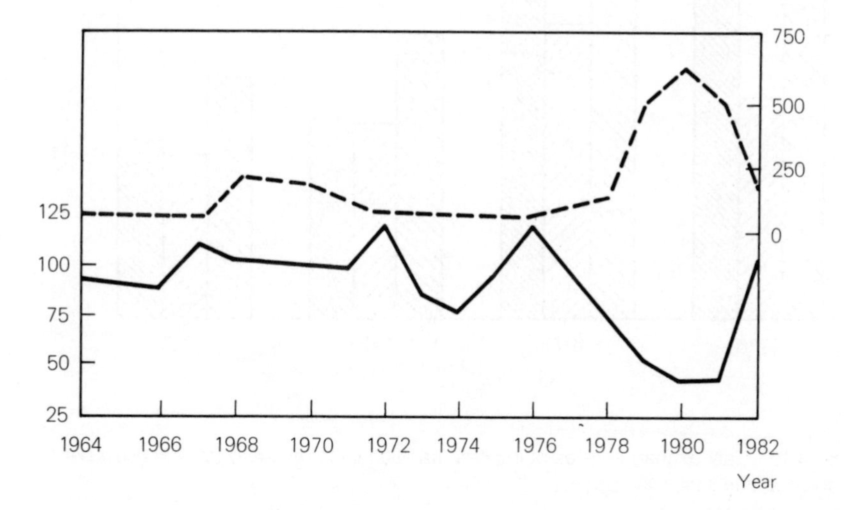

Figure 4.11 Travel and tourism spending abroad: ——, real exchange rate for financial transactions (1970=100); – – –, travel and tourism spending (million US dollars at constant 1960 prices)
Source: Banco Central

implicit tax and, unless it is replaced by an explicit tax, the REER for tourism falls below the effective rate for imports since the latter is affected by tariffs. In figure 4.12 we show that the effect of trade liberalization policies in 1976–80 was to equalize the REERs on tourism and exports while leaving an important gap between the REERs on imports and tourism. Of course, real appreciation also helps to increase the pro-tourism bias since a large part of tourism spending falls in nontradeable services, such as meals and hotels, the cost of which is reduced abroad relative to similar consumption at home. The implication is that choosing to postpone import liberalization in favor of export promotion not only slows down elimination of the pro-tourism bias, but actually strengthens it by allowing people to enjoy cheaper nontradeable consumption abroad. This outcome may be undesirable during a trade liberalization episode and was, in fact, the source of significant outflows of foreign exchange during the Martínez de Hoz episode, thereby contributing to the external problems faced by Argentina in the early 1980s.

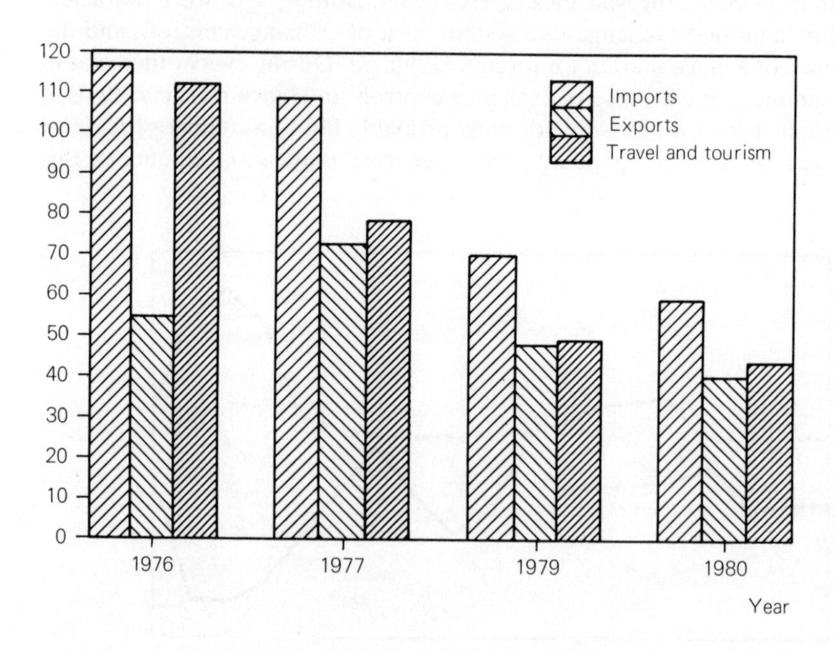

Figure 4.12 Real exchange rates of imports, traditional exports, and tourism (m$n per US dollar at constant 1960 prices)
Source: Own (see Appendix 1)

5

Inferences for the Timing and Sequencing of Liberalization Policies

From our previous discussion, some conclusions have emerged about the timing of export and import liberalization, the sequencing of trade and financial liberalization, and the synchronization between liberalization and stabilization policies. These conclusions are synthesized here. The conclusions related to the choice of an appropriate path for import liberalization, about which less can be inferred from the Argentine experience, are fewer and more tentative. Those that we have been able to derive are dealt with in the last section.

Does the Timing of Export and Import Liberalization Matter?

A generalized reduction in tariffs and quantitative restrictions on imports raises the equilibrium level of the RER, that is, the long-run sustainable equilibrium level of the RER is higher once import tariffs and QRs are reduced, given an initial structure of nominal protection that predicates a positive average rate of effective protection.

Export promotion policies, in contrast, lower the RER (defined as the nominal exchange rate multiplied by the foreign price of tradeables divided by the domestic price of nontradeables). The instruments used to promote exports generally include fiscal incentives such as tax rebates and financial incentives such as cheaper credit. However, they also include direct subsidies to inputs and drawbacks, which raise the EPRs of exportable industries. In a country like Argentina these promotion policies apply to nontraditional exports (mostly manufactures of nonagricultural origin); traditional exports, however, are generally subject to export taxes called *retenciones*. These are levied on exports of grains, beef, vegetable oils, wool, and other traditional products. A reduction in export taxes has the same qualitative effect on the RER as a subsidy increase granted to nontraditional exports, namely it lowers the RER's long-run equilibrium level.

Full trade liberalization assumes the elimination of all taxes and subsidies on foreign trade. In fact, however, the existence of trade distortions on the import side provides a second-best justification for export subsidies. Once tariffs are removed, the need for export subsidies is less evident. The question arises as to whether a separate export promotion stage should be a part of the trade liberalization package and where it should be placed in the policy sequencing. When the liberalization program includes reductions in export taxes, a related question is whether they should be reduced simultaneously with import taxes or sequentially.

Conventional wisdom indicates that, although equilibrium RERs tend to move in opposite directions depending on whether import tariffs or export taxes are removed, the effects of export and import liberalization on the relative prices and quantities of the goods produced and consumed at home are qualitatively the same.

This is true in a three-sector world with an exportable, an importable, and a nontradeable, where both exports and imports are taxed. Thus the relative price of importables with respect to nontradeables is $e(1 + t_i)$, where e is the RER and t_i is the tariff on imports. After a tariff reduction, this relative price will fall but, since e increases to equilibrate demand and supply of foreign exchange, the net reduction in the relative price of importables will be lower, in absolute value, than the fall in $1 + t_i$. However, the relative price of exportables in terms of nontradeables is $e(1 - t_x)$, where t_x is the tax on exports. Since the latter has not changed, this relative price increases in proportion to the rise in e.

The export tax reduction can be analyzed along the same lines. Here, t_m remains constant but, since e decreases, $e(1 + t_m)$ falls in proportion. The relative price of exportables increases owing to the fall in the export tax, but this effect is partially compensated by the reduction in e.

It follows that, in the two cases analyzed previously, the relative price of exportables increases while that of importables decreases. Under such circumstances, the timing of export and import tax removals should be of no concern to policymakers during a trade liberalization episode. However, there may be other activities in the economy for which the relevant effective RER is neither $e(1 + t_m)$ nor $e(1 - t_x)$. For example, for some traded goods which are not taxed or protected, the relevant relative price is just e. This price will increase or fall, as a result of trade liberalization, depending on whether import tariffs *or* export taxes on other traded goods are removed. Thus the unilateral elimination of export taxes on traditional exports, for example, will lower the effective RER of nontraditional exports. (This is simply a variant of the Dutch disease, where the problem originates in domestic policies rather than external shocks.)

Once invisibles (for instance, tourism), financial transactions, and smuggling enter the picture, further problems arise, since real appreciation encourages capital outflow through any of these channels. Foreign investment, however, is discouraged by a low RER and by the expectation that real depreciation will ensue when the process of import liberalization intensifies.

The problems of a unilateral liberalization of exports (that is, one which is not accompanied by a simultaneous liberalization of imports) are further aggravated by the existence of import restrictions in the form of quotas. When these restrictions are generalized, imports are very inelastic with respect to relative prices. Under such conditions, a cut in export taxes will be totally ineffective since the RER will fall in equilibrium to exactly offset the increase in $e(1 - t_X)$ brought about by the reduction in t_X. However, in the presence of import quotas, other components of the demand for foreign exchange, such as financial outflows, tourism, and contraband, may respond elastically to the fall in the RER. In that case, there will be some increase in traditional exports. Note, however, that the higher exports will simply finance more trade in invisibles, capital flight, and illegal activities, with an uncertain effect on growth and welfare.

Despite these problems, the strategy followed by many countries, including Argentina, has been to stimulate exports first. The argument supporting this approach is that export incentives generate trade surpluses, allowing reserves to accumulate which place the economy in a strong position for embarking on a subsequent tariff reduction program. The implicit assumption is that the government is able to forestall a resultant appreciation of the currency by imposing effective controls on capital mobility. Without this safeguard, however, the likely outcome is that the RER will fall and both imports and exports will increase with little improvement in the trade balance. The effect takes place as capital movements are influenced by one-sided expectations of appreciation linked to export liberalization. Capital movements are generally associated with the expectation of changes in the RER. To take an easy example: if the real interest rate on domestic assets is constant, the differential return between domestic and foreign assets is a function of the expected change in the RER. Now assume that the government announces a gradual elimination of export taxes without a simultaneous reduction in import tariffs. In this case the RER will be expected to fall. Private speculators will then sell foreign assets, provoking a quick and pronounced fall in the RER which will squeeze profitability in tradeable activities soon after the announcement of the export liberalization program. Although the damage could be reduced by limiting the degree of capital mobility enjoyed by the economy, the costs could be more effectively minimized by synchronizing trade reforms so as to maintain exchange rate stability whenever possible. Thus import and export taxes should be gradually and *simultaneously* reduced to prevent exchange rate expectations from being animated in one direction or another.

Should Trade Liberalization Precede Financial Liberalization?

When financial markets are liberalized faster than goods markets, export activities may experience adverse effects. One such effect highlighted in the Argentine experience arose from the greater emphasis on export liberalization and promotion than on import liberalization during the first stage of the Martínez de Hoz episode. According to our previous argument, this could have been a source of capital inflow provided that people responded rationally to expectations about the RER. However, regardless of this effect, it is still true that in an economy where foreign indebtedness is well below its desired level because of past restrictions on external borrowing, lifting those restrictions may initially induce excessive capital inflow as private investors try to close the gap between actual and desired debt. Such an overshoot is a source of temporary real appreciation which may hurt tradeable activities, especially when trade restrictions are still present. We can call this the Harberger–Edwards effect (Edwards, 1985).

Finally, the harmful effects of financial liberalization during an incomplete trade liberalization episode are accentuated if the government continues to run a large fiscal deficit, since the opening of the capital account reduces the ability to collect the inflation tax and makes it necessary to rely on domestic and/or foreign borrowing. In fact, under high capital mobility, domestic borrowing produces the same impact as foreign borrowing: it appreciates the RER by inducing private capital inflow.

Is There a Conflict between Stabilization and Liberalization?

It is clear by now that the credibility of a trade liberalization program and its short-run costs depend crucially on the use of appropriate accompanying policies. The Argentine experience gives further empirical support to the widely accepted view, raised by Krueger and National Bureau of Economic Research (1978), that many of the problems observed in trade liberalization episodes result from the failure to adjust the RER appropriately.

The role of exchange rate policy is to permit the adjustments in the RER necessary to avoid both external imbalances which condition the opening of the trade account, and production and employment losses which impose unnecessary costs on domestic industry. Such objectives are achieved by letting the nominal exchange rate float or, alternatively, by devaluing in response to (or even in anticipation of) falls in international reserves. We believe, however, that these kinds of policies are inescapable unless there is easy access to international financial markets, enabling the country to finance trade or current account deficits by running capital account surpluses. When such access is available, the government has to be very careful not to use capital inflow as a substitute for the necessary RER adjustment rather than as a means of facilitating it.

As an endogenous variable, the value of the RER depends on a wide range of policy variables, not merely on the management of the nominal exchange rate. In fact, nominal devaluations do not have lasting effects unless they are followed by contractionary fiscal and monetary policies. Aggregate demand policies affect the RER more when imports are subject to extensive QRs than when they are subject to tariffs, since, in the first case, demand shocks affect not only the price of nontradeables relative to exportables but also the price of importables which are protected by quotas or licenses.

The issue of accompanying macropolicies during a trade liberalization process acquires special importance when the policies are addressed to another task, such as fighting inflation. Although, in principle, there should not be a conflict between trade liberalization and disinflation (high foreign competition sets a limit to domestic price increases), a problem appears whenever anti-inflationary policies have the effect of lowering the RER at the same time as import tariffs are reduced competitively.

As a general conclusion, we can infer that the best accompanying policies during a trade liberalization episode are those that do not depress the RER in the short run below its sustainable equilibrium level. If disinflation is pursued by reducing real money supply under a dirty floating exchange rate system (or a crawling peg with a reserves feedback rule, as in 1977–8), the outcome will be real appreciation. However, it is well known that a fixed or controlled nominal exchange rate impairs the effectiveness of monetary policy even in the short run, provided that domestic and foreign assets are good substitutes. The use of the rate of devaluation or crawl as an active anti-inflationary instrument in this case, as in 1979–81, produces real appreciation to the extent that domestic inflation is stubborn or rigid. This, in turn, may be due to sticky expectations resulting from high fiscal deficits or excessive domestic credit expansion. However, there is increasing evidence that contractionary fiscal policies, such as deficit and government spending reductions, can be used to lower inflation without appreciating the currency above the level which makes trade liberalization an economically and politically feasible policy.

The Choice of an Appropriate Path for Import Liberalization

The following issues need to be assessed in choosing a route for import liberalization: (a) whether a one-stage or a gradual multistage liberalization should be preferred; (b) what kind of government assistance is deemed appropriate to reduce adjustment costs; (c) whether a separate stage to replace QRs by tariffs is desirable; (d) whether a uniform or discriminatory treatment of sectors is preferable in a gradual process; (e) what circumstances are appropriate to the introduction of a liberalization policy.

Unfortunately, clear and generally applicable inferences cannot be drawn from the Argentine experience regarding most of these issues. Import liberalization was partial, incomplete, and aborted. Moreover, its effects were obscured by real appreciation which laid a heavy burden on industrial output and employment. However, some of the facts can be used at least to illustrate some of the topics in question and for purposes of comparison with the other studies in this project.

Gradualism or One-stage Liberalization?

The problems associated with import liberalization usually take the shape of short-run adjustment costs arising from possible negative repercussions on (a) the balance of payments, (b) income distribution and (c) unemployment. Balance-of-payments problems only arise if the government fails to adjust the exchange rate appropriately. Therefore import liberalization has to be accompanied by exchange rate devaluation. However, policymakers are usually concerned about the effect of real depreciation on real wages. In a country like Argentina, this concern is reinforced by the fact that more traditional exports are food products, the prices of which rise with the exchange rate. If import liberalization conflicts with income distribution goals, the well-known answer of neoclassical theory is to use nondistortionary lump sum transfers, that is, transfers which do not interfere with the incentives to produce or consume in the margin. When such transfers are not feasible, however, the government will have to rely on other (second-best) policies. For example, if a tax on land exists instead of taxes on agricultural exports, the government might be able to raise that tax and subsidize food consumption to forestall wide fluctuations in income distribution. Otherwise, the government may increase export taxes temporarily and then reduce them gradually, as Krieger-Vasena did in 1967 (chapter 2).

Fear of unemployment is probably the main source of opposition to trade liberalization from workers and trade union leaders. If, during a liberalization process, expanding sectors grow more slowly than contracting sectors, some unemployment will result. Eventually, the problem will disappear provided that there is sufficient flexibility in real wages and high output response to price incentives. Perhaps the only way to avoid unnecessary unemployment costs due to real world rigidities is to combine gradualism and efficient government intervention in proper doses.

In Argentina, as chapter 3 shows, import liberalization was a gradual process in 1976–81, probably too gradual considering that it started in 1976, and not until 1979 was a five-year program of significant quarterly tariff reductions pre-announced. This program did not have a uniform tariff as the end target, but maintained some of the existing escalation. As noted by Medina (1980), excessive gradualism was hard to justify under these circumstances. Implementation was extremely slow for some industries but fast for others, creating a problem of discrimination among sectors to which we return below.

Adjustment Assistance

An essential function of the government during an ideal trade liberalization episode is to help resources move in the direction predicated by the new set of relative prices, that is, from import-substituting to export activities. What the government must *not* do is to engage in activities which, directly or indirectly, hinder labor or capital mobility in the appropriate direction or absorb resources that should be available to other sectors. Certain reinforcing measures are desirable; some are cost free, like pre-announcing tariff reductions in order to produce clear market signals, while others involve fiscal costs which may yield high social returns, for instance, subsidizing industrial reconversion, providing better infrastructure of roads, railways, and ports to encourage export activities, giving more support for training for workers in the expanding sectors, offering temporary unemployment compensation for dismissed workers in contracting industries, and so on. Sensible as this may sound, examples abound in Argentina of misguided government intervention designed to overcome the fear of unemployment on the verge of major reforms. Offering public posts to unemployed workers, starting costly public investment programs which increase the capacity of already oversized activities, and subsidizing industries with a high capacity to absorb unemployment but no leading role in a trade liberalization process, such as construction, have become common recourses of several administrations; Martínez de Hoz's was no exception. As shown earlier, government spending increased significantly between 1976 and 1981. Most of this increase was used to raise unproductive investment, wages, and employment in the public sector.

Replacement of Quantitative Restrictions by Tariffs

During the Martínez de Hoz episode, there was a separate stage for removing quantitative restrictions and replacing them by tariffs. Prohibitive tariff levels were cut in order to eliminate or reduce water, and most bans on imports were lifted along with licenses and quotas before the tariff program started. There were exceptions, however, which exacerbated sectoral discrimination; the most notorious was the maintenance of licenses on basic metal imports.

There are few doubts that the elimination of quantitative restrictions in 1977–8 was an appropriate first step toward a rationalization of trade policy. As well as eliminating many socially costly rent-seeking activities, the removal of QRs increased competition in the margin since, from that moment, increases in the demand for importables led to higher imports and not to higher domestic prices (except where commercialization services were important, since the cost of these services increased *pari passu* with real appreciation). Conceivably, under more favorable RER conditions, the elimination of QRs would have induced domestic producers to compete for increases in supply without overly affecting absolute levels of production and employment.

Discrimination

Special treatment was accorded to some industries, notably automobiles, steel, and paper, which led to harmful distortions. A few instances are noted below.

1. Import prohibitions were eliminated in 1977, except for automobiles and motors, for which they were maintained until 1978. In 1979, when the tariff program started, the ban was lifted, but the automobile industry continued to be favored by a special regime which assured high levels of protection for a longer time.
2. Import licenses disappeared in all industries except basic metals (steel, aluminum, and so on), where licenses continued to be administered by Dirección General de Fabricaciones Militares, a state holding controlled by the military.
3. Capital goods imports, in contrast, were liberalized much more quickly than the average. In April 1979, three months after the beginning of the tariff reduction program, tariffs were reduced to the levels originally scheduled for 1984. This measure was intended to encourage investment in manufacturing to foster industrial modernization. Thus the government increased effective protection in some industries by removing protection from capital goods. Meanwhile, steel (the main input of the capital goods industry) continued to be produced domestically at a price several times higher than the international price.
4. The paper and cardboard industry continued to be protected by high tariffs at the expense of other industries. For example, in 1980 fruit was produced in Argentina at a lower cost than in Chile, but packing materials were significantly more expensive. As a result, Argentina lost participation in world fruit markets to Chile.

Harmful discrimination was probably one of the most serious deficiencies of the import liberalization program implemented under Martínez de Hoz. Of course, we cannot infer from this that *any* discrimination is bad. It is always possible to find arguments for maintaining discriminatory incentives during at least the first stages of trade liberalization process to avoid the collapse of sectors that respond very strongly to tariff changes, presumably because they grew the past under the shelter of heavy import restrictions. Similar concerns are raised by factor specificity and geographical concentration, which may be higher in some sectors than in others. One problem with preferential treatment, however, is that discrimination necessarily imposes externalities on other sectors and leaves the door open for unwanted protection demands from pressure groups. Since these effects are generally at once important and unpredictable, there are good chances that the problems created by sectoral discrimination will be more intractable than those it was intended to solve. Soon after the pre-announced 1979 tariff reform had begun, Dadone and Swoboda (1979) voiced concern that the structure of the EPRs that would result from the reform bore little resemblance to the structure of NPRs set by the government. They surveyed a small sample of goods and found that, with nominal tariffs varying between zero and 50 percent, EPRs ranged from − 82 to 230 percent. After arguing that these differences in protection had neither been provided for nor planned by the authorities, they pointed out that, by the time the episode was supposed to end, some EPRs would have actually increased despite the pre-announced fall in the NPRs. Referring to Berlinsky's results, which show the rankings of NPRs and EPRs as highly correlated, Dadone and Swoboda maintained that:

> In Berlinsky's estimates of correlation coefficients, sectors are defined in broad aggregate terms, so that nominal tariffs and input–output coefficients are actually averages which smooth out the difference found here . . . [yet] entrepreneurs make their decisions not on the basis of average sector protection, but strictly on the basis of the EPR accorded to the specific commodity they produce. (Dadone and Swoboda, 1979)

Appropriate Circumstances

It is difficult to draw useful and generally applicable conclusions about what circumstances are appropriate for introducing liberalization. If anything, the Martínez de Hoz experience suggests that bad economic conditions at the beginning of an episode – high inflation, current account imbalances, capital flight, and recession – are not necessarily serious impediments to the introduction of a trade liberalization program. Both Martínez de Hoz and Krieger-Vasena succeeded in reversing adverse external conditions quickly and effectively means of proper exchange rate adjustment; they were also able to curb inflation. However, we may ask whether more intense import liberalization would have obstructed stabilization goals more significantly.

The importance of political circumstances in explaining the initial success of liberalization episodes is even more difficult to assess. Both the Martínez de Hoz and the Krieger-Vasena episodes occurred under non-democratic rule as an initiative of strong military governments. Trade unions, traditional defenders of the status quo as a way of preserving employment, were curbed, and an important source of opposition was thus neutralized. However, the influence of some pressure groups, like rent seekers, may have increased. In fact, the Argentine experience does not furnish conclusive evidence as to whether trade reforms are more easily implementable by democratic or *de facto* governments. In any case, it is never desirable for policies that promote economic freedom to be introduced by governments that do not believe in political freedom. Undoubtedly, the resistance to the trade liberalization programs of Krieger-Vasena and Martínez de Hoz was, to a large extent, motivated by the feeling that these policies had been introduced by authoritarian governments. Thus, to avoid reversals, those sectors of society that feel threatened by trade reforms should be able to air and sort out their differences in public forums where the mediator is a well-accepted democratic government.

Appendix 1 Methodology for the Estimation of Real Effective Exchange Rates

The REERs reported in chapter 2 (tables 2.16 and 2.17) and chapter 3 (tables 3.17 and 3.18) were estimated from data obtained at a five-digit SIC aggregation level. Our study deals with the sample of manufacturing activities selected by Berlinsky (1978) and Nogués (1978). These activities are interrelated through strong backward and forward linkages and have high degrees of internal output homogeneity. However, they are not directly related to the agricultural sector producing traditional exportable goods. Thus, in order to make the sample more comprehensive, we added five branches belonging to the foodstuffs sector which were also selected in a study by FIEL (1980).

For each activity, REERs were defined as follows:

$$\text{REER}_{\text{m}}{}^{i} = \text{NER}_{\text{m}}{}^{i}\,(1 + t_{\text{m}}{}^{i})\,\frac{P_{\text{f}}^{i}}{\text{GPL}}$$

$$\text{REER}_{\text{x}}{}^{j} = \text{NER}_{\text{x}}{}^{j}\,(1 + s_{\text{x}}{}^{j})\,\frac{P_{f}^{j}}{\text{GPL}}$$

where $\text{REER}_{\text{m}}{}^{i}$ is the REER for imports for activity i, $\text{REER}_{\text{x}}{}^{j}$ is the REER for exports for activity j, $\text{NER}_{\text{m}}{}^{i}$ and $\text{NER}_{\text{x}}{}^{j}$ are the nominal exchange rates relevant for imports and exports respectively, $t_{\text{m}}{}^{i}$ is the import tariff plus nontariff surcharge for activity i, $s_{\text{x}}{}^{j}$ is the export subsidy for activity j, P_{f}^{i} and $P_{\text{f}}{}^{j}$ are the foreign price levels for activities i and j, and GPL is the general price level measured by the domestic wholesale price index.

Nominal exchange rates for exports and imports are annual averages resulting from dividing exports and imports in current pesos by exports and imports in current dollars, using INDEC figures. This procedure permitted fairly accurate estimation of implicit sectoral exchange rates in the years when multiple rates existed (1965, 1973, and 1976 in our selection).

The US wholesale price index served as a proxy for foreign prices. Information on nominal protection (tariffs and export subsidies) was taken from the following studies.

Cuervo (1972): protection to domestic sales (import taxes) in 1965 and 1967.
Berlinsky and Schydlowsky (1977): protection to domestic sales and exports in 1969.
Nogués (1980): export protection (credit and fiscal subsidies) in 1973.
Nogués (1978): protection to domestic sales in 1976 and 1977.
FIEL (1980): protection to domestic sales and exports in 1979 and 1980.

Nominal rates of protection are shown in table A1.1; real effective exchange rates are reported in table A1.2. The units of measurement are pesos moneda nacional (m$n) per US dollar at constant 1960 prices.[1] The last column in table A1.2 shows the weights used to calculate averages and also to aggregate REERs at the three- and two-digit SIC levels. These weights represent the percentage of each activity in total manufacturing production as indicated by the 1974 economic census.

The following is the list of the 45 manufacturing activities included in the sample:

31110 Slaughtering, preparation, and preservation of meat
31120 Manufacture of dairy products
31132 Canning and preservation of fruits and vegetables
31151 Manufacture of vegetable oils
31172 Manufacture of biscuits
31174 Manufacture of dry pasta
32114 Spinning of textile fibers
32116 Weaving of textile fibers
32131 Manufacture of hosiery products
32201 Manufacture of shirts
34111 Manufacture of paper pulp
34112 Manufacture of paper and cardboard
35112 Liquid and compressed gas
35113 Manufacture of tanning products
35119 Basic industrial chemicals not elsewhere classified
35121 Manufacture of fertilizers
25122 Manufacture of pesticides
35131 Synthetic resins
35132 Manmade fibers
35210 Paints, varnishes, and lacquers
35511 Tire and tube industries
36201 Glass and glass products
36921 Manufacture of cement
37100 Basic iron and steel industries

1 The peso moneda nacional is an old currency unit equivalent to one billionth of the current austral, that is 1 ₳ = 10^9 m$n.

37200 Basic nonferrous metal industries
38131 Metallic tanks
38192 Manufacture of cans
38193 Stoves and heaters (except electrical)
38210 Manufacture and repair of motors and turbines
38220 Manufacture of agricultural machinery
38230 Manufacture of machinery for metal and wood work
38240 Special industrial machinery and equipment
38251 Manufacture of office machinery
38291 Manufacture of elevators
38292 Refrigerators, washers, air conditioners, and other electrical appliances
38310 Manufacture and repair of electrical industrial machinery
38321 Radio and TV equipment
38322 Communication equipment
38391 Manufacture of storage batteries
38392 Manufacture of lamps and electrical tubes
38393 Manufacture of electrical conductors
38422 Manufacture and repair of railroad equipment
38432 Motor vehicles, except tractors
38436 Tractors
38440 Motorcycles and bicycles
38510 Manufacture of professional and scientific equipment

FIEL (1980) deals with nominal and effective protection rates for all 45 branches, whereas Nogués (1978) only includes 40 activities in his study. NPRs in the activities omitted (the first five listed) are our own elaboration. In the work of Nogués (1980) and Berlinsky and Schydlowsky (1977), NPRs were available at the four-digit level of aggregation. Thus the same NPRs were assigned to all five-digit activities within a four-digit subsector. The NPRs reported by Cuervo (1972) correspond to activities classified according to the 1963 Input–Output Matrix, which we crossed with the SIC.

Table A1.1 Nominal protection rates on imports

Branch	*1965*	*1967*	*1969*	*1976*	*1977*	*1979*	*1980*
31120	n.a.	n.a.	n.a.	1.040	0.190	0.244	0.240
31132	2.083	0.801	0.057	1.013	0.207	0.303	0.303
31172	3.200	1.300	0.000	1.650	0.150	0.217	0.217
31174	3.200	1.100	0.000	1.100	0.150	0.217	0.217
32114	1.656	0.283	0.660	0.846	0.440	0.409	0.377
32116	2.754	0.736	0.660	1.257	0.679	0.548	0.507
32201	3.200	1.400	0.565	2.000	0.950	0.717	0.677
32131	3.250	1.400	0.897	2.000	0.950	0.667	0.647
34111	2.147	0.979	0.555	0.151	0.160	0.199	0.199
34112	1.887	0.802	0.555	0.300	0.300	0.601	0.568
35112	1.583	0.647	0.876	0.480	0.200	0.231	0.229
35119	1.923	0.776	0.876	0.636	0.350	0.427	0.398
35121	1.923	0.776	0.606	0.580	0.130	0.427	0.387
35121	1.850	0.900	0.606	0.900	0.400	0.346	0.329
35131	1.923	0.776	0.876	1.057	0.470	0.449	0.413
35132	2.136	1.112	0.876	0.950	0.400	0.503	0.462
35210	1.923	0.776	0.750	0.988	0.170	0.433	0.396
35511	1.400	1.100	1.040	1.100	0.450	0.771	0.731
36201	2.200	1.000	0.632	0.943	0.418	0.524	0.486
36921	1.750	0.600	0.150	0.660	0.110	0.237	0.237
37100	1.417	0.832	0.549	0.888	0.482	0.487	0.474
37200	2.343	1.127	0.722	0.685	0.445	0.523	0.495
38131	2.025	0.965	0.754	1.060	0.440	0.544	0.538
38192	2.079	1.047	0.754	1.060	0.335	0.525	0.512
38193	2.128	0.991	0.754	2.040	0.640	0.509	0.502
38210	1.586	0.992	0.879	0.840	0.690	0.599	0.559
38220	1.586	0.992	0.879	0.840	0.570	0.557	0.524
38230	1.586	0.992	0.879	0.840	0.690	0.584	0.545
38240	2.082	1.285	0.879	0.840	0.540	0.579	0.540
38251	1.892	1.111	0.879	0.840	0.690	0.554	0.521
38291	1.587	0.900	0.879	0.840	0.690	0.565	0.525
38292	2.198	1.229	0.879	1.740	0.840	0.584	0.551
38310	2.150	0.900	0.956	0.840	0.690	0.553	0.513
38321	2.166	1.343	0.956	0.938	0.707	0.603	0.567
38322	2.198	1.229	0.956	0.920	0.687	0.518	0.482
38391	1.844	0.942	0.781	0.875	0.438	0.490	0.467
38392	1.247	0.829	0.781	0.753	0.474	0.487	0.467
38393	2.198	1.229	0.781	0.900	0.500	0.527	0.487
38422	2.200	1.300	0.835	1.050	0.755	0.642	0.620
38432	5.210	5.210	1.119	1.332	0.946	1.552	1.419
38436	5.210	5.210	1.119	0.980	0.480	0.555	0.549
38440	1.586	0.992	0.441	0.980	0.980	0.829	0.787
38510	2.640	1.070	0.948	0.800	0.500	0.476	0.473
Un-weighted mean	2.217761	1.900023	0.728476	0.989116	0.499604	0.518883	0.491558
Standard deviation	0.822641	0.927062	0.267217	0.879961	0.933608	0.286005	0.392711
Coefficient of variation	0.371334	0.779028	0.366817	0.889644	1.362694	0.531193	0.798911

n.a., not available.

Table A1.2 Real effective exchange rates for a sample of industries, 1965–1980

Branch	*1965 IMP*	*1967 IMP*	*1969 EXP*	*1969 IMP*	*1973 EXP*	*1976 IMP*	*1977 IMP*	*1979 EXP*	*1979 IMP*	*1980 EXP*	*1980 IMP*	*Weights*
31120	n.a.	n.a.	0.827	n.a.	0.846	1.419	0.919	0.621	0.627	0.509	0.522	6.100
31132	1.974	1.538	0.911	n.a.	0.891	1.400	0.932	0.532	0.657	0.455	0.548	2.000
31151	0.610	0.717	0.708	0.711	0.456	0.759	0.750	0.493	0.603	0.424	0.504	3.400
31172	2.327	1.965	0.945	n.a.	0.832	1.844	0.888	0.632	0.614	0.516	0.512	1.200
31174	2.652	1.794	0.940	n.a.	0.832	1.416	0.888	0.640	0.614	0.516	0.512	0.600
32114	1.593	0.997	0.712	1.244	0.602	0.938	0.875	0.463	0.490	0.346	0.395	5.600
32116	2.252	1.349	0.712	1.244	0.602	1.147	1.020	0.493	0.539	0.381	0.432	5.800
32131	2.569	1.865	0.839	1.464	0.784	1.524	1.184	0.517	0.580	0.418	0.473	0.500
32201	2.540	1.805	0.840	1.173	0.801	1.566	1.320	0.496	0.622	0.434	0.488	6.300
34111	1.845	1.530	0.835	1.160	0.743	0.715	0.841	0.533	0.533	0.461	0.475	0.400
34112	1.693	1.411	0.835	1.160	0.743	0.808	0.942	0.573	0.712	0.541	0.621	3.000
35112	1.494	1.263	0.656	1.295	0.601	0.949	0.852	0.580	0.538	0.522	0.489	0.600
35113	n.a.	n.a.	0.656	n.a.	0.601	1.154	0.887	0.590	0.627	0.529	0.557	0.300
35119	1.690	1.362	0.656	1.295	0.601	1.049	0.958	0.595	0.624	0.532	0.556	2.600
35121	1.691	1.362	0.766	1.108	0.604	1.013	0.802	0.566	0.624	0.504	0.552	0.700
35122	1.653	1.457	0.766	1.108	0.604	1.218	0.994	0.584	0.589	0.565	0.529	1.600
35131	1.684	1.362	0.656	1.295	0.632	1.318	1.044	0.601	0.634	0.537	0.562	2.400
35132	1.823	1.620	0.656	1.295	0.632	1.250	0.994	0.591	0.657	0.527	0.582	1.500
35210	1.652	1.355	0.773	1.208	0.626	1.280	0.839	0.732	0.625	0.542	0.555	2.400
35511	1.320	1.576	0.804	1.259	0.653	1.169	0.888	0.495	0.668	0.435	0.567	1.600
36201	1.912	1.614	0.873	1.272	0.765	1.194	1.126	0.682	0.792	0.613	0.675	1.700
36921	1.657	1.240	0.873	0.896	0.752	1.229	0.887	0.603	0.631	0.545	0.560	18.200
37100	1.495	1.550	1.041	1.279	0.814	1.158	1.245	0.739	0.846	0.646	0.710	3.200
37200	2.068	2.174	0.926	1.422	0.820	1.179	1.248	0.553	0.852	0.453	0.720	0.700
38131	1.871	1.650	0.942	1.449	0.962	0.769	1.230	0.765	0.868	0.667	0.748	1.000
38192	1.904	1.719	0.942	1.449	0.906	0.769	1.140	0.753	0.858	0.667	0.735	0.700
38193	1.823	1.560	0.850	1.308	0.734	1.529	0.951	0.474	0.523	0.416	0.447	2.300
38210	1.552	1.673	0.937	1.531	0.953	1.169	1.257	0.656	0.743	0.599	0.633	2.500
38220	1.605	1.673	0.937	1.531	0.971	1.169	1.168	0.633	0.723	0.581	0.619	0.500
38230	1.494	1.673	0.937	1.531	0.969	1.169	1.257	0.659	0.736	0.602	0.628	2.100
38240	1.866	1.919	0.937	1.531	0.969	1.169	1.145	0.633	0.734	0.595	0.625	0.200
38251	1.816	1.773	0.937	1.531	0.874	1.169	1.257	0.660	0.722	0.603	0.618	0.300
38291	1.567	1.596	0.937	1.531	0.863	1.169	1.257	0.645	0.727	0.596	0.620	1.800
38292	1.864	1.739	0.858	1.401	0.759	1.377	1.062	0.488	0.546	0.439	0.453	1.100
38310	1.908	1.593	0.912	1.593	0.926	1.046	1.282	0.660	0.707	0.589	0.623	2.300
38321	1.826	1.825	0.835	1.459	0.796	0.872	1.005	0.494	0.542	0.433	0.486	0.500
38322	1.906	1.868	0.912	1.593	0.905	1.092	1.280	0.668	0.691	0.597	0.610	0.600
38391	1.756	1.628	0.953	1.451	0.830	1.066	1.091	0.640	0.678	0.575	0.604	0.300
38392	1.388	1.533	0.953	1.451	0.830	0.997	1.118	0.657	0.677	0.589	0.604	1.400
38393	1.775	1.868	0.953	1.451	0.830	1.081	1.138	0.645	0.695	0.579	0.612	1.300
38422	1.889	1.850	0.864	1.039	0.898	0.868	0.883	0.601	0.666	0.524	0.565	0.000
38432	3.609	4.737	0.800	1.513	0.839	1.211	1.138	0.497	0.930	0.460	0.773	7.000
38436	3.750	5.265	0.912	1.726	0.971	1.334	1.121	0.670	0.740	0.610	0.631	0.000
38440	1.528	1.519	0.800	1.029	0.625	1.028	1.158	0.485	0.667	0.447	0.571	0.300
38510	2.164	1.676	0.924	1.538	0.895	1.174	1.161	0.704	0.731	0.665	0.665	0.600
Unweighted mean	1.901	1.750	0.850	1.307	0.781	1.154	1.054	0.600	0.671	0.529	0.577	
Standard deviation	0.541	0.764	0.100	0.294	0.132	0.250	0.157	0.081	0.098	0.080	0.085	
Coefficient of variation	0.284	0.437	0.118	0.225	0.169	0.200	0.149	0.134	0.147	0.151	0.147	
Weighted mean	1.807	1.685	0.832	1.200	0.753	1.193	1.023	0.580	0.662	0.507	0.564	

n.a., not available; IMP, imports; EXP, exports.

Appendix 2 Investigation of Individual Sectors

The response of individual sectors during the Martínez de Hoz episode is dealt with in this appendix. The focus is on agriculture and manufacturing activities.

Output and Export Responses in Agriculture

Policy changes in 1976 and 1977 created favorable expectations in agriculture. REERs increased for most exports as a consequence of exchange rate unification and the fall in export taxes. REER improvements were shown in chapter 3 (see table 3.17). Only fruits and industrial crops did not experience an increase in REERs because export taxes were initially low in those cases. Output and export responses were immediate. The agricultural GDP and traditional exports rose significantly in 1976 and 1977. The surge is also apparent in the performance of individual activities, that is, food crops (cereals and oil seeds), fruits, beef, and edible oil. Only industrial crops experienced a fall in production. Another remarkable aspect of this period is the increase in yields for a number of crops, especially oil seeds. This was due to technological improvements (for instance, more intensive use of chemical fertilizers and adoption of new crop varieties) which were fostered by trade liberalization.

Immediately after 1977, however, REERs started to fall for every farming activity. This was the effect of domestic currency appreciation. The impact of this phenomenon on agricultural performance was clear and strong. After the 1976–7 boom, output growth decelerated and in 1980 production and exports fell. The financial reform and the fiscal and monetary policies implemented by the government also worked against the farmers. Given the tendency of agricultural relative prices to fall as the domestic currency appreciates, the real interest rate paid by the farm sector was higher than elsewhere in the economy. The difference between nominal interest rates and wholesale price increases for farm products was around 14 percent from July 1977 to December 1979 and 54 percent from January 1980 to March 1981 (annual averages). Thus capital intensive activities, such as livestock, wool production, fruits, and industrial crops, were more severely affected. Only cereals and oil seeds performed reasonably well over the period, although by 1980 and 1981 extreme overvaluation of the peso had also affected these two crops. In 1981 the situation of many farmers was critical. Paradoxically, relief came with the large devaluations which accompanied the collapse of the liberalization and stabilization programs.

Sectoral Responses to Changes in Real Effective Exchange Rates: the Case of Manufacturing

The methodology used to calculate individual responses in manufacturing is based on the following analytical framework. Each sector represents a particular manufacturing branch, and we are interested in obtaining partial-equilibrium estimates of sectoral effects of changes in REERs. Suppose that, for each branch, we define the following equations:

$$Q_i = D_i\left(\frac{P_i^{\mathrm{d}}}{P}, \frac{P_i^{\mathrm{f}}E(1 + t_i)}{P}, \text{other}\right) \tag{A2.1}$$

$$Q^*_i = S_i\left(\frac{P_i^{\mathrm{d}}}{P}, \text{other}\right) \tag{A2.2}$$

$$\frac{\mathrm{d}(P_i^{\mathrm{d}}/P)}{\mathrm{d}t} = \mathrm{b}_i\,(Q_i - Q^*_i) \tag{A2.3}$$

Equation (A2.1) states that the actual level of production Q_i is demand determined in the short run. This is because the domestic relative price P_i^{d}/P of commodity i is a state variable, the value of which changes over time but is fixed at a given moment in time. Thus producers sell whatever is demanded at the going price. (P_i^{d} represents commodity i's nominal price and P is a general price deflator.) In addition to its own relative price, the demand function D_i also includes the relative price of commodity i's closest foreign substitute and a set of "other" explanatory variables. The relative price of the imported substitute is the REER corresponding to the branch. The "other" variables may include real interest rates, credit availability, direct purchases by the public sector, indirect demand originating in government spending, real income, and income distribution, all of which are in turn affected by monetary, fiscal, and incomes policy.

Actual production does not always equal desired production. The value Q^*_i of desired production is shown in equation (A2.2) to be a function of P_i^{d}/P and other variables. These other variables are not the same as those included in the D_i function, although some of them, for example interest rates and credit availability, may interact both ways. Finally, equation (A2.3) accounts for "sticky" relative price adjustments in response to the gap between actual and desired production levels.

Thus, in our simple behavioral model the domestically produced good and the imported good are assumed to be imperfect substitutes. Relative price adjustments to changes in economic conditions are not instantaneous. Sectoral production has to fall below normal levels before producers let their relative prices decrease. This helps to explain why sectoral production and employment decreased in the face of increased foreign competition even before domestic relative prices fell.

Now assume that we reduce branch i's protection by decreasing the tariff t_i on commodity i. From equation (A2.1) it is clear that domestic production will fall as competing imports increase. If the RER depreciates while tariffs are reduced, the relative price of the import commodity will fall by less than the full reduction of the tariff. Clearly, the higher is the increase in the RER, the lower is the fall in the *effective* RER. However, if owing to accompanying macropolicies the exchange rate appreciates in real terms, the relative price of the imported good will fall by more than the tariff reduction and the effects on imports and domestic production will be larger. This is what happened to most manufacturing branches during the Martínez de Hoz episode. RER appreciation made imports more competitive and eliminated water in the tariffs where it existed, thereby exerting significant effects in domestic production. There were differences, however, in short-run sectoral responses across manufacturing branches. These can be found by calculating the partial elasticities of domestic production and imports with respect to the REER. The following information was available to us:

1 value added and employment figures corresponding to SIC two-digit industrial subsectors.
2 production and employment indices available at the three-digit (branch) level.
3 exports and imports in US dollars resulting from crossing the BTN and SIC classifications.

In addition, we chose the REER on imports (figures were listed in chapter 3, table 3.18) as the explanatory variable accounting for changes in imports, output, and employment. On the basis of this information, we calculated arc elasticities defined in the following way:

$$\epsilon_i = \frac{\dfrac{Y_{79}^{i} + Y_{80}^{i} + Y_{81}^{i} - Y_{75}^{i} - Y_{76}^{i} - Y_{77}^{i}}{Y_{75}^{i} + Y_{76}^{i} + Y_{77}^{i} + Y_{79}^{i} + Y_{80}^{i} + Y_{81}^{i}}}{\dfrac{R_{79}^{i} + R_{80}^{i} - R_{76}^{i} - R_{77}^{i}}{R_{76}^{i} + R_{77}^{i} + R_{79}^{i} + R_{80}^{i}}}$$

where ϵ_i is the arc elasticity for sector i, Y^i alternatively represents real output, imports (measured in US dollars at constant 1960 prices), and employment, and R^i is the REER of competing imports. The subscripts represent the years to which the data correspond.

An important limitation of our analysis is that we omit variables other than REERs. To include them would require the estimation of multiple elasticities by means of regression analysis using longer time series; this task is precluded by the lack of annual REER series.

Our elasticity results are ranked in tables A2.1 and A2.2 where sectors are disaggregated at the two- and three-digit levels respectively. They consistently show that the stronger responses to the fall in REERs during the Martínez de Hoz episode correspond to the branches supplying metallic products, machinery and equipment, textiles, clothing and apparel, and paper. The lower responses correspond to foodstuffs, chemicals, basic metals, and nonmetal mineral products like cement. The automobile industry (Branch 3843) is an interesting case: the response of imports and employment was high (elasticity coefficients ranked first in the two cases) but the effect on production was low (production increased despite the fall in the REER). The interpretation of this result is left for the next section. As for the rest, the results are hardly surprising: high efficiency in foodstuff production, transportation costs in the case of cement, and QRs imposed on basic metal imports explain their low elasticities.

Another indicator of structural changes in output and employment allocation is given by rank-order correlation coefficients. These were

Table A2.1 Sectoral elasticities at the Standard Industrial Classification two-digit aggregation level

REER elasticity of GDP			*REER elasticity of employment*		
Position in the ranking	*Sector*	*Elasticity value*	*Position in the ranking*	*Sector*	*Elasticity value*
1	34	0.36	1	38	0.70
2	32	0.27	2	34	0.53
3	31	0.22	3	32	0.47
4	38	0.22	4	35	0.45
5	36	0.06	5	36	0.39
6	35	− 0.06	6	37	0.35
7	37	− 0.14	7	31	0.23

Spearman rank-order correlation coefficients:
1 GDP versus REER = 0.697 (n = 7);
2 Employment versus REER = 0.607 (n = 7);
3 GDP versus EPR = 0.486 (n = 6) (excludes foodstuffs, beverages, and tobacco);
4 Employment versus EPR = 0.486 (n = 6) (excludes foodstuffs, beverages, and tobacco).
Constructed from data presented in chapter 3, table 3.17.

Table A2.2 Sectoral elasticities at the Standard Industrial Classification three-digit aggregation level

REER elasticity of production index			*REER elasticity of employment index*			*REER elasticity of imports*		
Position in the ranking	*Sector*	*Elasticity value*	*Position in the ranking*	*Sector*	*Elasticity value*	*Position in the ranking*	*Sector*	*Elasticity value*
1	381	0.93	1	384	0.85	1	3843/4	– 3.40
2	382	0.48	2	3843/4	0.85	2	381	– 2.51
3	322	0.40	3	385	0.82	3	322	– 2.18
4	383	0.38	4	382	0.76	4	385	– 2.12
5	385	0.36	5	321	0.71	5	383	– 2.10
6	341	0.27	6	351	0.54	6	384	– 1.65
7	321	0.24	7	383	0.54	7	362	– 1.54
8	352	0.11	8	322	0.53	8	321	– 1.45
9	355	0.10	9	381	0.52	9	341	– 1.13
10	311	0.09	10	362	0.50	10	382	– 0.98
11	362	0.08	11	341	0.49	11	311	– 0.75
12	351	0.03	12	352	0.43	12	352	– 0.68
13	369	– 0.01	13	371	0.40	13	355	– 0.65
14	372	– 0.33	14	369	0.39	14	351	– 0.52
15	384	– 0.36	15	372	0.30	15	369	– 0.33
16	3843/4	– 0.36	16	355	0.30	16	372	0.37
17	371	– 1.04	17	311	0.28	17	371	0.94

Spearman rank-order correlation coefficients:

1 production versus, REER = 0.677 (n = 17);
2 employment versus REER = 0.305 (n = 17) (not significantly different from zero at the 5 percent level);
3 production versus EPR = 0.547 (n = 16) (excludes foodstuffs);
4 employment versus EPR = 0.500 (n = 16) (excludes foodstuffs).

Constructed from data presented in chapter 3, table 3.17.

obtained by comparing relative variations in output and employment with relative variations in REERs between 1976 and 1980. The results are also reported in tables A2.1 and A2.2 and show a positive correlation, thereby suggesting that supply and factor allocation changed in the direction suggested by relative price incentives. The same conclusions result if EPRs are used instead of REERs.

The analysis of the response of nontraditional exports to price incentives requires further elaboration. Here, we cannot simply relate the percentage change in exports to the percentage change in exports REERs to calculate sectoral arc elasticities. If we did this, most elasticities would have the wrong sign since, during the Martínez de Hoz period, nontraditional exports increased despite the fall in their REERs. The important point, however, is that nontraditional export REERs fell proportionally less than import REERs, the former being affected by increases in export subsidies which compensated partially for RER overvaluation in the case of many manufacturing branches. Clearly, an improvement in these terms may actually increase exports, both in constant dollars and as a proportion of output.

Assume that a firm has some monopoly power when producing for the domestic market while facing a perfectly elastic export demand curve. Then, to maximize profits, the firm will resort to price discrimination. By doing this the price-discriminating firm is able to take advantage of increasing average returns which raise its benefits. When, owing to RER appreciation, the REERs on competitive imports and exports fall, the domestic demand curve shifts to the left and the export demand curve faced by domestic entrepreneurs shifts down. However, if import tariffs are simultaneously reduced while export subsidies are increased, the shift in the export demand curve will be smaller than the shift in the domestic market demand curve, especially if import responses are high in that sector. Thus, exports may increase even if the external price faced by domestic producers falls. This type of situation is typical of the Argentine manufacturing sector, which is characterized by a high level of industrial concentration (table A2.3).

Table A2.4 reports a ranking of export elasticities calculated as the percentage change in the export-to-production ratio divided by the percentage change in nominal incentives to exports relative to nominal protection to sales in the domestic market. The expression for the elasticity coefficient (branch i) is

$$n_i = \frac{\dfrac{X_{79}^i + X_{80}^i + X_{81}^i - X_{74}^i - X_{75}^i - X_{76}^i}{X_{74}^i + X_{75}^i + X_{76}^i + X_{79}^i + X_{80}^i + X_{81}^i}}{\dfrac{s_{79}^i + s_{80}^i + 2}{t_{79}^i + t_{80}^i + 2} - \dfrac{1 + s_{76}^i}{1 + t_{76}^i}}$$

Table A2.3 Industrial concentration in manufacturing activities, 1979

n	*Activity*	*b*	*Percentage share*
12	Textiles	2	55
20	Food	2	38
7	Sugar	3	68
5	Pack plants	2	83
6	Cosmetics	2	54
4	Tobacco	2	86
13	Automobiles and spare parts	3	60
5	Rubber	2	62
4	Cement	2	65
5	Tractors and agricultural machinery	3	85
13	Chemical products	2	28
9	Oil	1	61
8	Steel	1	35

n, number of firms in each activity out of the 200 largest enterprises in 1979; *b*, number of those firms with the share of the market given in the fourth column.

Source: based on *Anuario Prensa Económica*, 1980

Table A2.4 Sectoral elasticities of exports with respect to relative export incentives at the Standard Industrial Classification three-digit disaggregation level

Position in the ranking	*Branch*	*Elasticity*
1	385	2.60
2	322	1.42
3	362	0.93
4	381	0.92
5	351	0.74
6	383	0.66
7	372	0.56
8	352	0.50
9	321	0.40
10	384	0.35
11	311	0.29
12	382	0.18
13	371	− 0.07
14	369	− 0.25
15	341	− 0.33
16	355	− 0.44

Constructed from data presented in chapter 3, table 3.17.

where X^i is the export-to-output ratio in branch i (exports are expressed at producer prices, that is, prices which include export subsidies), s^i is the subsidy rate on exports (it is assumed that the level and structure of nontraditional export subsidies in 1976 was the same as in 1973, the year for which the Nogués (1980) estimation are available (see appendix 1) and t^i is the tariff rate of competitive imports.

The results in table A2.4 indicate that there is a high sectoral correlation between the ranking of export elasticities and the ranking of import elasticities (table A2.2). Industries in which sales to the domestic market were more severely affected by import competition also responded more to export opportunities. The difference between export and import REERs was high for some branches which exhibited high import and export elasticities. A good example is the capital goods industry. Although domestic sales and protection decreased significantly, credit subsidies to exports were particularly high and allowed some firms to significantly increase exports during the period, mostly to other members of LAFTA. Exports, however, were not to prevent falls in production in most cases.

Time Patterns of Sector Responses in Manufacturing

As indicated in chapter 3, most manufacturing REERs fell after 1976 as a result of real appreciation and trade liberalization. Therefore it is important to distinguish between changes in REER levels and changes in relative REERs when analyzing sector responses. The fall in the levels, along with other factors, help to explain the decrease in employment and production in almost all manufacturing branches during the late 1970s as well as the surge in imports. However, relative REERs must be used in explaining sectoral departures of output and employment from the average.

A characteristic common to all sectors is that layoffs increased more quickly than production declined. This process was facilitated by the loosening of restrictions in labor legislation and the ban on trade union activities after 1976. Those restrictions had prevented or made it expensive for firms to fire workers. By the mid-1970s it was evident that labor was overemployed in manufacturing and that some rationalization was needed.

Foodstuffs

Production and employment were less affected than the average. In particular, the behavior of production was less unstable in the food branch than in manufacturing in general, possibly because Argentina is an efficient producer of processed foods. In addition, we should note that the sector expanded significantly until 1978 under the influence of private investment promoted by the government (Schvarzer, 1978).

Textiles

Textile products and clothing were among the more affected branches. Tariffs on textiles decreased more than tariffs on other commodities. Changes in protection are even greater if EPRs are considered (see chapter 3, table 3.19). In fact, this sector was overprotected before 1976; in addition to high tariffs, QRs in the form of import licenses were common. When this situation ended, and given that import elasticities for textiles are relatively high, output and employment decreased more than the manufacturing average. Exports, which had expanded until 1978, declined thereafter while imports began to rise.

Paper

The Martínez de Hoz administration put a clear emphasis on stimulating paper production. In fact, this is one of the few cases in which the authorities showed an inclination to engage in import substitution. Between 1976 and 1978 officially promoted investment plans were approved for a total of over a billion dollars. A large part of this effort was devoted to the production of paper used in the newspaper industry, an input which was totally imported before 1970. Tariffs on imports were increased from 10 to 15 percent in 1976 and to 20 percent in 1977, a remarkable exception from the trade policies being pursued at the same time in other branches. As a result of these measures, production expanded steadily between 1976 and 1979 despite the 1978 recession. This situation did not last as the RER became severely misaligned in 1979 and after. Paper production, being a highly elastic importable, dropped significantly in 1980–1.

Chemicals

This is another sector in which investment promotion policies may have played a role in determining its performance during the 1970s. Serious efforts aimed at import substitution started in 1970 with most of the initiative coming from the government. By 1976 there were two major projects under way which involved the construction of chemical conglomerates in Bahía Blanca and Río Tercero. The investments combined public and private capital, the former predominating in the case of basic chemical products. Fabricaciones Militares, the military industrial complex, was directly involved in these projects which totaled more than US$900 million.

Commercial policy discriminated in favor of the chemical branch. Nominal protection increased in relative terms from 1976 to 1980. Exports were promoted and increased steadily during the 1970s and both production and employment performed better than the manufacturing average.

Steel and Other Basic Metal Industries

The most important nonsteel basic metal industry is aluminum, which is run by a mixed state–private monopoly. The steel industry, in turn, comprises a huge state enterprise (SOMISA), three smaller but still large private firms (Acindar, Dálmine, and Propulsora), and a few other intermediate firms. The armed forces have direct interests in basic metal production: Fabricaciones Militares supplies a high proportion of the capital invested in SOMISA.

Steel and aluminum were the only exceptions to the elimination of quota restrictions started in 1976. Import licenses protect the productive capacity of these industries: licenses are granted when domestic demand at the price set by local producers is higher than domestic supply. However, in practice, most imports are made directly by the domestic producers who, in turn, have a say in approving or rejecting consumers' import applications. As a result of this preferential treatment, steel production grew between 1978 and 1981 and imports fell. Thus the sector's performance diverged from that of most other sectors in the economy. Similar considerations apply to aluminum and other metals, although this branch was relatively more affected by the business cycle.

Capital Goods

Capital goods is a clear example of an industry affected adversely during the Martínez de Hoz episode. The sector was discriminated against by the trade policies pursued in the late 1970s in at least two different ways:

1. by an unscheduled acceleration in the rate of tariff reductions.
2. by the maintenance of high levels of protection in the industries supplying basic metal inputs.

Before the liberalization episode, capital goods imports were severely limited, except where domestic substitutes were not available. In 1976–7 quota restrictions were abolished but high tariffs were maintained. The tariff program announced in 1978 contemplated a gradual reduction in investment goods tariffs consistent with protection cuts in other sectors. The situation changed four months after the program was implemented: Resolution 493 of April 1979 reduced nominal tariffs on capital goods to the levels set initially in 1984. The reasons for such a dramatic change in the rules of the game are not entirely clear, but it can be deduced from official declarations that the authorities wanted to foster the incorporation of technologically advanced imported equipment to improve industrial efficiency in capital intensive branches. Thus, in order to favor some activities, the domestic production of capital goods was hurt. At the same time, domestic versus foreign price differentials for steel and other basic metal inputs (subject to quota restrictions) increased with real appreciation, inducing further EPR deterioration in capital goods branches. A study by the Secretary of Commerce quoted by Nogués (1983) has found that steel protection created sectoral transfers in excess of US$650 million a year during the period.

Table A2.5 shows a few examples of actual changes in protection once all effects are taken into account. Note that output and employment in branches 382 (nonelectric machinery) and 383 (electric machinery) performed much worse than the average as a result of the fall in EPRs.

Table A2.5 Changes in effective protection for a selected sample of five-digit manufacturing activities between 1979 and 1980 (percent)

		EPR	
SIC number	*Activity*	*1979*	*1980*
38220	Machinery and equipment used in agriculture	72.5	10.2
38230	Machines used in metal or wood work	73.7	22.1
38240	Machinery and equipment used in industry	85.1	12.0
38310	Industrial electrical equipment	63.2	22.6
38322	Communication equipment	55.0	23.3

Source: FIEL, 1980

Automobile Industry

The automobile industry received preferential treatment. Import prohibitions were not eliminated until 1978 and the sector was specifically excluded from the 1979–84 tariff program (Resolution 1634). The nominal duty on car imports was set at 95 percent in 1979 and the value was supposed to fall until a minimum 45 percent level was reached in 1984. In practice, however, the nominal protection afforded to car production was even higher owing to the incidence of other taxes on imports. The combined effect of all forms of taxation yields a true tariff of 132–92 percent for 1979 according to FIEL (1980). Another incentive was given by a mechanism through which domestic car manufacturers were allowed to import automobile parts duty free from LAFTA producers up to 6 percent of planned production. As a counterpart, firms had to export finished cars in order to compensate for the foreign exchange needed to purchase these parts. Since most of the latter came from Brazil, a relatively efficient producer, the arrangement implied a rise in effective production for Argentine manufacturers.

Even though the policies actually undertaken in 1976–80 were clearly biased in favor of the automobile industry, official declarations during the early days of the Martínez de Hoz administration sounded like the prelude to major liberal reforms. Not only was the sector excluded from the list of activities where investments were to be promoted, but the authorities declared their intention of changing regulations protecting the industry in order to make it more efficient. By 1976, the growth of the automobile industry had come to a halt, and further expansion was limited by the slow increase in population and in the replacement of used units. Therefore, unless producers were able to export, sustained expansion could not be resumed. Early in the process, the Minister of the Economy asked manufacturers to inform him whether they wanted to stay in the business or close, and private conversations with foreign representatives were actually held. At last, a new regime for the automobile industry was announced in 1978, but it fell far short of the expectations that had been aroused. By that time, however, some private decisions had already been taken: three plants closed (General Motors, Citroen, and the state-owned IME) and two others merged (Safrar-Peugeot and Fiat). As a result, employment decreased significantly, but production was less affected. In fact, it increased (despite the increase in imports) until 1980.

Appendix 3 A Model of Real Exchange Rate Determination, 1975–1985

The Model

We use a three-sector model with exportables, importables, and nontradeables, denoted x, i, and n respectively. Relative prices, measured in terms of nontradeables, are

$$p_x = \frac{P^*_x E}{P_n}(1 - t_x) \tag{A3.1}$$

$$p_i = \frac{P^*_i E}{P_n}(1 + t_i) \tag{A3.2}$$

P^*_x and P^*_i are the external prices of internationally traded goods, E is the nominal exchange rate, P_n is the price of nontradeables, t_x is the tax on exports, and t_i is the tariff on imports.

Now, let us define the RER as

$$e = \frac{P^* E}{P_n} \tag{A3.3}$$

where P^* is an index of foreign prices for tradeable goods. Expression (A3.3) allows us to redefine (A3.1) and (A3.2) as follows:

$$p_x = p^*_x e(1 - t_x) \tag{A3.1$'$}$$

$$p_i = p^*_i e(1 + t_i) \tag{A3.2$'$}$$

Here, the external prices are deflated by the general index P^* (the ratios are indicated by p_x^* and p_i^*). We note that, given external prices and commercial policy, p_x and p_i vary proportionately with the RER.

The equilibrium condition in the domestic goods market is

$$n^s(p_x,p_i)y = n^d(p_x,p_i)a \tag{A3.4}$$

This appendix draws on Cottani and García (1987).

where n^s and n^d are respectively the supply and demand for nontradeable goods as a share of real income (y) and real absorption (a).

Real absorption is the sum of public and private spending in the three goods. We assume that it depends on relative prices, real money balances, net capital inflows, and expected inflation. The absorption-to-income ratio is specified as follows:

$$a/y = f\left(p_x, p_i, \frac{M}{P_n y}, \frac{K}{P_n y}, \pi^e\right) \qquad \text{(A3.5)}$$

Changes in relative prices have ambiguous effects on the rate of absorption (Sachs, 1981). However, in a world of liquidity constraints, changes in p_x and p_i may exert direct effects on absorption. For example, RER appreciation increases real wages which raises consumption. Real money balances (M/P_{ny}) affect absorption through changes in private wealth and/or liquidity effects. Capital inflows net of factor payments ($K/P_n y$) can also raise absorption, by allowing a relaxation in foreign exchange constraints. Finally, expected inflation (π^e) is also included in (A3.5) since it generally reduces real interest rates which raises aggregate demand.

It is convenient to write

$$\frac{M}{P_n y} \equiv m\, e, \frac{K}{P_n y} \equiv ke \qquad \text{(A3.6)}$$

where m and k represent the supply of money and net capital inflows valued in foreign currency (for example, dollars), at constant foreign prices, as a proportion of real income, and e is the RER as defined in (A3.3).

Substituting (A3.1′), (A3.2′), and (A3.5) in condition (A3.4), and using (A3.6), implicitly defines the following function:

$$e = e(\overset{-}{m}, \overset{-}{\pi^e}, \overset{-}{k}, \overset{+}{t_x}, \overset{-}{t_i}, \overset{-}{u}) \qquad \text{(A3.7)}$$

This indicates that the RER that clears the market for nontradeable goods depends on the monetary and exchange rate conditions prevailing in the economy (m), the expected rate of inflation π^e, capital flows k, trade policy (t_x and t_i), and a variable that represents the external terms of trade (u). The expected signs of the partial derivatives are shown above each variable.[1] We assume that the price of domestic goods is flexible, so that the market always clears.

1 The signs that correspond to t_x and t_i are derived under normal assumptions of substitutability among the three goods. In the case of changes in the terms of trade, we assume that the income on the demand for nontradeables is higher than the substitution effect.

From (A3.7) it is possible to characterize the dynamics of the model, assuming a controlled rate of exchange and endogenous money supply. If we also assume that the equation is linear in the logarithms of the variables, e will change over time according to

$$\hat{e} = \hat{e}(\hat{m}, \hat{k}, \hat{\pi}^{e}, \hat{t}_x, \hat{t}_i, \hat{u}) \tag{A3.8}$$

where the circumflex above a variable indicates the percentage rate of variation, for example, $\hat{e} \equiv \log e - \log e_{-1}$. Note that $\hat{m}$ measures the monetary pressure on the RER for given values of the rates of devaluation, foreign inflation, and real growth, that is

$$\hat{m} \equiv \hat{M} - \hat{E} - \hat{y} - \hat{P}^{*} \tag{A3.9}$$

Monetary expansion in open economies is due to domestic credit creation and foreign reserves growth:

$$\hat{M} \equiv \frac{\mathrm{D}C}{M_{-1}} + \frac{\mathrm{D}R}{M_{-1}} \tag{A3.10}$$

where D is a first difference operator, that is $\mathrm{D}C \equiv C - C_{-1}$, $\mathrm{D}R \equiv R - R_{-1}$, and C and R are the stocks of domestic credit and foreign reserves respectively.

The inclusion of DR in (A3.10) allows us to incorporate the balance of payments in our analysis. Thus

$$\mathrm{D}R = EP^{*}y(ts + k) \tag{A3.11}$$

where ts is the trade surplus as a proportion of real income.

Net capital flows k are largely determined by international financial conditions and by domestic government decisions, that is, public sector borrowing and regulations on capital mobility. Although financial markets were liberalized in Argentina, the capital account was endogenous only in 1979 and 1980. An important part of the increase in external borrowing was due to the government and, as such, can be treated as exogenous.

In order to close the model, we need to specify an equation for the trade balance. Noting that the excess of income over absorption equals the trade balance,

$$ts = 1 - \frac{a}{y} \tag{A3.12}$$

Using (A3.5), we obtain the trade account equation as follows:

$$ts = h(\overset{+}{e}, \overset{-}{t_x}, \overset{+}{t_i}, \overset{+}{u}, \overset{-}{k}, \overset{-}{m}, \overset{-}{\pi^{e}}) \tag{A3.13}$$

where, as before, the sign above each variable shows its effect on ts.

Our model has two behavioral equations, that is, (A3.8) and (A3.13), and an identity which results from combining (A3.9), (A3.10), and (A3.11), and which provides the monetary link between the trade balance and the change in e. Real income and its rate of growth are assumed to be exogenous while the price of domestic goods is endogenous.[2] Policy variables are the rate of devaluation $\hat{E}$, domestic credit expansion DC/M_{-1}, and trade subsidies and tariffs t_x and t_i. Net capital inflows k, however, are determined by a combination of policy and external factors, and can thus be treated as exogenous.

At any given moment, the system can be solved for the value of $\hat{e}$, after which the level of the RER follows from

$$e \equiv (1 + \hat{e})e_{-1} \tag{A3.14}$$

The dynamic nature of the model appears more clearly when we combine (A3.8)–(A3.11) and (A3.13) into one equation:

$$\hat{e} = \hat{e}(e,z) \tag{A3.15}$$

where z is a vector of policy and nonpolicy exogenous variables. This expression defines a nonlinear difference equation in the RER which can be solved for a given sequence of past values of the exogenous variables to yield the dynamic path of e over time.

Estimation

The model was estimated using quarterly data from the first quarter of 1976 to the second quarter of 1985. Table A3.1 shows the definitions of the variables used in the estimation as well as the data sources.

It is extremely difficult to construct a time series of tariffs on imports which is useful for analyzing the impact of import liberalization on the trade balance and the RER. This is so firstly because tariffs are just one way of limiting imports, sometimes not even the most important if QRs are dominant. Secondly, in the presence of QRs, implicit tariffs calculated on the basis of domestic price–border price comparisons are influenced by nontrade policy instruments such as exchange rates, money supply, and government spending.

During the 1976–81 period, for example, collected tariffs as a proportion of imports increased and so did the differential gap between domestic and foreign prices of imported goods. The first effect was due to the move from

2 Strictly speaking, real income is not completely exogenous since it is measured in units of nontradeables and hence depends on the relative price of domestic *vis-à-vis* other goods. However, to preserve the mathematical simplicity of the model, we can ignore this effect without much loss in generality.

Table A3.1 Data used in the estimation of the model

Variable	*Symbol*	*Description*	*Source*
Nominal exchange rate	E	Bilateral, US dollar	Banco Central
Foreign price index	P^*	Wholesale, US	*International Financial Statistics*
Domestic price index	P_n	Consumer prices	Secretaria de Hacienda and INDEC
Export tax	t_x	Collected export taxes as a proportion of total exports	
Foreign terms of trade	u	Foreign prices of exports divided by foreign prices of imports	Cavallo, 1985b
Foreign price index of exports	P_x^*	Exports in dollars at current prices divided by exports in pesos at constant prices (index 1970 = 1.0)	Cavallo, 1985b
Foreign price index of imports	P_i^*	Imports in dollars at current prices divided by imports in pesos at constant prices (index 1970 = 1.0)	Cavallo, 1985b
Trade account surplus as a proportion of income	ts	Exports minus imports at constant 1970 prices divided by GDP	Banco Central
Money supply	M	M3 aggregate, i.e. M1 plus time and savings deposits at commercial banks and *financieras*	Banco Central
Foreign reserves	R	Reserves in gold and foreign currency, from the monetary statistics of the Banco Central	Banco Central
Domestic credit	C	M3 minus reserves	Banco Central
Net capital inflow as a proportion of GDP	k	Increase in foreign reserves (DR) minus trade surplus divided by GDP	Banco Central
Inflation rate	π	Quarterly rate of change in the consumer price index	INDEC

import licenses to tariffs and the elimination of duty exemptions which were common under the QR regime. The second effect was caused by real appreciation which raised the costs of commercialization services associated with imports. Thus, neither the collected nor the implicit measure of tariffs reflect the liberalization of imports which took place in 1977–81;

indeed, they reflect the opposite. Therefore, rather than using an incorrect measure of t_i, we omitted this variable on the assumption that this would reduce estimation biases in the regression.

In order to estimate equations (A3.8) and (A3.13) it was first necessary to specify the way in which economic agents form their expectations about current inflation. For that purpose, expected inflation was assumed to be based on the past knowledge of inflation rates. Thus an autoregressive model was estimated yielding the following results (t values are shown in parentheses below the coefficient estimates):

$$\begin{aligned} \pi_t &= \underset{(3.8)}{0.64}\,\pi_{t-1} + \underset{(1.5)}{0.23}\,\pi_{t-2} + \underset{(2.9)}{0.43}\,\pi_{t-3} - \underset{(2.3)}{0.34}\,\pi_{t-4} \\ \bar{F}^2 &= 0.68 \\ Q(12) &= 4.03 \end{aligned}$$

Longer lags had no additional explanatory power. The Q statistic indicates that the null hypothesis that the error item is white noise cannot be rejected at the 10 percent significance level.

Equations (A3.8) and (A3.13) were estimated using the two-stage least-squares (2SLS) method. A first estimation of equation (A3.8) indicated the presence of first-order correlation of the error term. The 2SLS technique was modified accordingly, using the procedure suggested by Fair (1970) to obtain consistent estimates of the parameters. The results are shown below:

$$\begin{aligned} \mathrm{D}(\log e_t) &= -\underset{(7.8)}{0.52}\mathrm{D}(\log m_t) - \underset{(4.5)}{0.38}\mathrm{D}\pi_t^e - \underset{(0.1)}{0.005}\mathrm{D}(\log u_t) \\ &\quad + \underset{(0.4)}{0.11}\mathrm{D}[\log(1 - t_x)_t] + \underset{(0.4)}{0.16}\mathrm{D}k_t \\ \bar{R}^2 &= 0.76 \\ \mathrm{DW} &= 1.87 \\ r(1) &= \underset{(2.5)}{0.42} \end{aligned}$$

where $r(1)$ is the autocorrelation coefficient of the error term. The coefficients of $\mathrm{D}(\log m_t)$ and $\mathrm{D}\pi_t^e$ are significantly different from zero and have the expected signs. All the other variables are statistically insignificant.

Equation (A3.8) was reestimated excluding $\mathrm{D}k_t$, $\mathrm{D}\{\log(1 - t_x)_t\}$ and $\mathrm{D}(\log u_t)$.

$$\begin{aligned} \mathrm{D}(\log e_t) &= -\underset{(8.5)}{0.51}\mathrm{D}(\log m_t) - \underset{(4.9)}{0.37}\mathrm{D}\pi_t \\ \bar{R}^2 &= 0.79 \\ \mathrm{DW} &= 1.95 \\ r(1) &= \underset{(2.7)}{0.42} \end{aligned}$$

This appendix draws on Cottani and García (1987).

When equation (A3.13) was estimated using the 2SLS method, preliminary results indicated the presence of trade balance seasonality. A fourth-order autocorrelation correction was used to take account of this. Additionally, a lagged value of x_t was included to allow for partial adjustment of exports and imports within the quarter.

A collinearity problem was detected between $(1 - t_x)$ and log m. (This was evidenced by the fact that the significance of any of these variables increased considerably when the other was eliminated.) Since only the coefficient of log $(1 - t_x)$ had the sign predicted by the theory (see equation (A3.13)), we chose to drop the collinear variable log m, along with K_t, and π_t^e which had statistically insignificant coefficients. The following regression resulted:

$$
\begin{aligned}
ts_t &= 0.03 + 0.44\, ts_{t-1} + 0.09 \log e_t + 0.19 \log(1 - t_x)_t \\
&\quad\;\; (2.4) \quad\;\; (3.7) \qquad\qquad (4.8) \qquad\qquad\quad (2.2) \\
&\quad + 0.06 \log u_t \\
&\quad\;\; (2.1) \\
\bar{R}^2 &= 0.83 \\
\text{Durbin's } h &= 0.96 \\
r(4) &= 0.71 \\
&\quad\;\; (5.10)
\end{aligned}
$$

where $r(4)$ is the coefficient of the fourth-order autoregressive model.

Note that the coefficient of log $(1 - t_x)$ is about twice the value of the coefficient of log e_t, indicating a higher response of the trade balance to changes in export taxes than to changes in the RER. Thus a 10 percent increase in one minus the export tax rate would generate an increase of almost two points in the trade balance as a proportion of GDP, while only half of that change would occur for a similar increase in the RER.[3] This result seems to indicate that exporters perceive a change in export taxes as a more permanent move in relative prices than an equivalent change in RERs. In fact, a rationale for this perception does exist in Argentina where the RER has been a far more volatile, and hence less reliable, indicator than t_x.

Simulations

Using the equations reported above and identities (A3.9)–(A3.11) and (A3.14) were used to simulate the path of e_t for the sample period 1976, quarter I, to 1985, quarter II. The actual (RER) and simulated (RERF) values are plotted together in figure A3.1. In general, the main turning

3 Long-term elasticities are about 80 percent higher once we account for the partial adjustment coefficient implied by the lagged variable.

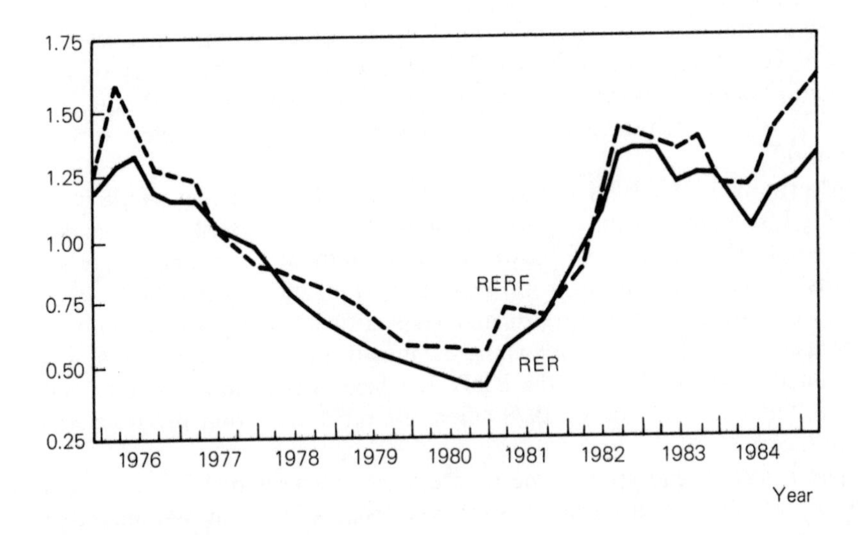

Figure A3.1 Actual and simulated real exchange rates, 1976–1985 (index 1970 = 1.0): RER, actual; RERF, simulated
Source: Cottani and García (1987)

points are reproduced by the simulations, although there appears to be a consistent, but not large, overestimation of the RER level.

To evaluate the performance of the model in simulating the actual evolution of e_t, several statistics were computed which are shown in table A3.2. The reported statistics indicate that, despite its simplicity, the model describes the behavior of the RER rather well.

To investigate the sources of real appreciation between the first quarter of 1976 and the first quarter of 1981, we simulated the evolution of the RER under alternative policy scenarios. Thus, RERFX in figure A3.2

Table A3.2 Statistical results from the simulations of the real exchange rate

Statistic	*1976.I–1981.I*	*1976.I–1985.II*
R.m.s.	0.11	0.13
R.m.s. percent	15.3	14.8
Mean RER	0.83	0.94
Mean RERF	0.90	1.03
U (Theil)	0.06	0.06

R.m.s., root mean square statistics; *U*, Theil's inequality coefficient.

represents the value that e_t would have attained had export taxes not been reduced after the first quarter of 1976. In other words, the vertical difference between RERFX and RERF accounts for the effect of the reduction in export taxes. Note that this effect lasts until the fourth quarter of 1978, after which the gap between the two curves becomes more or less constant.

Alternatively, RERFX can be interpreted as the RER that would have resulted from liberalizing exports and imports simultaneously in a manner that would have avoided surpluses or deficits in the trade balance. In other words, real appreciation from export liberalization could have been avoided if the increase in exports had been sufficiently compensated for by increasing imports to the level where balance-of-payments equilibrium was sustained without adjusting the RER. In place of that, imports remained controlled until the end of 1978 when the tariff reduction program was introduced.

The effect of excessive domestic credit creation coupled with a much lower rate of devaluation can be simulated from RERFX by assuming that monetary expansion proceeded in a less destabilizing fashion. Thus RERFC in figure A3.2 results from assuming that, between the first quarter of 1977 and the first quarter of 1981 (that is, immediately after the initial overshooting of the RER caused by the 1976 devaluation), domestic credit expanded at a rate equal to the sum of nominal devaluation, foreign

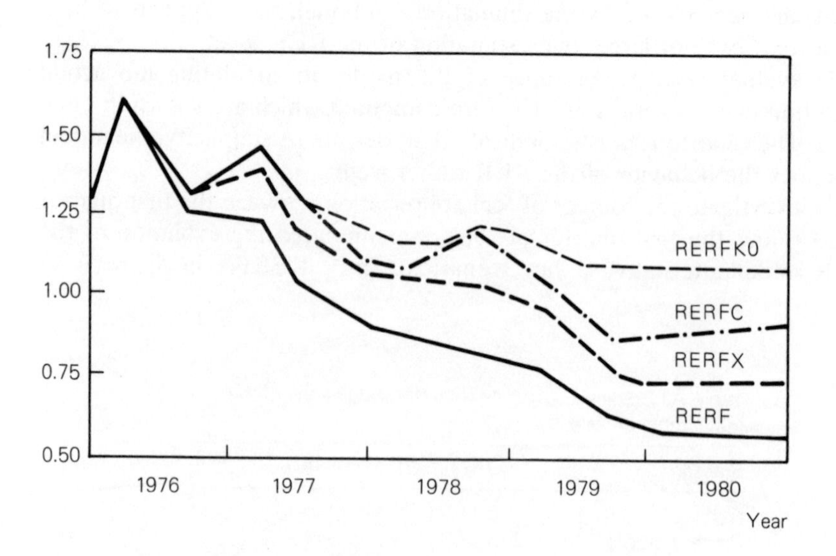

Figure A3.2 Simulated real exchange rate under alternative policy scenarios (index 1970 = 1.0): ——, RERF; – – –, RERFX; – · –, RERFC; – – –, RERFKO
Source: Cottani and García (1987)

inflation, and real output growth. For a given stock of foreign reserves, this rate yields the increase in money supply that is needed in the long run to achieve a domestic rate of inflation not higher than foreign inflation plus devaluation.

The rate of domestic credit expansion was actually higher than the "consistent level" during the second half of 1978 and, most notably, in 1980. Therefore the resulting pressure on domestic prices accounted for domestic currency overvaluation, as indicated by the difference between RERFC and RERFX. Note that this difference shrinks as a consequence of monetary contraction between the third quarter of 1977 and the second quarter of 1978.

Finally, the effect of capital inflow is measured by the spread between RERFK0 and RERFC, where RERFK0 is the trajectory of the RER that would have existed if, in addition to that which is stated above, net capital inflow had been null after the fourth quarter of 1977. It is clear from the figure that capital inflow exerted an important influence on the RER on two occasions: the "timid" financial opening of 1977, which led to reversal in 1978, and the more overt opening from 1979 to 1981.

In figure A3.3 the differences between each of the three previous curves and RERF were added to RER to obtain new plots where the actual (instead of a simulated) RER appears as a reference. The following conclusion emerges: of the total fall in the RER between the fourth quarter

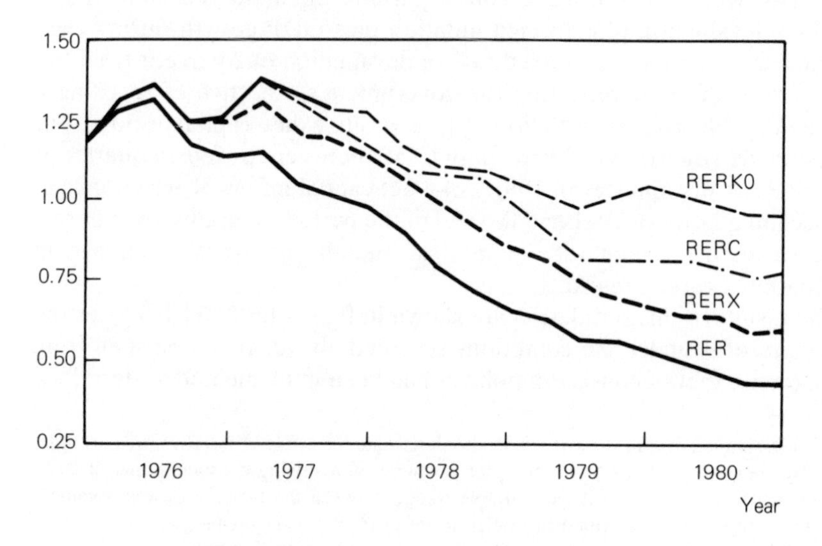

Figure A3.3 Actual real exchange rate and simulations under alternative policy scenarios (index 1970 = 1.0): ——, RER; – – –, RERX; – · –, RERC; – – –, RERKO
Source: Cottani and García (1987)

of 1976 and the first quarter of 1981, about 65 percent can be explained by the three factors analyzed before, namely export tax removals, excessive domestic credit expansion, and positive net capital inflows, with each factor having an almost equal weight in explaining the total variation. Therefore the monetization of the increase in reserves caused by capital inflows explains the real appreciation of 20 percent.[4]

Since the condition of zero net inflow seems rather stringent in the face of high international liquidity, we also simulated RER changes under a lower constraint. Thus it was assumed that if f_t had been equal to 0.5 percent of GDP during every quarter between the last quarter of 1977 and the first quarter of 1981, the resulting increase in foreign debt would have been "sustainable" in the sense that the economy would have reached its desired ratio of foreign debt to GDP by 1981. The new ratio would have stood at half the level it actually attained, and the resulting RER path would have been RERK (figure A3.4). Thus, if this assumption were adopted, the difference between RERK and RERC would be ascribed to the effect of "excessive" foreign borrowing. Note that, in this case, the portion of real appreciation explained by this factor is much lower than before (about half the previous gap).

Finally, a simulation was completed that covered the whole period under study (the fourth quarter of 1976 until the first quater of 1985). It was based on a hypothetical scenario including the following assumptions: (a) simultaneous liberalization of exports and imports compatible with trade balance;[5] (b) internal credit expansion equal to the sum of the nominal devaluation plus foreign inflation plus GDP growth during each quarter in the period; (c) a fixed rate of devaluation of 2 percent from the first quarter of 1981, reflecting the government's objective of reaching a low and stable rate of inflation; (d) a positive net capital inflow, but restricted to a quarterly 0.5 percent of GDP, between the fourth quarter of 1977 and the first quarter of 1981; (e) a net capital inflow of zero between the second quarter of 1981 and the end of the period to capture the net real increase in the foreign rate of interest and the unfavorable change in international capital markets.

The results of this simulation are shown in figure A3.5. RERS gives the trajectory of e_t under the conditions specified above. It can be seen from this exercise that, if consistent policies had been implemented as described

4 A fourth simulation (not shown) was run to determine the effect of foreign terms of trade. Thus, by comparing RERK0 with the plot obtained by assuming constant terms of trade throughout the period, a small and variable wedge between the two curves was obtained, indicating that the effect ascribed to foreign terms of trade was negligible.

5 As before, the measurement of this effect was accomplished by taking advantage of the fact that the level of the RER that would have resulted under this assumption equals the level that would have been sustained had export taxes been constant.

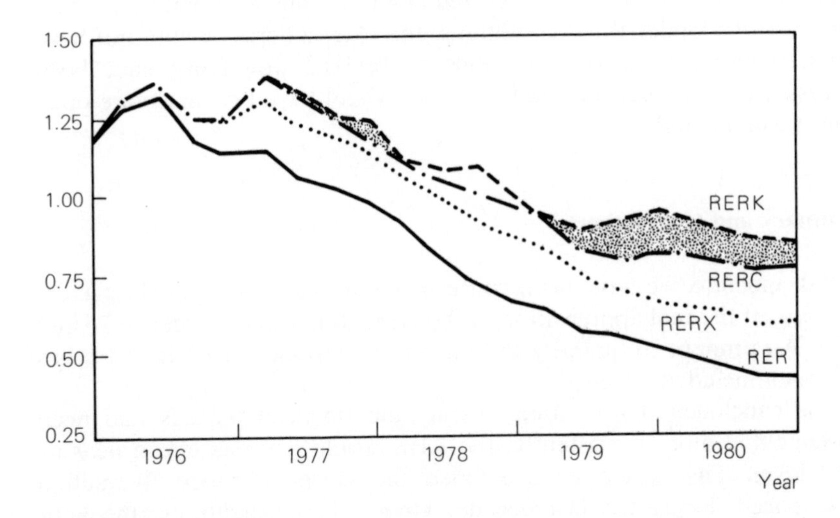

Figure A3.4 Simulated effect of unsustainable capital inflow on real exchange rate behavior (index 1970 = 1.0): ———, RER; · · ·, RERX; – · –, RERC; – – –, RERK
Source: Cottani and García (1987)

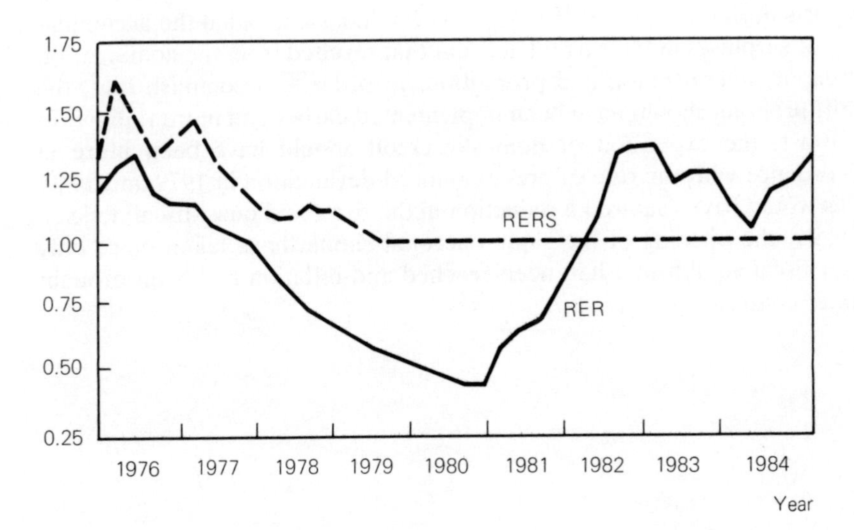

Figure A3.5 Actual and simulated real exchange rate, 1976–1985 (index 1970 = 1.0): RER, actual; RERS, simulation assuming a set of consistent policies
Source: Cottani and García (1987)

above, the RER would have stabilized at a level similar to that of the base year of 1970. Under these conditions, the external crisis would not have occurred and the maxi-devaluations of 1981–82 would not have been necessary even though the trade account would have become more open than it actually did.

Summary and Conclusions

In this appendix we have been concerned with the analysis of the factors that caused the real appreciation of the Argentine peso between 1976 and 1981. An attempt to quantify the relative importance of each factor has also been included.

It is concluded that if trade, fiscal, and financial policies had been implemented more consistently, the RER would have stabilized near its 1970 level. This would have avoided the sharp U-shaped fluctuation experienced during the last decade. Under these conditions, the anti-inflation program would have been successful, and the trade and financial reforms would have transformed the previously repressed economy into a free economy without experiencing exaggerated costs during the transition.

A more consistent trade policy would have allowed a greater increase in imports during the period 1977–8. This would have avoided the accumulation of surpluses in the current account that resulted from the combination of export liberalization and promotion. In order to accomplish that, the tariff program should have been implemented earlier and more rapidly. In contrast, the expansion of domestic credit should have been more in accordance with the rate of pre-announced devaluation in 1979 and 1980. This would have required a reduction in the fiscal and quasi-fiscal deficits. Finally, the opening of the capital account should have taken place only after fiscal equilibrium had been reached and inflation had been brought under control.

References

Alemann, Roberto (1969) "La reforma arancelaria en la República Argentina." In INTAL (Instituto para la Integración de América Latina), ed., *Hacia una tarifa interna común en América Latina*. Buenos Aires: INTAL.

Banco Central (1976) *Cuentas Nacionales de la República Argentina, Series Históricas*, Buenos Aires.

Banco Central (1977–85) *Estimaciones Trimestrales sobre Oferta y Demanda Global*. Output Statistics, quarterly.

Berlinsky, Julio (1975) *Protección Arancelaria de Actividades Seleccionadas de la Industria Manufacturera Argentina*. Buenos Aires: Ministerio de Economia.

Berlinsky, Julio and Daniel M. Schydlowsky (1977) "Incentives for Industrialization in Argentina." Boston, MA: Center for Latin American Development Studies, Boston University, Occasional Paper Series no. 1.

CADIE (Cámara Argentina de la Industria Electrónica) (1967) "Análisis de la reciente reforma arancelario-cambiaria." *Boletín Informativo Mensual*, no. 6.

Calvo, Guillermo A. (1985) "Fractured liberalism: Argentina under Martínez de Hoz." New York: Columbia University, Discussion Paper Series no. 275.

Cavallo, Domingo F. (1985a) "Exchange rate overvaluation and agriculture: the case of Argentina." Unpublished background paper. Washington, DC: World Bank, World Development Report 1986.

Cavallo, Domingo F. (1985b) "Long-term growth in the light of external balance policies. The case of Argentina." In *A Policy Manual for the Open Economy*. Washington, DC: World Bank.

Cavallo, Domingo F. (1988) "Argentina." Rudiger Dornbusch and F. Leslie C. H. Helmers, eds, *The Open Economy. Tools for Policymakers in Developing Countries*. Washington, DC: World Bank.

Cavallo, Domingo F. and Angel Peña (1983) "Déficit fiscal, endeudamiento del gobierno y tasa de inflación: 1940–1982." IEERAL, Estudio no. 26.

Cavallo, Domingo and Humberto Petrei (1983) "Financing private business in an inflationary context: the experience of Argentina between 1967 and 1980." In Pedro Aspe, Rudiger Dornbusch, and Maurice Obstfeld, eds, *Financial Policies and the World Capital Market: The Problem of Latin American Countries*. Chicago, IL: University of Chicago Press.

CONADE (Consejo Nacional de Desarrollo) (1967) "Protección aduanera efectiva en la Argentina." Unpublished paper.

Cottani, Joaquín and Raúl García (1987) "Real appreciation and the order of trade and financial liberalization: Argentina 1976–81." Unpublished paper. World Bank, Washington DC.

Cuervo, Miguel (1972) "Tariff protection in Argentina in recent years: a study on effective protection." D. Phil. thesis, Oxford University (unpublished).

Dadone, Aldo A. and Carlos J. Swoboda (1979) "La reforma arancelaria argentina." *Estudios* 2 (11), September–October.

de Pablo, Juan Carlos (1970) *Política anti-inflacionaria en la Argentina*. Buenos Aires: Amorrortu.

Díaz-Alejandro, Carlos Federico (1970) *Essays on the Economic History of the Argentine Republic*. New Haven, CT: Yale University Press for Economic Growth Center, Yale University.

Díaz-Alejandro, Carlos Federico (1983) "Good-bye financial repression, hello financial crash." New Haven, CT: Economic Growth Center, Yale University, Center Discussion Paper no. 441.

Edwards, Sebastián (1985) "The order of liberalization of the balance of payments: should the current account be opened up first?" Washington, DC: World Bank, Staff Working Paper no. 710.

Fair, Ray (1970) "The estimation of simultaneous equation models with lagged endogenous variables and first order serially correlated error." *Econometrica*, no. 38.

FIEL (Fundación de Investigaciones Económicas Latinoamericanas) (1980) "Apertura de la economía: el impacto de las modificaciones arancelarias." Mimeo.

FIEL (Fundación de Investigaciones Económicas Latinoamericanas) (1985) "El gasto público en la Argentina 1960–1983." Mimeo.

Frenkel, Roberto (1980) "El desarrollo reciente del mercado de capitales en la Argentina." *Desarrollo Económico* no. 78, July–September.

García Pareja, Victor and Maria Elena De Marchi (1984) "Quiebras y concursos en dos períodos recientes de la economía argentina." *Novedades Económicas*, no. 42.

Guía Práctica del Exportador e Importador y para tódo hombre de negocios, Buenos Aires, several issues.

IDES (Instituto de Desarrollo Económico y Social) (1967) "Situación de coyuntura." Buenos Aires: IDES.

IEERAL (Instituto de Estudios Económicos sobre la Realidad Argentina y Latinoamericana) (1986) "Estadísticas de la evolución económica de Argentina, 1913–1984." IEERAL, no. 39.

INDEC (Instituto Nacional de Estadísticas y Censos) (1976) *Censo Nacional Económico 1974*. Buenos Aires: INDEC.

INDEC (Instituto Nacional de Estadísticas y Censos) *Evolución de le Industria Manufacturera 1970–1981*. Buenos Aires: INDEC.

Krueger, Anne O. and National Bureau of Economic Research (1978) *Foreign Trade Regimes and Economic Development: Liberalization Attempts and Consequences*. Cambridge, MA: Ballinger.

Llach, Juan and Carlos Sánchez (1984) "Los determinantes del salario en la Argentina. Un diagnóstico de largo plazo y propuestas de políticas." IEERAL, Estudio no. 29.

Loser, Claudio (1971) "The intensity of trade restrictions in Argentina, 1939–68." Ph.D. dissertation, University of Chicago (unpublished).

Macario, Santiago (1964) "Proteccionísmo e industralización en América Latina." *Boletín Económico de la CEPAL*, 9.

Mallon, Richard and Juan V. Sourrouille, J. (1975) *Economic Policymaking in a Conflict Society: The Argentine Case*. Cambridge, MA: Harvard University Press.

Martirena–Mantel, Ana (1981) "Crawling peg systems and macroeconomic stability: the case of Argentina, 1971–78." In John Williamson, ed., *Exchange Rate Rules. The Theory, Performance and Prospects of the Crawling Peg*. London: Macmillan.

McKinnon, Ronald (1973) *Money and Capital in Economic Development*. Washington, DC: Brookings Institution.

Medina, Juan (1980) "Evaluación del plan de apertura de la economía argentina, 1979–1984." Buenos Aires: Centro de Estudios Macoeconómicos.

Nogués, Julio J. (1978) "Protección nominal y efectiva: impacto de las reformas arancelarias durante 1976–1977." Banco Central de la República Argentina, Ensayos Económicos no. 8.

Nogués, Julio J. (1980) "Trade, distortions and employment in the Argentine manufacturing sector." Ph.D. dissertation, University of Minnesota (unpublished).

Nogués, Julio J. (1983) "Protección comercial y cambiaria: una interpretación de la experiencia argentina durante 1976–1981." Banco Central de la República Argentina, Serie de Estudios Técnicos no. 52.

Ribas, Armando P., A. Castillo Marín, O. Mignini, and R. Vallebella (1967) "La capitalización en los distintos sectores de la actividad económica argentina. Análisis del proceso en la Argentina y sus perspectivas." Buenos Aires: FIEL, Libro FIEL, no. 2.

Rodríguez, Carlos (1980) "Gasto público, déficit y tipo de cambio real: un análisis de sus interrelaciones de largo plazo." Centro de Estudios Macroeconómicos de Argentina, Documento de Trabajo, no. 18.

Rodríguez, Carlos and Larry Sjaastad (1979) "El atraso cambiario en Argentina: mito o realidad?" Centro de Estudios Macroeconómicos de Argentina, Documento de Trabajo, no. 2.

Sachs, Jeffrey (1981) "The current account and macroeconomic adjustment in the 1970s." Brookings Papers on Economic Activity, 1.

Sánchez, Carlos, Fernando Ferrero, and Walter Schulthess (1979) "Empleo, desempleo y tamaño de la fuerza laboral en el mercado de trabajo urbano de la Argentina." *Desarrollo Económico* no. 73, April–June.

Sánchez, Carlos, Horacio Palmieri, and Fernando Ferrero (1976) "Desarrollo urbano y sector informal en la Ciudad de Córdoba." Geneva: International Labor Organization, Research Working Paper 02-19/WP.

Schvarzer, Jorge (1978) "Estrategía industrial y grandes empresas: el caso argentino." *Desarrollo Económico* 18 (71), October–December.

Wainer, Pedro (1970) "La protección aduanera efectiva en la República Argentina." Paper presented at the Reunión de Centros de Investigaciones Económicas, Universidad Nacional de Rosario.

Wisecarver, Daniel (1979) "Una contrareforma arancelaria?" *Mercado*, November.

Part II

Chile

Sergio de la Cuadra
Instituto de Economía
Pontificia Universidad Católica de Chile

Dominique Hachette
Instituto de Economía
Pontificia Universidad Católica de Chile

Contents

List of Figures

List of Tables

Acknowledgments

We are particularly indebted to Philip Brock, Armeane Choksi, Arnold Harberger, Michael Michaely, Julio Nogués, Demetris Papageorgiou, Pablo Spiller, Gert Wagner, and Daniel Wisecarver for their comments, critical and constructive, made at diverse stages of this work. Any remaining shortcomings are our own. We would also like to express our appreciation to our assistants François Oliger and Alexandra Lomakin, who painstakingly built up the basic information while making useful conceptual and methodological suggestions. Without the patient, efficient, and unstinting efforts of our secretaries Ana María Sagüez and Maria Elena Rozas, this work would not have taken readable shape. Finally, Philippa Shepherd has been extremely useful in the final edition with her incisive queries and her patient and careful revision of our draft.

Introduction

Like many developing countries, Chile has had a long tradition of protectionism toward manufacturing which intensified after the Great Depression of the 1930s. Post-depression growth, based on an import substitution strategy and well sheltered behind high trade barriers, became dependent on the roller coaster of copper prices – and soon lost momentum as a consequence of a very limited domestic market and increasingly inefficient additional import substitution. Aware of some of the basic shortcomings of the protectionist policy, three governments made modest attempts to liberalize in the 1950s and 1960s; unfortunately, all failed. However, unlike many countries in similar circumstances, Chile went on to mount a major and most ambitious project of trade liberalization between 1974 and 1979, which unified exchange rates, eliminated import prohibitions, export quotas, all tariff exemptions, and on-tariff barriers, and reduced a tariff schedule widely dispersed around an average of 90 percent to a flat 10 percent. This last experience has been successful. It has survived a major depression – in fact the most severe since the 1930s – and it has resisted the growing and sometimes acute pressures arising from dumping practices and protectionist policies in world markets, from the domestic financial crisis, and last but not least from the traditional rent-seeking lobbies which had been so successful in the past. It is true that the trade policy suffered from some adjustments between 1982 and 1985; however, the rules established after 1974 have not, in essence, been altered.

Why has protection been so pervasive in the history of Chile in the twentieth century? Were there particular circumstances – domestic and foreign – discouraging liberalization efforts? Why was one liberalization episode successful while the two which preceded it were short lived and speedily reversed? Is the success related to the appropriate timing and a particular sequencing, or is it a matter of sheer luck? Is it possible to liberalize trade while major stabilization efforts are carried out or while significant institutional adjustments are occurring simultaneously? Is a shock treatment likely to be more successful than a gradual one, and if not, how gradual should gradualism be? Are some preliminary steps necessary before any tariff reduction to make it workable and to take full advantage of its benefits? These are some of the interesting questions suggested by the analysis of the Chilean experience and covered by this investigation.

The period 1950–86 has been chosen, as it is characterized by a combination of liberalization episodes and the availability of basic information. We were able to identify three episodes of trade liberalization since 1950 – 1956–61, 1966–70, and 1974–9 – but we analyze only the first and last, since they furnish enough material to draw conclusions while the second (1966–70) was comparatively insignificant.

The aim of this research should obviously be qualified at the outset. Desirable objectives for research are easy to define: however, these must be limited by the exigencies of the analysis required for their realization. In particular, the foundations on which our conclusions are based necessarily vary in strength and credibility. Some have firm grounds with quantitative backing; others seem fairly well established, though scanty information makes the figures less than incontrovertible. Still others are informed guesses, derived from interpretation of the research and from the direct experience of one of the authors in the policymaking of 1974–82. Finally, perhaps, some may arise from intellectual inertia and prejudice springing from a priori theorizing. We hope that these are well outnumbered by the rest.

The investigation is presented in seven chapters and two appendices. An overview of the protection pattern that evolved in Chile between Independence in 1810 and 1986 is dealt with in the first chapter, which also includes, as a logical and numerical outgrowth, an index of liberalization constructed specially for the period 1950–86. In chapter 2 an attempt is made to explain the factors behind the rise in protection of the manufacturing sector after the depression of the 1930s, and also to find reasons for its durability. Brief descriptions are given in chapters 3 and 4 of both liberalization episodes from the point of view of the political and economic conditions before they started, of the removal of trade restrictions, and of the accompanying policies, and the reversal of the first episode is examined. Both chapters tend to bear out, with due qualifications, the condition that the worse political and economic conditions are, the easier it becomes to introduce major policy changes, liberalization included. The success and sustainability of liberalization policies during the two episodes are assessed in chapter 5. Selection of criteria for this sort of evaluation are necessarily somewhat arbitrary. Here, as yardsticks to analyze the success of liberalization, we chose the impacts on trade, on production, and on employment because, on the one hand, they seem to be related to what conventional wisdom has considered relevant and, on the other hand, they have been among the principal preoccupations of the government. The analysis of sustainability has been based not so much on the duration of trade liberalization as on the strength of opposing forces and policy's capacity to withstand them. In chapter 6 we address questions related to the appropriate sequencing of liberalization policies, such as the degree of gradualism, the desirability of separate stages for the replacement of quantitative restrictions (QRs), for export promotion, and for policies directed towards other objectives such as stabilization, financial liberalization, or distributional considerations, and the questions of uniform versus discriminatory treatment of sectors during the process of adjustment. Finally, the main conclusions of the investigation are tentatively summarized in chapter 7. The first appendix is methodological in content, while the second presents a Harbergerian type of estimate of the static benefits from the last liberalization episode.

1

A Historical Outline of Tariffs and Import Restriction Policies in Chile

The history of tariffs and import restrictions in Chile in the last two centuries can be divided into four subperiods: (a) 1810–1930, when tariffs were the principal instrument affecting imports; (b) 1930–50, with much higher protection than the previous period and wide use of QRs; (c) 1950–74, characterized by continued high protection and QRs interspersed with three attempts at liberalization (1956, 1959–61, and 1968–70); (d) 1974 to the present, when all previously existing protective devices were transformed into a uniform customs duty. In a gradual process started in 1974 a 10 percent rate was reached by mid-1979, which was increased to 20 percent after the deep recession of 1982.

From Independence to 1950

Since the beginning of the independent life of the nation in 1810, protectionism has been a potent force in Chile. Sustained by a pressing need to increase fiscal revenues, the success of protectionist pressure was reflected in a customs tariff with rates ranging from zero to 35 percent, with most articles being taxed at 30 and 35 percent. This state of affairs continued until the initiation in the 1860s of a political regime whose basically liberal economic ideology was expressed in a tariff policy that taxed the majority of goods at rates of 15 and 25 percent. A liberal stance was maintained until the end of the 1890s, when (in 1897) the government reinstituted a clearly protectionist policy. This move could be attributed to two factors: the protectionist campaign of the Sociedad de Fomento Fabril (SOFOFA), an entrepreneurs' organization for medium and large manufacturers, and the economic recession brought about by a drop in international prices during the late 1890s. Protectionist pressures continued to

More detailed discussion of the issues addressed in this chapter can be found in de la Cuadra and Hachette (1985, part I).

increase, revealing themselves in three important tariff modifications in 1916, 1921, and 1928.

The Great Depression of the 1930s had profound repercussions for subsequent economic policy. The closure of the economy to foreign trade resulting from reduced export earnings was reinforced by a policy of import restrictions. Furthermore, the government obtained comprehensive powers of discretionary intervention in the handling of foreign trade. In the foreign exchange areas, a commission was created to ration foreign currency, a system of multiple exchange rates was established, and the return of export earnings was made mandatory. Import tariffs came to play a secondary role in restricting imports, while other means, such as import licenses, lists of permitted imports, and prior deposits, became more important. These trade policies affected the development of imports for decades following the crisis: whereas in the 1920s, imports had reached an average level of 27 percent of gross domestic product (GDP) they remained at about a third of this level between 1930 and 1970.

World War II, with its inevitable reinforcement of the inclination towards import substitution policies, further reduced trade volumes. During the 1940s imports grew at an average annual rate of 3.1 percent, GDP at 3.3 percent, and industrial production at 6.4 percent; corresponding growth rates for the 1950s were 4.4 percent, 3.8 percent, and 4.4 percent respectively. A comparison of the two decades shows, on the one hand, an increase in the import income elasticity and, on the other hand, a reduction in the relative growth of the industrial sector. These figures support the contention that the easy stage of import substitution was over by the mid-1950s; further substitution became more and more inefficient, as evidenced by expensive products of poor quality. High inefficiency substitution is not dynamic; rather, it brings industrial growth to a standstill and generates some pressure to liberalize, which is what happened in the 1960s and early 1970s.

From the 1950s to the 1980s

Liberalization Attempts (1950–1970) and the Tariff Reform (1974–1979)

Three attempts to rationalize the import regime were made between 1950 and 1970. The first took place in 1956; the second, beginning in 1959, was in effect a continuation and intensification of the first. The main purpose was to make more use of the price system in regulating imports. With this objective in mind, the policymakers considered (a) replacing the multiple exchange rate system by a single rate, (b) eliminating QRs and replacing them by a list of permitted imports and prior deposits, (c) fixing tariffs at "reasonable levels," and (d) removing export quotas. Although equivalent tariffs may have been reduced between 1958 and 1962, the impact on effective rates of protection is not clear at all. The trend of alterations was biased toward reducing previous deposits and the so-called additional duties on intermediate and capital goods and equipment. This process came to an abrupt end in January 1962 when the foreign exchange crisis exploded.

Protection increased after this experience until the third attempt to rationalize import regulations in 1968. This attempt took the form first of replacing previous deposits by equivalent tariffs, and second of adjusting the tariff structure with a bias in favor of intermediate and capital goods, resulting in higher effective protection in several industrial subsectors.

The early 1970s saw a return to an interventionist trade regime, with multiple exchange rates and dominance of nontariff barriers. This was the situation when the 1974 tariff reform was initiated. The first step was to eliminate nontariff barriers and to announce tariff cuts, although well-defined targets were not announced until August 1975. These targets were redefined in December 1977, when a flat rate of 10 percent was established as the goal to be reached by June 1979.

An Inflationary Environment

The liberalization episodes sketched above were undertaken in the inflationary environment that characterized the entire period 1950–80. Average annual inflation in the decade of the 1950s was 35 percent, in the 1960s it was 27 percent, in the first half of the 1970s it was 233 percent, and in the second half it was 61 percent. The maximum rates reached in each subperiod were 84 percent, 45 percent, 508 percent, and 174 percent respectively.

The high inflation made stabilization a prime objective of economic policy; accordingly, the government directed a battery of instruments toward fighting inflation, with commercial policies in general, and the exchange rate in particular, playing a significant part. The resulting mixture of stabilization and resource-allocation objectives led to confused and contradictory uses of trade liberalization instruments. Exchange rate policy was particularly susceptible to these contradictions: on the one hand, it was to be used as an anti-inflationary device for revaluing the domestic currency;[1] on the other hand, devaluations were needed to compensate for lower restrictions on imports. This conflict imposed a heavy burden on the liberalization attempts of 1959–61 and 1979–81. In

1 Unless otherwise specified, the exchange rate will be defined throughout as the number of units of domestic currency per US dollar. A revaluation (devaluation) will be equivalent to a reduction (increase) in the nominal exchange rate, deflated by an index of domestic prices and multiplied by an index of international prices.

both instances, the abundant inflow of foreign credit biased the exchange rate policy in favor of the stabilization objective.

The Pattern of Protection

The restrictiveness of commercial policies, and the depth and durability of the liberalization attempts, can be assessed from the liberalization index (figure 1.1). The index constructed for this purpose combines five indicators: (a) QRs on imports (index), (b) the ratio of effective exchange rate to nominal exchange rate, (c) the ratio of black-market rate to official rate, (d) an export quota index, and (e) the implicit tariff rate (see table 1.1).

The liberalization index was reached through an iterative process by matching the five indicators constructed for the period 1950–85. When doubts arose, qualitative judgments based on the literature and on some debates among research team members were also ingredients in the final outcome, presented at the last column in table 1.1 and in figure 1.1. In view of this approach, the index is intended as no more than an ordinal arrangement of the intensity of liberalization (see appendix 1 for further details).

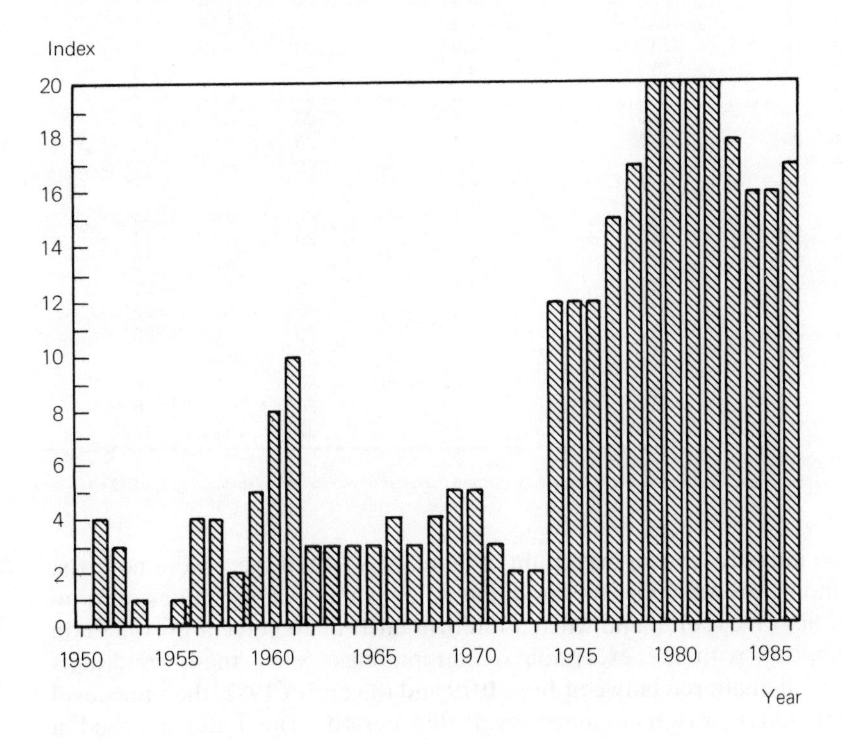

Figure 1.1 Index of liberalization

Table 1.1 Some indicators of trade control

Year	Quantitative control index	Effective exchange rate divided by nominal exchange rate	Black-market rate divided by official market rate	Export quotas index	Implicit tariff rate	Index of liberalization
1950	2	27.2	2.1	—	1.72	0
1951	4	26.0	1.0	9	1.67	4
1952	3	25.2	1.1	13	1.85	3
1953	2	21.1	1.7	13	2.17	1
1954	2	17.1	2.3	5	2.63	0
1955	4	18.9	2.8	8	2.73	1
1956	7	21.7	1.2	2	2.65	4
1957	6	21.0	1.3	1	1.48	4
1958	3	18.1	1.4	13	1.52	2
1959	6	21.7	1.0	13	1.46	5
1960	11	24.9	1.0	17	1.62	8
1961	12	27.1	1.0	18	1.69	10
1962	5	28.9	1.6	19	1.72	3
1963	5	26.2	1.7	20	1.48	3
1964	5	21.7	1.8	20	1.59	3
1965	4	25.2	1.7	20	1.43	3
1966	7	28.6	1.5	20	1.45	4
1967	7	30.1	1.6	20	1.49	3
1968	7	26.8	1.4	20	1.40	4
1969	8	23.3	1.5	20	1.43	5
1970	8	28.2	2.0	20	1.40	5
1971	5	25.7	4.5	20	n.a.	3
1972	3	22.1	10.5	20	n.a.	2
1973	1	15.2	9.6	20	n.a.	2
1974	20	19.5	1.4	20	n.a.	12
1975	20	12.4	1.2	20	n.a.	12
1976	20	13.5	1.1	20	n.a.	12
1977	20	13.1	1.1	20	n.a.	15
1978	20	18.5	1.0	20	n.a.	17
1979	20	6.4	1.0	20	n.a.	20
1980	20	6.2	1.1	20	n.a.	20
1981	20	6.2	1.1	20	n.a.	20
1982	20	6.2	1.1	20	n.a.	20
1983	20	9.3	1.2	20	n.a.	18
1984	20	14.9	1.2	20	n.a.	16
1985	20	16.2	1.1	20	n.a.	16
1986	20	12.4	1.1	20	n.a.	17

—, not applicable; n.a., not available.
The meaning of each index and the methodology used to build each time series is explained in appendix 1.

The index reached a maximum of 20 in 1979, when there were no QRs, no import prohibitions, no antidumping or countervailing duties, and no subsidies on exports, and when a uniform tariff of 10 percent prevailed on all imports with the exception of automobiles. Since these conditions remained unaltered between June 1979 and the end of 1982, the same level of the index was maintained over this period. The index reached a minimum of zero in 1950 and 1954; both years correspond to the most extensive use of QRs, while the other four indicators also showed high levels of restrictions. The 1959–61 liberalization reached its peak in 1961 when QRs were eliminated and imports were subject only to tariffs, though these were high and dispersed. It was decided arbitrarily to assign a value of 10 to year 1961.

Finally, some comments should be made on the behavior of the index in the last four years: in November 1982, surcharges – with rates ranging from 10 to 28 percent – were granted to 15 products; another 15 products were added to the list during 1983, and four more in 1984. In no case did the tariff plus the surcharge exceed 35 percent.[2]

The flat tariff rate was raised to 20 percent in June 1983 and to 35 percent in September 1984; it was then reduced to 30 percent in March 1985 and to 20 percent in June of the same year. Thus the yearly average rates were 15 percent, 24 percent, and 26 percent in 1983, 1984, and 1985 respectively. In 1986, the flat rate remained at 20 percent until the beginning of 1988, when it was reduced to 15 percent. The values of the index for the years following 1982 have been assigned on the basis of these average rates, assuming that uniformity was maintained except for the few surcharges that were granted.

2 However, the establishment of so-called "price bands" on wheat, sugar, and oil in 1985 implied, at least during that year, an implicit surcharge of over 35 percent. In addition, some products imported from countries belonging to the Asociación Latinoamericana de Integración (ALADI, I atin American Association for Integration) have received preferential tariff treatment.

2

Development and Sustainability of Protection

Manufacturing in Chile has been particularly heavily protected through import restrictions. The extent of this protection is attributable to several influences, principal among them being the unity and increasing political power of entrepreneurs in the manufacturing sector, pervasive ideologies identifying industrialization with economic growth, external shocks transmitted through terms of trade, capital flows, or both, and balance-of-payments problems stemming from the domestic policy mix. Geographical factors, natural resources, geopolitical pressures, costs of controls, and, in particular, factor specificity have also played their part.

The durability of protection has both political and economic foundations. Protection is sustained by the political power of the organizations it benefits – entrepreneurial associations, labor unions, politicians, and so on – whereas a liberalization program, in contrast, holds fewer attractions for politicians because costs tend to be immediate while the benefits will be reaped only in the long term. Such a program does not naturally draw supporters. Among the relevant economic considerations that help account for the durability of protection are market efficiency for both goods and factors of production, and factor characteristics such as specificity and mobility.

Development of Protection

Organized Pressures and Ideologies

Historians generally agree that the years following the War of the Pacific (1879–81) were a period of economic boom and, in particular, of great industrial expansion. In 1883 the leaders of industrial enterprises joined

More detailed discussion of these issues is given by de la Cuadra and Hachette (1985, part I).

forces, giving birth to the well-known organization SOFOFA. The main objective of this group was to obtain protection from external competition; four years after its foundation it made public its first report: *El Impuesto de Internación y Proyecto de Reforma del Mismo* (*The Import Tax and a Project for its Reform*).

The aims of organized industrial management were fostered by the economic recession of the second half of the 1890s, which was caused as much by internal as by external factors. Prominent among the former was a deflationary monetary policy consisting of a monetary reform to return to the gold standard (Fetter, 1937, pp. 107–17). Important among external influences was a drop in the international price of Chilean exports: in 1897 exports fell by 13 percent, and during that same year Law 980 was passed, establishing a customs tariff based on "the necessary protection of national industry."

As was pointed out in chapter 1, "necessary" protection to manufacturing continued to increase during the first three decades of the present century. In addition, in the 1930s state intervention became more active through the use of controls and with the creation at the end of that decade of Corporación de Fomento de la Producción (CORFO, a state agency devoted to promoting new industries, most of them in the import substitution sector; see Muñoz, 1975). Thus private sector pressures for higher protection were fueled by the direct interest of the government. These joint forces became increasingly active until 1970, when the Allende government assumed power.

The ideology that identifies industrialization with development has flourished in Chile ever since the first tariff schedule was enacted in 1811, with interruptions to its political predominance only during the second half of the last century and under the current military government, which has been in power since 1973. The ideology was nourished by academic opinion, by publications of the Economic Commission for Latin America (ECLA), and by the sustained rate of growth during the "easy substitution stage" of recuperation from the Great Depression (see chapter 1).

External Shocks

Between 1925 and 1982, Chile's economy suffered 12 recessions. (The beginning of a recession is defined as that year during which the rate of growth of the GDP is negative or during which it diminished by 5 percentage points or more, dropping to a level below 4 percent.)

Of these 12 recessions, eight were associated with a drop in exports either during the preceding year or during the same year, leading in turn to a real devaluation of the peso, that is, an increase in the exchange rate greater than the rate of inflation. This devaluation has invariably occurred,

Table 2.1 Recessions, exports, exchange rate, and import restrictions

Beginning of recession	Variation in nominal value of exports (%)	Variation in real rate of exchange[a] (%)	Direction of change of liberalization index	Change in foreign indebtedness (percentage points)
1930	−42 (1930)	154.0 (1932)	n.a.	4.4
1938	−28 (1938)	7.7 (1939)	n.a.	−6.2
1949	−19 (1949)	2.4 (1949)	n.a.	16.9
1954	−21 (1953)	1.5 (1955)	−	−2.4
1958	−20 (1957)	10.3 (1958)	−	−1.3
	−10 (1971)	—	+	—
1972	−15 (1972)	99.1 (1974)	−	−0.8
1975	−26 (1975)	46.4 (1975)	0	−4.1
	−16 (1981)	—	0	—
1982	−4 (1982)	21.3 (1982)	−	− 11.9

—, not applicable; n.a., not available.
0, No significant changes; −, decrease (more restrictions); +, increase (fewer restrictions).
[a] Nominal exchange rate multiplied by the US wholesale price index and deflated by Chile's consumer price index.

Source: de la Cuadra and Cortés, 1984

even after a delay of two years. Furthermore, import restrictions were increased on top of devaluation in the midst of these recessions (table 2.1).

The four recessions not associated with falls in exports took place in 1936, 1941, 1947, and 1967. Of these, three were strongly conditioned by external elements. In 1936 expenditure was restricted to confront the difficult foreign debt situation, in 1947 a significant capital flight occurred, and in 1967 terms of trade dropped while payments on foreign debt increased. The 1941 recession, caused by a large decrease in agricultural production, was the only one not related to external variables.

The above relationships, as well as the evidence presented in table 2.2, indicate that one influence in favor of closing the economy is the behavior of the international environment and its effects on the value of exports, the availability of external credit, and the interest rate on foreign debt. A reduced capacity to import brings more legal restrictions on trade, which tend to be maintained even after the situation improves. Import substitution policy, which is intended to diminish the external influences, can conversely be argued to have increased them. In the first place, the concentration of exports induced by import substitution made export earnings more unstable; it is even likely that fluctuations in the price of Chile's main export (copper) are inversely correlated with international interest rates. A policy of free trade, to the extent that it favors a wider range of exportable products, could attenuate the impact of external

Table 2.2 Exchange rate. Central Bank credit, fiscal policy and international reserves

Year	*Changes in nominal exchange rate (%)*	*Changes in domestic credit of Central Bank (%)*	*Inflation (%)*	*Changes in real exchange rates (%)*	*Changes in real domestic credit of Central Bank (%)*	*Fiscal policy* [a] *(index)*	*International reserves (million US$)*	*Index of liberalization*
1950	33	27	15	16	10	1.10	53	0
1951	25	35	22	2	11	1.05	55	4
1952	33	43	22	9	17	1.1	72	3
1953	17	45	25	−7	16	1.30	65	1
1954	35	48	72	−22	−14	1.24	37	0
1955	102	43	75	15	−18	1.25	83	1
1956	77	50	56	13	−4	1.12	76	4
1957	46	56	33	10	17	1.13	27	4
1958	25	19	20	4	−1	1.01	30	2
1959	32	87	39	−5	35	1.16	105	5
1960	0	47	12	−11	31	1.28	73	8
1961	0	32	8	−7	22	1.26	−5	10
1962	9	96	14	−4	72	1.33	15	3
1963	70	14	44	18	−21	1.29	−24	3
1964	37	47	46	−6	1	1.25	−17	3
1965	25	49	29	−3	16	1.23	35	3
1966	23	45	23	0	18	1.15	77	4
1967	26	38	18	7	17	1.09	54	3
1968	35	24	27	6	−2	1.09	125	4
1969	33	31	31	2	0	1.03	285	5
1970	29	40	33	−3	5	1.13	394	5
1971	3	193	20	−14	144	1.47	163	3
1972	71	196	78	−4	66	1.70	76	2
1973	454	714	353	22	80	2.19	167	2
1974	527	415	505	4	−15	1.44	94	12
1975	575	393	375	42	4	1.13	−129	12
1976	166	130	212	−15	−26	1.10	108	12
1977	65	113	92	−14	11	1.07	273	15
1978	47	32	40	5	−6	1.04	1,858	17
1979	18	17	33	−11	−12	0.93	2,314	20
1980	5	−18	35	−22	−39	0.88	4,071	20
1981	0	−15	20	−16	−22	0.93	3,775	20
1982	31	35	21	8	12	1.02	2,584	20
1983	55	169	23	26	118	1.05	2,629	18
1984	25	47	23	2	20	1.04	2,837	16
1985	63	71	26	29	36	1.03[b]	2,952	16
1986	20[b]	n.a.	20[b]	0[b]	n.a.	1.02[b]	n.a.	17

n.a., not available.
[a] Fiscal expenditure as a ratio of fiscal revenue.
[b] Projections.

Source: de la Cuadra and Cortés, 1984

fluctuations. In the second place, import substitution encourages restrictions on imports of raw materials, intermediate goods, and capital goods, and leads to the elimination of imports of final consumption goods. Therefore when imports have to be reduced, the burden can only fall on inputs, with a direct and immediate impact on GDP.

The Domestic Policy Mix

Along with the external influences postulated above, the domestic policy mix is likely to bear some responsibility for changes in the level of protection, particularly those in the direction of closing the economy. The argument is that a set of policies related to demand expansion – via the fiscal budget and/or domestic credit – together with exchange rate policies biased against the relative price of tradeable goods will generate a growing deficit in the balance of payments on current account. Such a disequilibrium can be maintained for a while depending on the availability of international reserves and/or capital inflows, but in the long run it cannot be sustained and is too often reduced by closing the economy.

In table 2.2 movements of fiscal, credit, and exchange rate policies are shown, together with the index of liberalization. It can be seen that for all episodes where restrictions on trade were tightened (1952–4, 1958, 1962, and 1971–3), the accompanying policies during the preceding years and/or during the same year were expansionary: the fiscal deficit increased, real domestic credit grew and the domestic currency was revalued (except in the 1958 episode). This policy mix further reduced the already permanently low level of international reserves, so that the economy tended to close even more.

The Geographical Factor: Natural Resources and Geopolitical Pressures

Some geographical characteristics may have helped to sustain the substantial protection of manufacturing through the early 1970s. Chile has had comparative advantages in natural resources, particularly in mining – nitrates and then copper. The relative productivity of these commodities, both within the country and among countries, was so high that, at the relevant equilibrium exchange rate with free trade, import-competing activities (manufactures in particular) could develop only with difficulty (this effect has been called the "Dutch disease"). High transport costs, acting as as natural protective barrier, would be insufficient to compensate for a relatively "low" exchange rate resulting from highly productive exports. Production of capital intensive manufactures would therefore be hampered by competition from products from foreign sources.

One indicator of Chile's comparative advantages in activities intensive in natural resources in the composition of exports, which were relatively free of artificial incentives during the period analyzed. From 1950 through 1980, on average about 78 percent of goods exports were mining products, 7 percent were agricultural, and 15 percent were manufactures. Furthermore, most manufactures (for instance, pulp, fishmeal, and so on) were intensive in natural resources, with relatively low industrial value added. This concentration in mining and mining-related exports changed drastically, but only at the very end of the period: mining products represented only 57 percent of goods exports in 1978–80, while manufactures jumped to 36 percent and the rest were agricultural products. Despite the change in composition, however, exports retained their high intensity in natural resources (table 2.3).

Geopolitical pressures to strengthen specific and geographically extreme regions – in particular Africa in the north and Magallanes in the south – helped to promote the artificial development of import substitution sectors, the most conspicious being automobile assembly in Africa during the late 1950s (see in particular Decree 303 and Law 13039 [1952]). The consequent significant migration towards at least one of these centers intensified political pressures to maintain the status quo and even to widen the range of import substitution activities.

Net migration to Tarapacá – the province in which Arica is located – rose from − 26,000 in 1960 to + 14,000 in 1970; it was the only province in the country to experience a reversal of migration trends during the 1960s. In addition, Tarapacá was one of the seven provinces (out of 25) to receive a positive influx of population, while being second only to the Santiago metropolitan area in terms of change in the absolute number of migrants.

Table 2.3 Composition of exports, 1950–1980 (percentage of total)

Sector	*1950*	*1955*	*1960*	*1965*	*1970*	*1975*	*1980*
Agricultural	11.8	7.4	6.5	3.3	3.0	5.3	7.2
Mining	83.4	84.8	86.4	81.5	85.8	67.6	55.6
Industrial							
(highly intensive in natural resources)[a]	4.5	7.3	6.9	15.1	11.2	24.9	36.2
(percentage of industrial exports)	n.a.	n.a.	n.a.	(68.6)	(64.7)	(58.8)	(68.7)

n.a., not available; the figures in parentheses are estimated values.
[a] Fishmeal and other fish products, paper and cellulose, semi-refined copper, and molybdenum oxide.

Source: Central Bank of Chile, *Balanza de Pagos*

Sustainability of Protection

Specificity of Factors of Production

The assumption is that demand for protection would depend on the rents obtained by factors of production in their current use, on the cost of moving to other uses and/or sectors, and on the cost of obtaining additional protection. In turn, rents obtained could be the consequence of specificity and of some degree of monopoly power of the factor or of the firm. The demand for protection is a function of the degree of factor specificity and monopoly power, the cost of factor mobility, and, of course, the cost of obtaining protection. The factors should therefore be calibrated in relation to the traditionally protected sector – manufactures and to some extent agriculture – during the period analyzed (1950–80) or at least during the subperiod of high protection (1950–74).

Labor

Two types of specificity could be distinguished: preferential and aptitudinal (Bhagwati and Srinivasan, 1983, p. 92).

Preferential specificity arises from differences among firms and between manufacturing and other sectors with respect to labor legislation, social security benefits, minimum salaries, and the like. Although differences across productive sectors in these areas tended to disappear after 1952, two general bottlenecks to mobility remained and contributed to involuntary wage and productivity differentials. One was a relatively more favorable treatment for white-collar than for blue-collar workers accompanied by across-the-line immobility; another was the more than imperfect severance pay system.

Severance pay, entitling workers to a month's wage for each year worked in the same firm upon dismissal (without regulated causes) and sometimes even on voluntary retirement, was supposed to be financed by the social security system. In practice, however, owing to financial constraints and collective bargaining, most firms offered this benefit from their own resources, often on terms better than those legislated. The implied cost induced firms to restrict labor turnover, at least for eligible employees. Generally, restrictions were imposed either by limiting the total benefit to "funds available" or by restricting the number of workers eligible for severance pay. The significant amounts involved meant that workers had no incentive to change jobs if these restrictions obliged them to forfeit the benefit. The result was relative immobility of both blue- and white-collar labor.

Aptitudinal specificity arises when a factor of production may have a comparative aptitude in producing one good rather than another. This aptitude is likely to be acquired through specific education, such as technical, university, vocational, and on-the-job training. The scanty information available on the basis characteristics of labor force education for 1958 (Gran Santiago) and for 1970 and 1976 for the whole country (de la Cuadra and Hachette, 1985, appendix table A.59) is not fully comparable between time periods, since coverage of secondary schooling changes for each time period and the level of disaggregation is not sufficient to build a more homogeneous set of data for the whole period. However, the information is adequate to suggest (a) that specialized education in the manufacturing labor force was lower than for most other sectors, apart from agriculture, (b) that general education – primary and secondary – predominated over specialized, with the specialist component representing only 5 percent, 8.6 percent, and at most 10 percent of the total in 1958, 1970, and 1976 respectively, and (c) that the mining sector seemed to be the tradeables sector with the highest specialization. In the absence of information on on-the-job training, or on the average age of workers in a sector as a proxy for on-the-job training, the tentative conclusion would be that aptitudinal specificity may exist but seems to be relatively insignificant.

However, a recent analysis of the adjustments of manufacturing firms to liberalization suggests that in the past the cost of training workers has generally been regarded as deterrent (Corbo and Sánchez, 1984). If so, firms incurring that cost would probably have taken measures to reduce the mobility of their labor force. In sum, specificity and the immobility arising from specificity may have been influences for maintaining protection, both from labor and management perspectives, but they do not appear to have been dominant ones.

Capital

Unfortunately the specificity of capital stock cannot be directly illustrated. Neither surveys nor direct evidence are available and there is even less information on the cost of adapting existing capital stock to new ones.

A special variant of specificity is *over-investment* or excess capacity in the highly protected import substitution industrial sector. It has been argued that the minimum size for capital investment in modern (protected) firms, given the limitations in the range of available technologies and the relative prices of productive factors, would be too large for the captive domestic market. The resultant excess capacity, with capital loss apparently unduly large and installed capacity wastefully idle, would in turn increase resistance to liberalization.

An index of capacity utilization was constructed for the period 1959–68, on the basis of information taken from a survey of 42 industrial firms, as a ratio of the industrial production index to a "maximum" industrial production index obtained by using linear interpolation through peaks of the index of industrial production (Corbo, 1971). The period 1959–68 was chosen because it was characterized by a "normal" rate of labor unemployment or state of aggregate demand. The results, which are shown below tend to support the hypothesis of overcapacity:

	1959	*1960*	*1961*	*1962*	*1963*	*1964*	*1965*	*1966*	*1967*	*1968*
Rate of capacity utilization (%)	82.6	76.7	78.2	79.7	81.7	81.4	77.7	78.8	78.0	77.5

Cost of Factor Mobility

Factor specificity to firms or sector, resistance to mobility, and the pressure exerted by owners to maintain protection increase in proportion to the cost of factor mobility.

Labor

Indirect evidence suggests that mobility costs, as measured by transportation costs and distance (as a proxy for information in which quality is taken to be inversely proportional to distance) deter migration (Coeymans, 1983). However, this consideration may not be as important as it seems, since (a) the mobility most relevant to the analysis here is either intra-sectoral (within manufactures) or intra-urban, (b) the industrial sector is concentrated geographically in a few urbanized locations, and (c) the regions in which activities alternative to traditional import substitution industries could develop if relative prices improved have traditionally been net exporters of migration. Consequently, such activities – in types, size, and coverage – could develop in these regions without depending on immigration, urban or rural, except where factor specificity was paramount.

Capital

Some characteristics of the capital market may have fostered the relative immobility of capital and correspondingly reduced the incentive to liberalize by increasing the cost of adjustment: (a) the segmentation of the financial market (lack of organized and flexible capital transactions, high information costs, and so on); (b) the extreme scarcity of medium- to long-term credit in the commercial banking sector for investment or adjustment; (c) the earmarking of commercial medium- and long-term credit for specific activities. In addition, restrictions on foreign investment could hamper the additional flexibility such investment might contribute to the adjustments required by liberalization (see in particular Instituto de Organización y Administración (INSORA), 1962; World Bank, 1965; Fuenzalida and Undurraga, 1968; Jeftanovic, 1980).

Medium- and long-term credit represented an extremely low percentage of total investment. During most of the period analyzed, commercial private banks were not allowed to concede loans with more than a one-year horizon. The State Commercial Bank and CORFO were the only sources of medium- and long-term credit. Public investment was partly financed through external debt accumulation and partly by CORFO's loans. The remaining financing – a small fraction – would be private sector investments, limited either by the availability of medium- and long-term funds from sources internal to the firms or by access to short-term financing. An earlier survey (INSORA, 1962) of "sources and uses of funds" in the industrial sector over the period 1949–60 suggests that internal sources were, as expected, the most important (de la Cuadra and Hachette, 1988, appendix table A.60). However, the most striking peculiarity of funding was the proportion of short-term financing – 87 percent of funding from external sources. In the United States for the same period, this was less than 50 percent.

Labor Unions

Some productive factors may have become specific to firms because of the strength of unions, while others may have been able to improve their position by negotiating increased protection or delays for any liberalizing effort. The justification for protectionist lobbying, adduced from its effect, has been discussed elsewhere (Mussa, 1974, 1984). In the framework of this analysis, it can be inferred that such lobbying, whether by capitalists or workers, appears reasonable. Did any such lobby exist? What form did it take? How successful was it? Can we find any relationship between the height of protective barriers and the lobby's power?

Only a few facts can be shown here in relation to unionization as a proxy for the lobby's power. From table 2.4 it can be seen that (a) manufacturing

Table 2.4 Unionized employed population by sector, 1956–1972 (percent)

	1956		*1960*		*1965*		*1970*		*1972*	
Sector	*1*	*2*	*1*	*2*	*1*	*2*	*1*	*2*	*1*	*2*
Agriculture and fishing	n.a.	2.8	1.3	3.3	1.4	3.1	25.0	24.9	45.7	28.3
Mining	n.a.	21.5	68.1	23.2	71.2	20.1	74.7	10.5	79.9	8.7
Manufactures	n.a.	40.5	31.2	32.3	29.3	42.9	41.5	32.7	46.2	29.9
Construction	n.a.	2.3	5.4	2.6	6.3	3.8	14.6	4.4	25.8	6.2
Public utilities	n.a.	2.6	79.5	3.1	54.2	3.4	73.9	2.6	61.7	2.0
Transportation	n.a.	9.6	20.7	9.2	18.4	9.1	27.9	8.1	36.0	8.4
Financial services	n.a.	4.1	11.6	1.6	13.2	1.8	21.4	1.8	30.5	2.0
Communal services	n.a.	n.a.	3.2	n.a.	3.6	n.a.	5.4	n.a.	5.9	n.a.
Others[a]	n.a.	16.6	n.a.	14.7	n.a.	15.8	n.a.	15.0	n.a.	14.5
Total	n.a.	100.0		100.0		100.0		100.0		100.0

n.a., not available.

(1) As a percentage of the employed population in the sector.

(2) As a percentage of the total unionized employed population.

[a] Includes communal services in columns (2).

Source: de la Cuadra and Hachette, 1985, part II, table A.52

has had the third highest proportion of unionized workers (columns 1), (b) unionized manufacturing workers constituted the highest proportion of total unionized workers (columns 2), and (c) before unionization in agriculture, mining unions were second in importance to industry, with each of the other sectors providing only a small fraction of the total unionized population.

A tentative conclusion that can be drawn from this information is that the manufacturing sector unions could have supported potentially substantial pressure for protection, despite the drawbacks of their modest average size (about 120 members during the period analyzed) and the organizational difficulties inherent in large numbers of small unions. Only the mining unions, by virtue of their size and conflicting interests, were in a position to challenge the power of the manufacturing unions. However, the mining unions would be unlikely to provide opposition because their significantly higher salaries would more than compensate for the likely negative impacts of protectionist policies on their purchasing power.

Market Organization

The high degree of concentration in the Chilean manufacturing sector during the period analyzed may well have contributed to the extent of protection of manufactures up to 1974. It could be (and has been) argued that direct government intervention has assured both monopolies (or quasi-monopolies) and high protection for firms in some subsectors, among them, for instance, sugar factories and refineries, producers of fertilizers and pesticides, petroleum refineries, and basic iron and steel industries. The government's indirect intervention in private sector firms – for instance, motor vehicles, tire and tube industries – has also enhanced both market power and the degree of protection.

The Cost of Control

Finally, we would expect that an economy that can enforce protective barriers at low cost would be more inclined to maintain protection. This argument implies that the net impact of a vector of tariffs is inversely proportional to the administrative cost of its enforcement. Chile enjoys two formidable natural barriers, the Pacific Ocean and the Andes. Only three important mountain passes and six lesser ones permit some access to Argentina and Bolivia, and most of them are closed during the winter. The only border relatively easy to cross is that with southern Peru.

3

First Episode, 1956–1961

Circumstances Surrounding the Introduction of Liberalization

Political Circumstances

Chilean history seems to suggest, with due qualifications, that the worse political and economic conditions are, the easier it becomes to introduce major policy changes, including liberalization. The state of general economic conditions, the political situation, and the external environment leading up to both episodes of liberalization illustrate this assessment.

General Ibáñez was elected in 1952 by a popular landslide. Not much more than a year later, however, discontent was seething in all quarters as a consequence of galloping inflation, widespread corruption and speculation, and a wide and growing gap between social sectors. Moreover, by his frequent recourse to the established political powers (parties) for policy support as time passed, the President lost the backing of the masses, who had become critical of traditional politics. During 1955, with the annual inflation rate passing 80 percent and external pressures piling on internal, General Ibáñez decided to carry out a stabilization program prepared by the US-based Klein–Saks consulting firm. However, the erosion of his domestic support during 1956 and 1957 made it impossible for him to follow the program strictly; the rightist coalition that had sustained the stabilization program evaporated in the wake of the program's failures and the problems it generated. Moreover, in preparation for the next presidential election, political parties felt it necessary to dissociate themselves from the Ibáñez government.

The government's failures brought the traditional division among parties back to the forefront of the political scene with the addition of a new force at the center: the Christian Democrats. Alessandri, the candidate of the right and of a significant share of independents, won a five-candidate race in 1958 with slightly less than 33 percent of the votes. Once firmly in power

A summary of the two liberalization episodes analyzed in this chapter is presented in table 3.1.

with the additional support of one of the two centrist parties – the radicals – he imposed an economic program inspired by the same basic principles as had fed the Klein–Saks stabilization program: strengthening of private property and of impersonal market mechanisms to solve economic problems. Washington and multilateral institutions gave him enthusiastic support.

Economic Conditions

At the inception of the first episode, the economy was a shambles. On the domestic front, inflation was high and growing, reaching 83.8 percent in 1955 (table 3.2); output growth was low and income per capita was even falling; industrial production was at a standstill while investment was so reduced that it barely reached half the average rate for Latin America. Public administration, but not fiscal revenues, had grown rapidly: the result of this imbalance was increasing and inefficient bureaucracy. In addition, social security benefits to public employees had been significantly increased. The inevitable ever increasing fiscal deficits were financed by Central Bank credit (table 3.2). Discontent mounted as salary readjustments, although automatic and equal to the previous year's inflation, implied a loss of purchasing power and benefited only organized labor – a small fraction of both total employment and Ibáñez's political support. Internal prices were completely divorced from external prices, leading to further resource misallocation.

On the external front, copper and export bonanzas came to a halt after the end of the Korean conflict, with exports falling in both volume and price. The policy consequence was to increase the number, depth, and intricacy of import controls: exchange rates, quotas, and prohibitions multiplied. This restriction was consistent with prevailing doubts about, if not contempt for, the market system, whose efficacy in resource allocation had shown serious limitations. Interventions on a case-by-case basis, whether based on lobby influence, ministers' preferences, or desires to please and strengthen the bureaucracy, generated a highly distorted system of incentives, where the private sector could move only conservatively and without any incentives to increase efficiency, to introduce technological changes, or to save. The economy was rather closed and found itself moving from one exchange crisis to another.

Gross inefficiencies in trade management generated serious import shortages hindering production in some sectors while severely limiting necessary export expansion and diversification. Massive devaluation (83 percent, 82 percent, and 50 percent in 1953, 1954, and 1955 respectively) led only to speculation and capital flight (table 3.2). Inadequate demand management prevented the devaluations from achieving the

Table 3.1 A sketch of two liberalization episodes: 1956–1961 and 1974–1981

Question	*1956 episode*	*1974 episode*
Broad nature	From QRs to method oriented to market prices, with modest tariff liberalization afterwards	Liberalization cum stabilization
Size; duration	Large; 5 years	Large; 6 years
Stages and targets	Two: elimination of QRs; reduction in tariffs	Three: elimination of water in tariffs, quantitative controls, and multiple exchange rates; tariff reduction, pre-established levels; reduction to new goal, a flat 10%
Economic circumstances before		
Balance of payments	Continuous pressure on scarce reserves	Rapid increase in commercial deficits faced with loss of reserves on top of quantitative controls and multiple exchange rates
Price of major exports	Falling after Korean War (copper)	Declining from 1969 with a large increase in 1973
Rate of inflation	High and growing	Galloping
Rate of growth	Low; extremely low investment	Falling
Degree of openness	Low	Low
Shocks	Through copper prices, wide fluctuations	Multiple: copper price fluctuation, widespread black markets and barter, significant reduction of private sector activities
Industrial production	Standstill	Widespread seizures reduced production
Fiscal	Growing bureaucracy and deficit financed by Central Bank	Growing deficits
Other	Massive devaluations and capital flights	Capital flights; private investments came practically to a halt

continued

Table 3.1 *Continued*

Question	*1956 episode*	*1974 episode*
Political circumstances		
Government	Unstable at first; stable during second stage	Strong with generalized support
Ideological shift	Slow but clear	Significant
Public perception and debate	First stage clear and none; second stage some	Not clear; very little debate
Administering arm of government	Central Bank	Ministry of Finance
International influence	Significant	Insignificant
Other	Widespread strikes and corruption at the start of episode	No activity of labor unions
Accompanying policies		
Policy objectives	Mainly stabilization	Stabilization, liberalization, improvement in resource allocation
Exchange rate	First stage, dual rate, one of them free; second stage, monthly fixed in nominal terms	Variable objectives: initially stabilization; later, balance of payments; still later, stabilization again
Export promotion	None relevant	None
Fiscal policy	First stage, reduced deficit; second stage, increased deficit	Elimination of fiscal deficit; privatization of many public enterprises; tax reform (value added and indexation of the basic system)
Monetary controls	Slightly contractionary on the whole; first stage, accent on reduction in high-powered money; second stage, accent on source of high generation (from domestic to foreign assets)	Central Bank cannot lend to public sector; issuance of index securities by Treasury; money supply control through domestic credit, freed interest rate; elimination of quantitative credit limits
Price controls	Widespread wages control; gradual freeing of prices	Eliminated

Implementation		
Stages, departure	Large first step; reversed second stage within 3 years	Full, no departure until 1982
Economic performance		
Prices	Successful stabilization	Slow but successful stabilization
Exchange rates	Initially consistent with liberalization; later inconsistent	Prices of tradeables relative to nontradeables rise significantly at the start, then almost a continued falling trend
Trade	Increase in trade as percent of GDP; export share, constant shift in import composition in favor of consumer and investment goods	Trade opening; both exports and imports rise as share of GDP; no traditional exports rise
Production	Decrease in tradeables (agriculture, in particular; manufacture, constant)	Relative increase of nontradeables; industrial sector adapted better
Income distribution	Improved with tariff reduction; worsened with special regimes and exchange rate policy	Worsened during stabilization, improved in the period 1979–81
Growth	Irregular, but more on average than over previous period	Acceleration
Wages	Unclear	Drastic reduction before the beginning of the episode; rise in the last stage
Employment	Increased at first, then reduced on average over at least next period	Reduction in tradeables; increase in nontradeables; overall increase in unemployment
Other		Falling real exchange rate during post-liberalization worsened unemployment and trade balance

Table 3.2 Circumstances before the first liberalization episode, 1956–1961

Year	*Inflation annual rate, end of year (%)*	*Fiscal deficit (% GDP)*	*Change in foreign reserves*[a] *(million US$)*	*Exchange rate ratio*[b]	*Growth rate of GDP (%)*	*Terms of trade (1977 = 100)*	*Unemployment (%)*
1950–3 (average)	29.2	2.2	2	1.5	6.0	120.8	n.a.
1954	71.0	3.1	– 15	2.3	4.4	113.6	n.a.
1955	83.8	3.5	26	2.8	1.4	126.9	n.a.

n.a., not available.
[a] Gross of revaluation.
[b] Ratio of black market to banking rate.

Sources: de la Cuadra and Cortés, 1984; de la Cuadra and Hachette, 1985, part I, table 17

required changes in domestic terms of trade. Finally, with the public image of the country deteriorating abroad, external credit was not forthcoming.

Extent of Liberalization

The 1956–61 episode was characterized by a shift from a discretionary system based on QRs to a more impersonal one, where the price mechanism played a more important role in determining imports. It is difficult to judge how significantly the level of protection was reduced. If the implicit tariff (defined below) is used, both the dispersion and the average tariff were lower. The nonweighted average tariff was reduced from 151 in 1959 to 102 in 1960, and then increased to 135 in 1961. The overall reduction from the 1959 level took place only in manufacturing, with no changes detected for the other sectors (agriculture and mining).

This episode has been arbitrarily located in the middle of the index (that is, the number 10 has been assigned to 1961) on the basis of the following criteria: the use of zero when all imports are controlled with QRs; the use of 20 when QRs are absent and there is a uniform and low tariff. Thus the number 10 could summarize a situation of no QRs and high and dispersed tariffs. According to changes in the index, this episode can be considered something more than a mild liberalization; in fact the index climbed from 4 in 1957 to 10 in 1961 (see figure 1.1 and table 1.1).

Removal and Reduction of Restrictions

QRs were replaced by a list of permitted imports (LIP). Items on the list could be freely imported, subject to a prior deposit. Initially in 1956, 530 items were included on the LIP with two categories of deposits, one ranging from 5 to 50 percent and the other from 100 to 200 percent. During the period 1957–9 new items were included on the LIP but in higher categories of prior deposits (going up to 10,000 percent). In 1960 the number of listed items kept increasing while prior deposits were reduced. By 1961, the number of items on the LIP reached 2,003, of which 89 percent were deposit free. The reduction in prior deposits was compensated for by a cost-equivalent tax on imports – the additional duty. These duties fluctuated between zero and 200 percent over the cost, insurance and freight (c.i.f.) value of the imported good.

To estimate the level of protection, an implicit tariff was defined as the sum of the costs imposed on imports by different regulating mechanisms such as nominal tariffs, special regimes, prohibited items, prior deposits, additional duties, and administrative controls (table 3.3).

Table 3.3 Implicit tariff, 1959–1961 (percent)

	1959		1960		1961	
Sector	Range	Average	Range	Average	Range	Average
Agriculture	n.a.	47	n.a.	42	n.a.	48
Mining	0–66	26	0–66	25	0–66	26
Industry	53–303	151	32–248	102	52–286	135

n.a., not available.

Source: Hachette, 1973b

Accompanying Policies

Exchange Rate Policy

During this period (which covers both the Ibáñez (1956–68) and the Alessandri (1959–62) liberalization attempts), the trend was to simplify the exchange rate system (figure 3.1). In April 1956 a dual exchange rate was established: the banking rate for merchandise trade, and the brokers' rate for all other transactions. The first was set on a dirty float system controlled by the Central Bank with the backing of credits obtained abroad. The second rate was allowed to float freely and served as a reference by which the Central Bank "set" the merchandise rate (table 3.4).

The changes implied a *de facto* devaluation. The regulation of the dirty float by the Central Bank came about through (a) the Bank's legal obligation to act as an intermediary for the public sector in foreign exchange transactions and (b) the combination of a flexible LIP and prior deposits. The consequence was increased stability of nominal and real

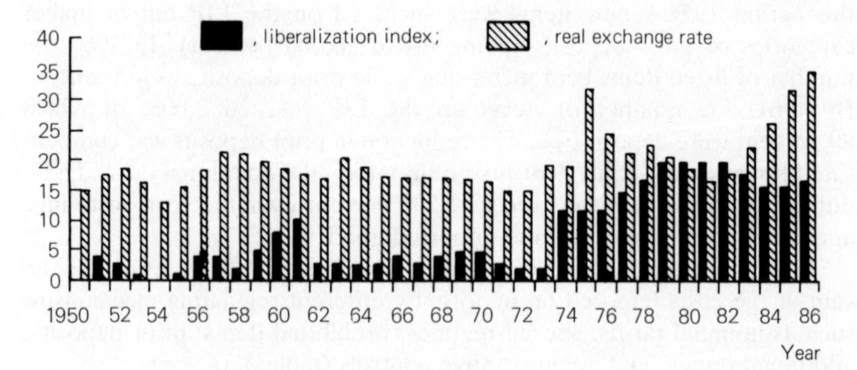

Figure 3.1 Liberalization index and the real exchange rate

Table 3.4 Nominal exchange rates, 1955–1962 (pesos per US dollar)

Year	Free rate (black market)	Special rate	Official or monetary fund	Bank market	Central bank
1955	0.554	0.01937	0.110	0.225	—
1956	0.534	—	—	0.459	0.507
1957	0.708	—	—	0.631	0.629
1958	1.055	—	—	0.828	0.817
1959	1.051	—	—	1.051	1.049
1960	1.051	—	—	1.051	1.049
1961	1.051	—	—	1.051	1.049
1962[a]	1.822	—	—	1.175	1.173

—, not applicable.

[a] The future bank market rate was established in 1962, but became significant only after 1963.

Sources: Libano, 1970; Lüders, 1968; Hachette, 1973b

exchange rates, compared with previous periods, at the cost, however, of significant and erratic changes in other trade restrictions.

Alessandri, arguing that exchange rate stability was critical to domestic price stability and to "the restoration of confidence in trade and credit management" (Alessandri, 1960, p. 115), extended the reforms of the previous administration by unifying the two previously existing markets, fixing the rate in nominal terms early in 1959 to remain constant until October 1962, and insuring full convertibility to attract foreign capital. Also, the Comisión de Cambios Internacionales (COCAIN) – the institution which had previously controlled foreign exchange allocation – disappeared, while the Central Bank took full responsibility for foreign exchange policy.

When a major foreign exchange crisis exploded at the end of 1961, exchange operations were suspended for three weeks and reestablished with (a) a fixed banking rate – the same as in previous years – for most trade operations and a freely fluctuating brokers' rate for tourism and capital transactions, (b) a delay of 90 days for exchange remittances in the case of import transactions, (c) the elimination of automatic access to foreign exchange, (d) the creation of a futures market for a few essential commodities and later on for exports, (e) a reduction in the scope of the LIP, and (f) increases in prior deposits.

Despite successive devaluations in the brokers' market and all the above-mentioned measures, foreign reserves kept dwindling. The authorities consequently decided to devalue the banking rate by 33 percent in October 1962 and to let it fluctuate freely thereafter.

Fiscal Policies

During the 1956–61 episode, the goals for fiscal policy of the Klein–Saks Mission (1956–8) initiated during the Ibáñez years differed from those of the succeeding Alessandri administration.

Klein–Saks

The Klein–Saks Mission framed fiscal policies to control aggregate demand, with only modest success (table 3.5). Public employees' real salaries were unevenly reduced (among sectors) and public investment remained almost constant in real terms, while transfers increased significantly in 1956 and 1957. Tax reforms were systematically postponed, with the exception of an increase from 3 to 5 percent for the general sales tax and to 15 percent for luxury goods.

Nevertheless revenues increased between 1956 and 1958 by more than could be explained by these changes alone and, despite proliferating exemptions given to regions and firms, as the foreign trade tax base (that is, imports and the nominal exchange rate) rose and as inflation was curbed.

Table 3.5 Fiscal situation, 1955–1962 (current prices)

	Revenue		*Expenditure*		*Deficit*	
Year	*(million escudos)*	*(% GDP)*	*(million escudos)*	*(% GDP)*	*(million escudos)*	*(% GDP)*
1955	129.6	14.1	161.6	17.5	32.0	3.5
1956	223.4	15.1	250.9	17.0	27.6	1.9
1957	318.4	15.6	360.5	17.6	42.4	2.1
1958	395.3	15.1	450.3	17.2	55.0	2.1
1959	583.6	15.9	678.9	18.4	95.3	2.6
1960	707.9	16.6	907.1	21.3	199.2	4.7
1961	808.2	16.9	1,015.8	21.2	207.6	4.3
1962	959.3	17.0	1,277.8	22.6	318.5	5.6

Information for the consolidated public sector is not available.

Source: de la Cuadra and Cortés, 1984, p. 116

Alessandri

Alessandri's government shifted fiscal policies toward reactivating the semiparalyzed economy. No major tax reform was contemplated initially. As in the preceding three years, limited and strictly enforced salary readjustments helped to curb aggregate demand and reduce the fiscal deficit – indeed, Alessandri's rhetoric was more emphatic than Ibáñez's about the need to limit salary raises drastically.

On the expenditure side, investment (in housing, public works, and decentralized public agencies) was increased substantially while tax exemptions for construction were generously distributed to stimulate complementary private investment. Tax exemptions were also given to fishing and some domestic import substitution industries to stimulate production.

The government hoped to finance the major part of the deficit with foreign loans to avoid inflationary pressures and to increase the availability of imported inputs required for the production drive. Unfortunately, a disastrous earthquake in mid-1960 meant that a great deal of money had to be spent on reconstruction. This was obtained from new taxes, created in 1960 and 1961, on income (particularly that accruing from copper mining), real estate, and luxury goods, and via a compulsory loan from foreign-owned copper mining. Meanwhile, lags in additional revenues and in expected foreign support brought pressures on the authorities to resort to Central Bank financing.

Monetary Policies

Monetary policy was intended to be consistent with stabilization policy, although the Ibáñez (Klein–Saks) and Alessandri subperiods show quite different approaches. During the three Ibáñez years, the accent was on reducing money supply and on redirecting credit away from the public and toward the private sector. During Alessandri's government, the accent was on eliminating QRs and shifting the source of Central Bank generation of high-powered money to foreign instead of domestic assets. (See table 3.6 and de la Cuadra and Hachette, 1988, appendix tables A.3 and A.4.)

Table 3.6 High-powered money, 1955–1962 (million escudos, end of year, and percent)

	1	2	3	4	5	6	7
		Credit to private sector					
Year	*Credit to public sector*	*Rediscount*	*Other*	*Foreign exchange operations*	*Other*	*Total*	*Variation (%)*
1955	26.2	17.8	5.3	5.6	−3.7	51.2	61.0
1956	31.6	25.6	17.1	5.3	−6.4	73.2	43.0
1957	49.4	41.4	24.7	−0.2	−23.7	91.6	25.1
1958	70.9	40.0	26.5	−4.1	−9.1	124.2	35.6
1959	174.8	15.1	67.3	1.4	−77.5	181.1	45.8
1960	293.6	6.3	77.6	−49.0	−65.0	263.5	45.5
1961	374.4	2.6	115.1	−164.4	−42.3	290.4	10.2
1962	815.7	—	156.4	−289.8	−184.2	498.1	71.5

—, not applicable.

Sources: Columns 1, 2 + 3, and 6, de la Cuadra and Cortés, 1984, statistical appendix, p. 74; columns 2 and 4, Arbildúa and Lüders, 1968, column 5, obtained by difference

Klein–Saks, 1956–1958

Increases in money supply were curbed by imposing absolute limits on the expansion of commercial bank loans, reducing the volume of rediscounts through a tighter rediscount rate, and reducing the rate of increase of direct Central Bank credit to both private and public sectors.[1] New banks were prohibited and credit quotas could not be augmented by increasing capital and reserves. The availability of credit was also made discriminatory: banks were instructed to expand credit chiefly to the agricultural, industrial, and mining sectors. Quantitative controls were slightly relaxed starting in 1957.

The previously uniform rediscount rate (nominal) was replaced early in 1956 by a relatively flexible rate structure depending on the percentage the rediscount would represent of the particular bank's capital and reserves; for agricultural credit the corresponding rediscount rate implied a relative subsidy. Quantitative limits for rediscounts were also established.

Import deposits, eventually to be replaced by tariffs, were instituted to freeze high-powered money. These deposits were percentages of the c.i.f. values of imported merchandise, frozen in Chilean currency, held at the Central Bank either until the merchandise arrived in the country or for 90 days; their impact was marginal.

Finally, the fiscal deficit during the subperiod (1956–8) was mainly financed by Central Bank credit.

Alessandri, 1959–1962

Quantitative controls on commercial bank loans were eliminated in the first semester of 1959 and replaced by reserve requirements. Legal provisions were introduced to allow banking operations in foreign currency, and a tax amnesty was decreed to stimulate the return of Chilean capital. In addition, savings and loan associations, whose operations could be indexed to the annual inflation were permitted. The government created a Joint Fiscal Account (CUF) at the State Commercial Bank to improve efficiency, to increase control, and to limit public sector access to Central Bank and commercial credit.

The real cost of credit was increased, mainly because of the drastically reduced rate of inflation. Nevertheless, the fall in inflation was reinforced by an increase in nominal interest rates, despite several measures to reduce them, including a lowering of the rediscount rate, elimination of the tax charged on interest, and a requirement that commercial banks lower their interest on one fifth of the increase in their loans.

1 The original plan was to reduce the rate of increase in the money supply by about 50 percent per year (Lüders, 1968, p. 220). This section is taken mainly from Lüders (1968).

After the 1961 exchange crisis and the reestablishment of a dual exchange rate, debtors in foreign currency were allowed to amortize their debt by recourse to the official market and, after October 1962, by means of newly issued US dollar bonds which could be bought with credit subsidized by the Central Bank.

Unfortunately, Central Bank credit to the public sector, instead of being bridled, virtually exploded during the 1959–62 subperiod, as table 3.6 shows. The resultant monetary expansion, though somewhat restrained by foreign exchange operations (specifically, use of foreign credits), was far from absorbed by them.

Domestic Controls

Wages

During the Ibáñez (Klein–Saks) subperiod (1956–8), automatic readjustments of public employee wages, the basic salary, and the minimum agriculture salary were eliminated (early in 1956). As a consequence, nominal wages increased by less than average inflation. To lessen the negative impact of readjustments which were lower than inflation, a minimum salary was created for workers in industry and commerce and above-average wage rises were given to specific sections of the armed forces. Social security taxes increased by 7 percentage points between 1956 and 1958.

The Alessandri subperiod (1959–61) also saw wages rising more slowly than average inflation, as expected. In addition, a new policy was set in motion to replace automatic readjustments applying to the entire private sector with annual collective bargaining at the firm level. In 1960, however, the government decided to return to the previous system. Furthermore, the authorities tried to reduce disparities in family allowances among social security institutions. Automatic readjustments were reestablished in 1962 for both the basic salary and the minimum industrial wage.

Prices

The Ibáñez (Klein–Saks) strategy was to free prices gradually with particular emphasis on stabilizing the supply of essential goods. This gradual freeing is summarized below (de la Cuadra and Hachette, 1988, appendix table A.5). Rents could be increased by less than previous inflation while prices of some public services, such as railway fares, were adjusted by more than the inflation rate of the previous year. Subsidies and tariff exemptions were granted for the import of necessary goods in 1956. Furthermore, to assure normal supplies, imports were stimulated while exports were curbed. Credit was obtained from the US government to import cereals (PL 480 Agreements) while compensation agreements were reached with some countries.

Under Alessandri most prices were freed between 1958 and May 1960. To assure steady and abundant supply, three PL 480 Agreements were signed, some products were exempted from tariffs, INACO's[2] operations were simplified and made more efficient, norms were dictated to control monopolies and other activities designed to limit competition, and consumer organizations were created to help authorities control speculation and reverse inflationary expectations.

As a consequence of the 1960 earthquake, and to avoid potential inflationary and speculative trends arising from the interruption of normal transportation and commerce, prices of most necessary goods were frozen at the level attained by May 20, 1960. Originally announced as short term, the measure was in fact extended indefinitely. Prices of goods produced by public enterprises were scarcely changed after 1960. It should be added at this stage that one likely reason for maintaining this policy was to reduce the impact of a relatively strict wage policy at a time when union power was growing quickly.

Export promotion policies were not significant during this episode.

Reversal

The main objective of the liberalization attempt initiated in 1956 had been the disappearance of QRs. It was essentially fulfilled on both the export and import sides by 1961. It could have remained so if the commercial balance had converged to a sustainable deficit. Unfortunately, this was not the case. Imports grew rapidly during the period 1956–61 while the export performance was modest – 86.8 percent and 25.6 percent respectively.[3] The combination of the elimination of QRs and an increase in GDP by 82 percent in nominal terms between 1959 and 1961, with a fixed nominal exchange rate, may have been the main force behind the large import expansion. It is difficult to assign the proper weight to each effect. However, it should be noted, despite an alternative hypothesis proposed elsewhere (Ffrench-Davis, 1973, pp. 82,89), that the income effect of the high growth in GDP together with the possibility of closing the gap between the effective and the desired stock of imported durable and capital goods, repressed for a long time through QRs, should not be omitted as part of the explanation of the rising commercial deficit.

2 Instituto Nacional de Comercialización, later renamed Empresa de Comercio Agrícola (ECA, Enterprise for Agricultural Commerce).
3 Statistical details are given in chapter 5.

The commercial balance, which was severely disturbed by these developments, worsened in 1961 when the credibility of the exchange rate stability was seriously shaken. Capital flight ensued which carried the foreign reserves to an unsustainable situation given the limited access to the foreign capital market. The banking system foreign reserves had reached US$164.8 million by then.

Unwilling to devalue to avoid both inflationary pressures and the disruption of the ongoing stabilization program, the authorities reduced the LIP by 700 items and established a prior deposit of 10,000 percent on all imports. These measures represented a major departure from the main target of the liberalization attempt and were maintained indefinitely thereafter. Furthermore, the government suspended the exchange operations for three weeks and reestablished them in early January 1962 with the following alterations: (a) a dual exchange market with a fixed banking rate (the same as in previous years) for most trade operations and a freely fluctuating brokers' rate for tourism and capital transactions; (b) an administrative delay of 90 days for exchange remittances for import transactions; (c) the elimination of automatic access to foreign exchange; (d) the creation of a futures market for a few essential commodities and later for exports; (e) reduction in the scope of the LIP; (f) increases in prior deposits.

Despite the initial devaluation of 40 percent in the brokers' market (and successive devaluations during 1962) and all the above-mentioned measures, the foreign reserves continued to dwindle. The authorities then decided to devalue the banking rate by 33 percent in October 1962 and to let it fluctuate freely thereafter. The consequence was a new devaluation which resulted in an average exchange rate for the last quarter of 1962 which was 47 percent above the average rate for the previous quarter. However, QRs and prior deposits were maintained.

4

Second Episode, 1974–1981

Circumstances Surrounding the Introduction of Liberalization

Political Circumstances

The Allende government came to power in 1970 supported by the Popular Unity (UP) coalition and slightly more than one third of the votes. By the same token, Congress was and remained firmly controlled by opposition parties during his tenure. Allende's aim was to establish a new socialist order which would eradicate dependence on the capitalist industrial economies, control of local markets by domestic and foreign monopolists, and the concentration of agricultural resources in the hands of a small feudal landowning aristocracy (World Bank, 1980). These forces were considered to have been principally to blame for Chile's poor economic performance since 1930.

The main long-run objective was, then, to establish firm control of productive activities by extending state ownership, creating a mixed area in which the state would enter into partnership with domestic and private entrepreneurs, and establishing strict rules for all remaining activities. State property was extended through expropriations and nationalizations, "within the bounds of Chile's democratic, constitutional process." Other more short-term objectives, such as the reactivation of the economy and the reduction of inflation, were also defined.

The revolutionary program for expanding state ownership became a matter for bitter conflict between Congress and the Executive. To make things worse, Congress considered that the President was increasingly by-passing it to carry out his objectives. The atmosphere became increasingly confrontational. However, conflict was not limited to government and opposition: "As time passed, increasing disagreement appeared with the UP coalition itself regarding the acceptable pace of reform, the need for concessions to obtain or retain the support of one or another group – e.g.,

See the sketch of this episode presented in table 3.1.

small shopkeepers and manufacturers, truck drivers – and the feasibility of achieving the Government objectives by traditional means" (World Bank, 1980, p. 61).

Furthermore, when inflation accelerated in 1972, expansionary and redistributive objectives were effectively abandoned, real income gains achieved in 1971 were eroded, even reversed, and tensions among early supporters of the regime grew rapidly and dangerously. Additional conflicts arose from the international arena, as traditional lenders withdrew their economic and political support which was only partially replaced by new sources from socialist and Latin American countries.

Allende's loss of control over the coalition which had brought him to power, together with the chaotic economic situation, led to a military coup on September 11, 1973. Political parties were prohibited and Congress was closed. "The new Government proclaimed its intention not only to restore economic stability and normalize relations with foreign creditors, but also to reverse the approach to economic development that Chile had pursued for four decades, of which the UP policies were seen as an exaggerated extension" (World Bank, 1980, p. 92).

Economic Conditions

Consistent with its objectives, the Allende government attempted a major shake-up of the economy, giving particular attention to the control of means of production and to redistributive measures. Policy measures included massive adjustments of wages and social benefits, expansion of government employment through new public works programs and simple additions to the government payroll, strict enforcement of controls on prices and availability of popular consumer goods, and significant expansion of social expenditure. Meanwhile, the means of production were brought under control by nationalization, expropriation, requisition, and outright intervention; compensation was considered in only a few instances.

Expansionary fiscal and monetary policies were the basic tools of the program; Congress would not approve additional taxes. While idle capacity, availability of foreign reserves, and the initial euphoria prevailed, progress toward objectives were spectacular (table 4.1). However, serious problems soon arose as aggregate supply became strained to its limit, subsidies increasingly distorted the price structure, the distribution system began to crumble, labor–management conflicts multiplied, foreign reserves were exhausted, and uncertainties grew as to the limits between private property and the so-called social area, and even as to basic rights and freedoms of production and consumption of specific goods.

Furthermore, inexperienced management, widespread private controls, and an inflated and higher-paid public sector work force all helped to erode

Table 4.1 Circumstances before the second liberalization episode, 1974–1981

Year	*Inflation annual rate, end of year (%)*	*Fiscal deficit (% GDP)*	*Change in foreign reserves*[a] *(million US$)*	*Exchange rate ratio*[b]	*Growth rate of GDP (%)*	*Terms of trade (1977 = 100)*	*Unemployment (%)*
1960–70 (average)	28.4	1.3	89	1.6	2.7	174.6	5.4
1971	22.1	8.3	−240	4.4	9.0	150.6	3.8
1972	163.4	12.3	−121	11.0	−1.2	145.3	3.1
1973	508.1	21.1	−21	15.0	−5.6	163.6	4.8

[a] Gross of revaluation.

[b] Ratio of black market to banking rate.

Sources: de la Cuadra and Cortés, 1984; de la Cuadra and Hachette, 1985, part I, table 17

fiscal savings and production. As a consequence, aggregate production declined precipitously in 1972 and 1973, decapitalization accelerated in numerous sectors, inflation jumped way over any previous historical levels, and shortages of goods developed at the retail level, while barter and generalized black markets even more seriously disrupted normal distribution channels and further eroded the tax base. Foreign reserves accumulated up to 1970 (table 4.1) – about two thirds of the equivalent of one year's imports – were lost during the period 1971–3 despite a sizeable increase in foreign debt. The money supply exploded while fiscal deficits surpassed 20 percent of GDP in 1973. Real income gains achieved in 1971 were eroded and even reversed. The drain of capital and technical and managerial expertise accelerated; labor productivity fell severely, as labor conflicts escalated, further reducing supply. The economic decline was exacerbated by a drop in world copper prices in 1971 and 1972, although this price rose spectacularly in 1973, and by the withdrawal of international credits from traditional sources.

Further Considerations

The chaotic political and economic state of affairs may have justified major changes in 1973, but do they completely explain the desire for a major liberalization, particularly on the part of a group (the military) well known among Latin American countries for their autarkic views? On the face of it, liberalization would seem a most unlikely option in such circumstances. No single answer satisfactorily accounts for the seeming contradiction; we can only offer some suggestions which together may be indicative.

In the first place, the new major long-run objectives of the government concerned the correction of fundamental disequilibria, which had long characterized the Chilean economy, and the organization of the economic system. Thus there were two main goals:

1. the achievement of a high and stable rate of economic growth which, in the government's view, had been jeopardized in previous decades by the combination of a faulty development strategy (based on import substitution) and an inadequate choice of instruments (tariffs, prohibitions, price and exchange controls, among others;
2. the achievement of full employment and the eradication of extreme poverty.

All economic objectives, whether imposed by necessity or chosen as instruments of policy, had to respect the guarantee of individual rights to property and of equality of opportunity in education, health, and social security. Effective economic decentralization also had to be achieved since it was considered a precondition for effective political decentralization and the basis for an efficient democratic organization.

The objectives were to be attained through a combination of means:

1. restoration of the market as the principal determinant of economic decisions;
2. restoration of the private sector as the main agent of development, (see in particular, Cauas, 1974, 1975; de Castro, 1979), a condition which would imply not only a revision of public sector responsibilities but also a drastic reduction in its size and involvement in economic activities;
3. nondiscriminatory treatment of all productive sectors to improve resource allocation;
4. development of an efficient financial market (previously nonexistent) to enhance savings and the allocation of investment;
5. the use of general economic tools, such as exchange rate, interest rate, and the money supply, to achieve the objectives outlined;
6. last but not least, a greater opening to foreign markets, a measure which was considered amply justified.

Although the authorities recognized that protection "had originated in part as a means of satisfying the legitimate aspirations to promote industrialization," they stressed that "various factors contributed to an accumulation of errors in the structure of the tariff system, so that it has become one of the most distorted elements in the nation's economy" (Gotuzzo, 1974). In particular, it "penalized the efficient non-industrial sectors (and the regional consumer who has to pay high protectionist prices when cheap imports are substituted for by expensive imports from the sub-region" (de Castro, 1979). In order to diminish the imports of luxury goods, it stimulated the use of scarce domestic resources to produce them domestically. It "permitted the creation and subsistence of national and foreign monopolies that produce locally at a cost several times that of international market" (Gotuzzo, 1974). Consequently, efficient firms became inefficient when obliged to buy locally. The structure and level of protection was also the cause of stagnation and limited diversification of export. However, more important from the dynamic point of view, it bridled growth by limiting the extent of the market, hindering savings (at least through foreign investment), and stimulating "prestige" investments. Finally, it tended to favor inefficient import substitution through integration exercises such as the Andean Pact which argued for a high and common tariff wall. Although the new authorities were willing to consider some sacrifices as a concession to integration, "the nature of these sacrifices must not be such as to conspire against a legitimate right to obtain the economic development required for the population" (de Castro, 1979).

New winds were blowing among new generations of professionals and within political ideologies in several Latin American countries (for instance, Mexico, Peru, Argentina, Brazil, and Uruguay), all characterized by an almost synchronized questioning of traditional development strategies based on import substitution. Many Chilean supporters of the new government shared these new viewpoints, although bureaucrats thought otherwise. Therefore, despite their inherent autarkic bias, the commanders of the armed forces came to see the usefulness of liberalization as an essential part of a coherent plan based on decentralization of economic and political activities.

In the second place, governments place a great value on "product differentiation." Since import substitution policy had been pursued actively since the 1930s by governments of different persuasions, from the far right to the far left, liberalization in 1973 might be attractive to the military government as a clear case of product differentiation.

In the third place, foreign institutions may have had some impact on policy decisions. Washington and international institutions supported liberalization actively. Although their loans were not significant, they assisted in debt renegotiations (1973, 1974, and 1975) and in improving the country's image abroad. Less directly, Chilean relationships with the Andean Pact may also have had some impact. The first steps toward opening the economy would win the support of the Pact's member countries only to the extent that they were consistent with those countries' views on the Common External Tariff (even though the Tariff's provisions were ambiguous, and remain undefined to this day). If the Pact countries had supported the new Chilean regime, the latter would have cut short or modified its liberalization efforts in line with their more protectionist views. In the event, the Chilean authorities may have accelerated the process as a consequence of the Pact countries' refusal of support.

Finally, a significant liberalization required more than political backing; it required a change in the composition of its supporters. As long as power was based on highly concentrated visible well-organized urban interests, significant liberalization would have been virtually impossible. The military, without direct ties to any of the traditional power groups or the traditional bureaucracy, were probably the only group capable of breaking the impasse.

Extent of Liberalization

By the time liberalization had been completed in the second episode (June 1979), the Chilean import regime could be considered one of the most open in the world. In fact there were no QRs, no prohibitions, no antidumping or countervailing duties, no subsidies on exports, and a uniform nominal tariff of 10 percent for all imports except for automobiles (some items imported from ALADI had tariffs below 10 percent). We therefore considered that the maximum figure of the liberalization index (20) could be assigned to this year (table 1.1), and since these conditions remained unchanged during 1980 and 1981, the same level of the index was attached to them.

In 1973 the index was 2, revealing that the economy was operating under a heavy load of trade controls (table 1.1). In 1974 the index jumped to 12, reflecting the elimination of a significant number of controls. This level of the index was maintained during 1975 and 1976 to show a pause in the pace of liberalization. The pace quickened in 1977, 1978, and during the first semester of 1979; values of 15, 17, and 20 respectively were attached to the index during these years.

Removal and Reduction of Restrictions

The Quantitative Restriction System and its Elimination

In 1973, there were 5,125 tariff positions. The following QRs constituted direct or indirect prohibitions on the import of 63 percent of them.

1. Imports of merchandise corresponding to 187 positions were directly forbidden.
2. Goods corresponding to 2,872 positions were subject to a 90-day non-interest-bearing prior deposit of 10,000 percent of the c.i.f. value in the Central Bank. This cost was prohibitive. Central Bank authorities, however, arbitrarily exempted certain importers from this tax.
3. Another 2,278 positions were subject to official approval. This required costly bureaucratic procedures and arbitrary official decisions and discrimination. It was found that official authorization was used to prohibit the import of 159 items.

All this meant that goods classified in 3,218 tariff positions were not allowed to be imported.

These restrictions were eventually eliminated as follows.

1. Direct prohibitions: the 187 tariff positions directly prohibited were reduced to only six in August 1976. This reduced group included caviar, manufactured synthetic fur articles, fine pearls, precious and semiprecious stones, synthetic or reconstituted stones in the rough, and color TV sets. The import of color TVs was authorized in April 1978, while that of the other goods was allowed in August 1981.
2. 10,000 percent prior deposit: this restriction was not legally eliminated until August 1976, although it had ceased to be applied before then. It was first reduced by the liberal granting of waivers, and was then effectively eliminated as automatic exemptions were established

for all but a few items. The reason given for not abolishing prior deposits explicitly was that, once abolished, General Agreement on Tariffs and Trade (GATT) provisions would make it impossible to reestablish them, and some government officials argued that they might conceivably be used in the future.

3 Official approvals: at the beginning of 1974, all quotas and official approvals required to initiate an import operation were eliminated.

Tariff Reduction

First Stage

In 1974 there were three general reductions, two in March and one in June, in accordance with the norms announced by the Ministry of Finance. The highest tariffs were thus drastically reduced. In March rates ranging from 220 to 750 percent were reduced to a single rate of 160 percent, those between 35 and 215 percent were reduced by 5 to 65 percentage points, and rates below 30 percent remained unchanged. In June 1974 the maximum tariff was reduced further. A fourth reduction went into effect in January 1975. This time, however, the lowest tariffs began to rise in an effort to approach the desired concentration of rates. Thus, within a year, the maximum tariff came down from 750 to 120 percent, the simple average tariff dropped from 105 to 57 percent, and the modal tariff declined from 90 to 55 percent.

Second Stage

During the second semester of 1974, the Tariff Policy Advisory Committee submitted to the Minister of Finance a proposal for tariff rates to be set at 25 percent, 30 percent, and 35 percent for raw materials, and semi-manufactured goods, and manufactured goods respectively. However, in the ensuing discussions of the economic and political benefits of the tariff the Committee encountered two significant obstacles.

The first had to do with the political consequences of taxing imported food at a rate of 25 percent. Food not only had been traditionally exempted from duties but also was frequently favored with preferential exchange rates and subsidies. The establishment of a "high" tax while eliminating subsidies for items integral to the budget of the vast majority of the population was considered politically explosive. However, if the uniformity objective was to be realized, any reduction in the tariff on foods would require a general reduction in tariffs.

The second drawback was the rather heavy discrimination against exports that would have been imposed by the 25–30–35 percent tariff scale. To mitigate this effect, it would have been necessary to establish export subsidies (considered undesirable for a number of reasons) or refunds of import duties paid on inputs (assumed to be administratively too cumbersome). The only alternative was a general reduction of the tariff level.

The Advisory Committee accordingly made a new proposal, according to which tariffs would vary between 10 and 35 percent, with a simple average of 19.7 percent and a mode of 15 percent. Out of a total of 4,985 items subject to tariff, only 288 could have exceeded 25 percent. The tariff scale from 10 to 35 percent was to be applied to goods according to the degree of processing: raw materials and goods not significantly processed were to be taxed at 10 percent, while the maximum rate for manufactured goods was set at 35 percent.

In August 1975 the President of the Central Bank announced the form that the tariff reform would take: the goal was a tariff structure of 10–35 percent, to be reached in five equal semi-annual reductions by the first semester of 1978. Since the proposed tariff structure incorporated a relationship between the rates for inputs and for final products, the actual structure was corrected as follows. The target rate of 10–35 percent was multiplied by three, and all tariffs exceeding these calculated rates were to be immediately reduced to that level; for example, if the final tariff level on raw materials was 10 percent, then the initial rate, say 120 percent, was to be reduced to 30 percent. At the same time, the difference between the adjusted tariff and the target tariff was further reduced by approximately 20 percent. Continuing with the example of raw materials, the rate was reduced by an additional 5 percentage points, thus reaching 25 percent (compared with the original 120 percent). Thus Decree 950 established both a new tariff at a lower rate and a different structure.

The first two of the intended semi-annual tariff reductions took place as scheduled in 1976, but in December of that year an exceptional modification occurred. According to Decree 1098, rates for all inputs, intermediate products, tools, and machinery not produced in the country were reduced immediately to the target rate. Then, after the third reduction in January 1977, it was decided to advance the remaining two, and the entire adjustment was completed by August 1977.

During 1977 businessmen began to question the wisdom of the 10 and 35 percent structure that had been chosen. The groups protected by the lowest rates argued that they were being discriminated against for no valid reason. A strong current of opinion against the discrimination emerged and, as the government had already excluded the possibility of high levels of protection, it took advantage of the situation to unify the tariff at the lower level.

Third Stage

On December 2, 1977, the Minister of Finance announced that there would be a uniform 10 percent tariff. On December 5 a general reduction was decreed in which the maximum rate of 35 percent was reduced to

25 percent, capital goods not produced in the country were immediately assigned to the 10 percent level, and remaining goods that had rates between 25 and 10 percent were distributed along a lower range. The same decree established that the tariff be reduced each month for the next 18 months; that is, the tariff would reach the single 10 percent rate in June 1979. Thus the process of tariff reform took five years and three months, achieving a uniform rate with only one exception: automobiles and other vehicles.

The schedule of tariff reductions which was in fact implemented is shown in figure 4.1, separated into three blocks corresponding to each of the three stages.

Complementary Measures

At the beginning of the second episode a consumption tax was in existence that taxed some imported goods more heavily than the equivalent domestically produced items. Among these were cigarettes, tobacco, alcoholic beverages, perfumes, and tires. This discrimination was abolished in 1977.

Import duty exemptions were plentiful until 1974, when it was decided that the public sector would pay the same taxes as the private sector and that no new exemptions would be introduced. The exemptions were so numerous that a complete list of existing legal provisions became available only in 1977 (Torres, 1977).[1] On the basis of that information, three decrees were promulgated to eliminate most exemptions, one in June 1978 and the other two in March and December of 1979. The majority of the exemptions disappeared, leaving only those corresponding to international agreements and a few others to be imported duty free, including documents consigned to shipping companies, plans, industrial drawings and the like, bank bills, nuclear reactors, particle accelerators, fire engines, airplanes and helicopters, and ships over 500 tons.[2]

In 1973 most imports of capital goods were legally exempt from tariffs. In practice, every productive activity enjoyed exemptions for the import of machinery and equipment. Therefore the inclusion of capital goods in the customs duty schedule was strongly opposed by interested sectors, and it was particularly difficult to apply the full tax to those goods not produced in the country. Consequently, the following system was used: for capital goods not produced in Chile the import duty was to be paid (without

1 The compiling of tariff exemptions revealed the existence of no less than 290 legal provisions benefiting private individuals, firms, productive sectors, regions, public institutions, etc.

2 Tariff reductions can be considered as a linear approach to targets, although some features of a radial reduction could be found in the second stage as tariff exemptions were eliminated.

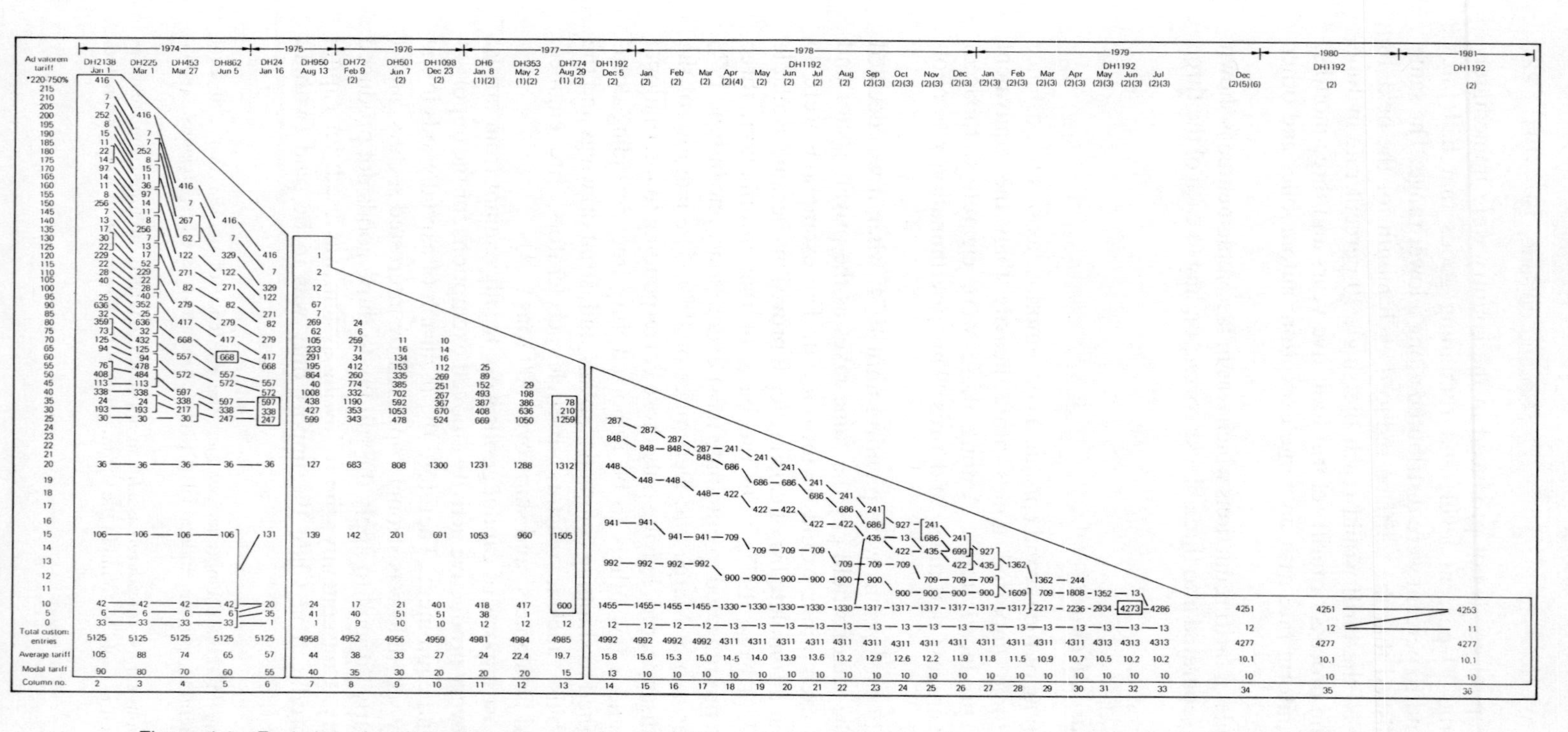

Figure 4.1 Evolution of tariff levels between 1974 and 1981 according to the number of tariff positions affected at every tariff level: (a) tariff positions corresponding to cars, trucks, other vehicles, and drills, which benefited from special tariff treatment, are not included and therefore the sum of the tariff positions of each column differs from the total indicated, but such positions were considered for the estimated average tariff; (b) DH667 of September 6, 1978, established a descending scale of tariffs for fuels derived from petroleum, which ended at 10 percent in July 1979; (c) the information presented in gray indicates the number of tariff positions corresponding to the target levels

interest) seven years after importation; for all other capital goods, the import duty was paid in a maximum of 14 semi-annual installments of no less than US$2,500 each, but in this case the balance of the debt was subject to an interest rate, established periodically by the Central Bank, similar to the market rate for loans in dollars.

Accompanying Policies

Exchange Rate Policy

The government considered the exchange rate to be a relevant standard for guiding resource allocation; its first decision, therefore, was to abolish the very extensive multiple exchange rate regime left by the previous government and to correct the overvaluation of the peso accumulated during the preceding three years. Devaluation was 229 percent in 1973, and for imports of food and raw materials, which had previously received a preferred rate of 25 escudos to the US dollar, the adjustment amounted to a devaluation of more than 1,000 percent. Between December 1970 and December 1972, the nominal exchange rate, deflated by the consumer price index (CPI), had thus been adjusted by 50 percent.

A crawling peg was reinstituted and maintained until 1979 (table 4.2). With a few minor exceptions, whether the periodic adjustments amounted to more or less than the previous inflation rate was determined by several considerations: (a) the accumulation of foreign reserves, (b) the lowering of nominal tariffs, and (c) the stabilization goal (table 4.3). That is, the exchange rate was adjusted by more than inflation when the price of copper fell (1975), when tariffs were reduced (August 1974 and December 1977), and when a fixed nominal exchange rate was announced for an indeterminate period (June 1979). Adjustment was less than inflation mainly to promote stabilization, when it became clear at the beginning of 1976 that the combination of fiscal, monetary, and exchange rate policies of 1975 had produced a dramatic turnaround in the balance of payments: the expected deficit had been reduced by 80 percent and foreign reserves had started accumulating. This below-inflation adjustment of the exchange rate lasted until 1982, first as an unannounced sliding peg until 1978 and then as a *tabla* (pre-announced), with either daily or monthly rates of devaluation, up to June 1979 when, after a devaluation, the rate was fixed with the intention of linking further domestic inflation with international inflation. A comparison of real exchange rates and the index of protection for the period 1950–86 is shown in figure 3.1.

Foreign reserves had increased by US$250 million during the first months of 1976. This favorable situation persuaded the government to start a stronger anti-inflationary policy. Simultaneously, the government com-

Table 4.2 Foreign exchange rates, 1974–1981

Quarter[a]	Nominal exchange rate (pesos US$)	Real exchange rate[b]	Effective exchange rate[c]	Real effective exchange rate[d]
1974				
I	0.371	26.50	0.768	54.87
II	0.545	23.70	0.987	42.91
III	0.790	23.24	1.343	39.50
IV	1.173	23.00	1.994	39.10
1975				
I	1.906	28.03	3.012	44.29
II	3.537	30.49	5.587	48.18
III	5.339	30.34	7.848	44.59
IV	6.800	29.96	9.588	42.24
1976				
I	9.190	31.69	12.498	43.10
II	11.510	28.35	15.078	37.14
III	12.820	23.52	16.410	30.11
IV	15.170	22.99	19.418	29.42
1977				
I	17.960	23.53	21.911	28.72
II	18.640	20.78	22.368	24.94
III	20.960	20.96	24.942	24.94
IV	24.710	22.10	28.911	25.86
1978				
I	28.350	25.34	32.319	28.88
II	30.810	23.76	35.123	27.08
III	32.290	23.31	36.488	26.35
IV	33.320	22.33	37.318	25.01
1979				
I	34.210	21.80	37.973	24.20
II	35.770	21.27	39.347	23.39
III	39.000	21.29	42.900	23.42
IV	39.000	19.10	42.900	21.01
1980				
I	39.000	17.91	42.900	19.70
II	39.000	16.67	42.900	18.33
III	39.000	15.66	42.900	17.23
IV	39.000	14.58	42.900	16.04
1981				
I	39.000	13.71	42.900	15.08
II	39.000	13.40	42.900	14.74
III	39.000	13.13	42.900	14.44
IV	39.000	12.81	42.900	14.09

[a] The rates are those of the first month of each quarter.

[b] Nominal exchange rate deflated by the CPI.

[c] Nominal exchange rate multiplied by one plus the nominal tariff. The nominal tariff is a weighted average of tariffs of agricultural and industrial products.

[d] Real exchange rate multiplied by one plus the nominal tariff.

Sources: Central Bank, *Boletín Mensual*; Aedo and Lagos, 1984

Table 4.3 Exchange rate policy and objectives

Period (month, year)	*Objectives*	*Underlying conditions*	*Real exchange rate adjustment*	*Change in rate of inflation*
First stage: 1974–5				
Jan 74–Feb 74	Stabilization	High price of copper	Revaluation	Deceleration
Mar 74–Jan 75	Stabilization	Terms of trade start declining	Devaluation	Deceleration
Feb 75–Jul 75	Balance of payments	Sharp drop in terms of trade and reduced supply of foreign credit	Devaluation	Acceleration
Aug 75–Jan 76	Balance of payments	Upturn in domestic activity	Devaluation	Deceleration
Second stage: 1976–7				
Feb 76–Nov 77	Stabilization	Significant improvement in balance of payments	Revaluation	Deceleration
Third stage: 1976–7	Support to tariff reduction and stabilization by the end of the period	Inflow of foreign capital starts at beginning of period	Devaluation	Convergence to constant rate
Post-liberalization: 1980–1	Stabilization	Rapid growth of foreign credit and international reserves	Revaluation fixed nominal rate	Constant in 1980 and convergence to US inflation in 1981

mitted itself to maintaining an equilibrated or surplus fiscal budget and to controlling Central Bank credit strictly. The fixed exchange rate of 39 pesos to the dollar was enforced until June 14, 1982, when the peso was devalued by 19 percent.

Export Promotion Policy

Consistent with its general market orientation policy, the government did not offer subsidies or special incentives to exports. The only special benefits came from (a) the rebate of the value-added tax introduced in 1975, (b) a rebate of import duties paid on inputs to be reexported, although limited to direct importers of inputs, and (c) a subsidy to fishing and tree planting.

Monetary and Financial Policies

The two main objectives of these policies were a more efficient allocation of credit and savings, and a reduction in the rate of inflation.

The principal policy actions for achieving the first were as follows:

1. the sale back to the private sector of most of the banking shares acquired by the state during the Allende government and a decree (December 1974) prohibiting state ownership of commercial bank shares;
2. a move toward multipurpose financial institutions by relaxing restrictions on the types of operations that could be undertaken;
3. the elimination of quantitative credit limits on commercial bank lending operations, and a progressive reduction of legal reserve requirements on deposits (de la Cuadra and Hachette, 1988, appendix table A.6);
4. the progressive raising and ultimate elimination of the legal ceiling on interest rates;
5. legal standardization of the indexation of financial assets and exemption of the resulting monetary corrections from income tax.

The most noteworthy policy actions for reaching price stabilization were as follows.

1. In the first stage, the Central Bank was prohibited from lending to public sector entities other than the central government, commercial banks, and financial institutions. In a second stage, prohibition by the 1980 Constitution of Central Bank lending to the public sector extended even to buying Treasury notes in the open market.
2. The Treasury issued indexed securities to provide noninflationary financing for the fiscal deficit.

3 Special credit lines from the Central Bank to the private sector were progressively eliminated. By 1978, the only lines remaining were for reforestation and housing.

The government gradually opened the Chilean economy to foreign capital between 1974 and 1981. Medium-term capital movements were progressively deregulated (through reductions in reserve requirements), with overall global limits on borrowing eliminated in 1979; the only limitation on total bank indebtedness is the maximum allowed debt-to-capital ratio (20 to 1). Restrictions on monthly inflows were eliminated in April 1980. Short-term financial credits (less than 24 months) were not allowed until 1981 (table 4.4).

Table 4.4 Balance of payments: capital account, 1974–1981 (million US dollars)

Year	*External debt accumulation (gross)*	*Public*	*Private*	*Reserves accumulation*
1974	626	n.a.	n.a.	−73
1975	324	331	158	−223
1976	−133	−189	121	237
1977	481	−59	298	165
1978	1,463	727	750	785
1979	1,820	228	1,324	1,256
1980	2,600	−72	2,596	1,760
1981	4,458	526	3,225	−299

n.a., not available.

Source: Central Bank of Chile, *Deuda Externa*

Fiscal Policy

The main objectives of fiscal policies between 1974 and 1981 were to reduce the size of the public sector, fiscal deficits, and distortions derived from taxes, subsidies, and pricing of public utilities. Different policies and reforms were instituted to pursue these aims.

Revenues

After implementing a package of tax measures in late 1973 and early 1974 as a stopgap solution to the presssing fiscal situation, a majore comprehensive reform was promulgated in late 1974. Its major features were as follows:

1 introduction of a value-added tax of 20 percent, replacing the old cascade-type sales tax;

2 taxation of undistributed corporate earnings;
3 elimination of a number of preferential situations, special rates, exemptions, loopholes, and taxes on capital gains;
4 indexation of the value of all business assets and liabilities as well as taxpayer liabilities for unpaid taxes;
5 an increase in rural and urban real-estate assessments and income tax rates, on top of a 10 percent additional surtax on income and property taxes.

Public Enterprises

Early in 1974 public enterprises were permitted to raise their tariffs and prices significantly and, from then on, were to follow a rule of self-financing (with due exceptions). Furthermore, most important public enterprises tended to apply marginal cost considerations to price their output.

Expenditure

Public expenditure was reduced, at least as a percent of GDP, throughout the period:

1 a general austerity program, which included an across-the-board reduction of between 15 and 25 percent in government outlays on goods and services, was launched early in 1975;
2 a program to reduce personnel resulted in close to 100,000 public employees (about 2.5 percent of the total labor force) being laid off between September 1973 and mid-1977;[3]
3 as part of fiscal restraint, and in line with the announced principle of fiscal subsidiarity, over 500 state-owned firms, which had accounted for a disproportionate part of the overall public sector deficit during the Allende administration, were sold to the private sector.

Consequently, during the period encompassing September 1973 to the end of 1975, the fiscal sector was subjected to a major policy shift which thoroughly altered its size, behavior, and role in the economy as a whole. The basic fiscal features achieved by 1976 were maintained, with only minor alterations, throughout the remainder of the period under study, while the consolidated public sector accounts showed a permanent positive figure for government savings and overall surplus (table 4.5). This consistent surplus found its counterpart in negative Central Bank lending to the public sector, with the exception of 1977 when sugar imports were heavily subsidized (de la Cuadra and Hachette, 1988, appendix table A.7).

3 Sjaastad and Cortés (1981) estimate a reduction of 91,000 in the period 1973–6 and another 45,000 between 1976 and 1980; Marshall and Romaguera (1981) show a reduction of 92,000 between 1973 and 1977, while Tokman (1984) presents an effective reduction of 94,600 between 1973 and 1979.

Table 4.5 Consolidated public sector accounts, 1973–1981

	1973	*1974*	*1975*	*1976*	*1977*	*1978*	*1979*	*1980*	*1981*
Percentage of GDP									
Current surplus	−4.1	6.2	6.5	10.4	7.7	8.9	10.2	10.6	5.5
Capital revenue	1.8	2.3	2.1	2.0	1.6	2.1	1.4	0.4	0.4
Capital expenditure	11.1	13.6	10.3	8.7	8.9	9.4	7.8	5.4	5.1
Net capital expenditure	−9.3	−11.3	−8.2	6.7	−7.3	−7.3	−6.4	−5.0	−4.7
Overall surplus	−13.5	−5.2	−1.7	3.7	0.4	1.6	3.8	5.5	0.8
In billions of pesos at 1977 prices									
Current surplus	17.8	18.0	16.4	27.2	22.6	27.7	34.4	38.5	21.1
Capital revenue	5.2	6.7	5.3	5.2	4.6	6.5	4.7	1.4	1.5
Capital expenditure	31.9	39.5	26.0	22.8	25.6	29.2	26.3	19.6	19.6
Net capital expenditure	−26.8	−32.8	−20.9	−17.6	−21.0	−22.7	−21.6	18.2	18.0
Overall surplus financing	−38.8	−15.1	−4.3	9.7	1.2	5.0	12.8	20.0	3.1
Foreign (net)	0.3	0.6	−6.1	−6.0	−0.6	4.0	—	−0.4	10.4
Domestic (net)	38.6	14.5	10.4	−3.9	−0.3	−9.0	−12.8	−19.6	−13.4
Central Bank	118.4	84.2	89.7	47.4	44.4	16.1	5.6	−0.4	−12.6
Total change in monetary base	44.0	19.7	15.6	19.5	15.7	12.6	11.3	9.4	−2.7

—, not applicable.

Source: IMF, *Recent Economic Developments*, various issues

Restrictions on Foreign Investment

In July 1974, a new foreign investment statute – Decree 600 – was promulgated with the express purpose of stimulating the inflow of capital and technology. It was refined after Chile withdrew from the Andean Pact in October 1976. The main features of the new scheme were as follows.

1. Repatriation of capital could not start until three years after entry.
2. There was no mandatory fade-out requirement.
3. The foreign exchange regime for capital repatriation and profit remittances must be as favorable as that applied to the acquisition of exchange cover for general imports.
4. Foreign investors were to receive the same treatment as national investors, with the exception of access to domestic credit. The statute also eliminated limits to profit remittances, offered foreign investors a choice of tax regimes on profits, ensured stability of the foreign exchange regime, and required a minimum time for the investment to remain in the country.

Domestic Controls

Prices[4]

The vast majority of price controls were eliminated by the end of 1973, when three categories of goods and services were created: those whose prices were to be freely determined, those whose prices were still to be fixed by the Direccíon de Industria y Comercio (DIRINCO) (about 30), and those whose prices were to be informed – freely set subject to approval from DIRINCO (about 20). To reduce the effect of price increases on low income families the government granted direct temporary subsidies for some goods. Items were switched between categories, although the lists did not change much during the period analyzed. After December 1980, any new price fixing required a law. Currently, less than ten prices are still legally fixed.

Labor market

Social security Starting in 1974, special discriminatory benefits were slowly eliminated, family allowances and retirement age were made uniform, and contribution rates were gradually reduced. The main reform, transforming the pay-as-you-go system into an obligatory personal savings and insurance program, was approved in 1980 and put into practice in 1981.

4 This section is based on Wisecarver (1983); see also de la Cuadra and Hachette (1988, appendix table A.8).

The labor code The Labor Plan of 1978 – and later the Social Security Reform of 1981 – reduced the cost of the employee to the employer by reducing legal severance pay, granting the right to dismiss workers without justifying the cause, limiting the application of minimum wages, granting absolute freedom of association, eliminating the exclusive right of one union in any firm, and eliminating the legal distinction between blue-collar and white-collar workers. Furthermore, all negotiations were to take place at the level of one firm, with obligatory arbitration if required. This labor reform plan also established a wage floor equal to the previous wage package, indexed by the CPI for the intervening period.

5

The Success and Sustainability of Liberalization

Success

In this section we attempt to evaluate the success of liberalization policies in Chile, based on the two episodes of liberalization analyzed so far. Selection of criteria for this sort of evaluation will necessarily be somewhat arbitrary. Here, three effects of liberalization – impacts on trade, on production, and on employment – have been chosen as yardsticks because, on the one hand, they seem to be related to what conventional wisdom has considered relevant, and, on the other hand, they have been among the principal preoccupations of the government.

Of course, success in these areas can be properly judged only when the full impact has let itself be felt. By that token, the first episode (1956–62) may have been too quickly reversed, while too short a time has elapsed since the second and more interesting episode (1974–9) for firm conclusions to be offered. Furthermore, many unrelated policy actions occurred simultaneously with the liberalization, making it difficult to distinguish the pure effects of liberalization. Despite these shortcomings, the analysis of these impacts may elicit useful observations and conclusions. The aim of this section is thus necessarily modest, attempting only to highlight the noteworthy characteristics of the observed impacts and adding judgments on success wherever these can reasonably be made.

This chapter covers both episodes. The decision to combine them was taken to facilitate comparisons which could lead to more general, although tentative, conclusions. Furthermore, the two most interesting and relevant texts to judge the success of liberalization – production and employment – would be applied only to the second episode.

Impact of Liberalization on Trade

The success of liberalization can be analyzed through two different criteria related to trade: the trade balance, and the volume and composition of exports and imports.

Trade Balance

In the long run, the trade balance should not be significantly affected by liberalization policies (capital flows and debt service will be the main factor behind any long-term disequilibrium). The adjustment to that long-run situation may, however, imply short-run disequilibria in one manifestation or another. Since the main worry of governments is usually the depletion of foreign reserves, development of negative trade balances could be considerd undesirable, particularly if the country's access to the world capital market is limited. Correspondingly, a positive trade balance, or a positive trend in the trade balance, could be considered a criterion of success for liberalization policies.

In this respect, liberalization appears to have been relatively unsuccessful during both episodes (table 5.1), thus carrying the seeds of its own destruction. However, several qualifications are in order which lead to a different conclusion. Ups and downs in the trade balance during the period analyzed suggest that the results can be explained by factors other than trade liberalization – terms-of-trade fluctuations and policies as to net indebtedness, aggregate demand, foreign reserves, and the exchange rate. These factors influenced the trade balance mainly through imports and to a lesser extent through exports (table 5.1).

As might be expected, the trade balance in both episodes of liberalization deteriorated concomitantly with an increase in the volume of imports related to (a) relatively buoyant demand and production conditions, with the exception of 1958–9, (b) a significant increase in foreign indebtedness (net of accumulation of foreign exchange), (c) a reduction in the real exchange rate, with the exception of the period 1956–7, and (d) a fall in the terms of trade, at least in 1958–9 during the first episode, and during the entire second episode (specific evidence for the relationship of these variables to components of trade balance is given below).

It may thus be difficult to tie the worsening of the trade balance unequivocally to liberalization. In the absence of a full macroeconomic model, however, the likelihood that liberalization harmed the trade balance cannot be disproved, although the above evidence suggests that its relative influence was rather limited.

Exports

Liberalization is expected to increase the volume of both exports and imports. Exports increased in real terms during both episodes, except during 1956–7 when their volume was slightly reduced (table 5.1). However, while the share of exports in GDP remained stable during the first episode, it increased during the second episode (table 5.2). This result is not surprising. Exchange rate adjustments were insufficient to stimulate marginal exports (almost nonexistent at that time), while the bulk of

Table 5.1 Trade balance and selected variables (annual averages)

	Net indebtedness (changes as % of imports)	*Change in reserves (% of imports)*	*GDP growth (%)*	*Terms of trade (% of change)*	*Real exchange rate (% change)*	*Exports (% change)*	*Imports (% change)*	*Trade balance (% of imports)*
First episode (at constant 1970 prices)								
Preliberalization								
1953–5	5.7	1.1	2.3	0.6	−5.6	n.a.	n.a.	26.8
Liberalization								
1956–7	11.0	−6.9	4.5	−3.9	16.8	−3.0	7.7	16.7
1958–9	9.1	1.2	1.6	−4.4	−3.3	9.0	−4.3	6.1
1960–1	26.4	−13.3	6.0	1.1	−5.4	0.8	53.6	−9.0
Post liberalization								
1962–3	36.4	−3.9	5.5	2.4	1.0	2.5	−0.4	−1.7
Second episode (at constant 1977 prices)								
Preliberalization								
1971–3	25.9	−10.7	0.5	−6.1	5.3	n.a.	n.a.	−0.4
Liberalization								
1974–5	36.7	−12.0	−6.2	−20.4	28.8	9.3	−5.9	12.9
1976–7	4.6	14.5	6.6	−1.8	−18.3	12.3	−9.1	18.7
1978–9	46.4	24.9	8.2	−1.8	−1.4	13.0	53.7	−11.0
Post liberalization								
1962–3	58.9	11.0	6.6	−15.6	−9.8	4.1	20.2	−28.1
1982–5	15.0	−14.0	−1.8	−1.8	20.4	7.4	−12.5	16.6

n.a., not available.

Source: de la Cuadra and Hachette, 1988

Table 5.2 Development of trade

	Exports (% GDP)	*Imports (% GDP)*	*Exports plus imports (% GDP)*
Episode 1956–61 (at constant 1970 prices)			
Before liberalization, 1953–5	15.4	7.7	23.1
During liberalization, 1956–61	15.7	9.1	24.8
After liberalization, 1962–3	15.2	10.8	26.0
Episode 1974–9 (at constant 1977 prices)			
Before liberalization, 1971–3	9.9	10.4	34.5
During liberalization, 1974–9	19.4	23.0	42.4
After liberalization, 1980–1	22.0	31.9	53.9
1982–5	25.5	22.2	47.7

Source: de la Cuadra and Hachette, 1988, appendix tables A.15 and A.29

export revenues and costs – from copper – were almost completely independent of the exchange rate. In addition, quotas severely limited the export potential (see de la Cuadra and Hachette, 1988, appendix table A.20).

The behavior of exports during the second episode of liberalization is more interesting. They increased regularly (in constant prices) from 1974 to 1981, a period which includes the post-liberalization years 1980 and 1981. They also increased as a share of GDP, even though the nominal exchange rate deflated by CPI fell substantially and continuously after 1975, a fall which cannot be attributed to the process of liberalization *per se*. In contrast, external conditions were favorable to nontraditional Chilean exports up to 1981,[1] stimulating exports during the period of liberalization and compensating more than fully for the fall in the exchange rate below its pre-liberalization period level during 1980–1 (table 5.3). However, the attribution problem remains. How much of that success story can be assigned to liberalization policies and how much to exogenous circumstances? The same question arises for imports.

One way in which liberalization affects exports and imports is through changes in their domestic prices relative to the prices of nontradeable goods. Consequently, the answer to the question requires estimating first the impact of liberalization on relative prices and then that of relative prices on exports and imports. The first impact, which includes the effects of both the tariff reduction and movements in the exchange rate related to

1 This is not reflected in the terms of trade, as their reduction is mainly due to the rise in import prices.

Table 5.3 Real exchange rate and export prices

Period	Real exchange rate (index, annual average)	Percentage change	Export prices (index, annual average)	Percentage change
1971–3	100.0	—	100.0	—
1978–9	133.4	33.4	151.6	51.6
1980–1	87.0	– 13.0	196.3	96.3

—, not applicable.
Data presented in the second and fourth columns are averages of indices. The real exchange rate is defined here as the nominal rate deflated by the CPI.

liberalization, has been estimated by Sjaastad (1981). He estimates that, as of 1970, tariff barriers in Chile were such that the same volume of trade would have been realized with a uniform tariff of about 90 percent. He assesses the impact that a tariff reduction from a uniform level of 90 percent (about its equivalent level in 1974) to 10 percent (its effective level in 1980) would have on domestic relative prices of exportables to nontradeable goods and of importables to nontradeable goods. The relevant parameters are obtained from an econometric analysis fed by time series data covering 1930–70.

Further, the effect of relative prices on export supply could be derived from price elasticity estimates[2] which, for noncopper exports, vary from 0.49 to 0.60. The main shortcoming of these estimates is that these elasticities are related to the exchange rate, defined differently from the ratio of relative prices of exportables (or importables) to nontraded goods since they take the CPI as a proxy for prices of nontradeables, even though the CPI is negligible and in the absence of a better approximation, the method described above was used. The results appear in table 5.4.

Changes in prices of exports, relative to nontradeables, as a result of the reduction of tariffs to 10 percent, explain about 16 percent of the rise in exports. The main positive impact on exports was the growth of Organization for Economic Corporation and Development (OECD) countries and the high income elasticities for Chilean exports during the period analyzed. The factor "Change in relative prices, other" (table 5.4) includes the impact of the 35 percent reduction in the real exchange rate between 1975 and 1979. Unfortunately, the item "Other" is large, but it can be partially explained by significant technological improvements and the maturing during the episode of investments made before liberalization. One of the most significant components of "Other" is that reduction in tariffs

2 Cline (1984), de Gregorio (1984, 1985), Desormeaux and Bravo (1984), Díaz-Alejandro (1984), Ivulic (1984).

Table 5.4 Factors explaining export and import trends over the period 1975–1979 (percent)

	Change in relative prices					
	Resulting from tariff reduction	*Other*	*Growth in OECD*	*Expenditure effect*	*Other*	*Total*
Export	16.4	– 54.9	57.3	–	81.2	100.0
Import	8.9	11.9	–	59.8	19.5	100.0

–, negligible.

Sources: IMF, 1985; own data

improved the profitability of exports by diminishing input costs. In addition, the depression of 1975 stimulated, for mere survival purposes, an export drive whose momentum lasted for several years. Finally, parallel to the process of liberalization and privatization, there was a significant shift in focus of new investments into products intensive in natural resources, such as paper, cellulose, ferromolybdenum, fishmeal, and fruits, which are all sold mostly in foreign markets.

Imports

Imports increased consistently (at constant prices), at least as a share of GDP, over long periods which include both liberalization years and the periods immediately before and after the episode (table 5.2). However, they behaved more erratically than exports during the liberalization periods. Once again, important factors other than liberalization were at work.

To be able to isolate the net effect of liberalization on imports would require the assignment of relative weights to each policy in effect at the time. In particular, the difficulty is to extract the impact of tariff reductions on the equilibrium exchange rate in order to obtain the net impact of liberalization on prices of imports relative to nontradeable goods. An approach parallel to the one used for exports was adopted. The expected change in relative prices of imports to nontradeables was obtained from Sjaastad's (1981) estimates. Combined with estimated price elasticities for imports – varying from – 0.29 to – 0.5 (see note 2) – these estimates allow a rough calculation of the impact of liberalization on imports during the second episode (table 5.4).

Again, the results are interesting, even taken as simple orders of magnitude. The impact on relative price changes resulting from liberalization is small given the significant change in tariffs. This is so because the import-competing sectors were in fact much less protected than they appeared to be.[3]

Other factors also explained the unexpectedly small impact: in particular GDP growth and expenditure financed through net indebtedness. In addition, falling real exchange rates fueled increased imports (see table 5.4, third column).[4] Finally, technological changes, particularly the use of more import intensive technologies, and adjustments to the stock disequilibria that existed at the start of the second liberalization episode may also help to account for the results shown. Some of these issues are discussed further below in our evaluation of the impact of liberalization on production.

As both exports and imports increased with liberalization, the economy became steadily more open in both episodes, as expected. These results hold regardless of the measure of openness used, such as the figures in table 5.2 which are based on actual values of exports and imports and not on what exports and imports (or exportables and importables) would have been had trade liberalization been the only policy in operation. Although higher shares of exports and imports in GDP were realized during trade liberalization, the share of tradeables in GDP was not altered significantly, implying increased specialization within tradeables, consistent with comparative advantages.

Furthermore, the foregoing analysis of reasons for both export and import trends suggests that changes in relative prices resulting from tariff reductions improved the trade balance during the second episode, *ceteris paribus*, since the volume of exports expanded more than the volume of imports. The behavior of exports clearly made the difference between the two episodes. Buoyant world prices, concentration of investments in exportables, previous investment coming to maturity at the time of liberalization, and last but not least a substantial increase in profitability through changes in relative prices were the engines of success for the second episode.

The Structure of Trade

Trade liberalization can be considered successful if it allows exports to diversify, if it stimulates nontraditional exports along the lines of compa-

3 As the incidence of protection in 1970 estimated by Sjaastad (1981) was heavily on the side of the export sector – the same relative prices could have prevailed in Chile in 1970 had the import duty been a uniform one at 27 percent with an export *duty* of 33 percent – a substantial increase in nontraditional exports could be expected as a direct consequence of the elimination of the implicit taxation of that sector.

4 The impact on the volume of imports of a reduction in the prices of importables relative to nontradeable goods is underestimated, because the effective relative prices used for purposes of measurement are the prices of imports deflated by the CPI which includes a high proportion of importables.

rative advantage, and if the pattern of imports is influenced by internal resource allocation more akin to comparative advantage. In these respects, liberalization was unsuccessful during the first episode but highly successful during the second.

The two episodes of liberalization differ strikingly in their impacts on trade composition. The composition of trade during the first episode remained unaltered, but it changed radically during the second episode when manufacturing and agriculture increased from an initial 11.9 percent of total exports to 32.3 percent during liberalization (table 5.5).

The only change in the structure of exports during the first liberalization episode was a slightly greater concentration of exports. It should be recalled that this period was one of rationalization of tariffs, modest changes in the real exchange rate, and a less than favorable external environment. Further, export promotion policy was almost nonexistent.

In contrast, during the second episode, nontraditional exports increased significantly, from 2.7 percent of total exports in 1971–3 to 34.7 percent in 1980–1, while manufactures went from 9.6 to 32.6 percent in the same period (measured at constant prices) (table 5.5). The share of mining was correspondingly reduced. The major growth is observed in products such as fishmeal, timber, cellulose, and molybdenum oxide which, although classified among manufactures, are highly intensive in natural resources. The results are consistent with expectations: liberalization, with a higher average real exchange rate than before and a normalized flow of inputs, allowed the country to make use of comparative advantages existing in sectors other than copper.

Agricultural exports were particularly buoyant during the second liberalization period (table 5.6): their average annual growth rate exceeded 25 percent during each of the three stages of liberalization. However, they dropped drastically in 1980–1 as a result of the 35 percent reduction in the real exchange rate, reduced trade with Argentina – a consequence of the Austral conflict (1979–81) which affected forestry products in particular – and the recession felt in OECD markets. But these factors are unrelated to trade liberalization *per se*.

The major impact of trade liberalization on the structure of imports was initially channeled through its effect on domestic demand and production, and is consequently analyzed in the relevant section. However, a few comments are in order here.

First, the change in the composition of imports is a byproduct of liberalization and of *other* policies. Second, the observed striking increase in the share of imports of consumer goods during the first episode is related to the proliferation of special import exemptions and the combination of high growth rates of aggregate demand with a fixed exchange rate – at least during the period 1959–61. This policy mix, partly financed by foreign savings, resulted in reduced production of tradeables and, consequently,

Table 5.5 Composition of trade – constant prices (percent)

	Exports				*Imports*		
	Mining	*Manufacturing*	*Agriculture*	*Nontraditional*	*Consumption*	*Intermediate*	*Capital*
Episode 1956–61							
Before liberalization							
1953–5	81.8	8.6	9.4	n.a.	29.3	43.5	27.1
During liberalization							
1958–61	83.6	8.8	7.7	n.a.	30.2	32.8	37.0
After liberalization							
1962–3	87.1	7.5	5.4	n.a.	36.0	29.2	34.8
Episode 1979							
Before liberalization							
1971–3	88.2	9.6	2.3	(2.7)	17.8	62.3	19.9
During liberalization							
1974–9	67.7	26.4	5.9	(24.7)	14.6	63.1	22.3
After liberalization							
1980–1	59.3	32.6	8.2	(34.7)	27.2 (34.7)	51.3 (45.5)	21.6 (20.4)
1982–5	57.4	34.4	8.3	(n.a.)	(34.1)	(52.1)	(13.8)

n.a., not available; the figures in parentheses are estimated values.
The classification of imports changed in 1981. The new classification was applied to the period 1980–1 to make comparisons possible.
Source: de la Cuadra and Hachette, 1988, appendix tables A.30 and A.33

Table 5.6 Trade in agriculture

	Pre-liberalization 1965–7)	Liberalization 1974–5	1976–7	1978–9	Post-liberalization (1980–1)
Exports (total)					
Annual rate of growth	5.9	44.3	27.0	25.6	−2.4
Percentage of total exports	3.5	5.5	8.5	11.5	13.0
Exports net of forestry					
Annual rate of growth	4.6	56.6	23.7	15.2	3.0
Imports					
Annual rate of growth	−0.6	−18.5	6.4	11.7	3.0
Percentage of total imports	19.7	23.5	22.5	13.0	12.5
Balance					
Current US$	−735.6	−724.9	−395.2	−222.6	−280.6

Source: Cox, 1983

diminished demand for raw materials and intermediate goods used in that production, while it stimulated imports of consumer goods. In addition, generous PL 480-financed agricultural imports went a long way toward explaining the increase in the share of imports of consumer goods and the reduction in the share of agricultural production. PL 480 agreements could be looked upon as a tool for both liberalization and stabilization, since they indirectly opened domestic agriculture to foreign competition and constituted an additional source of foreign financing to support a relatively low exchange rate.

The composition of imports does not seem to have changed as much during the second episode. When annual figures are compared, a definite trend appears favoring the relative increase of imports of consumption goods as compared with imports of intermediate products. These are interrelated phenomena, as imports of intermediate products are inputs in the production of consumption goods (de la Cuadra and Hachette, 1988, appendix table A.28). This change in composition seems to be consistent with expected effects of liberalization: increase of imports of consumption goods and the reduction in domestic production of import substitutes, primarily in traditional crops and in manufactures of both durables and nondurable consumer goods. A high share of manufactures produced in Chile before 1974 were assembly lines for consumer goods, the sector with the highest effective protection. Agricultural imports, however, became more concentrated in cereals, for which Chilean comparative advantages were the least evident.

Impact of Trade Liberalization on Output and Employment

Liberalization policies could be considered successful, in terms of production, first if they have a positive impact on growth, and second if the share of exportables within the GDP increases while that of importables decreases. Only general and largely qualitative conclusions can be drawn from the analysis of the impact of Chile's trade liberalization on production and employment during the second half of the 1970s. One reason for the elusiveness of quantitative data may be the difficulty of isolating trade policy effects from other contemporaneous policies and from external shocks. We have not fully succeeded in solving this problem, but offer some progress in separating the effects of the trade liberalization from those stemming from the 1975 recession and from the downward trend in the terms of trade which started in 1974.

The analysis in this section is limited to the second episode for lack of relevant detailed information on the first: it deals first with impacts in the aggregate, and then focuses on the behavior of manufactures. Even though this sector did not represent more than 27 percent of GDP in 1974, it has usually been regarded as the sector most affected in terms of production and employment be trade liberalization (Castañeda, 1984; Meller 1984; Tokman 1984). A less detailed review of the agricultural sector is also included (relevant information is scanty); this sector accounted for 9 percent of GDP in 1974. One tradeables sector – mining – has been left out of our sectoral analysis: its combination of importables (oil production) and exportables (other minerals, of which copper is the most important) does not appear to have been affected by liberalization. It represented 7.8 percent of GDP in 1974 and 7.4 percent in 1979.

Aggregate Impacts: Output

Product The deep recession of 1975 blurs conclusions about the impact of trade liberalization on the aggregate product. This recession, as discussed before, originated primarily in the external shocks of 1975 and in the adjustments necessary to break down the inflationary spiral and to tackle the severe scarcity of foreign reserves. Tariffs, although lowered, were still redundant as late as 1976. GDP recovery to the 1974 level took at least two years (1976–7), coinciding with the implementation of the second stage of the liberalization process (table 5.7).

The third stage was implemented after GDP had recovered to its pre-recession level. Therefore growth during this stage (averaging 8.3 percent) can be considered to be less affected by recuperation. The pace declined in the post-liberalization years (1980–1); nevertheless, the average rate of 1978–81 reached 7.3 percent, the highest figure for four successive years since 1935.

Table 5.7 Gross domestic product growth and liberalization stages

Stage	*Rate of growth (%)*
First	
1974	1.0
1975	−12.9
Second	
1976	3.5
1977	9.9
Third	
1978	8.2
1979	8.3
Post-liberalization	
1980	7.8
1981	5.5
1982	−14.1
1983	−0.7
1984	6.3
1985	2.4

Source: de la Cuadra and Hachette, 1988, appendix table A.15

Such growth rates make it hard to sustain the contention that trade liberalization injured aggregate product; unfortunately, the contrary cannot be proved either.

Composition of the gross domestic product The impact of the set of policies (monetary, fiscal, exchange rate, and so on) and other variables (foreign credit, terms of trade, and so on) on the composition of the GDP can be seen in table 5.8. The tradeables sector – agriculture and forestry, mining, and manufacturing – reduced its participation in the GDP. This decline is associated with a drop in the relative prices of tradeables and with a growing deficit in the trade balance. Such behavior is principally attributable to capital movements: when the marginal propensity to spend in tradeables is less than unity, their relative price must fall to absorb the capital inflow net of reserve accumulation. Conversely, when conditions of capital movements returned to normal, in the period 1982–5, the composition of GDP changed back in favor of tradeables, suggesting that liberalization *per se* could not explain significant changes in its composition (table 5.8).

Constant relative prices of exportables to importables were assessed in the above analysis, which obviously is not necessarily true during a process of trade liberalization and when international prices have been fluctuating. Fortunately, the internal P_X/P_M did not change significantly – the index at

Table 5.8 Gross domestic product composition, relative prices, and trade deficit (percent)

Stage	*Tradeables*	*Nontradeables*	*Relative prices*[a]	*Ratio of resource balance to GDP*
Liberalization				
1974–5	40.6	59.4	100.0	1.4
1976–7	40.0	60.0	95.4	0.0
1978–9	38.0	62.0	91.5	4.3
Post-liberalization				
1980–1	36.7	63.3	85.6	9.9
1982–5	38.3[b]	61.7[b]	80.0[b]	– 0.3[b]

[a] Ratio of tradeables to nontradeables.
[b] Only for 1982–3; information is not available for 1984 and 1985.

each stage is 1.00, 0.93, and 1.02 (de la Cuadra and Hachette 1985, part II, appendix table B.24).

Composition of tradeables The tradeables sector is a mix of exportables and importables.

The general opinion is that the industrial sector was the most affected by trade liberalization; however, the data show otherwise. In fact, the composition of tradeables did not change significantly during the period of liberalization (table 5.9). The most significant changes came during the post-liberalization period, characterized by a significant reduction in real exchange rates and, later, by deep recession during which the industrial sector suffered the most.

Table 5.9 Composition of tradeables (1977 prices) (percent)

Stage	*Agriculture and forestry*	*Mining*	*Manufacturing*	*Total*
Liberalization				
1974–5	23.0	19.3	57.7	100.0
1976–7	24.5	20.8	54.7	100.0
1978–9	22.8	19.6	57.6	100.0
Post-liberalization				
1980–1	22.3	19.8	57.9	100.0
1982–5	24.4	23.1	52.5	100.0

Source: Central Bank, *Cuentas Nacionales*

Aggregate Impacts: Employment

Despite the prolific research on causes of employment and unemployment in Chile during the period covered (see in particular Riveros, 1983;

Castañeda, 1984; Meller, 1984; Ramos, 1984; Tokman, 1984), the likely impact of liberalization on aggregate employment was analyzed carefully in only one paper (Coeymans, 1978a); unfortunately, even this paper could not be used. Since it gave the results of a simulation of equilibrium situations of comparative statics, between the final compared with the initial stage, it cannot help to predict the adjustment path of production and/or employment required to assess the effects of trade liberalization on short-term unemployment.

Furthermore, though most of the researchers directed their attention to employment in manufactures (and to the "destruction" of this sector), none except Riveros (1983) either seriously considered the choice of a proper methodology to evaluate the impact of tariff changes or recognized in the conclusions the influence of other factors, unrelated to trade liberalization, acting upon employment in manufactures. In fact, it became fashionable to postulate, in a deceptively simple way, a connection between liberalization and the reduction of employment in this sector after 1974. Further, only one author (Meller, 1984) mentioned the possibility of a positive impact of liberalization on other productive sectors – services(!); however, he presented no estimates of this impact.

As the issue of the employment (unemployment) effect of trade liberalization is of such importance, we have chosen *de novo* other methods of casting some light on the impact of liberalization on employment.

Trade theory models emphasize the effects of trade on the relative prices of productive factors. The most simple $2 \times 2 \times 2$ model, under assumptions of full employment, inelastic supply of factors, nonreversible production functions, and others, arrives at unambiguous conclusions. Its framework is static and, although the effects of growth on trade have been incorporated, the effects of trade on growth remain obscure. In this context, reference to employment appears mainly in discussions of the adjustment to changes in exogenous variables (for example, tariffs and other trade restrictions). The hypothesis in this model is that trade liberalization will favor the rate of use of the abundant factor and increase its relative price. The abundant factor is the one with the lower relative price, compared with the trade partner, under restricted trade.

Defective wage statistics combine with the lack of a time series for the price of capital to preclude any direct test of the effects of liberalization on the prices of labor relative to capital. However, if labor had been the abundant factor under restricted trade, then comparative advantages should be found in the labor intensive sectors. This hypothesis can be tested.[5]

5 When natural resources are considered, analysis of comparative advantage based only on capital–labor endowments should be limited to the processing of these resources, that is, to manufacturing activities. This does not guarantee that comparative advantages within the industrial subsector are not related to the domestic availability of natural resources.

If the labor intensity hypothesis is correct, we should expect the demand for labor to increase when the structure of production changes; its relative price would increase correspondingly and, for a given technology, some substitution of capital for labor would occur. This substitution was very significant in manufactures. In the next section it is shown that it may have been the result of (a) changes in the vector of products and (b) the introduction of new technologies in addition to likely relative price changes. However, information was insufficient for effective use of this factor intensity approach based on the classical theory models; another method had to be chosen to cast some light on the impact of liberalization on employment.[6]

Short of a macrodynamic general equilibrium model, a relatively simple approach was selected. It is based on a comparison between, on the one hand, observed employment and, on the other hand, simulated employment from "normal" rates of growth of sectors involved. The model is corrected for the so-called Allende effect, for the impact of the 1975 recession, and for the reduction in the terms of trade. It is more of a descriptive than an analytical type of approach. Its results may be consistent with the predictions of several trade models, but they are certainly consistent with the simplest $2 \times 2 \times 2$ type. At any rate, this model will not be our basic analytical framework as will soon be realized.

However, before this approach is presented a short account of the development of employment between 1974 and 1983 could be useful (table 5.10). Aggregate employment was reduced between 1974 and 1977, and after 1981. Employment increased in agriculture and nontradeables during the liberalization process (1976–9), while decreasing in mining and manufactures. Employment in mining even fell between 1974 and 1975 compared with the end of 1973, though the rate of growth appears positive as the average for 1972–3 was lower. During the first period (1974–5) most sectors lost employment when massive layoffs of public employees ensued as a result of a combination of a drastic reduction in fiscal expenditures, a stabilization program and the reduction of disguised unemployment generated during the period 1971–3 – the Allende effect.

The 1975–6 recession was a major cause of employment losses in nontradeables and also in agriculture and manufactures, whose output is basically demand determined in the short term. This assertion is supported by the marked reduction in employment that occurred during the second recession (1982–3) in the same sectors. Consequently, liberalization cannot be entirely responsible for the reduction in employment, as some authors have argued (see, in particular, Tokman, 1984).

6 Corbo and Meller (1977) have shown differences in the intensity of factor use of exportables and importables; however, their approach is too aggregated to be useful for our purposes.

Table 5.10 Employment growth (percentage of previous period average)

Sector	*1974–5*	*1976–7*	*1978–9*	*1980–1*	*1982–3*
Tradeables	−4.0	−3.2	3.0	0.3	−13.0
Agriculture	−6.3	7.3	1.1	1.2	−7.2
Mining	0.4	−4.7	−6.3	−7.8	−3.7
Manufactures	−5.9	−7.0	2.2	−0.5	−21.0
Nontradeables[a]	−5.7	−0.1	15.8	12.3	−10.2
Total	−5.0	−1.4	−10.2	7.4	−11.3

[a] Excludes employment in fiscal programs.

Source: Jadresic, 1985

Further, tariffs remained redundant until late 1976 while the real exchange rate rose significantly, so that until then the fall in employment, even in manufactures, could not have resulted from liberalization. What could be argued at best is that trade liberalization did not stimulate employment in manufactures until 1979, and had a negative impact during the remainder of the period, but certainly more modest than at first glance.

At a disaggregated level, trade liberalization initiated a substitution of imported inputs for domestic factors. Since the ratio of value added to value of production fell at an aggregate level, this latter substitution should not reduce the demand for labor, at any rate after the adjustment period. However, when a large deficit in the trade balance takes place, imports of intermediate products may replace corresponding domestic processes, reducing the demand for domestic factors in the short run. The impact of this substitution is estimated for the manufacturing sector (table 5.11). (No similar test was run for other sectors as information was not readily available.)

Methodology The basis of the methodology for measuring the aggregate impact of liberalization on employment is to simulate employment between 1976 and 1981, given an expected path of recovery from the 1975–6 recession, and to compare the values obtained with observed employment; the difference will be assumed to result from liberalization. Since other factors influenced the observed reduction in employment during those years, our simulation results were compared with observed employment levels of 1975, adjusted for the Allende effect and for the impact of the significant reduction in terms of trade, both of which, in different ways, reduced employment.

Table 5.11 Trade liberalization and change in the share of value added in gross value, 1976–1981

Subsectors	*Value-added substitution (%)*
Food products	−0.9
Wood product excluding furniture	−59.2
Beverages	−40.3
Printing and publishing	−8.9
Furniture and wood accessories	−20.6
Basic metal industries	−1.8
Tobacco	−2.7
Petroleum and coal	n.a.
Chemical products	−1.2
Paper and paper products	3.6
Nonmetal minerals	−4.8
Leather and leather products	n.a.
Rubber products	−39.9
Textiles	−22.1
Metal products	−27.1
Nonelectrical and electrical machinery	−10.1
Shoes and clothing	−62.2

n.a., not available.

Source: de la Cuadra and Hachette, 1985, part II, appendix tables B.37, B.58, B.59, and B.65

Basic to the methodology is an estimation of the impact of the recession. On the assumption that liberalization would not have directly affected nontradeables but that the recession and accompanying stabilization plan would, we simulated a path of "normal" development of nontradeables starting in 1974, based on the average growth of this sector between 1960 and 1970. The employment–output elasticity observed during that decade was used to simulate employment. When the results were compared with observed employment in the nontradeables sector, effective employment coincided with simulated employment only in 1979. That recovery took so long is not surprising; the recession was deep, and further efforts to break inflation engendered rather restrictive demand policies. It was then assumed that the annual rate of growth of output of each of the tradeables sector from recession between 1975 and 1979 would be proportional to the growth of output of nontradeables during the same period. The assumption seems tenable since economic recovery from recession should not presuppose any significant change in relative prices and in relative sectoral growth.

Implicit in the methodology, as suggested above, is the presumption that liberalization had no impact on employment in the nontradeables sector, which amounts to using employment in that sector as a numeraire by which the impact of liberalization on employment in tradeables is calculated. This assumption implies an upward bias in our estimate of the impact of liberalization on employment.

The tradeables sector was subdivided into three subsectors: agriculture, mining, and manufactures. A separate simulation of employment was prepared for each, with a common basic methodology (figure 5.1). The common methodology consisted in adjusting the annual growth of each sector between 1975 (the trough of recession) and 1979 (the year in which recession drew to a close) so that each would show a total growth during this period equal to the growth observed for the nontradeables sector. Output growth was then transformed into employment growth by using the relevant sectoral output employment elasticities obtained from the 1960–70 period. The annual change in employment thus calculated was added to the 1975 sectoral employment to obtain the relevant simulated values. In the case of mining and manufacturing, observed employment in 1975 had been corrected for the Allende effect (estimated as employment exceeding what would have been expected during the 1971–3 period on the basis of effective growth of output and normal employment–output elasticities). The agricultural sector did not need this correction because the growth of employment in this sector in the period 1971–3 was not significantly different from the estimation using normal employment–output elasticities.

Elimination of the overemployment due to the Allende effect roughly concided with the initiation of the liberalization period. Thus, had our methodology been applied without this correction, the negative impact of liberalization would have been overestimated. The simulated values were then compared with the observed values between 1976 and 1979; the difference (positive or negative) was taken to be the impact of liberalization. For the period 1980–1, the trend values explained above were compared with the observed values of employment in the same way, and again the difference was taken to be the impact of liberalization. The results are shown in table 5.12.

Table 5.12 Impact of trade liberalization on employment, 1976–1981 (thousands)

Sector	*1976*	*1977*	*1978*	*1979*	*1980*	*1981*
Agriculture	1.2	53.6	84.5	84.7	97.0	104.1
Mining	−1.2	−2.6	−6.9	−6.7	−6.7	−16.6
Manufactures	36.0	9.0	−16.0	−57.0	−57.0	−79.0
Total tradeables	36.0	60.0	61.6	21.0	33.3	8.5

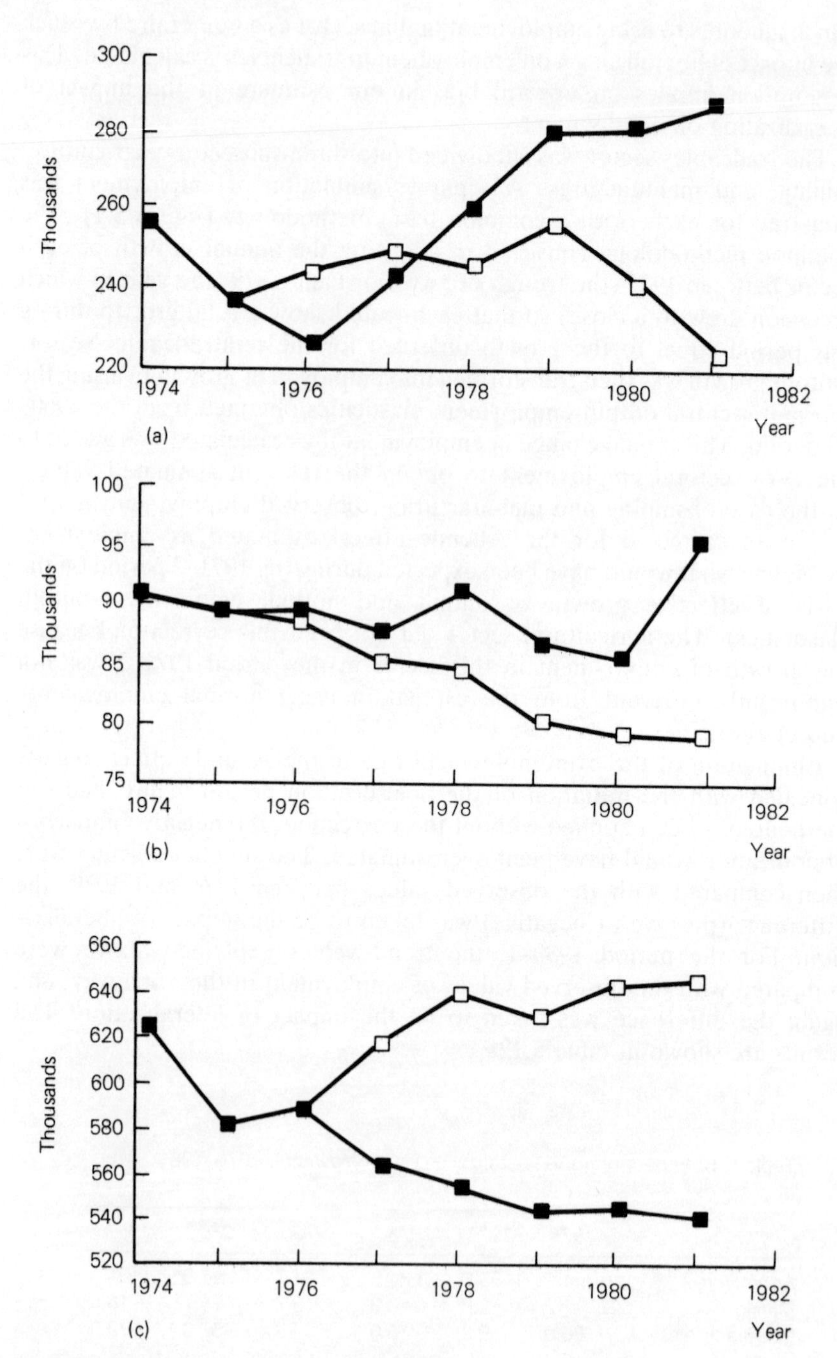

Figure 5.1 Simulated and actual employment in (a) manufactures, (b) mining, and (c) agriculture, 1974–1981: E_N, normal; E_E, effective

The impact of liberalization on employment overall was positive, despite its negative effect on manufactures. Employment in manufactures in 1974 represents 18.5 percent of total employment; the rates for agriculture and mining were 17.5 percent and 3.7 percent respectively. Losses in manufacturing employment were compensated for by gains in agriculture, and until 1977 even in manufacturing itself since tariffs were redundant up to 1976 while the real exchange rate had risen sharply. The results for the mining sector suggesting a negative impact are also misleading: employment in this sector fell primarily because of the severe reduction in personnel at the state-owned coal company – an action unrelated to liberalization efforts – together with significant adjustments in the so-called "small-mining" subsector (*pirquineros*) which is extremely sensitive to the downward trend in the price of copper. The sectoral results (which are analyzed in subsectoral detail separately for manufactures and agriculture below) must be viewed in the general context; taken in isolation they give a contradictory picture.

Sectoral Impacts: Manufacturing and Agriculture

The employment and output impact of trade liberalization on several subsectors of manufacturing and agriculture are analyzed in some detail in this section.

Manufacturing

Methodology The methodological approach employed, as discussed above, was to simulate the time path of production and employment for the various industrial subsectors based on their average rates of growth for 1960–70, adjusted to take into account the deep 1975 recession and the changes in terms of trade during the period of the projections. The resulting time path, including both adjustments, is called the "normal" path. Then, the liberalization impact was measured by the difference between the normal and the observed paths (figure 5.1).

The change in production ΔQ_L due to liberalization has been separated into two components: price effect (static effect) and supply effect (dynamic effect). The first is obtained by combining the change in relative price resulting from tariff reductions and the estimated supply elasticity. The second measures the difference between supply shifts under normal and actual (realized) paths. These effects are represented by the following equation:

$$\underset{\text{total effect}}{\Delta Q_L} = \underset{\text{price effect}}{\Delta Q_L{}^P} + \underset{\text{supply effect}}{\Delta Q_L{}^S} \qquad (5.1)$$

ΔQ_L is calculated as

$$\Delta Q_L(t) = [Q_E(t) - Q_E(t-1)] - [Q_N(t) - Q_N(t-1)]$$

where $Q_N(t)$ is the "normal" production in year t, $Q_E(t)$ is the actual production in year t, and $\Delta Q_L(t)$ is the change in production due to liberalization in year t, and the rate of change is calculated as

$$\frac{\Delta Q_L(t)}{Q_N(t)} \tag{5.2}$$

In the discussion of the results, all changes will be expressed as percentages of "normal" production Q_N.

On the basis of Q_N and the employment–output elasticity for 1960–70, we estimated the normal employment path E_N and compared it with the actual path E_E. The change in employment ΔE_L attributed to liberalization was also split into two effects: a scale and a substitution effect. The same procedure that was used to calculate ΔQ_L is used for calculating ΔE_L, with E_L^φ substituted for $Q_L{}^P$ and $E_L{}^\sigma$ substituted for $Q_L{}^S$. The scale effect estimates changes in employment corresponding to changes in production ΔQ_L, and the substitution effect captures changes in employment arising from variations in factor proportions. In equation form

$$\underset{\text{total effect}}{\Delta E_L} = \underset{\text{scale effect}}{\Delta E_L^\varphi} + \underset{\text{substitution effect}}{\Delta E_L^\varphi} \tag{5.3}$$

The results are presented as percentages of normal employment E_N.

Some comments about the components of the impact on production and employment of equations (5.1) and (5.3) are in order. The price effect $\Delta Q_L{}^P$ is defined as the change in production caused by the change in the relative price of the product in the corresponding sector, and is obtained by using the product's supply-price elasticity. The relative price p in sector j is defined as

$$P_j = \frac{P_j}{P_N} = \frac{1 + t_j}{1 + \omega \bar{t}}$$

and the percentage change between periods $s - 1$ and s is defined as

$$\frac{\mathrm{d}p_j}{p_j} = \left[\frac{1 + t_j}{1 + \omega t}_s - \frac{1 + t_j}{1 + \omega t_{s-1}} \right] \Big/ \frac{1 + t_j}{1 + \omega t}_{s-1}$$

where p_j is the absolute price in sector j, p_n is the price of nontradeables, t_j is the nominal tariff in sector j,ω is the omega factor defined by Sjaastad (1981), and t is the average nominal tariff of all sectors.

Hence our estimate is based on changes in the price of a sector's own tariff change relative to that of the average sectoral tariff rate. The measured changes embody a real exchange rate effect, given by the factor ω. The scale effect ΔE_L^φ of the employment impact measures the change in employment caused by the change in production due to liberalization, independent of changes in technology or in factor proportions that could have been induced by liberalization. The historical relationship between changes in production and employment in each sector was used to determine the required parameters.

The other two components to be obtained, the supply effect $\Delta Q_L{}^S$ in production and the substitution effect $\Delta E_L{}^\sigma$ in employment are more complex in the sense that they might have been caused by several simultaneous forces. The supply effect could be the result of changes in the size and number of firms in the sector, factor productivity (new technology), product composition, prices of productive factors, and so on. The identification of the relative importance of each influence is not possible at the level of aggregation used here. Only the magnitude and the direction of the resultant aggregate supply effect will be reported, since they shed some light on the size of the adjustment undertaken by different sectors.

Like the supply effect, the substitution among factors of production as a component of the employment impact, as measured here, may also have a number of different causes: changes in technology, production scale, size of firms, composition of products, and the like. The specific impact of each factor is not susceptible to separate measurement, but it would be interesting to assess the relative, although global, contribution of each to employment and output changes.

The methodology used has several limitations, the main one being the implicit assumption that the vector of variables affecting production and employment during the decade of the 1960s carries over reasonably well into the 1970s.[7] (We have corrected the vector, however, by two quite important events which occurred in the 1970s: the 1975 recession and the changes in the terms of trade.) This limitation is less serious when applied to large aggregates, such as total production or total employment in the manufacturing sector, than when applied to subsectors.

Impact on manufacturing output   The two initial years of the liberalization process, 1974 and 1975, are not important from the viewpoint of tariff reductions because that period was confined to reducing tariff redundancy (see chapter 4). The picture of those years is also confused by the 1975 recession. To appreciate the effects of liberalization, therefore, we concentrate here on the subsequent subperiods 1976–7, 1978–9, and 1980–1, defined earlier as the second stage, the third stage, and (since the tariff reform was completed by June 1979) the post-liberalization period respectively (see table 5.7). The results are as follows:

7 To the extent that the "normal" growth of manufactures during the 1960s was influenced by growing protection (see the index of liberalization shown in figure 1.1), estimates of the negative impact of liberalization during the 1970s will be biased upwards. This point should be recalled when the results are interpreted.

1 Manufacturing output was reduced by 20.4 percent between 1975 and 1979 (table 5.13). When the period is extended to include the two post-liberalization years (1975–81) the reduction reached 24.1 percent.

Table 5.13 Impact of trade liberalization on manufacturing production: total effect by subperiod (percent)

Subsector	*Stage 2* *1976–7*	*Stage 3* *1978–9*	*1976–9*	*Post-liberalization* *1980–1*	*1976–81*
Food products	30.1	−0.3	25.9	12.0	13.1
Beverages	−4.3	−17.2	−20.6	8.5	27.8
Tobacco	5.3	−19.7	−15.5	−17.6	−31.6
Textiles	−29.3	−24.1	−44.7	−10.7	−51.2
Shoes and clothing	−26.4	−25.0	−44.6	−28.0	−69.0
Wood and wood products	40.2	3.6	32.6	−32.2	0.2
Furniture	−2.8	64.2	61.7	31.7	93.8
Paper and paper products	−9.8	23.6	14.8	−4.5	10.1
Printing and publishing	3.2	−15.1	−12.7	4.6	−8.0
Chemicals	−11.4	−10.3	−18.8	1.2	−16.8
Rubber products	−11.1	−49.5	−55.1	−20.7	−69.2
Nonmetal mineral products	−24.5	−10.5	−27.9	17.9	−10.3
Basic metal industry	−49.6	−20.0	−53.9	−8.1	−53.0
Metal products	−39.0	−39.1	−64.7	−3.7	−62.2
Electrical and nonelectrical machinery	−35.7	−33.7	−58.7	19.0	−34.1
Others	−15.2	−17.0	−28.4	−8.0	−34.4
Manufacturing	−8.9	−13.6	−20.4	−4.7	−24.1

Source: de la Cuadra and Hachette, 1988, appendix table A.67

2 The impact was larger during the third stage than during the second (− 13.6 percent and − 8.9 percent respectively), and small during the post-liberalization years (− 4.7 percent).

3 Although tariffs remained at a 10 percent level throughout the post-liberalization period, liberalization still appears to have had a negative impact on output. Reasons for this include a possible lagged effect of trade liberalization on manufacturing production, inflation running at an average rate of 27 percent with the exchange rate fixed in nominal terms, and rapidly growing real wages. The last two reasons led to a change in the relative price of tradeables to nontradeables during 1980 and 1981, which could explain more than the 4.7 percent reduction in manufacturing output, implying high productivity increases for this sector.

4 During trade liberalization the price effect exceeds the total effect (− 29.9 percent versus − 20.4 percent) as import competition had a positive dynamic influence – higher productivity (table 5.14). The pace of

Table 5.14 Impact of trade liberalization on manufacturing production: total, price, and supply effects by subperiod (percent)

	Stage 2 1976–7			*Stage 3 1978–9*			*Post-liberalization 1980–1*		
Subsector	*Total effect*	*Price effect*	*Supply effect*	*Total effect*	*Price effect*	*Supply effect*	*Total effect*	*Price effect*	*Supply effect*
Food products	30.1	2.1[a]	28.0	−0.3	0.6	−0.9	−12.0	7.8	−19.8
Beverages	−4.3	−1.1	−3.2	−17.2	−1.6	−15.6	−8.5	−5.6	−2.9
Tobacco	5.3	−0.8	6.1	−19.7	−0.4	−19.3	−17.6	−5.6	−12.0
Textiles	−29.3	−27.8	−1.5	−24.1	−58.5	34.3	−10.7	−76.4	65.7
Shoes and clothing	−26.4	−16.5	−9.9	−25.0	−32.5	7.5	−28.0	−39.5	11.5
Wood and wood products	40.2	−17.0	57.2	3.6	−4.4	8.0	−32.2	−61.9	29.7
Furniture	−2.8	−17.0	14.2	64.2	−4.4	68.6	31.7	−61.9	93.6
Paper and paper products	−9.8	−20.4	10.6	23.6	−17.1	40.7	−4.5	−61.9	57.4
Printing and publishing	3.2	−8.1	11.3	−15.1	−28.9	13.8	4.6	−61.9	66.5
Chemicals	−11.4	−30.4	19.0	−10.3	−9.2	−1.1	1.2	−65.7	66.9
Rubber products	−11.1	−12.6	1.5	−49.5	−7.9	−41.6	−20.7	−65.7	45.0
Nonmetal mineral products	−24.5	−28.1	3.6	−10.5	−19.8	9.3	17.9	−71.6	89.5
Basic metal industry	−49.6	−25.9	−23.7	−20.0	−20.1	0.1	−8.1	−96.2	88.1
Metal products	−39.0	−35.0	−4.0	−39.1	−73.6	34.5	−3.7	−96.2	92.5
Electrical and nonelectrical machinery	−35.7	−37.7	2.0	−33.7	−35.3	1.6	19.0	−75.7	94.7
Others	−15.2	n.a.	n.a.	−17.0	n.a.	n.a.	−8.0	n.a.	n.a.
Manufacturing	−8.9	−14.2	5.3	−13.6	−15.7	2.1	−4.7	−40.9	36.2

n.a., not available.

[a] Coeymans' (1978b) estimates of price elasticity have a negative sign.

Source: de la Cuadra and Hachette, 1988, appendix A.67

the price effect is similar in the second and third stages and overshoots (that is, goes the "wrong" way) during post-liberalization, probably because of the large appreciation in the domestic currency.

5 The supply, or dynamic, effect is positive in the three subperiods (table 5.14) and very large during post-liberalization (36.2 percent). These results are interesting. Firstly, they suggest that, during the liberalization period, firms adjusted to augmented import competition by increasing productivity. Secondly, the very large and positive supply effect during post-liberalization suggests that all adjustments carried out by firms during the liberalization period may have had a significant impact on manufacturing productivity; in fact, this supply effect nearly compensated for the negative pressures on production stemming from the appreciation of the real exchange rate and the increase in real wages.

6 Trade liberalization also had a strong impact on the composition of manufacturing production (table 5.15). The importable subsectors suffered a very large cut in production: the six subsectors in this category experienced a negative impact ranging from − 64.7 percent (metal products) to − 27.9 percent (nonmetal mineral products). Of the three subsectors in the mixed importables and exportables category, two show results consistent with their mixes. The chemicals subsector, which is more importable than exportable (the trade ratios are 0.41 and 0.22 respectively), saw production reduced by 18.8 percent; paper and paper products, which is more exportable (the ratios are 0.10 for imports and 0.49 for exports), increased its production by 14.8 percent. The third subsector in this category, basic metal industries, appeared to suffer a large negative impact (− 53.9 percent). This result is explained by the very high rate of increase in production during the 1960s, which averaged 11.7 percent per year.[8] The exportable subsectors (wood and wood products and food products) increased their production as expected with relatively large supply effects. Four subsectors are included in the "domestic" category; of these, only furniture benefited from a positive impact on production, which was the highest impact of all positively affected subsectors.

7 Reduced production in the importable subsectors was largely determined by the price effect. Among importables, two of the six subsectors (rubber products, and shoes and clothing) reduced their supplies. This result suggests that foreign competition was an important spur to productivity. Supply increased in two of the three mixed importable–exportable subsectors, quite significantly in the more exportable paper and paper

8 The average was estimated only for the period starting in 1960 and ending in 1967, as production stepped up significantly between 1968 and 1970 to an extent that could be considered a "normal" long-term trend.

Table 5.15 Impact of trade liberalization on manufacturing production by type of product, 1976–1979

Product	*Import, export ratios*[a]	*Total effect (%)*	*Supply effect (%)*
Importables			
Electrical and nonelectrical machinery	(2.05)	−58.7	3.6
Metal products	(0.45)	−64.7	30.5
Textiles	(0.22)	−44.7	32.9
Rubber products	(0.20)	−55.1	−40.1
Nonmetal mineral products	(0.14)	−27.9	12.9
Shoes and clothing	(0.13)	−44.6	−2.4
Importables–exportables			
Chemicals	(0.41; 0.22)	−18.8	17.9
Basic metal industries	(0.19; 0.19)	−53.9	−23.6
Paper and paper products	(0.10; 0.49)	14.8	51.3
Exportables			
Wood and wood products	(0.34)	32.6	65.2
Food products	(0.11)	25.9	27.1
Domestic			
Tobacco	(0.02; 0.00)	−15.5	−13.2
Beverages	(0.03; 0.06)	−20.6	−18.8
Furniture	(0.01; 0.01)	61.7	82.8
Printing and publishing	(0.05; 0.02)	−12.7	25.1

The figures in parentheses are estimated values.
[a] When two ratios are presented, the import ratio appears first.

Source: import and export ratios, de la Cuadra and Hachette, 1985, part II, appendix tables B.39 and B.44; total effect and supply effect, de la Cuadra and Hachette, 1988, appendix tables A.9, A.67, and A.68

products industry. The two exportable subsectors showed high supply increases: 65.2 percent in wood and wood products and 27.1 percent in food products. Two of the four domestic subsectors augmented their supply, in the case of furniture by the highest percentage of all manufacturing subsectors (82.8 percent).

Two conclusions arise from these results: trade liberalization has had a significant impact on the productivity of the manufacturing sector; the production impact of liberalization was important and negative in those subsectors which enjoyed the highest nominal tariff protection when the process of liberalization was initiated, while the effect was positive and large in those subsectors with the lower initial tariffs (table 5.16).

Table 5.16 Impact of trade liberalization on manufacturing production (1976–1979) in relation to nominal tariffs (1976): rankings

Subsector	*Production impact (%)*	*Nominal tariff (%)*	*Production impact ranking*	*Tariff ranking*
Metal products	– 64.7	45	1	2
Electrical and nonelectrical machinery	– 58.7	40	2	4
Rubber products	– 55.1	38	3	5
Basic metal industries	– 53.9	30	4	9
Textiles	– 44.7	46	5	1
Shoes and clothing	– 44.6	44	5	3
Nonmetal mineral products	– 27.9	33	7	7
Beverages	– 20.6	29	8	10
Chemicals	– 18.8	34	9	6
Tobacco	– 15.5	23	10	15
Printing and publishing	– 12.7	33	11	7
Paper and paper products	14.8	29	12	10
Food products	25.9	26	13	14
Wood and wood products	32.6	27	14	12
Furniture	61.7	27	15	12

Spearman rank correlation coefficient is 0.7821 (99% confidence level).

Source: de la Cuadra and Hachette, 1988, appendix tables A.9 and A.67

Impact on manufacturing employment: the results

1 Figure 5.1(a) shows manufacturing activities, excluding those activities that are closer to services than to manufacturing such as repairs of different kinds.

Meller's figures for the liberalization period (1974–9) do not differ significantly from Jadresic's data. They show that actual employment in 1979 was the same as in 1974. Since the sector was able to regain its pre-recession employment level, it could be argued that import competition did not harm employment in manufactures, and the employment contraction in 1974–5 was due only to recession. This interpretation of the figures could be considered a minimum estimate of the impact of the trade liberalization on employment in manufactures.

A comparison of E_E with E_N by the end of the liberalization period (1979), however, indicates a negative impact of the tariff reduction. Meller's figures show employment in that year as 8.6 percent lower than "normal" (see table 5.17); Jadresic's corresponding figure is 10.4 percent. This alternative interpretation – that is, basing the estimation on a comparison of effective employment with the historical trend – could be considered the upper limit for estimating the employment impact. Since, because of incomplete information, our projection of E_N did not account

Table 5.17 Impact of trade liberalization on manufacturing employment: total effect by subperiod (percent)

Subsector	*Stage 2* *1976–7*	*Stage 3* *1978–9*	*1976–9*	*Post-liberalization* *1980–1*	*1976–81*
Food products	21.6	−8.5	12.1	−7.8	4.0
Beverages	0.5	18.6	19.0	−20.4	−1.5
Tobacco	−39.7	10.4	−19.7	8.3	−21.5
Textiles	−12.6	−15.8	−26.5	−25.0	−50.3
Shoes and clothing	−4.9	24.1	19.2	−18.3	1.0
Wood and wood products	−1.3	49.4	50.6	−31.5	19.1
Furniture	−13.0	30.8	18.3	5.4	23.7
Paper and paper products	23.6	−35.7	−15.1	0.3	−14.5
Printing and publishing	28.0	−7.1	15.5	−8.0	7.4
Chemicals	29.3	−4.2	18.1	−11.9	5.4
Rubber products	20.2	−50.6	−39.5	−17.5	−53.0
Nonmetal mineral products	57.8	−43.3	−11.7	−17.8	−29.6
Basic metal industry	0.9	−26.1	−25.3	−25.9	−50.1
Metal products	−6.3	3.5	−2.3	−12.4	−14.7
Electrical and nonelectrical machinery	−8.6	−42.8	−49.1	−5.1	−50.1
Others	−6.3	−40.0	−44.8	−10.9	−52.9
Industry	−2.5	−10.8	−8.6	−14.0	−22.4
	1.9[a]	−12.1[a]	−10.4[a]	−3.9[a]	−14.0[a]

Changes in employment for each stage were calculated with respect to the year previous to the stage.
[a] According to data from Jadresic (1986).

Source: de la Cuadra and Hachette, 1988, appendix table A.68

for the negative investment in the manufacturing sector in the years 1973–5, the result is probably an overestimation.

Actual employment is higher than normal in 1976 because firms, with the upturn in the economy in 1976, held off dismissal of superfluous workers to avoid costs of recontracting them later. For the post-liberalization years E_E is lower than E_N. Why did employment behave that way when tariffs were no longer being reduced? One explanation is that liberalization had a delayed effect on employment.

While this is true, other variables are also important in explaining why actual employment was less than normal. The most significant of these was the change in relative prices during 1980 and 1981 and particularly in real wages. Wages increased in US dollar terms by 90 percent between 1979 and 1981.[9]

9 The reduction in the real exchange rate is a roundabout way of expressing an increase in real wages in US dollars, since the most relevant price of nontradeables is the price of its least mobile factor of production. In fact, real wages increased by only 26 percent during the same period, when deflated by the GDP deflator. This is still a higher percentage but it can be explained by a combination of a low base (the real wage was lower in 1979 than in 1970) and significant increases in productivity illustrated in this section.

2 Increased real wages during post liberalization should have reduced demand for labor, in particular by stimulating labor-saving technological changes. This presumption is confirmed by the results presented in table 5.18. The substitution effect during the post-liberalization period amounts to −11.6 percent, representing 83 percent of the total employment effect. The adverse effect on employment during this period can thus be explained almost entirely by changes in relative prices, while tariffs for possible delayed effects, played virtually no part.

3 For manufacturing as a whole, the impact of liberalization on employment was positive but small (2.5 percent) in the period 1975–7 and negative (−10.8 percent) in the years 1977–9. The positive result was explained in point 1 above (table 5.17).

4 Two thirds of the total effect on employment is explained by the scale effect during 1977–9. This result suggests that the changes in technology were significant in explaining the difference during the last stage of liberalization.

5 The employment impacts of trade liberalization differ substantially among subsectors. (Since the following comments refer to the subsectors and the scale effect is proportional to the overall production impact already discussed, we discuss substitution effect only.) Therefore liberalization implied an important change in the composition of employment within the industrial sector. For the period 1975–9, the impact was positive for seven subsectors and negative for nine (table 5.19).

6 A very striking result is that the effect on employment fluctuates for 13 of the 16 subsectors. Within the stages of liberalization a monotonically negative impact appears in only three of the 16 subsectors. This result (summarized in table 5.20) illustrates a separate aspect of the phenomenon of labor reallocation, making it a two-dimensional problem: firstly among subsectors in a given period, and secondly within any given subsector between periods. This second type of reallocation could be explained by factors that influence the sectors' factor intensity, such as changes in technology, firm size, composition of production, and so on. This explanation is consistent with the fact that a similar pattern of ups and downs was not found when the impact of liberalization on output was analyzed.

7 Although in the aggregate the substitution effect explains only one third of the total effect, it is nonetheless important and acts in a different direction at the subsectoral level (table 5.21), suggesting the influence of many factors which combine to produce this effect, while operating with differing intensity and direction among subsectors and over time. As mentioned before, such factors may include changes in technology, firm size, composition of production, and so on.

Table 5.18 Impact of trade liberalization on manufacturing employment: total, scale, and substitution effect by subperiod (percent)

	Stage 2 1976–7			*Stage 3 1978–9*			*Post-liberalization 1980–1*		
Subsector	*Total effect*	*Price effect*	*Supply effect*	*Total effect*	*Price effect*	*Supply effect*	*Total effect*	*Price effect*	*Supply effect*
Food products	21.6	20.8	0.8	−8.5	−0.2	−8.3	−7.8	−8.3	0.5
Beverages	0.5	−0.6	1.1	18.6	−2.6	21.2	−20.4	−1.3	−19.1
Tobacco	−39.7	−0.2	−39.5	10.4	0.8	9.6	8.3	0.7	7.6
Textiles	−12.6	−13.2	0.6	−15.8	−10.8	−5.0	−25.0	−4.8	−20.2
Shoes and clothing	−4.9	1.6	−6.5	24.1	1.5	22.6	−18.3	1.7	−20.0
Wood and wood products	−1.3	1.6	−2.9	49.4	0.1	49.3	−31.5	−1.3	−30.2
Furniture	−13.0	−1.1	−11.9	30.8	26.3	4.5	5.4	13.0	−7.6
Paper and paper products	23.6	−13.0	36.6	−35.7	31.4	−67.1	0.3	−6.0	6.3
Printing and publishing	28.0	2.5	25.5	−7.1	−11.8	4.7	−8.0	3.6	−11.6
Chemicals	29.3	−10.6	39.9	−4.2	−9.6	5.4	−11.9	1.1	−13.0
Rubber products	20.2	−9.3	29.5	−50.6	−41.6	−9.0	−17.5	−17.4	−0.1
Nonmetal mineral products	57.8	−46.1	103.9	−43.3	−19.7	−23.6	−17.8	33.6	−51.7
Basic metal industry	0.9	−11.9	12.8	−26.1	−4.8	−21.3	−25.9	−1.9	−24.0
Metal products	−6.3	−6.6	0.3	3.5	−6.6	10.1	−12.4	−0.6	−11.8
Electrical and nonelectrical machinery	−8.6	−30.3	21.7	−42.8	−28.6	−14.2	−5.1	16.2	−21.3
Others	6.3	−13.7	7.4	−40.0	−15.3	−24.7	−10.9	7.2	−18.1
Industry	2.5	−4.6	7.1	−10.8	−7.1	−3.7	−14.0	−2.4	−11.6
	1.9[a]	−4.6[a]	6.5[a]	−12.1[a]	−7.1[a]	−5.0[a]	−3.9[a]	−2.4[a]	−1.5[a]

Changes in employment for each stage were calculated with respect to the year previous to the stage.
[a] Calculated using data from Jadresic (1986).
Source: de la Cuadra and Hachette, 1988, appendix A.68

Table 5.19 Impact of trade liberalization on employment: total effect 1975–1979 (percent)

Subsector	*Positive impact*	*Subsector*	*Negative impact*
Wood and wood products	50.6	Electrical and nonelectrical machinery	−49.1
Furniture	18.3	Others	−44.8
Shoes and clothing	19.2	Rubber products	−39.5
Beverages	19.0	Tobacco	−29.7
Chemicals	18.1	Textiles	−26.7
Printing and publishing	15.5	Basic metal industries	−25.3
Food products	12.1	Paper and paper products	−15.1
		Nonmetal minerals	−11.7
		Metal products	−2.3

Source: de la Cuadra and Hachette, 1988, appendix table A.68

Table 5.20 Employment impact on manufacturing subsectors: total effect

Number of subsectors	*1976–7*	*1978–9*
8	+	−
5	−	+
3	−	−

Table 5.21 Impact of trade liberalization on employment: substitution effect, 1975–1979 (percent)

Ranking subsector	
Labor for capital	
1 Nonmetal minerals	80.3
2 Wood and wood products	46.4
3 Chemicals	45.3
4 Printing and publishing	30.2
5 Beverages	22.3
6 Rubber products	20.5
7 Shoes and clothing	16.1
8 Metal products	10.4
9 Electrical and nonelectrical machinery	7.5
Capital for labor	
1 Paper and paper products	−30.5
2 Tobacco	−29.9
3 Basic metal industries	−8.5
4 Food products	−7.5
5 Furniture	−7.4
6 Textiles	−4.4

Substitution effects for the subperiods 1975–7 and 1977–9 were added to obtain the substitution effect for the whole period.
Source: de la Cuadra and Hachette, appendix table A.68

Table 5.22 Impact of trade liberalization on manufacturing employment by type of product, 1975–1979 (percent)

Product	*Import, export ratios*[a]	*Total effect*	*Substitution effect*
Importables			
Electrical and nonelectrical machinery	(2.05)	−49.1	7.5
Metal products	(0.45)	−2.3	10.4
Textiles	(0.22)	−26.5	−4.4
Rubber products	(0.20)	−39.5	20.5
Nonmetal mineral products	(0.14)	−11.7	80.3
Shoes and clothing	(0.13)	19.2	16.1
Importables–exportables			
Chemicals	(0.41; 0.22)	18.1	45.3
Basic metal industries	(0.19; 0.19)	−25.3	−8.5
Paper and paper products	(0.10; 0.49)	−15.1	−30.5
Exportables			
Wood and wood products	(0.34)	50.6	46.4
Food products	(0.11)	12.1	−7.5
Domestic			
Tobacco	(0.02; 0.00)	−29.7	−29.9
Beverages	(0.03; 0.06)	19.0	22.3
Furniture	(0.01; 0.01)	18.3	−7.4
Printing and publishing	(0.05; 0.02)	15.5	30.2

The figures in parentheses are estimated values.
[a] When two ratios are presented, the import ratio appears first.
Source: import and export ratios, de la Cuadra and Hachette, 1985, part II; total effect and substitution effect, de la Cuadra and Hachette, 1988, appendix table A.68

8 As expected, liberalization reduced employment in the importable subsectors. The impact is strong, ranging from − 2 to − 49 percent (table 5.22). An exception is shoes and clothing, for which employment increased by 19 percent. Although employment overall fell in the importable sectors, they became more labor intensive with liberalization; that is, they substituted labor for capital to compete more efficiently with imports. Of the six subsectors, only textiles became more capital intensive. This may be the result of a change in the composition in the subsector and of the considerable obsolescence in its productive capacity at the outset of liberalization. No detailed information is available to confirm this hypothesis.

9 Employment increased in the two exportable subsectors, in one of them (wood products) very substantially (51 percent). For food products, a

negative substitution effect reduced the impact. Employment increased for only one of the three mixed importables–exportables subsectors, but for three of the four domestic subsectors.

An important conclusion arising from these results is that the liberalization impact on industrial employment was positive within the exportable and domestic subsectors and negative in the importable subsectors.

Agriculture

Impact on Agricultural Production Estimates of the impact of liberalization on agricultural employment in the aggregate were presented in the first part of this chapter; since lack of data precludes pursuing the issue at the subsectoral level, we refer here only to the effects on production.

The main impact of liberalization policies on agricultural production was to change its composition, favoring, as expected, the exportable subsectors: fruit, vegetables, and forestry. The more important features of this subsector's development during and immediately after the second liberalization episode[10] (1974–9 and 1980–1) were as follows.

1 The rate of growth was lower than for the economy as a whole (table 5.23). Although higher than during the previous period (1965–70), this rate of growth was lower than the authorities had expected, given their working assumption that liberalization was likely to promote agricultural growth.

Table 5.23 Agricultural production (percent)

	Average annual growth	
Measure of production	*1965–70*	*1974–81*
GDP	5.7	5.5
Agriculture value added[a]	2.1	2.6
Sectors' gross value of sectoral production[b]		
Crops	– 1.9	0.7
Livestock	5.9	3.5
Wine	– 3.9	0.9
Vegetables	11.5	1.0
Fruits	n.a.	4.9

n.a., not available.

The rates of growth are estimated between two-year averages to lessen the impact of weather conditions on agricultural production.

[a] Includes forestry.

[b] Detailed information on forestry is not available.

Source: Cox, 1983

10 Detailed information is not available for the first episode of liberation.

2 The increased rate of growth over the previous decade may still look like a success for liberalization policies, given that the period 1965–70 was characterized by generous direct government support to that sector while the liberalization period saw this support removed. However, reality is not that simple. During trade liberalization, markets and institutions related to the support of agriculture were privatized, property rights to land were confirmed, and land could be more freely sold. All these made for reshuffled property rights, which probably improved resource allocation though not necessarily income distribution. Although it is true that subsidized credit to agriculture was eliminated (in 1977), it is equally true that lowered protection for several products – the protection for others increased with liberalization – was offset by a price-stabilization fund (*poderes compradores*) for wheat, maize, rice, and oilseeds up to 1977 (and for milk products, meat, wool, and even poultry, beans, onions, and potatoes in some years). In addition, maximum and minimum prices for wheat, oilseeds, and sugarbeet were in place up to 1980 to reduce the impact of external price variability. Consequently, agriculture's higher rate of growth in the late 1970s compared with the 1960s can be solely attributed to the combination of policies favoring agriculture, some of which in fact delayed the expected adverse effects of liberalization on products such as cereals and cattle.

3 The apparent success of cattle raising during liberalization is in fact the result of the virtual ban, since 1980, on the import of cattle as part of a program to eliminate foot-and-mouth disease. This activity should therefore properly be classified under nontradeables, at least for the period concerned.

4 Forestry growth accelerated during the period 1975–81 owing to favorable external market conditions and a planting effort (table 5.24) stimulated by DL 701 (1974) and DFL 2565 (1979) which considerably increased existing subsidization of planting costs. The process of planting was also transferred from the Consejo Nacional Forestal (CONAF, National Forestry Council) a public institution, to the private sector, which by 1980 was responsible for over 90 percent of that activity.

5 Nevertheless, liberalization affected the composition of agriculture in stimulating exportables (see table 5.6).

Sustainability

The duration of trade liberalization alone is not a sufficient measure of its sustainability; more significant are the strength of opposing forces and the policy's capacity to withstand them.

Table 5.24 Composition of agricultural production

	Pre-liberalization	Liberalization			Post-liberalization
	1965–70	1974–5	1976–7	1978–9	1980–1
Agriculture (% GDP)[a]	8.8	9.0	9.3	8.1	7.6
Sector (% of agriculture gross value of production)					
Crops	36.4	32.1	34.1	31.3	29.0
Livestock	47.6	45.9	42.0	43.1	49.2
Wine	5.6	5.6	6.2	6.0	5.1
Vegetables	10.5	10.5	11.7	13.0	9.7
Fruits	n.a.	6.0	6.1	6.6	6.9
Forestry, average annual planting (thousand hectares)	22.2	69.4	100.5	65.5	82.9

[a] Agriculture value added as percentage of GDP. Agriculture here includes wood.

Source: Central Bank of Chile, *Indicatores Económicos y Sociales*, 1960–82; Cox, 1983

Opposing Pressures

During the six and a half years that have elapsed since the implementation of liberalization (completed in June 1979) the policy has been subjected to strong attacks. Apart from a few concessions which have not, in our view, affected the fundamentals, the trade liberalization policy appears to have successfully resisted these pressures.

The principally external pressure that the policy has had to contend with came from the international recession that began in 1980. The effects, which were transmitted to the Chilean economy through reduced demand for its exports, increased international interest rates, and a liquidity squeeze in international financial markets (table 5.25), were profound: the GDP plunged, unemployment jumped from 11.2 percent in 1980 to 23.7 percent in 1982, and the economy had to reduce consumption and investment appreciably in order to adjust its current account deficit (table 5.26).

Not surprisingly, the 1982 recession eroded the government's political power. High unemployment and reduced real wages substantially weakened the political base; bankruptcies and high indebtedness made a rift between the entrepreneurial community and the executive branch. The repercussions were felt in internal pressures brought to bear against the policy: workers and entrepreneurs saw in the political weakness of the government an opportunity to regain privileges and franchises lost during liberalization; officials sought to exploit this vulnerability to rebuild their own political support. At the same time, commercial policies being

Table 5.25 External shocks

Year	*Terms of trade, first semester (index 1980 = 100)*	*LIBOR 180 days year average (%)*	*Net foreign debt (million US$)*	*Net change of debt (million US$)*
1980	100.0	14.2	7,010	—
1981	84.3	16.7	11,768	4,758
1982	80.4	13.4	14,576	2,808
1983	87.5	9.9	15,408	832
1984	83.2	11.2	16,821	1,413
1985	78.5	8.6	18,089[a]	1,268

—, not applicable; LIBOR, London interbank offering rate.
[a] Projected.
Source: Central Bank of Chile, *Boletín Mensual*, various years

Table 5.26 Gross domestic product, unemployment, and current account, 1980–1985

Year	*GDP (% change)*	*Unemployment (%)*	*Deficit in current account (million US$)*
1980	8.1	11.2	1,971
1981	5.5	12.4	4,733
1982	−14.1	23.7	2,304
1983	−0.7	22.5	1,117
1984	6.3	18.8	2,060
1985	2.4[a]	16.3[a]	1,307[a]

[a] Projected.
Source: Central Bank of Chile, *Boletín Mensual*, various years

adopted by trading partners facing their own foreign currency shortages had been revitalizing internal protectionist pressure. Consequently, entrepreneurial organizations such as the Production and Trade Confederation, the Manufacturers Development Association (SOFOFA), the Asociación Industrial Metal-Mecánica (ASIMET, Metal Mechanics Industrial Association), and the Sociedad Nacional de Agricultura (SNA, Agriculture Association) campaigned to protect their markets from foreign competition.

Changes in Trade Liberalization Policies

In the face of these considerable pressures for renewed protection, the actual changes in trade policies made since liberalization seem remarkably moderate. The tariff policy since June 1979 has been subject to two types of modification: the application of countervailing (discriminatory) duties, and changes in the level of the uniform tariff. The idea of a uniform tariff has been maintained ever since 1979; the only deviations are for the application of surcharges in agreement with the GATT Code of Compensatory Duties and commerce within the framework of ALADI.

The GATT Code, allowing the imposition of discriminatory duties on imports from certain countries without danger of retaliation, had been signed by Chile in 1979. It became legally binding only in 1981 (Ministry of Foreign Affairs Decree 300) when commercial policies of other countries contending with recession made it a relevant mechanism for protecting markets from imports subsidized in their countries of origin and from alleged dumping.

Surcharges

According to the GATT Code, a signer country can apply a compensatory duty to imports which have been subsidized by the exporting country, following a pre-established procedure which it is unnecessary to describe in detail here. However, it so happens that in the history of GATT, there has not been a single case in which a small country has been able to apply a compensatory duty on imports from a large country, because it does not have the "power" to do so. For example, when Chile intended to levy compensatory duties on a limited number of imports from Brazil, the pressures against doing so at diplomatic levels were such that the GATT mechanism did not work. For this reason, Chile had to use general surcharges, that do not discriminate among countries, instead of GATT's compensatory duties.

The application of surcharges, beginning in November 1982, was firmly restricted to a few products with a limit such that the basic tariff plus the surcharge did not exceed 35 percent. Surcharges were levied on 15 products in 1982 and 1983, and on four products in 1984; a few were eliminated later on so that, as of 1986, 16 products were under the system (table 5.27).

From the initiation of the system in November 1981 until December 1984, the authorities received 123 requests reporting subsidized imports, 60 of which were disallowed on grounds of insufficient supporting information. Of the 63 cases investigated, 35 were granted a surcharge (though in one case the recommendation was not enforced). In sum, the application of surcharges has not so far opened the door to general tariff increases.

Movements in the Uniform Tariff

The uniform 10 percent tariff established in June 1979 remained unaltered until June 1983, when it was increased to 20 percent. When the Minister of Finance announced this change of policy, he offered to establish a

Table 5.27 Surcharges applied

Product	*Initial surcharge (%)*	*Surcharge as of Sep 1984 (%)*	*Surcharge as of Dec 1986 (%)*	*Date of enforcement*
1 Preserved fish	16	15	—	12 Nov 82
2 Matches	12	15	5	12 Nov 82
3 Condensed milk	18	10	—	4 Nov 82
4 Leather footwear	18	15	—	12 Nov 82
5 Wool fabrics	10	15	9	12 Nov 82
6 Cement	21	15	—	12 Nov 82
7 Fabric for bags	16	15	6	12 Nov 82
8 Cotton yarn	15	15	—	12 Nov 82
9 Aluminum	20	15	—	12 Nov 82
10 Powdered milk	28	15	15	12 Nov 82
11 Butter	16	15	15	12 Nov 82
12 Cheese	12	15	15	12 Nov 82
13 Water meters	22	15	—	12 Nov 82
14 Acrylic yarn	15	15	—	12 Nov 82
15 Cotton fabrics	20	15	6	12 Nov 82
16 Continuous filament yarn	15	15	—	8 Jan 83
17 Clothing	15	15	5	8 Jan 83
18 Toys	4	15	—	15 Mar 83
19 Cookies	10	15	—	15 Mar 83
20 Propylene bags	23	15	—	15 Apr 83
21 Beverage bottles	6	15	—	28 Apr 83
22 Flat glass	7	15	10	28 Apr 83
23 Corduroy fabrics	15	15	8	20 Jul 83
24 Tires	15	15	8	28 Sep 83
25 Wheat flour	15	15	15	28 Sep 83
26 Towels	15	15	5	5 Nov 83
27 Candies	15	15	—	9 Dec 83
28 Rugs and carpets	15	15	5	9 Dec 83
29 Bed sheets	15	15	7	9 Dec 83
30 Steel cables	15	15	—	9 Dec 83
31 Refrigerators	15	15	—	9 Apr 84
32 Floor polishers	15	15	—	9 Apr 84
33 Blenders	15	15	—	9 Apr 84
34 Metal gabions	15	15	0	3 Aug 84
35 Single-phase electric meters	—	—	6	28 Jun 86
36 Domestic textile appliances	—	—	5	28 Jun 86

—, not applicable.

Source: Central Bank of Chile, *Boletín Mensual*

timetable for returning to the 10 percent tariff, citing in defense of this change "only the temporary necessity to increase tax revenues." It was also explained that tariff differentiation was rejected because of "the damage it would cause to a correct allocation of resources" (Central Bank, *Boletín Mensual*, June 1983).

Six months later (December 1983) the same Minister announced the decision of the government "to maintain the tariff at the 20 percent level, and not to reduce it to 10 percent by the end of 1985, as had been the original purpose" (Central Bank, *Boletín Mensual*, December 1983). The authorities intended by this means to reconcile the exigencies of higher tax collection that had originally been used to justify the change in tariff, with the adaptations to the 20 percent level already carried out by producers and investors.

In September 1984, a new Minister of Finance decided to increase the uniform tariff from 20 to 35 percent, and at the same time to devalue the domestic currency by 23.6 percent. The authorities justified the tariff increase cum devaluation as "a way to impede a deterioration of the external sector and the consequent loss in reserves and fiscal disequilibrium, not financeable without Balance of Payment problems and/or inflation" (Central Bank, 1984, p. 44).

These new policies were received with disapproval by a large section of the population, including most manufacturers. Thus the tariff reduction announced by the new Minister of Finance in February 1985 was well received (Central Bank, *Boletín Mensual* 684, February 1985). This reduction was to be implemented in the first semester of 1985 and 1986, to reach levels of 30 percent and 25 percent respectively. The first adjustment was made in March 1985, but the second one was anticipated and enlarged: in June 1985, the tariff was back at 20 percent. At the time of writing (February 1986) the discussion of this issue has faded away, although the supporters of tariff differentiation have not abandoned their efforts.

Sustaining Pressures

Most countries facing such a deep recession, a huge balance of payments problem, and a growing protectionist lobby would have gone much further in reinstituting protection – at any rate, this is what happened in most other Latin American countries. One reason why these pressures were resisted in Chile was the determination of successive Ministers of Finance to maintain the policy unaltered. As described above, only one Minister (appointed in 1983) modified the tariff policy, and his tariff increases (of 1983 and 1984) were largely reversed by another. The tenacity of the policymakers kept trade liberalization in place long enough for groups to develop who had a vested interest in defending it. Reversal would financially damage those groups who had reoriented their resources towards the objectives of liberalization. Specifically, a new group of producers has been created in the export sector: exports have diversified significantly and the absolute number of exporters has increased enormously, while substantial investment has been made in the exportable sector. For this new group, a reversal of the tariff policy will bring unfavorable relative prices; consequently, they make their opinions felt when changes in policy are discussed.

Further, liberalization has been maintained long enough to bring about a complete reorganization of production structures in the import-substituting sectors. Lines of production unable to compete with imports disappeared; new lines and new products developed according to the new set of relative prices, and resources were invested in modernizing several plants. Thus a reversal in the tariff policy today would obviously impose high costs on the firms that adjusted to new policies. By the same token, most "old firms" that might have benefited from a reversal have disappeared, leaving as potential beneficiaries only a few producers of import substitutes who might obtain rents.

In our opinion, the above reasons may go a long way toward explaining why the change of tariffs enacted in 1983 was mild, and why the larger increases in 1984 did not last for more than six months. Another reason for the durability of the policy is that, after almost ten years of debate, the entrepreneurial organizations have failed to reach an agreement on a new tariff schedule to be proposed to the government. Such disunity among entrepreneurs comes from the opposition between those favoring low tariffs, (mainly exporters and merchants) and others (rent seekers in the importable sector).

This brief account of the post-liberalization period shows that it has been maintained free of QRs with a very limited use of surcharges and a uniform structure which seems to have stabilized at 20 percent. In our view, this is a case of successful sustainability because it has survived strong attacks resulting from external shocks, the deep recession of 1982, and ensuing natural erosion of support for the government. Its durability has been increasingly insured because sustainability breeds on itself. *Contrari sensu*, it becomes increasingly difficult to reduce tariffs the longer they remain in force.

6

Timing and Sequencing of Liberalization: Salient Points from the Chilean Experience

The remaining questions identified by the original research proposal (see the preface to this volume) as key issues to be tackled in determining a route and timetable for a liberalization policy are addressed in this chapter. Issues that have already been dealt with, implicitly or explicitly, in preceding chapters are the circumstances appropriate for introducing liberalization (chapter 3), the length and speed of the process (chapter 4), and the choice of a uniform treatment of productive activities (chapter 5). Additional comments on these issues will be made in the concluding remarks.

The other issues require more detailed analysis, based on both the relevant aspects of the Chilean story told in preceding chapters, which will simply be referred to here, and on additional material, specific to the topic, which will be presented and discussed in more detail.

Part of this material will refer to theoretical arguments which could be made for or against the different issues presented here; all these arguments could have been used during the liberalization process to justify actions carried out, but not all of them were presented, at least explicitly, at the time. Nevertheless, we still found it useful to include them here.

One-stage or Multistage

The two Chilean liberalization episodes each took about five years to implement. In our definition, this constitutes a gradual as opposed to a one-shot liberalization, even though it can be considered rapid by comparison with episodes of sustained liberalization in other countries: the two episodes could certainly have been longer, but they could also have been shorter. Here we are concerned firstly to examine how much the gradual approach contributed to the durability and success of the second episode,[1] and secondly, as a contribution to the wider debate, to consider the pros and cons of an even more (or even less) gradual approach.

Arguments in Favor of the Gradual Approach

A principal objective in the design of a liberalization policy is to minimize losses from factor unemployment while quickly reaping the benefits of improved resource allocation. Liberalization entails changes in the productive structure, particularly among tradeables, leading to unemployment during the adjustment process, closures of some firms and openings of others, changes in market signals, and so on. These considerations lend support to the gradual approach adopted in 1974–9. However, the view that factors could adjust relatively quickly together with the desire to reap the benefits of liberalization rapidly, justified the relatively short length of the tariff reduction period.

Effects on Labor

Bearing in mind that the 16 percent unemployment rate in Chile during the 1976–81 episode cannot be ascribed solely to trade liberalization (see chapter 5), the adverse effects of the policy on employment in the aggregate appear inconsiderable (table 5.18). However, for a realistic assessment of the burden imposed on the labor market we must look to the intersectoral and intrasectoral effects, since changes ensuing from liberalization tend to require accelerated labor mobility.

In Chile, the labor market needed significant improvements to achieve the necessary employment flexibility. This is reflected in the contrast between the relatively insignificant impact on employment as a whole and the variation from one sector to another (agriculture, mining, and manufacture), and particularly among industrial subsectors (from – 49.1 percent for electrical and nonelectrical machinery in 1975–9 to 50.6 percent for wood products during the same period).

Intersectoral effects might be expected to be significant, since liberalization would likely favor nonurban sectors, requiring labor to move out of urban activities, and corresponding changes in skills. In any event, the evidence presented in chapter 5 suggests that intrasectoral dislocations within the manufacturing sector were more important. Increased employment opportunities in rural regions – the beneficiaries of the resource reallocation – simply reversed the traditional export of labor to urban areas; immigration to cities stopped, and the downward trend of agricul-

1 The first episode does not present these features and lacks essential information relevant to conclusions on the issue of gradualism.

tural employment was checked. As a result, while liberalization policies may have eased adjustments by postponing migration, the adjustments required within the manufacturing sector were exacerbated by loss of human capital and substantially changed skill requirements, another argument in favor of gradualism.

One danger of a multistage gradual approach could be seesaw effects: one stage reduces production while the next increases it, or vice versa, creating costly adjustments. Such affects only occurred in five sectors – food products, tobacco, furniture, paper and paper products, and printing and publishing – of which only three were significant in terms of employment (see chapter 5). Apart from these special cases, calling at best for differential treatment for the sectors in question, the gradual approach thus appears to have been justified.

Effects on Capital

Capital losses derived from adjustment to liberalization would depend on the size and type of impacts of liberalization and the degree of specifity of the factor within firms. The size and type of impacts on production have been analyzed in chapter 5. The aggregate results suggest that adjustments were relatively modest. However, the detail by industrial subsector gives another picture: the production impact varies during the whole period on tariff reduction (1976–9) from − 64.7 percent for metal products to 61.7 percent for furniture. Nine sectors out of 17 took a loss of production of more than 20 percent as a consequence of liberalization. Furthermore, it has been assumed that adjustments entailed both changes in lines of production and technological changes, with additional potential for capital losses.

No information is available on capital specifity. Nevertheless, it is likely that capital losses may have been heavy in a few subsectors, and could have been alleviated if the process had been more gradual. In particular, it seems strange that investment in tradeables took quite a long time to become significant. One likely reason for this apparent lag was the reluctance to recognize capital losses incurred by firm owners (and potential investors). This retardation was possible given the monopolistic structure of importables (in production and imports) and the use of credit to finance losses instead of new activities.

Information and Relative Prices

An argument in favor of gradualism is that adjustment requires time to obtain information on relative prices, markets, and alternatives opened (or closed) by liberalization; further, relative prices of the new steady state equilibrium take time to become established for the reason just given and because markets do not always work as smoothly as desired. Results shown in table 6.1 suggest that the evolution of domestic prices in tradeables was

Table 6.1 Comparison between trends in effective exchange rates and prices, 1974–1981

	Textiles			*Nonelectrical and electrical machinery*			*Shoes and clothing*			*Chemicals*		
Year	*(1) EER*	*(2) Prices*	*(1)/(2)*	*(1) EER*	*(2) Prices*	*(1)/(2)*	*(1) EER*	*(2) Prices*	*(1)/(2)*	*(1) EER*	*(2) Prices*	*(1)/(2)*
1974	6.2	3.0	2.1	4.7	3.3	1.5	6.6	3.2	2.1	4.8	4.0	1.2
1975	28.7	15.8	1.8	26.3	16.7	1.6	31.2	17.4	1.8	25.4	20.7	1.2
1976	66.7	54.7	1.2	67.3	58.6	1.2	66.9	58.1	1.2	66.7	53.3	1.3
1977	100.0	100.0	1.0	100.0	100.0	10.0	100.0	100.0	1.0	100.0	100.0	1.0
1978	137.6	158.6	0.9	138.4	141.8	1.0	137.4	155.4	0.9	143.2	147.9	1.0
1979	153.0	209.8	0.7	158.4	220.1	0.7	152.6	232.4	0.7	166.1	198.6	0.8
1980	159.9	284.8	0.6	166.3	287.9	0.6	159.5	337.2	0.5	174.8	264.4	0.7
1981	159.9	324.6	0.5	166.3	301.7	0.6	159.5	280.2	0.6	174.8	306.3	0.6

Source: de la Cuadra and Hachette, 1988, appendix tables A.10 and A.18

not tied to the evolution of effective exchange rates. This may be due to the level of aggregation of sectors chosen. However, these results are also consistent with scattered information on prices obtained for 20 products, which showed a three-year time lag for adaptation to new tariffs even after water had been eliminated from them.

Other Aspects

Subsidies could have been granted to accelerate the process of adjustment. However, one important goal of the authorities at that time was the rapid reduction of fiscal deficits, which were the main source of inflation. Consequently, funds were not available to hasten the liberalization process in this way.

Synchronization with export development, to avoid major shocks in the trade balance and in employment in the context of an inefficient and initially closed capital market, would also suggest that gradualism was desirable. It is true that in the Chilean experience export behavior could have permitted an even less gradual approach, but only when looked upon *ex post*. Reasonable doubts could have arisen at the start of the liberalization period with respect to both export performance and the opening of the capital market. In fact, when doubts were allayed liberalization accelerated, going even further than initially designed to a uniform and low tariff rate of 10 percent.

Arguments against Gradualism

Rapid liberalization is preferable if domestic production of tradeables is highly inefficient, low in labor intensity, or uses highly depreciated capital. In Chile, capital had been rapidly depreciated in several industrial subsectors before the inception of the second liberalization episode, with the result that liberalization policies caused less capital loss than otherwise. This fact could help to explain the lukewarm opposition shown to liberalization despite the known, articulated, and strong protectionist views offered by the industrialists' organization (SOFOFA) in the past.

The only available evidence on this issue is shown below (table 6.2). Unfortunately, this time series was built assuming a constant depreciation rate over time and is aggregated. Dispersed information suggests, however, that depreciation accelerated significantly, at least during 1970–3, as a result of fears of nationalization or takeovers, or because of mismanagement following expropriation. Consequently, the index of capital stock presented here is most probably overvalued between 1970 and 1977. In any event, the figures suggest that capital in manufacturing started to fall before water was eliminated from tariffs – about 1976–7 – and even before the liberalization policy was announced, making adjustments easier than otherwise. Information does not allow us to distinguish trends among manufacturing subsectors.

Table 6.2 Index of capital stock for manufacturing (end of year)

		Stage 1		*Stage 2*	*Stage 3*	*Post-liberalization*
1965	*1970*	*1973*	*1975*	*1977*	*1979*	*1981*
82.3	100.0	99.0	95.6	91.0	91.9	96.1

Source: Coeymans, 1986

The mild resistance of workers to the liberalization policies might seem at first sight to have warranted a more rapid tariff reduction. During the first stages of trade liberalization this cooperative behavior arose from the existing combination of high real exchange rates and tariff redundancy; later on, resistance was weakened by significantly reduced union powers and high unemployment arising from the 1975 recession and stabilization policies.

Where past experience has created a lack of credibility, a more rapid *fait accompli* implementation seems called for. Lack of faith in the permanence of reforms is self-fulfilling: it retards any major adjustment and further fuels pressures on the authorities to reverse the policy. In fact, the avalanche effect on imports following the replacement of quantitative controls by tariffs (the Klein–Saks experience of 1956–7) was probably propelled by doubts as to the durability of the policy. In such circumstances a rapid liberalization may carry enough credibility to persuade economic agents to postpone imports until the stage is completed; this may be favorable to the trade balance in the short run.

However, it is difficult to believe that the lack of credibility of the trade liberalization policy was a paramount consideration for the second episode.[2] Doubts disappeared when the civilian economic team consolidated its position as managers of the economic policy in 1976, when they took charge of the key economic offices: the ministries of finance, economy, and mining, and the Central Bank. Significant changes in the composition of industrial value added began to occur early in 1976, but did not cease in 1979 when tariffs had already reached their final level: import-competing industries continued to reduce their share, while exportables and nontradeables increased theirs (see chapter 5). Investments were made in most sectors; new technologies were adopted to reduce costs and new lines of production were opened, while significant improvements were made in product quality (Corbo and Sánchez, 1985).

The only relevant available piece of evidence consistent with the view taken here on credibility at least does not disprove it. It compares the behavior of different types of assets of the import substitution sectors with those of the exportable sector during the period 1977–80. A sample of about 80 firms shows a lesser growth of fixed assets among import substitutes than expected from producers in a sector believing in the stability of the tariff reduction. However, the textile sector represents an exception in the results. But this is not an unequivocal sign of lack of credibility. The significant accumulation of fixed assets in this sector could be the result of modernization efforts to adopt to the new rules – a decision taken on the basis of mistaken perceptions of relative prices and interest rates. Anyway, too much weight should not be given to this sector's being the exception to the rule observed.

The same sample suggests a reduction of the ratio of fixed assets in total assets of the import substitution firms to those of the exportable sector. This result is again consistent with credibility in the tariff reform. Firms which would be affected negatively by changes in relative prices and conditions of competitivity would tend to reduce, relative to others, the importance of factors specific to them. Hence fixed assets would be among the likely candidates. By the same token, liquid assets of the importable sector should have experienced the highest rate of growth, which they did. Furthermore, when firms bankrupted between 1978 and 1980 are included in the sample, the import substitute sector shows a significant accumulation of inventories during 1977 and 1978, at least compared with the exportables. However, this result could be consistent with errors of prediction with respect to relative prices, which is not an unlikely consideration given

2 Frankel et al. (1985) attempt to demonstrate that firms did not believe in the liberalization process. Unfortunately, their demonstration is shaky and goes against the acknowledged perception of the business community at the time. Any remaining doubt about the sustainability of trade liberalization at the end of 1977 was dissipated by the political consolidation of the economic team which lowered the tariff to 10 percent without eliciting a reaction from the business community. Against the views of these authors see Coloma and González (1986).

the structural changes occurring in the economy at that time. Consequently, the business community seems to have believed in the stability of the tariff reform.

This conclusion is confirmed by their behavior post-liberalization. Industrial firms have adapted themselves efficiently to the low tariff barrier enforced after 1979, although adjusted upward later on, *without* any major investment. Even bankrupted firms in 1982 were facing new relative prices and conditions of competitivity successfully once financially amended. Both considerations tend to prove that they were fully adapted to new conditions probably by 1981, which implied credibility in the tariff reform.

Although some businessmen disagreed on the uniform 10 percent tariff level and on the speed of adjustment, they publicly expressed satisfaction with the substance of the liberalization policy. They may not have believed that a fixed nominal exchange rate would be maintained in an inflationary context, but they acted as if they believed in the stability of the liberalization policies. Consequently, shock treatment was not predicated by considerations of credibility during the second episode of liberalization.

If the export sector had been characterized by high price elasticity and high labor intensity, a more rapid implementation might have been indicated. These characteristics, however, prevailed only in the wood products industry (excluding furniture), whose exports reached no more than 9 percent of exports of manufacturers during the period 1974–81 (less than 3 percent of total exports).

In sum, the gradual strategy for trade liberalization was on the whole more appropriate than shock treatment, at least during the second episode. In particular, the strategy was justified by the exigencies of resource mobilization within sectors of production, as a consequence of the significant reduction in tariffs and the far from perfect performance of both labor and capital markets. The gradual strategy also allowed the major institutional reforms and their accompanying price changes to take effect, thus giving the relevant signals for adjustment. Finally, political stability and support for liberalization was crucial to maintain gradualism and to lessen the significant burden of adjustment.

A Separate Stage for Replacing Quantitative Restrictions by Tariffs

Arguments in favor of a separate stage for dismantling QRs lend support, by definition, to the multistage strategy discussed above; they should consequently be considered in that context as well as in relation to the specific issue addressed here.

Analysis of the two liberalization episodes suggests that the replacement of QRs by tariffs may have had some impact, though not very significant, at the beginning of both periods. This impact was cushioned during both

Table 6.3 List of permitted imports – number and share of items

	Apr 1956		*Aug 1956*		*Jul 1957*		*Jun 1958*		*Apr 1959*		*Sep 1960*		*Dec 1961*		*Dec 1962*		*Oct 1963*	
Product	*No.*	*Share*	*No.*	*Share*	*No.*	*Share*	*No.*	*Share*	*No.*	*Share*	*No.*	*Share*	*No.*	*Share*	*No.*	*Share*	*No.*	*Share*
Mining	42	7.9	46	6.6	48	6.0	48	5.0	54	3.4	57	3.1	57	2.8	47	3.4	46	3.4
Natural products of fishing and forestry	6	1.1	9	1.3	13	1.6	13	1.4	16	1.0	20	1.1	20	1.0	12	0.9	12	0.9
Products of animal kingdom (livestock)	15	2.8	22	3.1	25	3.2	27	2.8	34	2.1	42	23.0	46	2.3	37	2.7	36	2.7
Agricultural products	31	5.9	30	4.3	32	4.0	40	4.2	54	3.4	57	3.1	58	2.9	42	3.1	42	3.1
Food products	7	1.3	9	1.3	9	1.1	12	1.3	27	1.7	35	1.9	38	1.9	18	1.3	18	1.3
Beverages and liquors									8	0.5	10	0.5	10	0.5	0	0	0	0
Tobacco manufacturing									5	0.3	6	0.3	6	0.3	0	0	0	0
Textiles industry	27	5.1	30	4.3	31	3.9	31	3.2	68	4.3	69	3.8	75	3.7	34	2.5	33	2.5
Chemical industry	87	16.4	113	16.1	141	17.7	159	16.6	385	24.1	403	21.9	466	23.3	309	22.5	295	22.0
Metallurgical industry	101	19.1	112	16.0	127	16.0	142	14.8	175	11.0	212	11.5	228	11.4	171	12.5	171	12.7
Machinery, equipment, and tools	29	5.5	119	17.0	140	17.6	195	20.4	344	21.6	450	24.5	475	23.7	331	24.1	332	24.7
Materials and equipment for transport	25	4.7	32	4.6	39	4.9	50	5.2	80	5.0	91	4.9	104	5.2	64	4.7	60	4.5
Miscellaneous manufactured items	159	30.0	177	25.3	190	23.9	240	25.0	341	21.4	383	20.8	414	20.7	302	22.0	292	21.7
Coins and precious metals	1	0.2	1	0.1	1	0.1	1	0.1	5	0.3	4	0.2	6	0.3	6	0.4	6	0.4
Total	530	100	700	100	796	100	958	100	1,596	100	1,839	100	2,003	100	1,373	100	1,343	100

Sources: Hachette, 1973b; Sierra et al., 1967

episodes by realignments in the exchange rates; furthermore, during the first episode the list of permitted imports was only gradually increased (table 6.3) which prior deposits were used flexibly after 1956 throughout the period.

The recession of 1975, a year after the elimination of most QRs in the second episode, may have hindered excessive above-optimal imports. In legal terms, QRs did not disappear until August 1976 when the prior deposit of 10,000 percent was eliminated.[3]

If QRs exist before liberalization, it might be desirable to initiate trade liberalization by replacing them by water-excluded tariffs at the prevailing exchange rate. However, tariff equivalence of quotas is difficult and administratively costly to determine, unless quotas have previously been auctioned. Tariffs fixed to replace them will thus be somewhat arbitrary, and consequently will have to be adjusted iteratively to reach the desired level.

The lifting of QRs might induce an abnormally high demand for imports at the relevant prices – c.i.f. plus tariffs – and a credibility gap with respect to the permanence of the policy. After the period of adjustment, however, demand growth for imports will return to "normal" levels. Containing increases in imports may require a higher exchange rate than would be justified by the equivalent tariff rates in the long term, although the use of the capital market could be more efficient. Such a high exchange rate would stimulate exports at the start of the liberalization process, and could be retained when further liberalization measures, requiring further appreciation of the "equilibrium" exchange rate, are taken in subsequent stages.

Therefore a separate stage for QR replacement seems to be in order to establish relative prices, awareness of which is important to both policymakers and firms. Policymakers need to know the price or tariff equivalence of QR barriers to determine the quantitative targets of liberalization, its adjustment costs, and its expected benefits, duly balanced by political considerations. It would be impossible for the authorities to reach even a rough estimate of the magnitude involved on which to base reasonable decisions if protection were reduced straight from nontariff barriers or water-in-tariff situations (table 6.4). The firms, for their part, need to understand the impact of policies to make decisions relevant to resource reallocation. This is true even if the only liberalization policy in question is the elimination of QRs, and is a more difficult task when substitution of tariffs for QRs is only one among many other market-oriented economic policies such as elimination of price controls, ending of all sorts of

3 This prior deposit nevertheless continued to be enforced for some time for the import of a few items (see chapter 3).

Table 6.4 Tariffs (percent)

Subsector	Implicit 1974	Nominal 1974	Nominal 1977
Food products	20.8	83	18
Beverages	16.0	112	21
Tobacco	17.6	100	18
Textiles	37.1	141	31
Shoes and clothing	47.0	160	32
Leather and leather products	39.1	104	23
Wood products (excluding furniture)	9.4	90	18
Furniture and wood accessories	10.7	90	18
Paper and paper products	25.7	97	21
Printing and publishing	4.5	114	26
Chemicals	39.7	66	19
Petroleum and coal	30.7	68	11
Rubber products	31.3	63	28
Nonmetal minerals	26.8	79	21
Basic metal industries	21.2	60	20
Metal products	38.4	91	31
Nonelectrical and electrical machinery	45.1	75	26

Implicit tariffs were obtained from price comparisons.
Sources: Coeymans, 1978b; Aedo and Lagos, 1984

subsidies, tax reform, and so on, as was the case in the 1974–9 trade liberalization.

A variant of the QR replacement stage, extremely relevant for Chile in both liberalization attempts but more so in the second one, is the need for a special stage to normalize commercial policies, which, among other things, implies the following:

1. the elimination of tariff exemptions (to firms, public sector institutions, specific regions);
2. the elimination of multiple exchange rates and export quotas;
3. the need to define tariff rules for capital goods, foreign exchange, and other relevant policies related to foreign reserves, and for credit policies (see chapter 4).

Experience suggests that the elimination of import exemptions, shown to be significant in the case of Chile, fostered interest in opening the economy still further. The regions, public enterprises, and firms which were positively affected became active supporters of liberalization policies.

A Separate Stage for Export Promotion

Sustainability and success of liberalization efforts depend in good measure on the ability of exports to grow *pari passu* with imports. The behavior of exports, as explained in the discussion of the impacts of liberalization on trade in chapter 5, was a crucial element in the success of the second episode, as opposed to the first.

The question is whether liberalization requires deliberate export promotion to ensure its success and, if so, how best to sequence the promotion to make it as effective as possible.

In addressing the question, a distinction must be made between export promotion policies proper – that is, deliberate moves to create a pro-export bias – and (a) policies with the more limited objective of reducing anti-export bias, such as the import substitution strategy following by Chile up to 1974, (b) policies which happen to stimulate exports as a side effect of a quite different primary objective, such as the exchange rate policy adopted during the second liberalization episode, and (c) incentives to exports which are an independent outcome of external forces, such as the export drive propelled by the recession.

Before examining the Chilean experience as evidence for or against the desirability of an overt export promotion policy, we need first to determine whether exports were a bottleneck for liberalization, and second whether such a policy existed.

During the first episode, export growth was hesitant and slow, and was insufficient to keep up with import growth and falling external prices. Conversely, rapid export growth in the second episode outstripped imports (table 6.5) in an environment that remained favorable to export prices at least until 1980. Furthermore, the wider export diversification desirable to offset destabilizing fluctuations in the terms of trade that may follow liberalization did not occur during the first episode, but did during the second. On both counts, therefore, while exports may have been a bottleneck during the first episode, they were not in the second (see chapter 5).

Does the existence or lack of an export promotion policy account for the differing behavior of exports during the two episodes? According to our analysis (chapter 4) export promotion policies as such were not significant during either episode. Although DL 409 allowed the refund of tariffs paid on imports of inputs reexported later, this instrument was operational only for the large exporting firms involved in copper, or for traditional noncopper exports, such as wood, paper and cellulose, and fishmeal, which accounted for a large share of the increases in exports. In addition, forest plantation, the basis for one of the most successful surges in noncopper exports, was subsidized to some extent for several decades. More signifi-

Table 6.5 Exports, real exchange rate, and external prices (percent)

Period	*Real exports (average rate of growth)*	*Real exchange rate for exports (average rate of growth)*	*External prices (average rate of growth)*
First episode			
1956–7	−3.0	27.0	−7.1
1958–9	9.0	3.8	−1.5
1960–1	0.8	−8.3	0.0
Post-liberalization			
1962–3	2.5	2.5	1.5
Second episode			
1974–5	9.3	53.3	0.9
1976–7	12.3	−14.4	4.4
1978–9	13.0	−1.6	17.2
Post-liberalization			
1980–1	4.1	−21.4	−2.4

Source: de la Cuadra and Hachette, 1988, appendix tables A.4, A.8, and A.23

cant was the role played by the exchange rate, which was designed in the first episode to be consistent with the stabilization plan and arising in the second from devaluation to compensate for tariff reductions and the effects of recession (see chapter 4). In neither case were they part of a deliberate export promotion policy; indeed, during the first episode their effect may even have been negative (table 6.5).

The opposite was true during the second episode, when a higher average real exchange rate prevailed – in index terms 111.1, compared with 70.5 and 90.2 respectively in the preceding Allende and Frei eras. The high rate no doubt acted as an instrument of export promotion, but only temporarily; during the post-liberalization period it dropped below pre-liberalization levels (to 67.7). Arguably more significant than the boost provided by the temporary above-equilibrium exchange rate were the expectations of the maintenance of a realistic exchange rate over the medium term. Businessmen at the time argued more for a stable realistic rate than for an artificially high one.

Exchange rates therefore appear to have been a reasonable substitute for an explicit export promotion policy during the second episode. Such a policy might nevertheless have been needed if unequal responses of resources to the pull by exportables and the push by importables were entailing costly adjustments to the liberalization. This effect is particularly worrisome when export development requires factor mobility to activities intensive in natural resources, such as mining, forestry, and specific agricultural subsectors, because it is harder to move resources across sectors and from urban to nonurban activities than within sectors and between urban activities. As explained earlier in this chapter, the dislocations during the second episode did not seem to have been compelling enough to have warranted further export promotion to accelerate absorption of unemployment coming from import substitution industries.[4]

Another reason why the lack of an aggressive export promotion policy does not appear to have been a major drawback is that nontraditional exports found three conditions extremely conducive to growth: the dramatic recession of 1975 and the resulting rise in the exchange rate, the maturing by that date of investments in exportables (for example, wood, ferromolybdenum, and, to a lesser extent, fruit) and favorable markets abroad.

Export Promotion – Some Conclusions

Some tentative conclusions on the case for export promotion seem to be in order.

The export behavior observed during the liberalization episodes does not rule out the desirability of accompanying export promotion policies during the liberalization process. Nor, on the other hand, does it rebut the hypothesis that export promotion may be superfluous if the reduction in tariffs is significant, if external markets are favorable, and if the exchange rate is "appropriate."

As long as there is an anti-export bias, exports should be "promoted" in the sense of reducing this bias. This strategy does not appear to justify a special stage; it merely needs to be initiated early in the liberalization process. In this connection it seems preferable to apprise firms of prospective opportunities, in particular those related to exports, during the first stage of liberalization.

Previous comments may imply that the best way to promote exports is to raise the real exchange rate substantially in the first stage of liberalization, if this is feasible, and then to try to maintain it throughout the liberalization process. An overvalued exchange rate may be in order during the liberalization period if the following conditions hold:

1 nontraditional exports are elastic to the exchange rate (econometric estimates vary from 0.49 to 0.60);

4 Export activities developed during the 1970s required significant investments to compete in foreign markets. Nevertheless, investments continued despite low domestic savings and limited openings in the capital market up to 1978. This is another sign of the relatively favorable environment for exports during the second episode.

2 it makes tariff adjustments easier once the latter are defined and carried out strictly according to the predefined schedule;
3 the overvaluation of the exchange rate of the first stages anticipates its equilibrium value when the process of liberalization is over.

Unfortunately, this overvaluation, even as an export "promotion" tool, gives the wrong signals to import substitution if it is not accompanied by tariff reduction. This is why the major reallocation adjustments in production and employment did not occur during the first stage, since the drastic exchange rate adjustment compensated more than fully for the tariff reduction. Undervaluation has a similar effect on both exportables and importables. Furthermore, overvaluation of the exchange rate could be unpopular if previously existing export quotas and subsidies to food imports are being eliminated at the same time: the poorest would suffer doubly through regressive changes in relative prices and unemployment generated by the first steps of liberalization (Hachette, 1973a). This may well have happened in Chile between 1974 and 1977, exacerbated by the 1975 recession: certainly, income distribution seems to have deteriorated dramatically at that time.

Consequently, a stage characterized by exchange rate overshooting may be less appropriate than a stable exchange rate policy, maintained throughout the liberalization process. Furthermore, the Chilean experience suggests that the "real exchange rate" may not be a feasible policy instrument since the government cannot control the price level. Only tariff reductions and real shocks such as terms-of-trade fluctuations may have some impact on the real exchange rate.

What could substitute for exchange rate overvaluation as a stimulus for exports? Real exports are fostered by good information dissemination, marketing facilities, new markets, attractive prices, relative prices not blurred by inflation, adequate financing, infrastructure, and so on – all factors which affect the elasticity of exports with respect to the exchange rate. If any, the first stage in the process of liberalization would be the most suitable for a special export push so that the game plan can be set out simultaneously for exports and imports. However, liberalization may not need to be postponed to accommodate export incentives if the implicit bias derived from tariffs on imports in largely compensated for by other measures. For example, the Chilean experience suggests that low tariffs, open trade, credit availability (mostly foreign), attractive exchange rates, and favorable world prices (coupled with higher efficiency and lower operational cost of parts) stimulated significant development of noncopper exports without additional explicit "promotion" policies.

To the extent that the combination of overshooting of exchange rates, tariff reductions, and refunds for tariffs paid on imported inputs could be classified as export promotion in the Chilean case, it affected the industrial subsectors differentially and resulted in discrimination. Unfortunately, it is impossible to judge the efficiency of this reform of promotion; consequently no reasonable comment can be advanced on the appropriateness of the "policy."

The basic hypothesis of this section has been that export promotion, while not essential, was not necessarily undesirable. Exports might have grown faster with a deliberate aggressive "promotion" policy, particularly when world markets were slumping as during the first episode analyzed in this research. The recession may have acted *de facto* as a stage characterized by export promotion through undervalued domestic currency, but the effects of this incentive, unlike the reduction in anti-export bias brought about by tariff reduction, did not persist beyond 1979.

The Contribution of Other Policies to Sustaining Liberalization

Policies carried out simultaneously with liberalization measures are briefly summarized and discussed here as a prelude to drawing conclusions about their role in the durability of liberalization. The discussion here centers on how far they were compatible with liberalization efforts: in this, it differs from the discussion of the topic in chapter 5, which dealt with pressures and changes in trade policies during the extended post-liberalization period (1982–6).

Liberalization efforts were aborted in the first episode and came under strong pressure in the second episode after almost three years of a fixed nominal exchange rate. Further, relative prices turned significantly against tradeables in both cases, as aggregate demand followed an expansionary path which inflated wages and the prices of nontradeables, making imports more attractive and the production of both exportables and importables ever less profitable. In addition, significant increases in money income increased pressures on the trade balance.

The reasons for these developments differ, however, from one episode to the other. During the first, the authorities were unable to curb expansionary fiscal and monetary policies during the two years preceding reversal. Efforts to finance a greater share of the deficits from external sources were insufficient because they were not accompanied by adequate neutralization of the monetary effects of this policy – domestic credit increased by 33.5 percent in 1961, while wages were rising by 24.5 percent during the same year.[5] Finally, independently of domestic policy, Chile's export prices were falling while its terms of trade were rising.

Conversely, during the second episode domestic expenditures increased rather as a result of positive developments arising from the earthshaking

5 CPI increased by 9.6 percent on a calendar year basis, but inflation was accelerating.

policies followed after 1973: a significant GDP growth rate – 7.5 percent annual average between 1976 and 1979 – which was internally considered a "boom" and externally closely watched and loudly praised, in some quarters at least. In addition, projections of the growth of GDP were becoming more than optimistic: "8 percent annual average growth until the year 2000" (Piñera, 1977). Both elements, together with significant changes in the political model and major institutional adjustments, may have given rise to expectations of significant improvement in permanent income. As actual incomes were below permanent incomes, expenditure rose faster than income, financed by reduced domestic savings and significantly increased demand for foreign credit. Large and increasing foreign debt ensued.

Despite restrictive fiscal and monetary policies, expansionary financial policies substantially augmented domestic credit in both 1980 and 1981 (table 6.6). Furthermore, labor legislation approved in 1979 began to stimulate a rise in real wages. The combination of financial and labor legislation policies in a context of optimistic expectations and fixed nominal exchange rates produced a change in relative prices against tradeables, reducing their competitiveness and widening the trade gap (table 6.7). As long as foreign capital was available and the country was considered creditworthy, capital kept flowing in and foreign reserves accumulated. However, an explosive situation was developing as London interbank offering rate (LIBOR) went up in 1981. Debt had been growing fast, in particular within the tradeables sector, to counteract the apparently temporary loss of competitiveness. Borrowing accelerated to finance the rising debt service. The explosion came with world recession and the virtually simultaneous contraction of the capital market: many firms went bankrupt and the financial system with them. One June 14, 1982, the peso was devalued, and a year later tariffs were raised to 20 percent – maintaining the uniform structure.

Table 6.6 Annual growth of credit and debt (percent)

	Domestic credit			
Year	*Total*	*Public*	*Private*	*External debt*
1980	80.9	4.1	85.1	30.6
1981	21.3	– 27.5	45.3	40.2

Source: Central Bank of Chile, *Boletín Mensual*

A final comment may be in order. Although an important ingredient in the failure to maintain the 10 percent tariff, the fixity of nominal exchange rate is far from being the whole explanation of the reversal.

Table 6.7 Development of relative prices, 1979–1982

Quarter	*Tradeables / Nontradeables*	*Tradeables / Wages*
1979		
I	0.955	1.003
II	1.000	1.000
III	1.132	1.051
IV	1.042	1.032
1980		
I	1.025	0.920
II	1.004	0.864
III	0.966	0.832
IV	0.895	0.736
1981		
I	0.845	0.687
II	0.780	0.631
III	0.726	0.579
IV	0.702	0.569
1982		
I	0.649	0.542
II	0.660	0.549
III	0.886	0.755
IV	1.003	0.963

Source: Corbo, 1983

First Episode, 1956–1961

The main policy effort was directed toward stabilizing the economy with less government participation in economic matters.

During the first subperiod (Ibáñez, 1956–8) the fiscal deficit dropped significantly, while both high-powered money growth and wage adjustments were reduced. This combination, supported by a more generous use of external resources and a reduction in the growth of nominal income, reduced the impact of liberalization on imports and consequently was in accord with the intended trade rationalization (table 6.8). However, monetary growth may have been insufficiently bridled in 1957 and 1958, limiting both the anti-inflationary impact of the stabilization program and its effect on the demand for imports.

To check the decline in GDP growth in 1958 and 1959, Alessandri chose, at the beginning of the second subperiod (1958–61), a combination of

Table 6.8 Some economic indicators, 1956–1962

Year	*Fiscal deficit (% GDP)*	*High-powered money (% change)*	*GDP growth (current prices)*	*Consumer prices (% change)*	*Nominal wages (% change)*	*Nominal interest rate*[a]	*Nominal exchange rate*[b] *(% change)*	*Use of external resources*[c] *(million US$)*
1956	1.9	43.0	60.2	37.7	46.5	23.6	95.2	23.0
1957	2.1	25.1	38.4	17.2	30.2	26.4	47.4	135.0
1958	0.2	35.6	28.4	32.5	20.0	30.5	27.7	66.0
1959	2.6	45.8	40.3	35.2	36.7	32.8	32.0	6.0
1960	4.7	45.5	15.9	5.5	0.0	33.6	0.0	105.0
1961	4.3	10.2	12.3	9.6	24.5	27.5	0.0	296.0
1962	5.6	71.5	18.0	27.7	16.4	26.2	14.7	185.0

[a] Credit cost (de la Cuadra and Hachette, 1985, Part II, table 14).
[b] Import exchange rate: average of mining, agriculture, and manufacturing.
[c] Capital account balance minus the change in foreign reserves.

Sources: de la Cuadra and Hachette, 1988, appendix tables A.0, A.6, A.15, A.25, A.42, A.46; and, Universidad de Chile, 1963a

expansionary fiscal and monetary policies. Later in 1959, in recognition of the importance of devaluation for inflationary expectations, the exchange rate was fixed in nominal terms until 1961 and fiscal deficits were further increased (though partly financed by foreign savings) (table 6.8).

The combination of policies chosen during 1958–9 was inconsistent with liberalization efforts, but the effect was not felt immediately; exports increased by about 9 percent at constant prices, while imports were delayed as a consequence of a reduction in economic activity. Similarly, the effect of the policies of 1960–1 (equally inconsistent with liberalization efforts) was somewhat offset by the elimination of mandatory wage rises in 1960, the increased use of external resources, and the significant reduction of monetary growth in 1961. Unfortunately, the increase in economic activity fueled by fiscal expansion, combined with *de facto* wage rises and an exchange rate fixed since 1959, generated strong pressures on imports and foreign reserves. The inability of exports to grow (related to a falling real exchange rate on top of high protection), the growing lack of faith in the viability of the pegged exchange rate, and the drying up of external resources underline the increasing incompatibility of other policies with liberalization efforts, which consequently stopped altogether and were reversed in 1962. Further, the nominal interest rate increased, becoming positive in real terms in 1960 and 1961 for the first time in many years. This development did not stimulate the required investment in any sector – least of all in tradeables. Nor was the freezing of prices of most "necessary goods" after the 1960 earthquake instrumental in stimulating investment in exportables, because these controls would generate expectations of export quotas to lessen inflationary pressures and speculative trends.

Second Episode, 1974–1979

Again, stabilization policies dominated during this episode. Other considerations were significant, however, and developed in step with these measures: an effectively market-oriented economy and its privatization, the elimination of sectoral discrimination, and the organization of an efficient financial sector.

While tariffs contained water until 1976, the vector of policies was not inconsistent with liberalization. In fact, the choice of policies adopted during the recession may have stimulated liberalization.

When the price of copper declined abruptly as a consequence of the international recession by mid-1974, the potential balance-of-payments crisis became obvious. The basic dilemma was whether to resort to international financing or to make internal adjustments. The second option was chosen because of (a) the belief that the decline in copper prices would not be transitory, (b) the precarious conditions under which Chile would have had to seek external financing, particularly in view of its extremely low creditworthiness, and (c) the desire not to postpone long-run policies, particularly the open-trade policy, despite the more active opposition arising from increasing unemployment generated by the recession.

Adjustments were made through expenditure-reducing policies such as contractive fiscal and monetary measures, and expenditure switching such as a substantial increase in the nominal exchange rate (table 6.9). The volume of imports consequently fell while exports rose. The policy was also instrumental in preparing for further stages: the exchange rate established in 1975 may have remained biased upward afterward as world market conditions improved and capital flowed into Chile after 1976 (table 6.9, last column).

From 1976 to 1979, when tariffs reached their final uniform level of 10 percent, fiscal and monetary policies could be considered mildly expansionary, while the periodic devaluations started to play an active anti-inflationary role. Relative prices of tradeables to nontradeables fell consistently throughout this period. However, the high average real exchange rate accompanied by almost constant real wages and falling interest rates could still be considered compatible with liberalization. In fact, exports grew at constant prices more rapidly than imports. The lessons learned during the recession bore fruit: foreign markets had been opened as a simple matter of survival. The production of exportables was increasing regularly, pressures to shift policies had almost vanished, and employment was increasing in both the tradeables and nontradeables sectors.

However, inflation was still over 30 percent in 1979. Then the government decided to link domestic inflation to international inflation by pegging the exchange rate, as Alessandri had done in 1959 for similar reasons. Simultaneously, the government maintained a fiscal surplus while drastically reducing the credit of the Central Bank. Unfortunately, prices of nontradeables did not adjust immediately: inflation was still 31.2 percent in 1980 while nominal wages were increasing at the rate of 48.7 percent and 30.0 percent during 1980 and 1981 respectively. Moreover, the 30-day real interest rate rose from 0.5 to 3 percent in 1981. As a consequence, imports jumped from 19 percent of GDP in the period 1978–9 to 23 percent in 1980–1, while exports fell from 17 to 16 percent – a disturbing trend, sustained only by a rapid increase in the use of foreign resources (table 6.9). However, when exports continued to fall in 1982, fueling doubts about the viability of the pegged exchange rate and the creditworthiness of the country, foreign credit suddenly ceased to be available and capital flight exploded. (In fact, this happened after the financial markets of both Mexico and Argentina were closed, and simultaneously with the reduction in world liquidity.) Bankruptcies multiplied during 1981 and 1982 in the tradeables sector as the sharp rise in the interest rate made itself felt; devaluation came by mid-1982.

The main losses suffered by the tradeables sector did *not* occur during the liberalization period but during the *post-liberalization* period, after the 10 percent tariff had been reached and when the exchange rate, supported by growing capital movements, went out of line in relation to wages and interest rates (table 6.9). The decreased competitiveness of tradeables and the increased pull of resources in nontradeables reduced the tradeables sector from 37.8 percent of GDP in 1979 to 36.4 percent in 1981. In particular, the GDP of manufactures remained constant despite a 10.1 percent rate of growth of GDP overall at 1977 prices.

Table 6.9 Some economic indicators, 1974–1981

Year	*Fiscal deficit*[a] *(% GDP)*	*High-powered money (% change)*	*GDP growth (current prices)*	*Consumer prices*[b] *(% change)*	*Nominal wages (% change)*	*Nominal interest rate*[c]	*Nominal exchange rate*[b] *(% change)*	*Use of external resources*[d] *(million US$)*
1974	5.2	222.6	702.1	375.9	645.3	n.a.	484.4	273.0
1975	1.7	259.0	285.3	340.7	365.8	411.3	490.2	584.0
1976	– 3.7	281.6	263.0	174.3	253.7	350.7	165.8	– 215.0
1977	– 0.4	114.2	123.7	63.5	146.8	156.4	65.1	459.0
1978	– 1.6	59.9	69.4	30.3	49.4	85.3	47.0	1,234.0
1979	– 3.8	44.7	58.4	38.9	59.9	62.0	17.6	1,200.0
1980	– 5.5	34.8	39.2	31.2	48.7	47.0	4.7	1,921.0
1981	– 0.8	– 8.9	19.9	9.5	30.0	51.9	0.0	4,323.0

n.a., not available.
[a] Consolidated public sector; the minus sign indicates surplus.
[b] Official CPI, December to December.
[c] Interest account balance minus the change in foreign reserves.
[d] Capital account balance minus the change in foreign reserves.

Source: de la Cuadra and Hachette, 1988, appendix tables A.0, A.6, A.15, A.25, A.42, A.46, and A.54

It could be argued that the capital flow merely reflected an adjustment made by Chilean economic agents toward an optimum stock of foreign debt, and consequently could not be blamed for the policy inconsistencies noted above. However, even if the assumption of optimum size of foreign debt is accepted, it should be recognized that the speed of adjustment to the desired stock led to an overshooting of relative prices of nontradeables to tradeables during 1980–2, and then to a reduction of exportables and importables below the size that would have prevailed in "normal" conditions. It might also have generated costs in terms of additional unemployment and under-use of productive capacity, bankruptcies and asymmetrical reactions of factors, once relative prices returned to long-run "equilibrium" conditions.

Further Conclusions

The opening of the capital market suggests additional comments in relation to its consistency or inconsistency with liberalization in the light of the Chilean experience.

1 The speed more than the degree seems to have been relevant in the opening of the capital market. Sustaining liberalization required that relative prices of tradeables to nontradeables should not change substantially after 1979 or even 1980. With a fixed exchange rate and constant tariffs, this would entail no significant alterations in prices of nontradeables, and consequently no major increase in aggregate demand, monetary supply, or high-powered money, given the demand for foreign savings and the demand for money. The impact of the flow of foreign savings on high-powered money became increasingly difficult to neutralize without generating problems for financial institutions other than the Central Bank. The authorities resorted to repaying central government debts to the Central Bank during 1981 to avoid expansion of high-powered money, with some short-term success. Unfortunately, the effort came too late, since inflation did not fade out until the end of 1981, while real wages kept rising, limiting the impact of restrictive monetary policy on prices of nontradeables.

2 The authorities expected the domestic real interest rate to fall rapidly as a consequence of the fast opening of the capital market. Unfortunately, this did not occur. A combination of low domestic savings with a fast increase in the demand for credit arising from optimistic expectations of consumers and producers, the privatization of public firms, and the need of most enterprises to increase their very low working capital may explain the

prevailing high interest rates. Thus, even on this count, a slower opening of the capital market would have been warranted.[6]

3 The high cross-supply elasticity observed between domestic and foreign savings would also justify a low and a slow degree of opening of the capital market (Foxley, 1985) as external credit would displace domestic savings while adding to foreign debt.

4 The sustainability of liberalization will depend on maintaining the stability of relative prices, a difficult task when terms of trade are highly erratic. Capital market policies may unfortunately compound this difficulty, since the supply of foreign credit has also exhibited considerable instability, as well as being procyclical.

5 New provisions introduced in the labor legislation in 1979 increased the dissonance between liberalization measures and the anti-inflationary policies by adding downward inflexibility in salary readjustments at the crucial moment when inflation was being reduced to international levels. The wage floor for negotiations was established as the current nominal wage inflated by the average rate of inflation of the previous year. Since inflation was coming down, the real wage floor was rising. It is difficult to assess the impact of this legislation on employment in tradeables. Probably, as shown above, labor arrangements in the tradeables sector were more the result of choices of new technology and lines of production, and of developing new sectors, than of relative prices of factors. The large substitution effect estimated in table 5.21 points in that direction. Nevertheless, this floor may have become significant after 1980, and particularly in 1981, when the margin of competitiveness for producers of tradeables had faded out.

The transfer of public firms to the private sector may have been a policy inconsistent with liberalization, although only marginally. Savings may have dropped to the extent that the proceeds of sales did not increase public savings proportionately. The presumption is that sales of enterprises to the private sector allowed an increase in social programs, among other things, but the evidence is still insufficient. Now, this reduction in savings may have limited investment in tradeables, since some exportables required significant investments in pulp and paper, mining ventures, and so on. The reduction in interest rates which would have stimulated investment in tradeables were also curbed by "distress borrowing" (Harberger, 1985). Excessive debt was enhanced by the massive credit extended to the sale of public enterprises; the weak financial situation of some of these resulted in

6 A factor which aggravated the disequilibrium produced by liberalization was the high interest rate differential and abundant credit to finance imports, which reduced the effective cost of imports in relation to import substitutes.

even more pressure on the interest rate and consequently constrained investment in the tradeables sector among others.

Uniform versus Discriminatory Treatment of Sectors in a Gradual Process

The 1974–1981 Experience

The outcome of the liberalization process was a similar treatment for all imports with two exceptions: ALADI imports and the automobile sector. Effective protection thus became fairly homogeneous for most importables sectors. However, the gradual strategy entailed discriminatory treatment among sectors while it was in process of implementation in Chile for the following reasons.

1 Although tariff redundancy may have been eliminated for some sectors during the first stage, it is not clear that it was taken out of *all* sectors during that stage.

2 Since nominal tariffs varied initially between zero and more than 500 percent, it would have been impossible to treat all sectors homogeneously because tariff changes were expressed as a similar change – either nominal or relative – or because the time horizon to reach the final tariff level was identical for each sector.[7] *De facto*, the norms established under gradual trade liberalization were stricter for the traditionally more inefficient most protected sectors, which would have more adjustment difficulties. Furthermore, as initial effective protection varied widely among sectors, it would have been impossible to carry all of them to a common denominator without treating them differentially in the process of adjustment. An apparently simple rule of reducing effective protection of all sectors by some constant and common λ per unit of time would have been hampered by the following:

(a) the extreme difficulty of obtaining even a rough estimate of effective protection for all sectors of the economy;
(b) the hopeless task of reducing (or increasing) effective protection symmetrically, when one good produced by one sector may be an input for several sectors protected differently at the outset;
(c) the volatility of relative prices among nontradeables;
(d) the fact that a few sectors would increase their effective protection in the process of adjustment, while most would decrease theirs (this was particularly true for some important food products).

7 "Homogeneously" in terms of the effect of tariffs on net incentives but not in terms of designing the tariff reduction scheme.

3 *De facto*, discrimination was also introduced in December 1976 by reducing special tariff rates for inputs, intermediate products, tools, and machinery and products in the country (Decree 1098).

4 One indication that sectors were not treated uniformly is protests from businessmen about the 10–35 percent structure chosen initially. Those facing the lower tariff felt discriminated against, and opposed that discrimination; their opposition was used by the authorities to justify unification of tariffs, in the hope of ultimate unification of effective protection.

5 Automobiles were left out of the general treatment. The justification was never clear. Several arguments were given: employment, transfers of technology, and geopolitical (or strategic industry) considerations. Nevertheless, according to the rules established early in the process of liberalization, tariffs for the automobile assemblies were supposed to reach 10 percent in 1986. Although tariffs have been lowered through time according to schedule, they have been replaced by "consumption taxes" which discriminated in favor of domestically produced automobiles and which imply effective tariffs higher than 10 percent.[8]

Some Lessons

Given the sluggish and inefficient labor and capital markets, discriminatory treatment to lessen adjustment costs could have been justified by the following.

1 High initial specialization (see comments above) with the resulting high costs of reconversion. However, it would seem that institutional ties with foreign firms (for instance, multinationals) in a wide spectrum of related products may have favored the conversion of some firms. The Chilean experience suggests that producers of importables used "wide contacts" at the start of the trade liberalization in order to shift from being industrial producers to being importers of similar goods, abandoning production altogether. In other cases, where oligopoly existed, these contracts were used to maintain control of the market without altering production plans, or to postpone adjustment as a means of reducing capital losses. It is difficult to be precise, however, on the importance of this phenomenon. It appears to be fairly widespread, for example, automobiles, durables, electronics, paper, tobacco, plastics, laboratories, some foods (instant coffee for instance), and some textiles and clothing. Most foreign and some domestic firms followed this pattern. Some producers shifted lines of production more rapidly as a consequence of greater factor mobility

8 Recently, since December 1985, this sector has been subject to the general tariff system, which had risen from 10 percent in 1983 to 20 percent in 1987, and, starting in 1987, to the general tax system. The discrimination made through the ill-named "consumption tax" is due to be eliminated gradually during 1987 and 1988.

derived from being multinationals. In general, the degree of specialization in production increased with liberalization.

2 High costs involved in rehiring by firms after dismissals in the previous stage. Five sectors may have suffered from this effect during the process of liberalization: tobacco and furniture (all domestic), wood and wood products (exportable), and shoes and clothing and metal products (importable). Four sectors suffered from a modest change in tariffs. However, three of them were producers of final goods, although their production did not represent more than 11 percent of gross manufacturing product. The other sectors produced intermediate and primary goods. On both counts, it would be difficult to justify a different path for liberalization. In particular, a slower reduction in tariffs, mostly for producers of intermediate and primary goods, would create problems for users of these inputs.

3 The importance of the resource push (measured by the employment impact). Again, eight sectors showed a significant resource push during the 1976–9 episode of liberalization: tobacco, textiles, paper and paper products, rubber products, nonmetal mineral products, basic metal industry, electrical and nonelectrical machinery, and others. All these are producers of intermediate and primary goods or are of mixed composition. It has been shown that adjustment costs seem to have been particularly high in these cases, when the cost is measured in terms of unemployment generated by liberalization. On this account, these sectors may have merited some special consideration in the process of liberalization – for instance, a slower reduction in tariffs. However, on the cost side we have to include (a) the costs imposed on other sectors, for which they produced inputs, and (b) the recognition that some industrial subsectors will not be economically viable in the context of Chilean comparative advantage. The latter is clearly the case for basic metal industry and nonelectrical and electrical machinery. Consequently, they would close, at least partially, sooner or later.

Reconversion loans and support to shift labor would probably be better instruments for reducing adjustment costs than reducing the speed of tariff reduction.[9]

9 There are many arguments for discriminatory treatment among activities, such as the following:

wide initial dispersion in nominal and effective tariffs;
wide initial dispersion in factor intensity;
wide dispersion in domestic value added in the gross value of production;
a lower objective for liberalization with respect to tariff levels;
a high degree of interdependence among productive sectors and, particularly within the industrial sector, among subsectors;
scarce information on production processes at a relatively disaggregated level;

From the above, it appears that discriminatory treatment of sectors could not be avoided during the process of liberalization, for considerations of administrative feasibility and as a consequence of their differences in industrial organization (oligopolistic in production and trade versus competitive; multinational versus domestic). It also appears that costs resulting from the unavoidable discriminatory treatment can be reduced by "rapid" rather than by "slow" gradualism.

---

significant changes in relative prices of goods and services (final, intermediate) particularly among nontradeable inputs of tradeables sectors;
a large number of special treatments to start with (defining tariff exemptions);
a highly specialized tradeables sector at the inception of liberalization.

These rules apply for both importables and exportables. However, applying them at the same time as implementing policy can reasonably be considered impossible, or at least very costly and difficult to justify for those discriminated against.

7
Conclusions

In this chapter we draw together what we consider to be the main conclusions of this investigation. The discussion relates to the timing of trade liberalization, its length and speed, its sequencing, and a pot pourri of other conditions for successful liberalization, concluding with the question of the sustainability of trade policies.

Chile experienced two episodes of liberalization in a little less than 30 years – the first (1956–61) unsuccessful and the second (1976–9) successful. At the time of writing, the second has been sustained for seven years since it ended (1979) with only minor reversals – minor at least compared with the extent of liberalization carried out between 1976 and 1979. Although most conclusions derive from the second sustained episode, both because it was successful and because of data availability, inferences are also, where appropriate, drawn from the first episode.

The *timing* of trade liberalization policies is appropriate whenever the authorities obtain a minimum domestic consensus to carry them out and world markets are open to the country's exports. The consensus can be (and in this instance was) obtained either as a reaction to earlier unsatisfactory political and economic conditions or from the support of power groups for new authorities who offer some kind of policy package – trade liberalization policies included – based on "product differentiation" with respect to the previously dominant ideologies. With due qualifications, the worse political and economic conditions are, the easier it becomes to introduce major policy changes. If foreign support – from governments, international organizations, or simply from the silent experience of friendly countries – can reinforce the domestic willpower to carry these policies out, so much the better. Furthermore, improved export prices stimulate exports, strengthening the viability of liberalization. All these ingredients were present, both before the first trade liberalization attempt in 1956 and, mostly nearly, in 1973, before what can be regarded as the most substantial liberalization effort carried out by any country during the twentieth century.

The later episode suggests two comments that illustrate and further reaffirm the importance of the main conclusions about timing. One is that governments seem to set such a high premium on "product differentiation" that the major trade liberalization could be carried out by military authorities well known in the world context for their *autarkic* views. (The fact that the previously chaotic situation was propitious for initiating the policies is an incidental bonus.) The other observation is that, as long as the political power in Chile was based in highly concentrated well-organized urban interests, significant liberalization would have been virtually impossible. In such circumstances a meaningful liberalization program required a radical political shake-up; this was provided by the military regime. We can envisage different sets of circumstances which would call for different schemes.

Another basic conclusion is that the gradual implementation of trade liberalization policies was appropriate during the second episode, but not during the first. This conclusion stands despite the relatively short length of the second episode (1974–9), the comprehensiveness of changes, and the rapidity of implementation. It should be recalled that, during that span, multiple exchange rates faded, QRs, export quotas, and import duty exemptions (which covered more than 50 percent of imports) were eliminated, and tariffs, dispersed in 1973 between zero and 750 percent around an average of about 90 percent, were converted to a flat 10 percent in June 1979.

The absence of balance-of-payments problems during the second episode of liberalization supports this argument. The trade balance was not negatively affected by liberalization policies, since imports did not overshoot after the elimination of QRs in 1974 and the initial rapid reduction in tariffs immediately after; furthermore, exports expanded rapidly in terms of both aggregate growth and diversification. The large deficits appeared only after 1977 as a consequence of massive capital inflow, although they did not represent more than 20 percent of exports between 1978 and 1981.

Several factors explain this positive result. In the first place, the significant recession of 1975 stopped any overshooting of imports which could have resulted from the simultaneous elimination of QRs and exemptions. Furthermore, for mere survival, former producers of import substitutes became exporters, learning by doing and opening new markets for new products, behavior that not only sustained the trade balance in the middle of the crisis but also formed a foundation for a major export drive later on. In the second place, the authorities adopted a policy leading to a very substantial increase in the real exchange rate both to counteract, in the short run, the threat of rapidly decreasing export value posed by the sharply falling copper prices in world markets and to stimulate, in the long term, an export-led growth strategy. The exchange rate rose so high in

1975 that, despite an almost continuous appreciation of the domestic currency after 1975 until 1982, the average real rate remained higher during that period than during the previous two decades. Thus it is no coincidence that exports grew fast in this environment. In the third place, foreign debt accumulated before 1974 was renegotiated, relieving the burden of debt service and potential balance-of-payments problems in the short term. Finally, the announcement of future tariff reductions may also have led to a postponement of imports.

Employment was also affected by the trade liberalization policies. This is probably the most sensitive issue associated with the policies, and particularly with the pace of their application. According to the results of our investigation, aggregate employment was not negatively affected by the trade liberalization. This result, derived from both a microanalysis and a macroanalysis, conflicts with the views of some analysts of the period who look at the problem from rather a limited microviewpoint. We show that, on the whole, employment tends to increase in the tradeables sector, which includes both exportables and importables. This trend is concomitant with a major change in the composition of employment: employment is reduced among importables, but increases among exportables. This optimistic result of course hides a major problem caused by the frictional unemployment arising from the significant reduction in manufacturing employment, resulting from external shocks and stabilization policies at a time of very large overall unemployment. Though sector-specific unemployment was compensated for by greater employment in other sectors, in the short run workers could not adapt their skills overnight to transfer into the exportable sectors. However, this short-term dislocation does not prompt the conclusion, reached by some analysts, that consequently trade liberalization created unemployment and lost production. These adjustment costs should be considered more than redressed by changes in the structure of production consistent with improved resource allocation, quality changes, and modernization in the tradeables sector. Even if the future development of the industrial sector is less labor intensive than in the past, higher productivity in manufactures and in other sectors, as well as greater growth potential and higher development of labor intensive sectors, will have justified such policies in the long run. Furthermore, unemployment in manufactures (and mining) was more than offset by labor absorption in agriculture, so that the net impact was positive even at the time. Unfortunately, the reduction of employment in manufacturing continued after the end of the process of trade liberalization. However, this was essentially the consequence of the continued revaluation of the domestic currency as a result of the massive capital inflow after 1978, and not of trade liberalization.

A major outcome of liberalization was that rural–urban migration stopped altogether; the traditional and worldwide trend was even reversed, because exportables were intensive in the use of natural resources. Thus a side effect of the liberalization policies has been a greater decentralization of the economic activities within the country.

The second episode of liberalization suggests that, despite the general proposition that gradualism was appropriate, the schedule of tariff reductions may not have been the most appropriate. In fact, three years (1974–6) were left to cut down "true" tariffs. A more rapid elimination of the redundancy in tariffs, say one year, and a slower reduction of the true tariffs, say the other five years, would probably have been preferable. Ideally, if the margin of redundancy could have been satisfactorily assessed in advance, the redundancy might have been eliminated overnight.

Although its formula for sequencing policies for a successful and sustainable trade liberalization may not be universally applicable, the sequencing of the second episode was suitable, with the exception of special features related to the capital market. The Chilean experience suggests several related points which may be worth stressing. In the first place, the liberalization should obviously start with the elimination of QRs and other gross distortions such as multiple exchange rates, before considering reduction in tariffs. A special stage also seemed necessary (chapter 6) at the beginning of the liberalization process in 1974 to normalize commercial policies by eliminating tariff exemptions and by defining tariff rules for capital goods which had been imported free of tariffs in the past, and to specify other relevant policies for exports and imports; all these steps were important as they tended to put all potential exports and imports on the same footing right at the outset and as the elimination of import exemptions fostered interest in opening the economy still further.

The behavior of exports was crucial in the success of the second episode as opposed to the first episode. It was not the result of a special stage designed for that purpose; rather, the comparison of the two episodes indicates that setting the basic conditions for successful exports – the reduction of the anti-export bias and the establishment of a real exchange rate consistent with liberalization and the trade balance – is more important than a special stage for promoting exports. In addition, both characteristics should be kept relatively stable over time. Of course, if exports had also been "promoted" by creating an anti-import bias, they could have been successful after 1956, during the first episode, and after 1974 they could have done even better, but this does not alter our main contention. Nevertheless, an important caveat should be added. The Chilean experience indicates that a "high" real exchange rate cannot be maintained for a long time artificially since the government cannot control the price level unless tariffs are reduced permanently. It follows that a significant reduction in tariffs should preferably be coupled with exchange rate management consistent with the trend of trade balance during the entire process of liberalization and subsequently.

Stabilization policies do not appear to pose any significant problem for the sequencing of trade liberalization. However, they may pose a major problem for its success and sustainability if the exchange rate is used as a stabilization instrument to affect price expectations, as is likely to be the case. In both episodes fixing the exchange rate subjected trade liberalization to considerable strain, as there was little downward flexibility and adjustments had to be made on a quantity basis, with obvious and immediate social or political consequences. This policy is unfortunate *at any time* during trade liberalization episodes, as explained in the previous paragraph. So, if a choice is possible, it would be better to start a major trade liberalization policy after overvaluation derived from stabilization policies is over.

Overvaluation of the domestic currency could also be the consequence of a greater than expected capital inflow maintained for several years – an experience unlikely to repeat itself in Chile in the near future. Again, the conclusion remains unaltered because the reason for overvaluation is immaterial to the issue discussed here. However, if the liberalization of the capital market results in an inflow of capital considered to be relatively stable through a long period, because it is an equilibrium flow and because conditions in the world financial markets also look relatively stable, the optimum sequencing of market openings should favor opening the capital market first.

A symmetrical conclusion should be reached for the sequencing of any other policies with expected significant impacts on resource allocation, such as the freeing of prices, the elimination of subsidies, and the deepening of the market-oriented economy as occurred after 1973. All of them should preferably be carried out (as was the case between 1974 and 1979 in Chile) before or, if not, during the application of the trade liberalization policies, to insure consistency of the resource-allocation decisions. In the same vein, the coincidence of the privatization of public firms with the process of liberalization may not have been adequate because the resulting reduction in private savings available for investment did not allow the higher investments in new concerns, related to the export sector in particular and to the tradeables sector in general, required for a successful liberalization. Although the essence of the above arguments is that everything else should ideally have been done before trade liberalization, we should quickly add that the appropriate political timing for the liberalization could have faded away in the meantime.

Discriminatory treatments could not be reasonably avoided in the process of liberalization because of administrative costs. A relatively rapid reduction in tariffs is likely to reduce the costs associated with discriminatory treatments in the process of adjustment.

One important lesson of the second episode is that liberalization policies acquired more strength and support, in fact became more *sustainable*, as consumers and producers became increasingly aware of their benefits. The direct beneficiaries of these policies proliferated to include public enterprises, some import substitute producers with higher effective protection than previously, producers of nontradeables, and last but not least exporters, whose lobby grew stronger as exports were diversified. The united opinion of officials responsible for most macro policies and for different public institutions, that liberalization was needed, further strengthened the credibility of the policies in the eyes of producers and consumers.

Therefore, despite unfortunate consequences for tradeables sectors as a result of massive capital inflow (1980–2), compounded by inadequate labor legislation, a new critical recession (1982), unemployment of over 25 percent (1982–5), a financial crash (1982–3), stringency of foreign reserves from continuously falling terms of trade and high debt services (1982–6), growing protectionism in world markets, and even a campaign led by entrepreneurial organizations to protect the domestic market from foreign competition (1982–4), the essential features of liberalization policies – low and flat tariffs, high real exchange rates, and absence of QRs and discriminatory treatments – were maintained. An attempt in 1984 to modify tariffs significantly did not last; some surcharges were applied to counter specific cases of dumping, but they were firmly restricted to a few products. The failure of this attempt was not even criticized by the traditionally stubborn supporters of high and discriminatory tariffs. The durability of this episode has been increasingly insured because sustainability breeds on itself.

Political continuity is an important explanation of the durability of the second episode; in other words, decisions related to liberalization policies were not subjected to contradictory political influence. These arguments do not, however, permit the conclusion that the benefits of liberalization have been so widely and deeply endorsed that it could not be overturned in a significant political shake-up. Pressure groups of entrepreneurs will always exist to seek protection, but it is likely that problems would come more from politicians than from these groups. There seems to be a complete dissociation between the entrepreneurial groups and the politicians who would take over with a change of regime.

Appendix 1 The Index of Liberalization

The Information Base

In this appendix we explain the selection of information used to construct an ordinal index of liberalization, and then present the analytical framework used to derive the index. The index itself is given in table 1.1 and figure 1.1.

If the process of liberalization is understood to be a move toward an equalization of domestic to international relative prices, then the best index of liberalization should be a direct comparison between domestic and international prices for a wide range of tradeable goods and services. The estimate of an implicit tariff rate (ITR) would serve the purpose. The ITR is defined as the ratio of the domestic price (net of normal distribution costs) to the c.i.f. price minus one. For Chile, this index is available with significant coverage for only three years – 1961, 1968, and 1969 (table A1.1).

The estimation of an ITR for the other years met with considerable difficulties. Chilean ITRs cannot generally be calculated by simply adjusting the c.i.f. prices by the amount of legal tariff rates and other legal charges because QRs sometimes create import premiums and because there are numerous exemptions from the legal rates. Therefore direct comparisons should be used. However, the periods 1950–60 and 1970–4 were characterized by widespread price controls as well as by generalized parallel or black markets for these same goods. Unfortunately, available data are limited to official prices and scattered parallel prices.

In the absence of ITRs for the whole period, an alternative would be to turn to effective protection rates, defined as the ratio of the difference between value added and international value added to the international value added. Available estimates for 1961, 1968, and 1969 were completed by a series of two-digit industrial subsectors for the period 1974–9. The resulting series is still far from satisfactory: the coverage for the period 1950–73 is very limited and is restricted to manufactures after these years.

Table A1.1 Implicit tariff rates, effective protection rates, and domestic resource costs in Chile, 28 sectors, selected years (percent)

	ITR			*Effective protection rate*						*DRC*	
Trade goods sector	*1961*	*1968*	*1968*[a]	*1961*	*1961*[b]	*1967*	*1968*[a]	*1975*	*1979*	*1961*	*1968*
1 Agriculture and forestry	43	1	19	50	145	−7	15	27	10	250	111
2 Fishing	21	n.a.	n.a.	25	n.a.	n.a.	n.a.	n.a.	n.a.	n.a.	n.a.
3 Coal mining	37	n.a.	n.a.	31	n.a.	n.a.	n.a.	n.a.	n.a.	n.a.	n.a.
4 Iron mining	2	n.a.	0	−7	n.a.	n.a.	−12	n.a.	n.a.	n.a.	n.a.
5 Copper mining	0	n.a.	0	−14	n.a.	n.a.	−10	n.a.	n.a.	n.a.	180
6 Nitrate mining	1	n.a.	0	−6	n.a.	n.a.	−11	n.a.	n.a.	n.a.	60
7 Stone, clay, and sands	66	n.a.	n.a.	64	n.a.	n.a.	n.a.	n.a.	n.a.	n.a.	n.a.
8 Other mining	46	n.a.	6	40	n.a.	n.a.	−6	n.a.	n.a.	n.a.	82
9 Food products	82	32	27	2,884	217	365	3	105	10	253	97
10 Beverages	122	7	n.a.	609	164	−23	n.a.	119	13	259	n.a.
11 Tobacco	106	9	n.a.	141	1	−12	n.a.	68	11	47	n.a.
12 Textiles	182	99	n.a.	672	462	492	n.a.	138	14	n.a.	n.a.
13 Footwear and clothing	255	23	29	386	318	16	5	164	14	1,916	52
14 Wood and cork	35	0	24	21	30	−4	22	93	15	210	161
15 Furniture	129	0	30	209	127	−5	18	58	11	241	73
16 Paper and paper products	55	44	27	41	49	95	14	114	17	683	164
17 Printing and publishing	72	0	n.a.	82	77	−15	n.a.	75	12	297	n.a.
18 Leather and leather products	161	25	15	714	325	18	−20	98	13	2,109	55
19 Rubber products	102	125	n.a.	109	137	304	n.a.	55	15	77	n.a.
20 Chemical products	94	38	24	89	107	64	14	53	13	356	75
21 Petroleum and coal products	50	55	n.a.	45	−26	1,140	n.a.	101	13	47	n.a.
22 Nonmetallic mineral products	139	27	n.a.	227	179	1	n.a.	87	14	n.a.	n.a.
23 Basic metals	66	25	28	198	74	35	21	86	17	n.a.	380
24 Metallic products	59	80	n.a.	43	45	92	n.a.	101	15	217	n.a.
25 Nonelectrical machinery	84	56	12	85	73	76	−9	72	13	150	59
26 Electrical machinery	105	162	26	111	92	449	10	72	13	131	50
27 Transport equipment	84	150	21	101	68	271	1	n.a.	n.a.	118	50
28 Other manufacturing	125	n.a.	18	164	129	n.a.	4	n.a.	n.a.	175	41
Equally weighted arithmetic mean	83	48	18	254	133	168	3	90	13	419	106
Standard deviation	58	51	11	552	117	282	13	33	2	598	80
Range	255	162	30	2,898	488	1,127	42	137	7	2,109	339

n.a., not available.

[a] For subsectoral exports only.

[b] Corrected for specific differences between world and domestic prices of intermediate goods imports.

Sources: Behrman, 1976; Aedo and Lagos, 1984

Estimates for the domestic resource cost (DRG) – the value of domestic resources (at opportunity costs) employed in earning or saving a dollar of foreign exchange in the domestic production of a good – are even scarcer. Only two estimates are available: for 1961 and 1968. Both rely heavily on basic information from 1962 and marginally, in the second case, from 1968 (table A1.1). The main shortcomings of the estimates are the high level of aggregation and the lack of a proper definition of the shadow price of capital.

In view of these deficiencies, it was decided to reach an ordinal index of intensity of liberalization through an iterative process, by matching several independent indexes constructed for the period 1950–80 or for some subperiod thereof. The indexes chosen were as follows: QRs, nominal exchange rate, real exchange rate, effective exchange rate, effective exchange rate premium included, and percentage of imports to GDP.

Qualitative judgments based on the literature, when doubts arose, and debates among the team's members were also ingredients of the outcome, which is presented as the final column of table 1.1 and figure 1.1. Specific comments will be made on each of the indices chosen.

Index of Quantitative Restrictions (IQR)

IQR is based on an estimate prepared by Ffrench-Davis (1973) and extended to include the years 1950, 1951, and 1970–80. The intention of the Ffrench-Davis index is to summarize the effects of prohibitions, quotas, administrative delays, prohibitive tariffs, and advance deposit requirements. A monthly account of all restrictions expressed quantitatively (for example, the number and coverage of restrictions) was transformed into an annual qualitative index ranging from zero to 20. The ordinal increase meant a reduction in restrictions or an increase in the degree of liberalization. The index was completed by adding value obtained by using the same methodology for 1950, 1951, and 1970–80.

To include the period 1970–80, the Ffrench-Davis index had to be adjusted downward; the index was considered to be over-inflated for our purposes because 1961, the most open year during the period analyzed (1952–70), had received the maximum of 20. Yet this value assigned by the Ffrench-Davis index corresponds only to a relatively open year when the situation is compared with the years 1979 and 1980. Perfect comparability in the IQR cannot be assured because the final qualitative judgment was made by two different people. However, a check of consistency between the two studies did not reveal significant discrepancies: the results based on our criteria and those of Ffrench-Davis were similar.

Ratio of Effective Exchange Rate to the Nominal Exchange Rate (ERR)

The nominal exchange rate was estimated as an average of exchange rates applied during the relevant periods weighted by the value of goods imported for each exchange rate category. To obtain the effective exchange rate, several elements were added to the nominal exchange rate: (a) tariffs effectively paid as a percentage of total imports, (b) the cost of advance deposits, (c) the financial cost of future market transactions. The cost of advance deposits was estimated by using the weighted average of the percentage of import values that have to be deposited and of the length of time until they mature. The percentages ranged from 10 to 10,000 and the maturity period from 30 to 180 days.

The result, expressed as a ratio of annual imports, was added as a surcharge to the nominal exchange rate. Another surcharge to the nominal exchange rate was the financial cost of making transactions with future rates instead of spot rates. This cost arises from the domestic currency deposit the importer was required to make, for a period ranging from 56 to 120 days, in order to operate in this market.

Ratio of Black-market Rate to Official Rate (BMR)

The BMR is used here to indicate tightness of controls in the foreign exchange market. As such, it is related to the severity of international trade restrictions. It can also be considered as an effective exchange rate for some marginal transactions of goods, services, and capital, because tariffs, taxes, and other charges are generally avoided when the black market is the source of foreign exchange.

Behrman (1976) has found econometric support for this hypothesis in two correlations: first by correlating the price level deflated by the black-market exchange rate with the Ffrench-Davis quantitative index, and second by correlating the difference between the price level deflated by the legal nominal exchange rate and the price level deflated by the black-market exchange rate with the Ffrench-Davis index. The period covered starts with the initiation of the last attempt at stabilization with liberalization. This ratio can be interpreted as a measurement of the cumulative pressures for another liberalization attempt (in the foreign exchange market) due to the disequilibrium system, and thus leading to speculative capital flight. In fact, the BMR used here could also be considered as an index of economic and political expectations. Consequently, it is not free from ambiguity; its use was checked for evidence of political turmoil, expectations of major devaluations, and capital flight.

The official rate used is the one which has traditionally prevailed for the majority of international goods transactions.

Exports Quotas Index (EQI)

Export quotas existed up to 1962, when they were completely eliminated (de la Cuadra and Hachette, 1988, appendix table A.20). These quotas, officially at least, directly restricted trade. How restrictive they actually were is difficult to assess, since information on international demand, domestic excess supply, and the relevant prices for these products was not available. Consequently, it was assumed that the restrictive impact of export quotas was proportional to its size.

The index was obtained by collecting the information available on 17 products for which export quotas had existed during some part of the period. A specific index was constructed for each product with 1951 = 100 as the base year. To avoid unit problems the value of the index for year t was obtained by using the ratio.

$$\frac{\text{quota product } j\text{, year } t}{(\text{quota product } j\text{, year } 0 + \text{quota product } j\text{, year } t) \, / \, 2}$$

The value of the quota assigned for a year free from export quotas was taken to be the maximum quota that had prevailed previously or later. This is rather arbitrary, although it was found that there was not much difference between the maximum quota and the mode of export of these products when free from quotas.

Implicit Tariff Rate (ITR)

The ITR is an effective exchange rate, deflated according to price level, and including premiums.

The rate is based on a comparison of international and domestic prices for 220 products. These time series were normalized to be consistent with the 1961 ratios of domestic to c.i.f. price estimates used for computing 1961 effective protection rates. Unfortunately, this "ideal" index for liberalization effort reflects a combined pattern of elements not directly related to trade controls, such as distribution margins, international shipping, quality differentials, monopolistic power in domestic markets, and time lags between changes in foreign and domestic prices. Changes over time in all or any of these factors would distort the impact of trade controls. However, these elements could not be separated from the pure tariff cum premium effect. Another deficiency of the index is its incompleteness: it only goes up to 1970.

The remaining indicator, the tariff collection ratio, needs no explanation.

Index for the Period 1983–1986

The index for the period 1983–6 was constructed considering only nominal tariffs since there were no QRs. Although tariffs were raised after 1982 the uniform structure was maintained, except for 34 products subject to surcharges (see chapter 5). By comparing these tariffs with the average nominal tariffs in the years preceding 1980 and applying the criterion that, among equal average tariffs of different dispersion, the average tariff structure with lower dispersion has a higher value in the index, the values shown in table A1.2 for the period 1983–6 were obtained.

Table A1.2 Estimates for the index of liberalization, 1976–1986

Year	Average tariff (%)	Tariff minimum	Range maximum	Index
1976	33	10	70	12
1977	22	10	50	15
1978	14	10	35	17
1979	11	10	16	20
1980–2	10	10	10	20
1983	15	10	10	18
		20	20	
1984	24	20	20	16
		35	35	
1985	26	30	30	16
		30	30	
		20	20	
1986	20	20	20	17

The average tariffs are calculated for the year. Values for the index also represent an estimate for the year – hence the blank spaces.

Analytical Framework for an Ordinal Index of Restrictions

Definitions

We define the ordinal index of restrictions (OIR) as a function of a vector of trade restriction indicators:

$$\text{OIR} = f(\text{TCR}, \text{ERR}, \text{IQR}, \text{EQI}, \text{ITR}, \text{BMR})$$

where TCR is the tariff collection ratio (ratio of tariff revenue to total imports), ERR is the exchange rates ratio (ratio of effective exchange rate to nominal exchange rate), IQR is the index of quantitative import restrictions, EQI is the export quota index, ITR is the implicit tariff rate, and BMR is the black-market rate ratio (ratio of the black-market rate to the official rate). These trade restriction indicators have been defined and discussed in the previous section.

We will consider imports M to be a function of the OIR and a vector $(X_1 \ldots X_n)$ of other variables such as the GDP, the mix of economic policies, foreign credit, etc.:

$$M = \phi(\text{OIR}; X_1, \ldots, X_n)$$

Hypothesis

1 When the OIR increases the TCR can increase or decrease depending on the level of the OIR. Then

$$\left.\frac{\partial \text{OIR}}{\partial \text{TCR}}\right|_{0 < \text{OIR} < \text{OIR}^*} > 0$$

$$\left.\frac{\partial \text{OIR}}{\partial \text{TCR}}\right|_{\text{OIR} > \text{OIR}^*} < 0$$

We postulate that $\frac{\partial M}{\partial \text{OIR}} < 0$ for all levels of OIR. On the basis of this relationship we can establish the following:

$$\text{dOIR}(\text{dTCR} > 0; \text{d}M < 0) > 0$$
$$\text{dOIR}(\text{dTCR} < 0; \text{d}M > 0) < 0$$
$$\text{dOIR}(\text{dTCR} > 0; \text{d}M > 0) < 0$$
$$\text{dOIR}(\text{dTCR} < 0; \text{d}M < 0) > 0$$

Following this, we can determine unambiguously the sign of

$$\frac{\partial \text{OIR}}{\partial \text{TCR}}$$

by inspecting the combined changes of TCR and M.

2 The ERR is a composite of tariff collection, the cost of prior deposits, and the financial cost of future market transactions. Therefore, the same considerations as applied in point 1 are valid for this indicator.

3 No discussion is required of the positive correlation between OIR and IQR, i.e.

$$\frac{\partial \text{OIR}}{\partial \text{IQR}} > 0$$

4 The symmetry between tariffs on imports and taxes on exports is also applied to quotas; therefore

$$\frac{\partial \text{OIR}}{\partial \text{EQI}} > 0.$$

5 The ITR is a mix of tariffs t, markups m, and "premiums" p due to QRs; this relationship will be represented by

$$\text{ITR} = \varphi(t, m, p); \frac{\partial \varphi}{\partial t}, \frac{\partial \varphi}{\partial m}, \frac{\partial \varphi}{\partial p} > 0$$

Some empirical evidence shows that, at least in the short run, the following holds:

$$m = m(t; p); \frac{\partial m}{\partial t}, \frac{\partial m}{\partial p} < 0$$

when t and p decrease. If the increase in markup more than compensates for the decrease in t or p, then

$$\frac{\partial \text{ITR}}{\partial t} = \overset{(+)}{\frac{\partial \varphi}{\partial t}} + \overset{(+)}{\frac{\partial \varphi}{\partial m}} \; \overset{(-)}{\frac{\partial m}{\partial t}} < 0$$

$$\frac{\partial \text{ITR}}{\partial p} = \overset{(+)}{\frac{\partial \varphi}{\partial \varphi}} + \overset{(+)}{\frac{\partial \varphi}{\partial m}} \; \overset{(-)}{\frac{\partial m}{\partial p}} < 0$$

This can result in an ambiguous relationship between OIR and ITR, which should be considered when the index of liberalization is being analyzed. We cannot be sure that a higher ITR implies a higher OIR because $\partial \text{ITR}/\partial t$ or $\partial \text{ITR}/\partial p$ can be negative for diminishing t and p.

6 The BMR is determined by exchange rate controls and capital movements channeled through the black market. Thus BMR can increase owing to an outflow of capital even though exchange controls have not changed. Therefore this indicator should be considered with caution as a proxy for exchange controls: $\partial \text{OIR}/\partial \text{EMR} > 0$ for constant capital movements.

Building the OIR This framework allows us to capture changes in the OIR. The signs +, −, and 0 are used for an increase, decrease, and no change in each indicator. More plus than minus signs for a year mean a higher OIR compared with the previous year, and so on. The procedure permits comparison only with the adjacent years.

Appendix 2 Static Benefits from Liberalization

In line with Harberger (1959), the static benefit from liberalization can be measured by the difference between the social and market values of incremental exports resulting from the reduction in trade restrictions. (This methodology will be applied to each sector later on.) The change in exports is measured by the increase in the ratio X/Y of exports to GDP, and the benefit is approximated by

$$\frac{\Delta W}{Y} = \frac{1}{2} \Delta T \frac{\Delta X}{Y}$$

where W is welfare, Y is the nominal income, and T are tariffs.

The Ratio of Exports to Gross Domestic Product

For any year t, the ratio is

$$\frac{X}{Y} = \frac{X_R P_X \pi}{Y_R P_Y}$$

where X_R are the real exports, P_X is the export price index, π is the nominal exchange rate, Y_R is the real income, and P_Y is the GDP deflator. We are interested in changes in the X/Y index produced by changes in X_R and not in those corresponding to fluctuations in relative prices ($P_X\pi/P_Y$). Accordingly we will first estimate an export-to-GDP ratio defined as

$$R_{XY_t} = \left(\frac{1 + r_x}{1 + r_y}\right)^t$$

where r_X and r_Y are the real growth rates of exports and income respectively.

To express the export increase in terms of percentage of GDP, although independently of relative price fluctuations, we will take as a base-year ratio X_0/Y_0 corrected by an average relative price of exports to GDP deflator as year zero may not have been a "normal" year:

$$\left(\frac{X}{Y}\right)_t = \left(\frac{1 + r_x}{1 + r_y}\right)^t \frac{X_0}{Y_0} \frac{\overline{P}_X \pi}{\overline{P}_T}$$

where X_0 are the real exports in the base year ($t = 0$), Y_0 is the real income in the base year ($t = 0$), and P_X, π, and P_Y are the average prices during a given period. $(x/y)_t$ will be calculated for the period 1960–81. The base year for X and Y was 1960, and the subperiod 1960–70 was chosen for the estimate of the averages $\overline{P}_X$, π, and $\overline{P}_Y$.

The behavior of the two indices R_{XY} and (X/Y) is shown in table A2.1. R_{XY} averages 1.00 for the period 1960–70, 1.83 for the period 1976–9 and 1.77 for the period 1980–1. This means that during the liberalization period the export-to-GDP ratio increased by 83 percent compared with the average in the 1960s, or, in terms of $(x/y)_t$, the ratio was 11.4 percent in the

Table A2.1 Export ratios

	Export growth rate (%)	*GDP growth rate (%)*	R_{XY}[a]	(X/Y)[a]
1960	–	7.3	1.00	0.1136
1961	7.1	5.6	1.01	0.1148
1962	5.5	4.0	1.03	0.1170
1963	0.6	6.7	0.97	0.1102
1964	10.5	3.0	1.04	0.1182
1965	7.2	0.6	1.11	0.1261
1966	4.0	11.0	1.04	0.1182
1967	1.4	3.4	1.02	0.1159
1968	−0.8	3.3	0.98	0.1114
1969	−1.1	3.9	0.93	0.1057
1970	2.8	2.0	0.94	0.1068
1971	8.3	9.1	0.93	0.1057
1972	−12.6	−1.0	0.82	0.0932
1973	−0.6	−5.8	0.87	0.0989
1974	49.4	1.0	1.28	0.1454
1975	8.1	−12.9	1.59	0.1807
1976	25.1	3.5	1.93	0.2193
1977	7.9	9.9	1.89	0.2148
1978	6.0	8.4	1.85	0.2102
1979	−2.7	8.1	1.66	0.1886
1980	18.4	7.4	1.83	0.2079
1981	−1.4	5.5	1.17	0.1943

–, negligible.

[a] See definitions in text. The values used for estimating (X/Y) are $P_X = 1.23$, $\pi = 4.265$, $P_Y = 5.00$, and $X_0/Y_0 = 0.1083$.

Table A2.2 Tariffs by import category

I	*T (%)*	*II*	*T (%)*	*III*	*T (%)*	*IV*	*T (%)*
Food products	30	Shoes and clothing	49	Textiles	47	Machinery	43
Beverages	32	Furniture	30	Leather products	34		
Tobacco	28	Printing and publishing	36	Wood products	30		
		Rubber products	39	Paper products	35		
		Nonmetal minerals	36	Chemicals	35		
		Metal products	47	Petroleum	20		
		Domestic appliances	50	Basic metals	32		
				Agriculture	21		
				Mining	21		
Average tariff	30		41		31		43
Weight of imports	0.141		0.161		0.485		0.212

1960s and 20.8 percent in the period 1976–9. Therefore we will consider an increase in exports of 9.4 percent of GDP (Harberger's estimate in 1959 was 10 percent as an optimistic upper limit).

The Change in Tariffs

An average change of t was obtained in four categories of goods: I, food, beverages, and tobacco; II, consumption goods except those in I; III, raw materials and intermediate goods; IV, machinery and equipment. The average change in the tariff in the period 1976–9 is calculated using

$$\Delta T = \sum_{i=\mathrm{I}}^{\mathrm{IV}} \frac{\Delta M_i}{\Delta M} \Delta T_i$$

where ΔT_i is the change in the average nominal tariff in group i between the fourth quarter of 1976 and the fourth quarter of 1979 (simple averages were taken), ΔM_i is the change in imports of group i in period 1976–9, and ΔM is the change in total imports in the period 1976–9.

The Static Benefit

The change in welfare can now be expressed as

$$\begin{aligned}\Delta W &= \frac{1}{2} \sum_{\mathrm{I}}^{\mathrm{IV}} \frac{\Delta M_i}{\Delta M} \Delta T_i \left[\left(\frac{X}{Y}\right)_{x(76\text{–}9)} - \left(\frac{\hat{X}}{Y}\right)_{\mathrm{X}(60\text{–}70)} \right] \\ &= \frac{1}{2}(0.245)(9.44) \\ &= 1.16\end{aligned}$$

The values of the variables are given in table A2.2. This means that the static benefit from liberalization is around 1.2 percent of GDP. Harberger's higher limit was 2.5 percent assuming $\Delta T = 0.5$ and $\Delta X/Y =$ 10 percent.

References

Aedo, Cristían and Luis Felipe Lagos (1984) "Protección efectiva en Chile 1974–1979:" Instituto de Economía, Pontificia Universidad Católica de Chile, Documento de Trabajo no. 94.

Alessandri, Jorge (1960) "Mensaje Presidencial," May 21, 1960. Santiago: Departmento de Publicaciones de la Presidencia de le República de Chile, Imprenta de la Penítenciería.

Arbildúa, Beatriz and Rolf Lüders (1968) "Una evaluación comparada de tres programas anti-inflacionarios en Chile: una década de historia monetaria 1955–1966." *Cuadernos de Economía*, 5 (14), 25–105.

Behrman, Jere Richard (1976) *Foreign Trade Regime and Economic Development: Chile, Special Conference Series on Foreign Trade Regimes and Economic Development, National Bureau of Economic Research*, vol. VIII. New York: Columbia University Press.

Bhagwati, Jagdish and T. N. Srinivasan (1983) *Lectures on International Trade*. Cambridge, MA: MIT Press.

Castañeda, Tarsicio (1984) "Evolución del empleo y desempleo y el impacto de cambios demográficos sobre la tasa de empleo en Chile: 1960–1983." Departamento de Economía Universidad de Chile, Documento de Investigación no. 64.

Cauas, Jorge (1975) "Report on the state of public finance." In J. C. Mendez, ed., *Chilean Economic Policy*. Santiago: Dirección de Presupuesto (DIPRES).

Central Bank of Chile (1984) *Informe Económico de Chile*.

Central Bank of Chile, *Balanza de Pagos*.

Central Bank of Chile, *Boletín Mensual*.

Central Bank of Chile, *Cuentas Nacionales*.

Central Bank of Chile, *Deuda Externa*.

Central Bank of Chile, *Indicadores Económicos y Sociales 1960–1982*.

Cline, William R. (1984) *International Debt: Systemic Risk and Policy Response*. Cambridge, MA: MIT Press.

Coeymans, Juan Eduardo (1978a) "Liberalización del comercio exterior y sus efectos sobre la asignacioń de recursos y empleo." *Cuadernos de Economía*, 15 (45), August, 183–245.

Coeymans, Juan Eduardo (1978b) "Reforma arancelaria, precio del cobre y asignación de recursos." Instituto de Economía, Pontificia Universidad Católica de Chile, Documento de Trabajo no. 60.

Coeymans, Juan Eduardo (1983) "Determinantes de la migración rural–urbana en Chile según origen y destino." *Cuadernos de Economía*, 20 (59), April, 43–64.

Coeymans, Juan Eduardo (1986) "Estimations of the capital stock," unpublished paper. Available at Pontificia Universidad Católica de Chile.

Coloma, Fernando and Pablo González (1986) "Credibilidad de la política comercial," Pontificia Universidad Católica de Chile, Documento de Trabajo no. 102.

Corbo, Vittorio and Patricio Meller (1977) "Sustitución de importaciones, promoción de exportaciones y empleo: el caso chileno." Santiago: Programa de Empleo para América Latina y el Caribe, Investigaciones sobre Empleo no. 4.

Corbo, Vittorio and José M. Sánchez (1984) "Impact on firms of the liberalization and stabilization policies in Chile: some case studies." Instituto de Economía, Pontificia Universidad Católica de Chile, Documento de Trabajo no. 91.

Corbo, Vittorio and José M. Sánchez (1985) "Adjustment by industrial firms in Chile during 1974–1982." In V. Corbo and J. de Melo, eds, *Scrambling for Survival: How Firms Adjusted to the Recent Reform in Chile, Uruguay, and Argentina*. Washington, DC: World Bank, Staff Working Paper no. 764.

Cox, Maximiliano, ed. (1983) *Agriculture Chilena, 1974–1982: Políticas, Evolución y Campesinado*. Santiago: Desarrollo Campesino.

de Castro, Sergio (1979) "Failure of protectionist policy in Chile." In J. C. Mendez, ed., *Chilean Economic Policy*. Santiago: Dirección de Presupuesto (DIPRES).Cauas, Jorge (1974) "Report on the state of public finance." In J. C. Mendez, ed., *Chilean Economic Policy*. Santiago: Dirección de Presupuesto (DIPRES).

de Gregorio, José (1984) "Comportamiento de las exportaciones e importaciones en Chile. Un estudio econométrico." Corporación de Investigaciones Económicas para Latinoamérica, Estudio no. 135, 53–86.

de Gregorio, José (1985) "Deuda externa, escenario económico externo y cuenta corriente en Chile: perspective para el período 1985–1990." Corporación de Investigaciones Económicas para Latinoamérica, Nota Técnica no. 68.

de Gregorio, José (1986) "Principales aspectos de la política cambiaria en Chile: 1974–1985." Corporación de Investigaciones Económicas para Latinoamérica, Nota Técnica no. 81.

de la Cuadra, Sergio and Hernán Cortés (1984) "Recesiones económicas, crisis cambiarias y ciclos inflacionarios, Chile: 1926–1982." Instituto de Economía, Pontificia Universidad Católica de Chile.

de la Cuadra, Sergio and Dominique Hachette (1985) "The timing and sequencing of a trade liberalization policy: the case of Chile. Part I: Documento de Trabajo no. 98; Part II: Statistical Appendix." Background paper available at Instituto de Economía, Pontificia Universidad Católica de Chile.

de la Cuadra, Sergio and Dominique Hachette (1985) "The timing and sequencing of trade liberalization policies: Chile, statistical appendix." Available from the Brazil Department, World Bank, Washington, DC.

Desormeaux, Jorge and Luis Bravo (1984) "Modelo agregado de la balanza comercial: Chile 1974–1982." Paper presented at the Annual Meeting of Economists, Punta de Tralca.

Díaz-Alejandro, Carlos Federico (1984) "In toto: I don't think we are in Kansas anymore." *Brookings Papers on Economic Activity*, September.

Fetter, Frank W. (1937) *Monetary Inflation in Chile*. Santiago: Universidad de Chile.

Ffrench-Davis, Ricardo (1973) *Políticas Económicas en Chile 1952–1970*. Santiago: Ediciones Nueva Universidad.

Foxley, Juan (1985) "Ahorro interno y ahorro privado: realidad y perspectivas para Chile 1985–1990." Santiago: Centro de Estudios del Desarrollo.

Frankel, Jeffrey A., Kenneth A. Froot, and Alejandra Mizzala (1985) "Credibility, the optimal speed of trade liberalization, real interest rates, and the Latin American debt." Mimeo. Washington, DC: World Bank.

Fuenzalida, Javier and Sergio Undurraga (1968) *El Crédito y su Distribución en Chile*. Santiago: Lambda.

Gatica, Juan and Molly Pollack (1986) "Fuentes del cambio en la estructura del sector industrial chileno: 1967–1982." Programa Regional de Empleo para América Latina y el Caribe, Documento de Trabajo no. 274.

Gotuzzo, Lorenzo (1974) "Three years to end protection; new tariff schedule under study." In J. C. Mendez, ed., *Chilean Economic Policy*. Santiago: Dirección de Presupeusto (DIPRES).

Hachette, Dominique (1973a) "Efectos redistributivos de las políticas cambiarias y arancelarias sobre el ingreso personal, 1958–1961." *Cuadernos de Economía*, 10 (30–1) August–December, 51–131.

Hachette, Dominique (1973b) "Revaluation of the escudo and distribution of income." Ph.D. dissertation, Department of Economics, University of Chicago.

Harberger, Arnold C. (1959) "Using resources at hand more effectively." *American Economic Review*, 49, May, 134–146.

Harberger, Arnold C. (1985) "Observations on the Chilean economy, 1973–1983." *Economic Development and Cultural Change*, 33 (3), 451–62.

IMF (International Monetary Fund) (1985) *World Economic Outlook*, April, Washington, DC.

IMF, *Recent Economic Developments*, various issues. Washington, DC.

INSORA (Instituto de Organización y Administración) (1962) *El Financiamiento de la Industria en Chile*. Santiago. Universidad de Chile.

Ivulic, Ivan (1984) "Modelo de comercio exterior, período 1975–1983." Paper presented at the Annual Meeting of Economists, Punta de Tralca, December.

Jadresíc, Esteban (1985) "Evolución del empleo sectorial: Chile, 1970–1983." Corporación de Investigaciones Económicas para Latinoamérica, Nota Técnica no. 79.

Jadresíc, Esteban (1986) "Elasticidades empleo-producto de la economía chilena." Corporación de Investigaciones Económicas para Latinoamérica, Nota Técnica no. 85.

Jeftanovic, Pedro (1980) "El mercado de capitales en Chile, 1940–1978." Departamento de Economía, Universidad de Chile, Documento de Investigación no. 39.

Libano, Dolores (1970) "El tipo de cambio en Chile desde 1948." Mimeo. Central Bank of Chile.

Lüders, Rolf (1968) "A monetary history of Chile." Ph.D. dissertation, Department of Economics, University of Chicago.

Marshall, Jorge and Pedro Romaguera (1981) "La evolución del empleo público en Chile 1970–1978." Corporación de Investigaciones Económicas para Latinoamérica, Nota Tecnica no. 26.

Meller, Patricio (1984) "Análisis de problema de la alta tasa de desocupación chilena." Corporación de Investigaciones Económicas para Latinomérica Estudio, no. 14, September, 9–41.

Muñoz, Oscar (1975) "Estado e industrialización en el ciclo de expansión del salitre." Corporación de Investigaciones Económicas para Latinoamérica, Estudio no. 6.

Mussa, Michael (1974) "Tariffs and the distribution of income; the importance of factor specificity, substitutability and intensity in the short and long run." *Journal of Political Economy*, 82 (6), 1191–1203.

Mussa, Michael (1984) "The adjustment process and the timing of trade liberalization." National Bureau of Economic Research, Working Paper Series no. 1458, September, 1–98.

Piñera, José (1977) "Hacia un desarrollo integral." *Informe Económico 1976–1977*, Colocadora Nacional de Valores.

Ramos, Joseph (1984) "Estabilización y liberalización económica en el cono sur." Comisión Económica para América Latina y el Caribe Estudios e Informes, no. 38. Santiago de Chile: Naciones Unidas.

Riveros, Luis (1983) "Efectos de la apertura comercial sobre el empleo: un análisis de desequilibrio." Universidad de Chile, Estudios de Economía no. 21, 2nd Semester.

Sierra, Enrique, Sergio Benavente, and Juan Osorio (1967) *Las Políticas de Estabilización en Chile: 1956–1966*, vol. II. Santiago: Universidad de Chile.

Sjaastad, Larry A. (1981) "Protección y el volúmen de comercio en Chile: la evidencia." *Cuadernos de Economía*, 18 (54–5), August–December, 263–92.

Sjaastad, Larry A. and Hernán A. Cortés (1981) "Protección y empleo." *Cuadernos de Economía*, 18 (54–5), August–December, 317–60.

Tokman, Víctor (1984) "Reactivación con transformación: el efecto empleo." Corporación de Investigaciones Económicas para Latinoamérica, Estudio no. 14, 105–27.

Torres, Cecilia (177) *Compendio de Disposiciones Legales Relativas a Franquicias Aduaneras Vigentes*. Santiago: Central Bank of Chile.

Universidad de Chile, Instituto de Economía (1963a) *La Economía de Chile en el Período 1950–63*, vol. II, *Cuadros Estadísticos*. Santiago: Universidad de Chile, Instituto de Economía.

Wisecarver, Daniel L. (1983) "Economic regulation and deregulation in Chile since September 1973." Mimeo. Pontificia Universidad Católica de Chile, December. Published 1986, "Regulación y deregulación en Chile: 1973–1980." *Estudios Públicos*, 22, 115–69.

World Bank (1965) *El Mercado de Capital en Chile* (out of print).

World Bank (1980) *Chile, an Economy in Transition*, Washington, DC: World Bank Country Study.

World Bank (1981) "Chile: economic memorandum." Washington, DC: World Bank, Report no. 2406–CH.

Part III

Uruguay

Edgardo Favaro
University of Chicago
Minister of Planning, Uruguay

Pablo T. Spiller
The Hoover Institution
University of Illinois

Contents

List of Figures

List of Tables

Acknowledgments

We would like to thank Javier de Haedo, Isabel Miguez, and Eduardo Sciandra for helpful technical assistance. Helpful comments were provided by project participants and in particular by Arnold Harberger and the project directors. The completion of the tariff levels was facilitated with the help of the directors and employees of Comas and Garretano, the Banco de la República Oriental del Uruguay, the Banco Central del Uruguay, and the Oficina de Planeamiento y Presupuesto.

1

Introduction

The post-war history of Uruguay took Uruguayans and foreign observers alike by surprise. This small country, with a well-educated and stable population of just above 2 million in the 1940s, enjoying a relatively high standard of living, was expected to achieve the dream of becoming the "Switzerland" of South America. Instead, Uruguay's experience during the second half of this century has been one of stagnation, inflation, and instability, not very different, in a sense, from the other Latin American countries.

The Uruguayan political system responded to the major events of the first half of this century by increasing the extent of government intervention in the economy. By 1950 Uruguay's public sector comprised all major public utilities (electricity, water, telecommunications, and railroads), and had state monopolies in the provision of insurance, alcohol, and petroleum refining. The economic impact of the public sector, however, extended well beyond its productive role. By 1950 Uruguay had a very well developed welfare system, providing coverage unparalleled in the region.[1] Public employment seemed to be part of the welfare system, as public sector employment was the major driving force behind much of the employment growth in the post-war period. Finally, and perhaps more importantly, after the 1930s Uruguay pursued a policy of import substitution, with foreign trade restrictions reaching their highest level in the early 1970s.

By then, however, the dreams of becoming the "Switzerland" of South America were shattered and replaced by the reality of stagnation. By the late 1960s economic stagnation and the development of the urban guerrilla movement paralyzed the political system as well. A military coup followed in 1973.

Thus, Uruguay reached the early 1970s with an overtaxed agricultural sector, an export sector almost totally based on agricultural products, a labor market characterized by emigration and public employment, a

1 For a description of the development of the Uruguayan welfare state, see Finch (1980).

depreciated industrial capital stock, and a strongly regulated financial sector with recurrent capital flight and currency crises. Thus the ability of the Uruguayan economy to respond to the oil shock of 1973 by maintaining its foreign trade structure intact was very limited. Further import substitution was impossible, and an export drive was required. In July 1974 the military appointed a new economic team which responded to the balance-of-payments crisis generated by the oil shock and the initial accommodative policies by introducing major foreign exchange, trade liberalization, and taxation reforms (tables 1.1 and 1.2).

The economy reacted to the new reforms with a flexibility unseen during the post-war era. From 1974 to 1981 the annual rate of growth was at record levels, with an average of 4 percent for the period, the ratio of investment to gross domestic product (GDP) also reached a record level of 20 percent, and the emigration process that started during the 1960s was reversed by 1981. Foreign trade increased substantially, as did capital

Table 1.1 Summary table for the 1974–1982 episode

Broad nature	From 1974 to 1978, elimination of quantitative restrictions and reduction of maximum tariff levels; from 1980 to 1982, gradual announced tariff reduction
Targets	Export growth strategy
Economic circumstances before	
Balance of payments	Before 1974 deficit; afterwards, current account deficit
Prices of exports	Low
Rate of inflation	Average in the 3 years before the reform, 62%
Rate of growth	Average in the 3 years before the reform, 2.5%
Terms of trade	Abrupt decline
Political circumstance	
Type of government	Military administration
Ideological shift	Yes
Accompanying policies	
Exchange rate	From 1974 to 1978; passive crawling peg; during the rest of period, announced devaluation program
Export promotion	Yes; use of export subsidies
Fiscal policy	Reduction in fiscal deficit until 1981; deficit in 1982
Monetary policy	Accommodating during most of the period
Capital movement	Absolutely free
Economic performance	
Employment	Increased steadily until 1981
Inflation	Erratic initially; decreasing at end of period
Growth	Average above 4%
Exports and imports	Deficit widened; diversification of exports
Wages	Real wages fell until 1978; increased later

Table 1.2 Policy changes in the 1974–1982 liberalization episode

Date	*Policy changes*
1974	Elimination of quantitative restrictions and reduction of maximum tariff levels
	Liberalization of foreign exchange transactions and international capital flow
1978	Unification of the exchange market and beginning of an announced program of devaluations
	Announcement of a gradual reduction of tariff levels
1980	First stage of the tariff reduction program
	Anticipated departures from the tariff reduction program
1981	Second stage of the tariff reduction program
1982	Third stage of the tariff reduction program. Step back in the program in June, and suspension of its implementation at end of year

inflow. Furthermore, the structure of imports and exports changed. While before the reforms traditional exports accounted for more than 75 percent of total exports, following the reforms they accounted for only 40 percent. Similarly, following the trade reforms, the share of intermediate goods in total imports almost halved. Clearly, the reforms had a substantial impact on the performance and structure of the economy. An index of trade liberalization is given in figure 1.1.[2] The ratio of investment to GDP is given in figure 1.2 and a measure of the degree of openness of the economy is given in figure 1.3.

In 1982, in the midst of a deep recession, the trade liberalization program was first partially reversed and then stalled. By then, however, the success of the reforms in reallocating resources away from the import-competing sectors was significant. The degree of openness and the share of the export sector in GDP declined by 1982. However, these indices never reached pre-reform levels. The failure of the trade liberalization reforms to provide further aggregate structural changes to the economy does not necessarily derive from the trade liberalization program itself. Accompanying policies may have impacted more strongly on the economy than the trade reforms themselves.

However, the experiment was successful in other dimensions. First, it provided the Uruguayan economy with new export industries and markets; second, it increased the efficiency of its industries; third, the structure of the export sector was permanently changed; fourth, and perhaps most

2 This index is based on three underlying factors: the level of the average nominal tariff, the index of implicit tariffs developed as the ratio of the domestic to the foreign terms of trade, and the share of intermediate goods in total imports (excluding oil). A more detailed explanation of the index is given below.

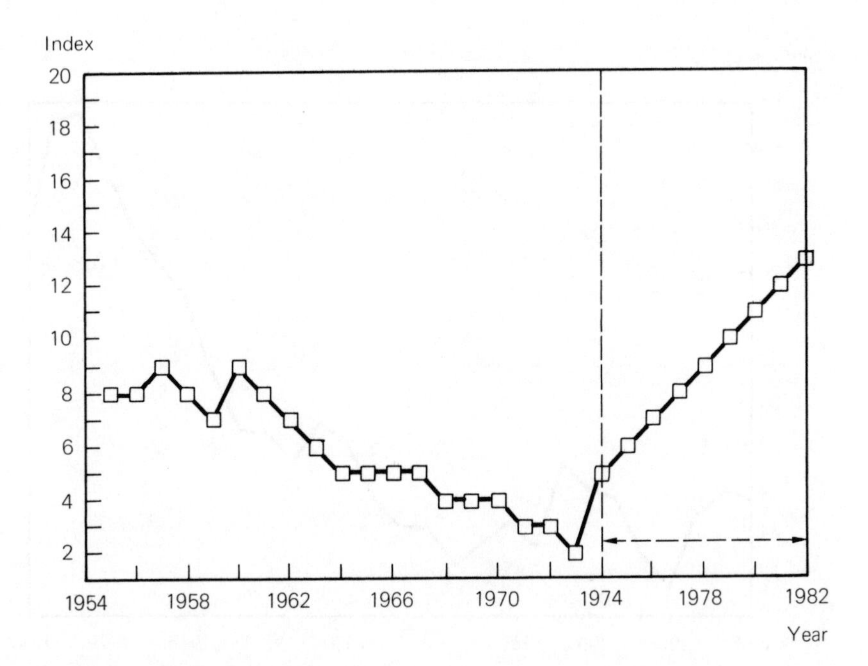

Figure 1.1 Index of trade liberalization

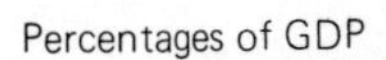

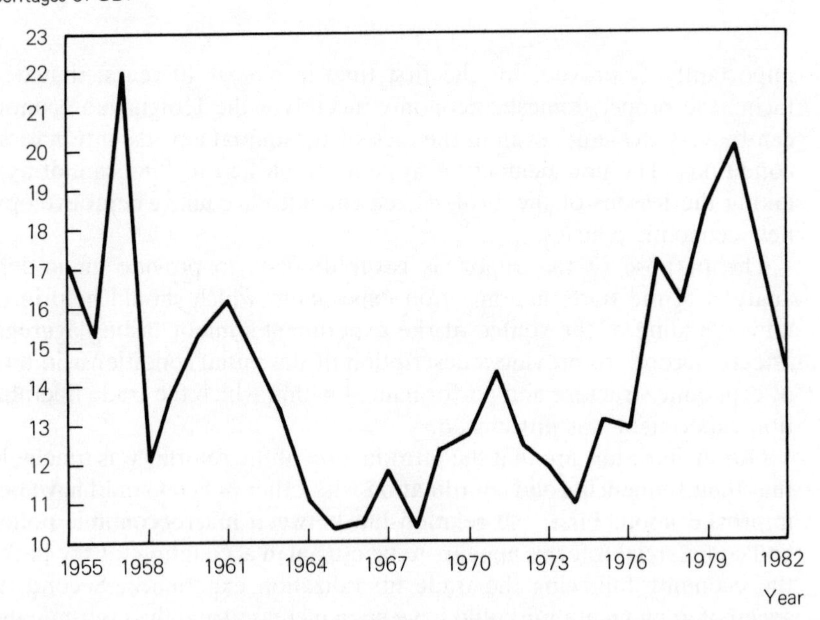

Figure 1.2 Ratio of investment to gross domestic product

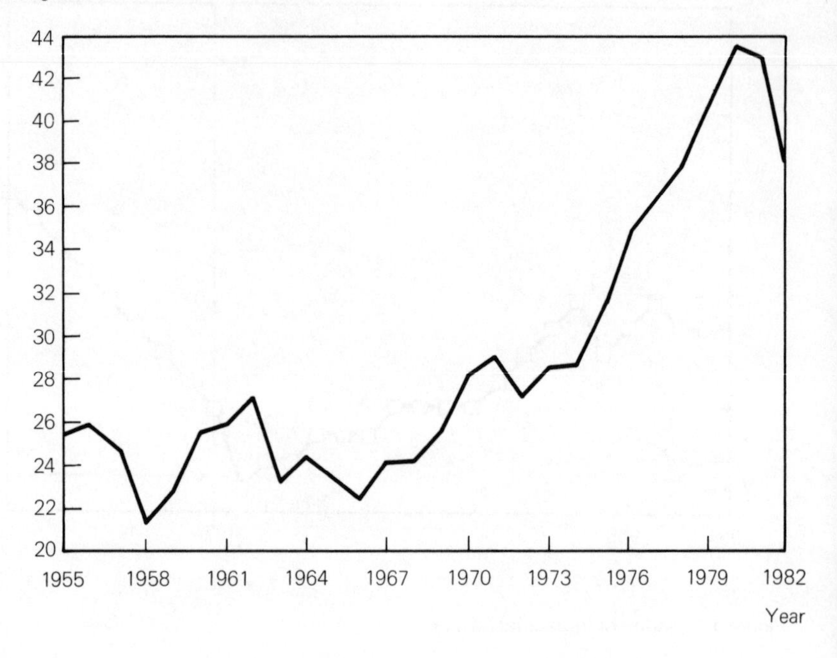

Figure 1.3 Degree of openness (exports plus imports divided by gross domestic product)

importantly, it proved, for the first time in almost 40 years, that when facing the proper domestic economy incentives the Uruguayan economy can be very dynamic, even in the face of substantial adverse international conditions. The new democratic system established in 1984 cannot avoid taking the lessons of the 1974–82 reforms into account when developing new economic policies.

The purpose of this report is twofold: first, to provide an in-depth analysis of the trade liberalization experiment which should help in our understanding of the source of the experiment's minor lasting aggregate effects; second, to provide a description of the initial conditions (in terms of economic structure and performance) within which the trade liberalization experiment was introduced.

Our main results are that the introduction of the reforms was timely, but that their sequencing and coordination with other policies could have been improved upon. First, the relationship between macroeconomic policies and commercial reforms appears to be crucial in accounting for the path of the economy following the trade liberalization experience. Second, the speed of implementation could have been increased and the discriminatory nature of the early stages could have been reduced without serious adverse employment effects. Both changes would have allowed the reforms to have more lasting effects, and may have generated potential support for its continuation. An analysis of the economic background, policies, and performance during the post-war period is given in chapter 2, the trade liberalization reforms as well as the economic policies and performance following them are analyzed in chapter 3, and the timing and sequencing characteristics of the trade liberalization experiment are analyzed in detail in chapter 4.

2

The Uruguayan Economy in the Post-war Period, 1945–1973

The Economic Background

The Pattern of Stagnation

The performance of the Uruguayan economy since the Great Depression differs dramatically from the pattern observed from 1870 to 1930.[1] The main economic sector – agriculture – stagnated after 1930, while the industrial sector did not experience a sustained process of growth except for the period 1945–55 under the joint influence of strong import substitution and expansionary government expenditure policies. From 1945 to 1955 the annual rate of growth was 4.8 percent; however, in the next 18 years the economy stagnated and the growth rate slowed down to 0.7 percent (table 2.1).

The Capital Stock

The capital stock grew until the late 1950s. However, a low level of gross capital formation resulted in a stagnant stock of capital up to the early 1970s. The average ratio of investment to gross national product (GNP) fell during the 1960s, and the overall 1955–73 ratio averaged barely 12.1 percent, which is probably about the level required to keep the stock of capital constant over time. In addition, available measures of capital productivity show a very low average during the 1960s and early 1970s, and a very strong recovery of this average return during the period 1975–82 (Favaro and Spiller, 1988, appendix table 2.2).[2]

1 During that period the Uruguayan economy experienced a remarkable dynamic growth rate, which explains the high level of income per capita observed in the country during the first decade of the century (Díaz, 1979).

2 The average return on capital was estimated at around 4–6 percent for the period (Harberger and Wisecarver, 1978; Cámara Nacional de Comercio, 1986).

Table 2.1 Growth and trade statistics

Year	*%GDP*	*%GDP$_n$*	*%EXP*	*%IMP*	*INV/GDP*	*Openness*
1955	n.a.	n.a.	n.a.	n.a.	17.11	25.47
1956	1.74	0.39	29.05	−9.20	15.26	25.86
1957	1.01	−0.40	−33.77	18.08	22.08	24.82
1958	−3.60	−4.95	36.43	−37.79	12.16	21.35
1959	−2.80	−4.18	−9.18	15.93	14.11	12.93
1960	3.63	2.31	−0.94	26.75	15.35	25.60
1961	2.84	1.54	22.86	−4.89	16.24	24.03
1962	−2.30	−3.51	−14.15	13.42	14.82	27.27
1963	0.51	−0.68	4.39	−23.26	13.24	23.35
1964	1.98	0.84	3.84	9.42	11.14	24.53
1965	1.25	0.17	28.01	−23.70	10.39	23.45
1966	3.35	2.31	−11.33	10.86	10.52	22.51
1967	−4.10	−5.02	−6.68	11.78	11.86	24.24
1968	1.60	0.72	14.47	−7.45	10.35	24.27
1969	6.07	5.31	−0.11	22.96	12.14	25.62
1970	4.71	7.10	5.29	22.92	12.74	28.25
1971	−0.97	−1.50	−7.17	7.96	14.35	29.12
1972	−3.56	−3.92	−7.06	−11.10	12.45	27.27
1973	0.83	0.69	1.11	8.74	11.30	28.66
1974	3.11	3.15	22.28	−6.26	10.99	28.80
1975	4.44	4.63	23.02	8.04	13.12	31.48
1976	2.60	1.96	27.23	3.55	12.91	34.97
1977	3.40	2.87	5.32	11.06	17.18	36.61
1978	2.30	1.78	4.58	8.84	16.01	38.22
1979	6.17	5.65	6.56	21.63	18.67	41.25
1980	5.75	5.20	5.41	16.75	20.14	43.61
1981	−1.29	−1.94	9.00	−10.48	16.76	43.08
1982	−10.04	−10.73	−25.51	−19.64	14.02	37.20

All series are based on real 1978 prices: %GDP, percentage change in real GDP; %GDP$_n$, percentage change in real GDP per capita; %EXP, percentage change in real exports; %IMP, percentage change in real imports, INV/GDP, investment-to-GDP ratio; Openness, ratio of exports plus imports to GDP.

Sources: Banco del Uruguay, *Producto e Ingreso Nacionales*, several issues; Direccion General de Estadística y Censos, *Anuario Estadístico*, several issues

Table 2.2 Share of major sectors in the gross national product, 1955–1980

Sector	*1955*	*1960*	*1965*	*1970*	*1975*	*1980*
Agriculture	16.6	14.2	15.9	16.3	12.5	11.1
Manufacturing industry	22.0	23.1	22.9	23.0	24.3	25.2
Electricity, water, and gas	1.3	1.7	2.0	2.3	1.3	1.4
Contruction	6.1	6.1	3.9	4.3	3.7	5.2
Wholesale and retail trade	16.4	15.2	14.7	14.8	15.4	17.3
Transportation and communications	8.5	8.9	8.9	7.1	6.6	6.9
Remainder	29.1	30.8	31.8	31.3	36.1	32.4

Source: Banco Central del Uruguay, *Producto e Ingreso Nacionales*, 1982

The Labor Force

A similar story of stagnation and contraction can be told for the labor force. The rate of population growth has been low during the whole century according to international standards.[3] It was 1.7 percent between 1908 and 1963 and 0.6 percent between 1963 and 1975. The slow population growth is attributable less to birth and mortality rates (which would presuppose a much higher population growth than actually took place) than to emigration (Favaro and Spiller, 1988, appendix table 2.3). Emigration had a significant effect on population and the labor force during the 1960s and 1970s in terms of both its magnitude and the characteristics of the emigrants. Emigrants were by no means a random sample of the population: they were mostly young (between 15 and 34 years of age), they were more educated than the average, and 55 percent of them were males.

Paralleling the emigration process, there was a reduction in the rate of male participation in the labor force and a corresponding increase in female participation: the rate of growth of employment between 1963 and 1975 was 1.1 percent for men and 2.4 percent while the overall rate of growth of occupation was 1.4 percent. The economically active population grew at a rate of 0.7 percent.

The reduced participation of males in the labor force and the substantial emigration of the 1960s and early 1970s can be understood as a rational response to diminishing opportunities in the domestic labor market. That the private sector was unable to stimulate the labor market can be seen from the fact that, of the 160,000 new jobs created between 1963 and 1975, at least 45,300 were in the public sector.[4] (This expansion of employment opportunities in the public sector may explain why the stagnation of the private sector did not generate substantial unemployment – the rate of recorded unemployment averaged 7.9 percent between 1965 and 1975.[5]) During this period of stagnation the level of education of the population rose: specifically, the percentage of the population who completed a university degree in 1963 (5 percent) had doubled by 1975.

3 Urban population accounted for 80.8 percent of total production in 1963 and 83 percent in 1975. Total population according to the 1975 census is 2.8 million.

4 Data on employment in the public sector for 1975 – except for employment in public utilities – as well as employment in the same government services are available from the 1967 Census of Public Employees. By comparing the data from both sources we estimated the number of new jobs in the public sector. Since employment in the public sector was presumably higher in 1967 than in 1963 the number of new jobs in this sector was underestimated using this approach.

5 From 1975 on, however, major cyclical movements occurred driving the rate of unemployment to less than 6 percent and up again to 14–16 percent during the 1982–3 recession.

Thus economic stagnation implied a substantial change in the labor force. Educated males postponed their entry into it and many emigrated, while women increased their participation in it. The result was popular discontent. The economic system was generating educated youngsters with no domestic opportunities.

The stagnation is also illustrated by the fact that from 1955 to 1975 the composition of both the GNP and foreign trade remained virtually unchanged (tables 2.2 and 2.3). The only significant trends were the decreasing role in GNP played by agriculture and the increasing significance of government services and the like. Similarly, before 1972–4 the major exports were natural-resource-based products (beef, wool, and hides), while the composition of imports shows a decreasing share of consumer and capital goods since the post-war period.[6] Neither exports nor imports grew significantly from the end of World War II to the end of the 1970s (see table 2.1). The sluggishness of foreign trade is even more remarkable in view of the explosive growth of world trade during the period. The proportion of trade within Latin American countries increased from the early 1960s, mirroring preferential trade agreements under the Latin American Free Trade Association (LAFTA). Similarly, the degree of openness of the economy fell until the mid-1970s (see table 2.1).

Table 2.3 Share of traditional exports in total exports in selected years between 1961 and 1982 (percent)

Year	*Share*
1961	90.9
1965	86.2
1969	74.5
1973	73.3
1977	43.0
1980	39.3
1982	39.5

Sources: Banco Central del Uruguay, *Boletín Estadístico*, various issues; *Indicadores de la Actividad Económico–Financiera*, various issues

In summary, after a short period of growth generated by the import substitution experience, the post-war period is characterized by stagnation, an increasingly closed economy, a level of capital formation below

6 Since new technologies appear, in general, embodied in new capital goods the decreasing role of capital inputs is an indicator of the low role of technological change occurring in the period.

depreciation allowances, almost no population growth, widespread emigration, and no indication of technological innovation. Thus the history of the capital stock and of the labor force during the post-war period shows very close similarities. The outward population movement reflects the parallel destruction or stagnation of the capital stock during the same period, and the low average return on capital parallels the low productivity of labor in the public sector. The structure of the economy remained almost unchanged except for a small increase in the share of manufacture and government services. Furthermore, GNP per capita decreased during most of the period.

The absence of economic growth for almost two decades (1955–73) and the contrasting sustained growth from 1974 to 1981 are interesting in themselves in view of the enormous economic expansion of the world economy during the former period and its contraction during the latter period. The clear indication is that the sources of economic stagnation should be sought among domestic circumstances and variables rather than among external factors.

The Pattern of Inflation

The second pervasive phenomenon of the post-war period is persistent inflation. The history of post-war monetary policy shows high rates of money creation, inflation, and increasing monetary and exchange rate instability (see table 2.4). In most chronic inflationary experiences, particularly in Latin American countries, money creation is explained by credit expansion to the public sector to cover fiscal disequilibria. The Uruguayan experience, however, does not reflect this pattern before the mid-1960s. Fiscal performance before the period 1963–6 although deficitary, was not a source of major credit expansion (table 2.5): from 1948 to 1962, fiscal deficits averaged less than 1 percent of GDP. During the next two decades,

Table 2.4 Rate of growth of exports and imports, 1946–1982 (percent)

Period	*Exports*	*Imports*
1946–51	9.2	16.5
1951–6	−1.8	−11.0
1956–61	−4.2	0.2
1961–6	1.2	−4.9
1966–71	2.1	6.9
1971–4	22.9	28.6
1974–82	14.3	10.0

Sources: Banco Central del Uruguay, *Boletín Estadístico*, various issues; *Indicadores de la Actividad Económico–Financiera*, various issues

Table 2.5 Fiscal deficit as a percentage of government expenditure and gross domestic product, 1948–1983

Period	*Deficit/expenditure*	*Deficit/GDP*
1948–50	4.3	0.5
1951–4	9.7	1.1
1955–8	5.9	0.7
1959–62	6.6	1.2
1963–6	28.4	4.1
1967–71	19.1	3.1
1972–4	16.8	2.8
1975–80	9.4	1.5
1981–3	19.1	4.3

Sources: Banco Central del Uruguay, *Boletín Estadístico*, various issues; *Indicadores de la Actividad Económico–Financiera*, various issues

however, fiscal deficits increased threefold, becoming a major source of credit expansion and, when financed by external savings, of the appreciation of the domestic currency.

Up to the mid-1940s monetary policy was orthodox. In subsequent periods, however, the rate of money creation considerably exceeded the trend in the demand for money. The downward trend in international reserves and the continuous build-up of the net external debt confirm the existence of an excess money supply over the whole period (table 2.6). The

Table 2.6 Balance of payments, 1946–1983 (million current US dollars)

Year	*Current account*	*Capital account*	*Change in reserves*
1946–50	20.1	−69.2	−49.1
1951–5	−134.8	47.9	−86.9
1956–60	−219.8	147.9	−71.4
1961–5	−15.5	−80.3	−95.8
1966–70	13.1	−33.4	−20.3
1971–4	−125.3	32.7	−92.6
1975–8	−549.9	687.5	137.6
1979–81	−1,471.8	1,706.5	233.7
1982–3	−290.5	−291.9	−582.4

Sources: Banco Central del Uruguay, *Boletín Estadístico*, various issues; *Indicadores de la Actividad Económico–Financiera*, various issues; Instituto de Economía, 1968

main source of money creation during the first stage of the inflationary process was credit expansion to the private sector through the widespread use of discounting at subsidized interest rates by the Banco de la República Oriental del Uruguay (BROU).[7] The use of subsidized interest rates implied a significant transfer of resources for those sectors which benefited from public sector credit, and the administration of subsidized credit lines became a powerful source of income distribution and wealth transfer.

From 1955 to 1959 the rate of growth of money creation accelerated, resulting in the first serious post-war attempt at stabilization from 1959 to 1962. From 1962 to 1967 the rate of growth of the money supply rose steadily until a second stabilization attempt was made between early 1968 and late 1970. The attempt ultimately failed, after a major fiscal deficit in 1971, and the rate of inflation increased up to 1973.

The sharp growth in the money supply in the post-war period was paralleled by persistent and increasing inflation and periodic balance-of-payments crises. During most of the period the authorities relied on a fixed exchange rate regime. As inflation soared, the real value of the Uruguayan currency eroded and periods of stability alternated with exchange crises, administrative exchange controls, loss of reserves, increased external debt, and finally large-step devaluation.[8] The ratio of the financial to the commercial exchange rates provides a measure of exchange pressure and suggests the presence of exchange controls during the period (table 2.7).[9] This ratio shows that equilibrium prevailed up to 1949 when a significant discrepancy appears for the first time. From 1951 to 1959 the gap between the rates widened, and a major devaluation was adopted as part of the 1959 exchange reform, which included the elimination of multiple exchange rates and a short period of freedom in foreign currency transactions as well as a floating exchange rate regime.[10] The exchange and tariff reform of 1959 was followed by four years of stability in the foreign currency market. In 1964–5 a major discrepancy again developed between the financial and commercial exchange rates, and this was repaired in 1966. From 1966 to 1970, although exchange controls prevailed, the ratio of the two rates was kept within tolerable limits. Finally, in 1971 a major discrepancy appeared

7 The BROU is a public commercial bank which also performed Central Bank functions up to 1966.

8 Up to 1959 there were multiple exchange rates. The commercial rate quoted for this period stands for the basic exchange rate for commercial transactions. The financial rate is the exchange rate that prevailed for other market transactions and is a proxy for the market value of foreign exchange during periods of strong exchange market repression.

9 A commercial rate well below the financial exchange rate induces an excess demand for foreign currency which can only be sustained with exchange controls and administrative rationing. Extremely repressive periods show up in significant gaps between both exchange rates. In general these periods are followed by stabilization attempts and step devaluation.

10 In practice, however, the exchange rate was never allowed to float freely.

Table 2.7 Exchange rate, 1945–1983[a]

Year	*Financial (F)*	*Commercial (C)*	*F/C*
1945	1.82	1.899	0.96
1946	1.78	1.899	0.94
1947	1.83	1.899	0.96
1948	2.06	1.899	1.08
1949	2.63	1.899	1.38
1950	2.62	1.90	1.38
1951	2.24	1.90	1.18
1952	2.69	1.90	1.42
1953	2.92	1.90	1.54
1954	3.20	1.90	1.68
1955	3.39	1.96	1.73
1956	4.04	2.33	1.73
1957	4.11	3.03	1.36
1958	7.09	3.01	2.36
1959	10.07	3.58	2.81
1960	11.29	11.30	1.00
1961	11.04	11.01	1.00
1962	11.07	10.98	1.01
1963	14.87	14.30	1.04
1964	21.01	16.64	1.26
1965	50.06	30.76	1.63
1966	68.52	64.49	1.06
1967	110.45	105.78	1.04
1968	234.23	233.85	1.00
1969	253.50	250.00	1.01
1970	261.27	250.00	1.05
1971	458.01	250.00	1.83
1972	834.43	536.01	1.56
1973	896.17	865.85	1.04
1974	1,621.71	1,196.23	1.36
1975	2.66	2.26	1.18
1976	3.69	3.34	1.10
1977	4.73	4.67	1.01
1978	6.09	6.06	1.00
1979	7.85	7.86	1.00
1980	9.10	9.10	1.00
1981	10.81	10.82	1.00
1982	13.93	13.91	1.00
1983	34.55	34.54	1.00

[a] From 1945 to 1974 in pesos; from 1975 on in new pesos.

Sources: Banco Central del Uruguay, *Boletín Estadístico*, various issues; *Indicadores de la Actividad Económico–Financiera*, various issues

between the two exchange rates and a period of tight restrictions on foreign exchange transactions was again in force up to late 1974.

In summary, the post-war macroeconomic history of Uruguay combines stagnation with high rates of money creation and acclerated inflation. The excess money supply prevailing during most of the period resulted in domestic price instability, a persistent downward trend in foreign currency reserves, a misaligned value of the domestic currency, and an ever-increasing external debt. Furthermore, the volatility of relative prices associated with monetary instability appears to be responsible for at least part of the poor investment performance during the period.

Attributes of the Main Economic Sectors

Agricultural Sector

Agriculture accounted for 16.6 percent of GDP in 1955 but only 11.1 percent in 1980. This declining share is strongly related to the sector's poor economic performance as shown in the low and declining rate of growth experienced in the most recent decades. This sector's performance, however, can be understood in the face of the extremely discriminatory exchange rate, tariffs, and tax policies. In particular, high protection barriers for the industrial sector constituted an indirect tax on the agriculture sector, reducing incentives for introducing modern technology.

During the post-war period, most of the sector's output was concentrated in a few product lines, with beef and milk accounting for over 90 percent of the value of livestock production, and wheat and sunflowers being the main agriculture crops.[11] The sector's productivity did not change substantially during the period. Productivity in wheat, corn, and sunflowers increased slightly, but these trends are related more to the improvements in land use than to technological innovation. In contrast, rice, which in the late 1970s became a major export crop, shows an increase in yield as well as in total area under cultivation. Productivity in the livestock sector remained stagnant over these decades: while the total land area allocated to livestock farming increased by 0.2 percent annually, beef output grew by 0.4 percent and wool production contracted. The low levels of productivity growth have traditionally been associated with inefficient lot sizes. This association, however, is not wholly compatible with the

11 The government cereal price policy introduced strong incentives to expand wheat production in the early 1950s. This policy resulted in a type of inmiserizing growth of the overall sector during the period. The change in cereal price policies during the 1960s explain the declining share of agriculture crops in the sector's gross value of production in the following period. Wool lost significance within the cattle breeding sector from 1955 to 1974 but strongly recovered after the first oil shock.

evidence. In the first place, the sector became more concentrated during the period. The total number of firms has been decreasing, at least since 1961: the number of firms in the lowest size range (less than 198 hectares) decreased whereas the number in the range 500–2,499 hectares increased. The increase in the average lot size reflects a change in output mix, as the share of cattle breeding in total has been increasing. Smaller firms have a stronger orientation towards arable farming. To explore the issue of the inefficiency of lot size, we analyze the extent of economies of scale in the agricultural sector using the "survivor's technique."[12] The data (Favaro and Spiller, 1988, appendix table 2.12) show a fairly wide range of gross value of production within which there are no diseconomies of scale. There seem to be diseconomies in the extremely large lot sizes (5,000 or more hectares). Economies of scale seem to be exhausted between 500 and 2,499 hectares.

Since the increase in lot sizes over the period was not concentrated on the largest holdings, lot sizes cannot be responsible for the stagnation in productivity that characterizes the sector. However, during the period the sector is characterized by low levels of investment. Although there was an upward trend in improved pastures and machinery, investment in these items remained low for the overall period. This low investment level may explain the low rate of growth of the sector during the last decades.

In summary, the agricultural sector has stagnated since the Great Depression. Although government price policies created sporadic incentives to increase crop production, these were insufficient to induce sustained growth. Stagnation is not related to structural attributes such as inefficient lot size, as is usually asserted, but to consistently low investment which, in turn, is a predictable outcome of the substantial protection afforded to the industrial sector.

Industrial Sector

The post-war performance of the industrial sector parallels that of the economy as a whole. After 1945, the industrial sector expanded rapidly (7.7 percent on average from 1945 to 1955), fueled by a strong import substitution policy.[13] However, from 1955 until the mid-1970s the industrial sector stagnated, gross capital accumulation declined, and the sector experienced no major structural changes. Most of the contraction in capital accumulation is explained by a decline in investment in machinery and

12 We classified the share of agricultural capacity (measured by the number of hectares allocated in each size bracket) coming from each size bracket over time. When the share of a given size bracket falls, we suspect that it is relatively inefficient. For details see Stigler (1983).

13 The rapid industrial growth in the period 1945–55 resulted in an increase in the share of the manufacturing industry in GDP from 16.8 to 22 percent over the decade.

equipment, which prompts the further inference that there may not have been major technological innovation during the period. Furthermore, except for a decline in the share of textiles the composition of the manufacturing industry remained unchanged during the period.

The policy of import substitution clearly impacted upon the structure of the industrial sector. First, it became more concentrated over the period (Favaro and Spiller, 1988, appendix table 2.13).[14] The increase in the degree of industrial concentration may have resulted from the substantial entry barriers raised by the import restrictions regime.[15] Second, tariff protection promoted the development of sectors which were relatively capital and skill intensive, whereas export-oriented sectors tend to be less capital and skill intensive. To analyze this difference in factor use, we first classify the sectors by their share of net imports in total consumption (table 2.8) and then analyze their evolution over time.[16] Observe first that, until the early 1970s, there were no changes in the exposure of the various sectors to international trade (that is, in their T classification). However, from 1974 on, several sectors became export oriented (for instance, clothing, leather, and footwear).

To analyze the factor usage of the various sectors we calculate capital-to-labor ratios based upon energy consumption,[17] and a measure of labor skill intensity based upon differences in wages and salaries across industries (see chapter 4, table 4.13).[18] We also develop alternative indicators of labor

14 Using the share of firms in the gross value of production we build up a Herfindahl index corresponding to 1968 and 1978. In most sectors the index shows a significant increase in concentration.

15 First, the existence of prohibitive tariffs did not allow competition with foreign products and a pattern developed where whatever was domestically produced was not imported and vice versa. Second, existence of restrictions on the import of capital goods and the presence of quota-allocation privileges for incumbent firms turned out to be a restrictive set of barriers to the entry of new firms up to the mid-1970s.

16 The statistic T is defined as net imports (imports minus exports) divided by consumption (gross value of production plus imports minus exports). The criteria of classification used are as follows:

exportable, if $T < -5.0$
import-competing, if $5.0 < T < 70.0$
non-import-competing, if $70.0 < T$
marginal trade, if $5.0 < T < 5.0$

17 The index is based upon data on all sources of energy power consumption (not expenditure) at the three-digit level for 1982. There is no comparable source of information for other periods.

18 A proxy for labor skills at the three-digit level was developed by estimating the quotient between total wages and salaries paid and the hypothetical value of this aggregate had the industry used unskilled labor.

Table 2.8 Industry classification based on statistic *T* for selected years between 1955 and 1982[a] (percent)

ISIC code	*1955*	*1959*	*1961*	*1964*	*1968*	*1971*	*1974*	*1978*	*1980*	*1982*
311	−4.8	−6.2	−9.5	−32.7	−26.8	−27.7	−32.9	−18.3	−30.6	−25.6
312						9.0	11.6	−0.3	10.8	−6.8
313	11.2	4.2	0.9	0.7	0	0.3	0.5	1.1	4.0	n.a.
314	4.1	51.9	22.6	20.4	n.a.	6.9	5.9	0.4	0.4	0.2
321	−60.1	−27.8	−20.4	−25.5	−18.3	−17.4	−12.0	−31.1	−27.7	−96.3
322–4	−1.8	0.4	0	0	n.a.	n.a.	−12.1	−10.1	−50.4	−81.1
323	n.a.	n.a.	n.a.	n.a.	n.a.	−1.2	−60.0	−49.5	−1.9	−80.5
324	0	0	0	0	0	2.2	n.a.	−41.1	−30.7	−38.4
331	10.4	4.2	13.4	n.a.	13.8	17.0	14.7	17.6	16.7	n.a.
332	0.2	0	0	0	0	0	n.a.	−2.2		
341	46.5	38.3	28.3	31.5	19.2	20.1	11.7	11.8	9.2	12.5
342	1.3	0.7	1.2	4.4	3.5	1.4	8.4	−0.2	−0.9	−0.6
351	26.1	33.5	22.4	28.1	23.8	47.3	46.5	61.5	61.5	41.8
352						14.3	13.9	9.3	11.4	4.5
353	5.7	38.1	9.1	5.3	17.8	4.2	3.7	n.a.	n.a.	1.7
354						93.7	49.5	22.9	0	0
355	4.7	1.0	0	4.4	0.5	−2.9	−10.2	−5.6	−3.4	0.7
356–90	−28.4	20.5	24.8	21.2	12.4	n.a.	35.5	4.3	16.3	9.0
361	15.1	8.9	3.4	0.5	−8.2	−13.9	−20.0	−24.7	3.6	−4.6
362						−1.3	−3.5	−21.7	−10.9	−0.3
269	0	0	0	0	0	−2.9	−6.6	−11.1	−9.5	−3.2
371	53.3	57.7	44.8	47.0	27.7	39.6	54.2	51.0	42.9	11.1
372						51.5	55.8	68.4	54.0	6.4
381	36.6	36.6	29.4	19.6	11.2	6.7	6.7	10.2	45.4	19.9
382	76.4	n.a.	62.4	55.8	34.6	53.8	48.1	75.3		77.1
383	38.1	29.1	23.1	16.9	10.5	14.1	10.5	30.0	39.0	38.3
384	35.1	25.8	36.2	25.4	6.5	26.7	21.7	30.1	36.3	31.8
385	0	0	0	0	0	0	0	0	0	89.3
390	n.a.	n.a.	n.a.	n.a.	n.a.	5.5	−1.9	8.5	31.4	37.0

n.a., not available.

[a] The statistic *T* is defined as net imports (imports minus exports) divided by consumption (gross value of production plus imports minus exports). The criterion of classification used is as follows:

exportable,	if $T < -5.0$
import-competing,	if $5.0 < T < 70.0$
non-import-competing,	if $70.0 < T$
marginal trade,	if $-5. < T < 5.0$

Sources: Banco Central del Uruguay, *Producto e Ingreso Nacionales*, various issues; Dirección General de Estadística y Censos, 1968, 1978

skill and capital intensity.[19] Since the difference measures of capital–labor intensity and labor skill intensity are highly correlated, in subsequent analysis we use the initial measures presented in table 4.13. By examining

19 An alternative labor skill measure is developed based on the share of unskilled workers and employees in each labor category (see Favaro and Spiller, 1988, appendix table 2.16), and an alternative indicator of capital–labor intensity across sectors is developed based on the number of jobs per million dollars of value added at the three-digit level (see Favaro and Spiller, 1988, appendix table 2.17).

tables 4.13 and 2.8 we can conclude that export activities are in general low capital–labor and low labor skill intensive.

In summary, after a decade of growth from 1945 to 1955 characterized by import substitution, the manufacturing industry stagnated. During the 1960s and early 1970s a sharp contraction in investment was observed. Firms within the import substitution sectors were largely uncontested during the period as foreign competition was severely curtailed and significant barriers to entry developed before 1974.

The Pattern of International Trade

Commercial Policy

The purpose of this section is to describe briefly the main characteristics of the commercial policy regimes in force from 1945 to 1974. For expository convenience we distinguish three stages of the tariff regime.[20] The first stage runs from the end of World War II to the exchange and tariff reform (ETR) of 1959; the second stage covers the period 1959–68, when quantitative restrictions were eliminated, and the third stage spans the years 1968–74, when the authorities again relied on nonprice trade restrictions.

First Stage, 1945–1959

Uruguay, like many other countries, reacted to the depression of the 1930s by introducing price and quantity restrictions on foreign trade. During the early 1930s, these measures included increases in border tariffs (*tarifas consulares*) as well as prohibiting the introduction of some products into the country and requiring that importers pay transactions in gold. Meanwhile, an exchange control regime was developed in which the BROU assumed control of foreign exchange operations, including those derived from exports. This regime of protection was fashioned during the 1930s in a disorganized manner. In 1941 a bill on export and import control (EIC) was approved which summarized all the measures taken in the previous decade.

The EIC bill created the Board of Export and Import Control to oversee allocation of the assignment of foreign exchange among institutions – public or private, industrial or commercial. The BROU, in turn, was in charge of the assignment of foreign exchange by country and item.

The EIC board, comprising government as well as private sector representatives, controlled the origin, destination, and value of exports

20 The tariff and tax regime is identified in this study as the set of price and quantity restrictions devised to protect domestic production against foreign competition.

and imports, intervened to allocate foreign exchange among users, and authorized imports. Every year the BROU set a foreign exchange budget and determined priorities according to currency availability. The BROU periodically assigned foreign exchange by country and item after accounting for its own needs as well as those originating in the government debt service. Items accorded priority raw materials, some consumer goods considered of first necessity, drugs, intermediate products and capital goods for the agricultural sector, and raw materials and machinery for the manufacturing sector.

The EIC bill was permeated by a discriminatory spirit. Its second article established that imports of raw materials to be manufactured in the country were privileged against the import of the final good. The assignment of foreign currency to import goods which were produced in the country, although not prohibited, was restricted.[21] Paralleling the assignment of foreign currency by country and item and the identification of priorities, the law established norms for the distribution of currency among users. The attributes considered as relevant to obtain foreign exchange were the need each firm showed, the number of employees and their salaries, the volume of activity, and the time that the firm had been established in the market. Any firm interested in importing had to ask permission from the EIC Board. It should be noted that the individual quota determination regime was not perfected until ten years later.

The EIC bill introduced different exchange rates according to the way a certain good was classified. Three broad classes were established: first necessity goods, intermediate products, and luxury goods. Those which were not classified under the necessity or intermediate product categories belonged to the third class.

The EIC regime had a varied performance. During the period when international trade was severely curtailed owing to war and protectionism, the system had a rationale which was absent in the post-war period when deregulation started and world trade exploded. During the post-war years, particularly in the 1950s, a regime originally devised as an exceptional mechanism became a powerful instrument for promoting certain industries while directly or indirectly punishing others. In the late 1950s there was a feeling that the system implied widespread inefficiency. This feeling was translated into a major reform of the tariff and exchange regime in 1959.

Second Stage: The 1959 Reform

Before the 1959 reform the tariff and exchange regulations were based on a barter trade model. The country should import from those countries which, in turn, imported from Uruguay. At the same time the system

21 It was recognized, however, that this type of restriction had to be administered with restraint to avoid abuse.

promoted imports of raw materials and intermediate products rather than finished goods.

The 1959 ETR attacked the first aspect of the EIC regime, eliminating bilateralism and unifying the exchange rate. The ETR established that the price of foreign exchange was to be determined freely in the market according to the supply and demand for foreign currency.

The ETR eliminated quantity restrictions as well as import prohibitions, and substituted quantity restrictions by price restrictions. These new tariffs were established in addition to existing border tariffs and the executive power was authorized to introduce, when necessary, deposits in advance to perform an import transaction. The new tariffs[22] were not levied on cost, insurance, and freight (c.i.f.) prices but on administered prices which, in many cases, were higher than the true prices. Although import prohibitions were eliminated, the administration was authorized to prohibit temporarily imports of luxuries or of goods considered to be competitive with domestic products.

In addition, the ETR levied taxes on exports of traditional products such as beef, wool, hides, etc. These taxes were used to favor domestic manufacture of goods based on natural resources, for fiscal purposes, and also to keep the domestic price of exportable goods low. The latter carried significant weight in the consumer market.

After 1962–3, the liberalization spirit ebbed and the economy evolved again into a very restrictive regime until a new stage of quantity restrictions was established after 1968.

Third Stage, 1968–1974

In 1968 an exchange control administered by the Central Bank was created. The new regime did not formally introduce prohibitions or quantity restrictions; however, prohibitions were in fact administered through a system of high tariffs and exonerations. It should be noted that this characteristic of tariffs was present in the second stage as well.

This aspect of the tariff regime shows up once we notice the difference between the actual tariff revenue and the amount that should have been collected had the theoretical tariffs been effectively charged. The exonerations come not only according to type of good and user or importer, but also with the preferential trade agreement treatment.

The quantity restriction regime worked as follows. Each importer was assigned a quota, within the limits authorized by the licenses. The importers could then perform transactions without further restrictions except for paying the tariff dues corresponding to the commodities involved in each operation. Any import in excess of the limit imposed by

22 These tariffs are called *recargos* and are not collected by the border authorities but by the BROU. The *recargos* are levied on administered rather than on c.i.f. prices.

the license level was subject to the further requirement of an advance deposit, for a six-month period, of up to 12 times the peso equivalent of the c.i.f. value of the imports. Since the average rate of inflation between 1968 and 1974 was 48.5 percent, this requirement was equivalent to an *ad valorem* tariff level of 260 percent in the extreme case of a twelvefold six-month advance deposit. Thus the inflation tax during this period made marginal imports beyond the license limits prohibitively expensive. In practice, the regime had an important loophole, by which firms that argued the impossibility of maintaining their level of activity were granted an increase in their license allocations.

There are two ways in which a licensing regime can become more stringent over time: first, when the level of authorized licenses within comparable periods of time is reduced; second, when the marginal tax treatment which applies for imports beyond the license limits becomes more expensive. Both approaches were implemented during the period 1968–74.

As observed before, licensing setting was related to *recargo* levels; however, in practice the regime had exemptions and specific treatments according to the origin and destination of the commodity. Goods imported under LAFTA "manufacture complementation agreements" received preferential treatment; commodities considered for national priority were exempted from paying tariffs and also from license constraints.

In summary, the exchange control regime during the period 1968–74 was extremely severe; it was removed at its highest level of repression by the 1974 reform.

The Evolution of Trade Restrictions

The purpose of this section is to develop some broad indicators of the level of restrictiveness involved in the commercial policy pursued in the post-war period. In the absence of time series data of effective protection rates we relied upon the following indicators: the composition of imports, the behavior of nominal tariffs, and the trajectory of the domestic terms of trade. For the post-war period, all three indicators show a continuous increase in the level of trade restrictions until the introduction of the 1974 trade liberalization reforms. From then on, the three indicators show a continuous reduction in the level of trade restrictiveness.

The Composition of Imports

The composition of imports is affected by the tariff structure. The higher is the level of tariffs on final goods with respect to the level of tariffs on intermediate products and raw materials, the higher is the proportion of the latter in total imports. Periods where the protection regime is more restrictive are characterized by a reduction of the share of final goods in

Table 2.9 Composition of imports, 1951–1982 (millions of US dollars and percent)

Year	*Final goods (million US$)*	*Total goods (million US$)*	*Ratio of final goods to total imports (%)*	*Ratio of final goods to total imports (excluding oil) (%)*
1951	211.9	373.0	56.8	60
1952	132.5	256.9	51.6	57
1953	41.3	195.2	46.7	49
1954	136.8	274.5	49.8	43
1955	108.5	226.0	48.0	53
1956	71.6	205.8	34.8	40
1957	99.8	226.4	44.1	45
1958	48.3	134.6	35.8	42
1959	61.8	214.1	28.9	41
1960	75.2	207.3	36.2	43
1961	107.4	205.9	51.4	58
1962	127.1	230.5	55.1	62
1963	91.1	176.8	51.5	58
1964	81.9	198.4	41.3	46
1965	66.2	150.7	43.9	51
1966	54.2	164.2	33.0	40
1967	94.0	171.4	42.2	63
1968	50.8	159.3	31.9	37
1969	91.9	197.3	46.6	52
1970	94.6	233.1	40.6	46
1971	91.9	222.1	41.4	47
1972	53.6	200.3	26.7	34
1973	76.8	284.8	27.0	32
1974	108.9	486.7	22.4	31
1978	221.4	757.3	29.2	40
1980	643.7	1,680.3	38.3	51
1982	341.6	1,057.9	27.3	53

Sources: Banco Central del Uruguay, *Boletín Estadístico*, various issues; *Indicadores del la Actividad Económico–Financiera*, various issues

total imports. Table 2.9 shows that the share of final goods in total imports fell, with some sporadic upturns, until the introduction of the 1974 trade liberalization experiment, when final goods underwent a sharp recovery.[23]

23 It is important to recognize that, although the index is affected by the level and structure of tariffs, it is also influenced by other factors such as the relative price of import components and the business cycle. The issue of relative price of import components is particularly relevant after 1973, since the weight of oil in intermediate products goes up significantly and the latter increases its share as well, as can be seen by comparing the fourth and fifth columns of table 2.10. The second issue is more difficult. During a recession, the demand for consumer durables and capital goods has a stronger decline than the average good demand, while during a recovery it moves up faster than the average. That is, the demand for consumer durables and capital goods has a higher volatility than that for the average good.

Level of Nominal Tariffs

Nominal tariffs were extremely high during the post-war period until 1974 (table 2.10). Our estimation of the average nominal tariff is based on a sample of products whose tax treatment was studied in detail for the whole period. In order to go from the sample to the aggregate measure, since weights on the gross value of production at this level of disaggregation are missing, we take the average of the level of tariffs of all the products included in one sector at the four-digit International Standard Industrial Classification (ISIC) level (the average level for this sector). The measures shown in table 2.10 are obtained by applying the weights of each sector to the gross value of production. In table 2.10 a simple average is constructed using the raw data from the sample. The sample mean, standard deviation, and coefficient of variation are taken as the relevant measures of average protection and tariff dispersion.

Table 2.10 Weighted average tariff rate for selected years between 1961 and 1982 (percent)

Year	*Rate*
1961	384.4
1964	684.1
1968	578.1
1971	534.5
1974	452.4
1979	69.5
1980	62.3
1982	52.7

The estimation is based on a sample of products whose tax treatment was studied in detail for the whole period. Average tariffs were calculated for four-digit ISIC sectors. Figures in the table were obtained by weighting four-digit ISIC sectors by their gross value of production.

The table shows that the average tariff was very high compared with any standards during the whole period. There is an upward trend in the tariff rate up to 1974 followed by a significant fall in the final period.[24] (If gross value of production weights are used, however, the path of tariffs looks different between 1964 and 1974.)

The tariff rates obtained are well above other estimates for the country in selected years made by other authors. There are two possible explana-

24 Note that the standard deviation as well as the coefficient of variation went up from 1964 to 1974, and both show a significant fall afterwards. Moreover, although the average tariff fell almost 20 points between 1979 and 1982, the coefficient of variation remained unaltered.

tions for this difference. First of all, implicit tariff measures were used in almost all other studies. Second, when nominal tariffs were estimated they included intermediate products in the sample, thus lowering the average significantly. We found, however, that this fact does not explain the whole wedge. Most authors disregard border taxes levied on administered prices, considering that they are insignificant. Our findings indicate that they are extremely significant in many cases. Another possible source of differences may be the introduction of errors when comparing administered prices with estimates of c.i.f. prices. As estimates of c.i.f. prices we used data on prices of similar goods recorded for some products and some years by the BROU. In addition, we estimated the unit value of imports using eight-digit data. We compared this unit-value data with the estimate of the c.i.f. value available, and later with the administered price, to adjust the *ad valorem* rate correspondingly. Although the procedure cannot be criticized since it was used systematically for every year, there is no reason why, although giving a biased measure, it should distort the perception of movements towards or away from free trade.

The Implicit Tariff

The implicit tariff is defined as the ratio of the domestic to the foreign terms of trade. Let P_{imp}^{D} (P_{imp}^{F}) and P_{exp}^{D} (P_{exp}^{F}) be the domestic (foreign) price levels for importables and exportable goods. In the absence of transportation costs,

$$P_{imp}^{D} = P_{imp}^{F}(1 + t)e \text{ and } P_{exp}^{D} = P_{exp}^{F}(1 + s)e$$

where e is the exchange rate, t is the *ad valorem* import tariff, and s is the *ad valorem* export subsidy. Then an index of the implicit tariff is given by

$$1 + t^{*} = \frac{P_{imp}^{D}/P_{exp}^{D}}{P_{imp}^{F}/P_{exp}^{F}}$$

where an upward movement in the ratio suggests a move toward trade restrictions. The implicit tariff index constructed for the period 1955–80 shows a continuous movement toward severe restrictions, except for the early 1960s, followed by a move toward trade liberalization after 1974 (table 2.7).

In summary, commercial policy was severely restrictive in the period 1945–74. While most countries reduced tariff barriers and eliminated quantity restrictions during the late 1940s and early 1950s, Uruguay adopted increasingly protectionist policies which isolated the economy from foreign competition. The share of final products in total imports declined steadily as tariff barriers increased, and a pattern of trade developed in which no good produced domestically was allowed to be imported, and no imported item was domestically produced.

3

The Trade Liberalization Experiment of 1974–1982

The period in which the trade liberalization experiment was introduced represents a major break with the three preceding decades. Dynamism and change characterize this decade. In order to be able to evaluate the performance of the trade liberalization experiment, the circumstances under which it was introduced and the accompanying policies, as well as the performance of the economy as a whole, need to be analyzed in detail.

In this chapter we provide, in the first section, an overview of the performance of the economy and the main economic policies undertaken during the period. In the second section we analyze the nature and components of the trade liberalization experiment, and in the third section we discuss the other reforms and accompanying policies undertaken during the period.

Main Economic Trends and Economic Policy

The energy crisis that started in 1973 had a dramatic impact on the Uruguayan economy. The threefold increase in the price of oil and the restrictions imposed by the European Economic Community (EEC) on beef imports resulted in a severe external crisis during 1974 and a terms-of-trade loss equivalent to 2.1 percent of GDP. A fiscal deficit equivalent to 30 percent of government expenditure and 4.4 percent of GDP developed as the government increased subsidies in an attempt to sustain real income levels while national income was experiencing a decline. Wage and price policies and an accommodating monetary policy contributed to an inflation rate which exceeded 100 percent during 1974. The balance of payments went from a current account surplus of US$37.1 million and a net reserve gain of US$6.4 million in 1973 to a current account deficit of US$118.0 million and a net reserve loss of US$79.8 million for 1974 associated with the expansionary policies pursued in the wake of these major crises.

The military regime which took power in June 1973 following a decade of political and economic paralysis initially responded to the energy crisis – applying the income redistribution–government intervention policies of the Batellista tradition. Very shortly, however, the new regime realized that the Uruguayan economy was too rigid to be able to accommodate these major shocks. A new approach was needed. In July 1974 the military regime appointed Alejandro Vegh Villegas as Minister of the Economy. Vegh Villegas, a highly respected Harvard-trained economist and engineer, formed a new economic team characterized by its commitment to liberalize the economy.[1] The new team started a program of far-reaching reforms, whose basic objectives were to improve economic efficiency and to promote and diversify nontraditional exports.

From 1974 to 1977 the government removed import licensing and quotas, fully deregulated the foreign exchange market and freed international capital movements, liberalized the capital markets, tightened controls over public sector expenditures, improved the economic performance of public utilities, reformed the tax system, decontrolled many consumer prices, and reduced social security taxes on labor.[2] From 1978 onward a second wave of economic reforms was pursued.

Among the economic policies introduced in this period four stand out: a major stabilization program based on the announcement of the future exchange rate, a gradual tariff reduction program, a tax reform which widened the application of the value-added tax (VAT) coupled with a further reduction in social security taxes, and a program of deregulation in the agricultural sector.

This period, then, can be divided into two major periods. While from 1974 to 1978 the authorities tried to reduce the fiscal disequilibrium, to promote nontraditional exports, and to keep the pace of devaluation at a level that would avoid a real appreciation of the domestic currency, from 1978 to 1982 stabilization was the main concern of the economic team. The exchange rate was used to pursue a stabilization purpose, and resulted, under circumstances of high domestic nominal interest rates and open international capital flow, in a strong appreciation of the Uruguayan peso with a substantial deterioration in the performance of the export-oriented sectors. The private sector responded to the innovative reforms introduced in 1974 with a dynamism unseen during the last 30 years. GDP grew from 1975 to 1978 at an average rate of 4.1 percent, and boomed to 4.7 percent in the next three years. Capital accumulation resumed, with the stock of capital growing at a rate of 6–8 percent, and the average investment-to-

1 The new team was formed by José Gil Díaz, a young economist formerly at the Secretary of Planning and Budget, as President of the Central Bank and José Anichini as Director of Planning and Budget.

2 Vegh Villegas resigned in 1976 and was replaced by his former deputy V. Arismendi.

GDP ratio increased from 11.81 percent in 1964–73 to 15.72 percent in 1974–81 (see table 2.1).[3] A similar rebound occurred in the labor force. While emigration accelerated during the early 1970s, it peaked in 1974 and decreased steadily in subsequent years.[4]

Following the reforms, the manufacturing industry experienced significant changes. While up to the early 1970s only the food, textile, and nonmetallic mineral industries were export oriented, from 1974 onwards other activities, among them the clothing and footwear industries, evolved from marginal trade to export-oriented sectors (see table 2.8). Export-oriented activities boomed from 1974 to 1978; the increased significance of nontraditional industrial sectors is associated with the outward-looking growth strategy which prevailed during the period. Nontraditional exports, which accounted for 25 percent of total exports in the early 1970s, reached more than 50 percent by the late 1970s (see table 2.3). The rate of growth slowed during the next four years. Those sectors which led the recovery from 1974 to 1978 contracted as the real exchange rate experienced a real appreciation. From 1978 to 1982, economic growth was led mainly by domestically oriented activities. The different performance of the nontraditional export sectors in the two subperiods can be related to the trajectory of the real effective exchange rate faced by each economic sector. Table 3.1 shows that the real effective exchange rate for exports increased from 1974 to 1977, but fell continuously afterward. However, the real effective exchange rate for imports fell dramatically for a few sectors from 1974 to 1977, while it showed a continuous and smooth decline for all sectors from 1977 to 1981 (table 3.2). The pattern of the real effective exchange rate during the two subperiods reflects the different macroeconomic and exchange rate policies followed in each period.[5]

The macroeconomic performance of the two subperiods differs substantially. The economic team appointed in the aftermath of the oil crisis was faced with a fiscal deficit equivalent to 4.4 percent of GDP and a severe external crisis. In the last quarter of 1974, the monetary authorities started enforcing a gradual reduction in the level of the fiscal deficit. However, the level of the fiscal deficit did not decrease before 1976 (see table 3.3). As

3 Note that investment in machinery and equipment grew faster than the average and that the public sector increased its share in overall gross capital formation. Note also that although investment increased, the level of gross capital formation is only significant from 1976 on.

4 Observe, however, that emigration remained high up to 1978.

5 The real effective exchange rate is also a function of the performance of real wages. Real wages, as measured by official indexes, experienced a sustained decline during the period. However, the quality of Uruguayan wage indices is doubtful. During the 1974–7 period they do not record the wages and salaries effectively paid, but rather those which resulted from the minimum increments determined periodically by the government. After 1977 they record the five wage and salary increases, starting, however, from an uncorrected base. The wage information is also inconsistent with data available from two economic censuses on the earnings of workers and employees.

Table 3.1 Real effective exchange rate (exports deflator, average wage level), 1974–1981 (1974 new pesos)

ISIC Code	*1974*	*1977*	*1978*	*1979*	*1980*	*1981*
311	1.48	1.90	1.94	1.80	1.45	1.30
312	n.a.	1.81	1.83	1.73	1.39	1.29
313	1.55	2.81	2.60	2.33	1.87	1.62
314	1.42	2.39	2.48	2.32	1.97	1.79
321	1.35	1.94	1.93	1.74	1.41	1.26
322	1.58	2.18	2.01	1.39	1.42	1.29
323	1.44	n.a.	n.a.	n.a.	n.a.	n.a.
324	1.59	2.53	2.27	2.32	1.79	1.54
331	1.59	n.a.	n.a.	n.a.	n.a.	n.a.
332	1.63	n.a.	n.a.	n.a.	n.a.	n.a.
341	1.46	2.13	2.05	1.96	1.65	1.51
342	1.37	2.54	2.38	2.34	2.16	2.02
351	1.43	2.52	2.34	2.38	2.13	2.03
352	1.39	2.23	2.18	2.49	1.61	1.51
355	1.49	2.18	n.a.	2.09	1.81	1.70
356	n.a.	2.70	2.46	2.48	2.28	2.05
361	1.50	2.27	2.32	2.20	1.75	1.77
362	1.55	2.29	2.31	2.20	1.71	1.75
369	1.55	2.25	2.29	2.19	1.76	1.75
381	1.37	2.41	2.30	2.14	1.67	1.63
382	1.50	n.a.	n.a.	n.a.	n.a.	n.a.
383	1.37	1.65	1.57	1.36	1.01	0.81
384	1.34	2.09	2.10	1.97	1.59	1.48

n.a., not available.

The real effective exchange rate is calculated as $E(1 + t)P^F/P^D$ where E is the exchange rate, t is the sector-weighted legal tariff (for imports) or export subsidy, P^F is the sector producer price index in the US (base 1974) and P^D is the respective domestic price index (also with base 1974). Thus the 1974 entry is the nominal effective exchange rate. E is measured as the (nominal) commercial rate.

Sources: tariffs and subsidies, our compilation except for 1981 for which the source is Centro Investigaciones Económicos, 1984; wages, Dirección General de Estadística y Censos, Encuesta Anual de Actividad, *Economica, Industrias Manufactureras*, various issues; exchange rates, Banco Central del Uruguay, *Boletín Estadístico*, various issues

the country received a significant capital inflow (see table 2.6), government sector financing needs did not result in the crowding out of private investment during the period. The current account deficit during these years mirrors a fiscal disequilibrium and an excess of private investment over savings. From 1974 to October 1978, Uruguay's exchange rate policy consisted of a crawling peg regime, which tried to keep the devaluation

Table 3.2 Real effective exchange rate (imports deflator, average wage level), 1974–1982 (1974 new pesos)

ISIC Code	*1974*	*1978*	*1979*	*1980*	*1981*	*1982*
311	3.61	3.22	2.17	1.60	1.31	1.47
313	3.77	5.11	3.57	2.53	2.25	2.20
314	1.59	2.66	2.47	1.97	1.78	2.33
321	24.37	3.29	2.19	1.67	1.49	1.75
322	17.09	3.09	3.49	2.64	1.41	2.65
323	16.49	2.15	2.17	1.52	1.21	1.45
324	3.16	3.72	2.35	1.78	1.52	1.68
331	1.51	4.56	3.95	2.51	1.98	1.92
332	3.32	3.95	3.30	2.39	1.99	2.08
341	3.32	3.72	2.90	2.31	2.08	2.35
342	n.a.	n.a.	3.81	2.90	n.a.	2.81
351	2.27	4.31	3.68	2.99	2.39	2.64
352	4.21	4.96	3.43	2.04	2.10	2.19
353	n.a.	2.24	n.a.	n.a.	2.69	n.a.
355	10.41	3.82	3.73	2.84	2.09	2.37
356	6.22	5.88	4.21	3.41	3.44	2.88
362	17.08	3.08	3.78	2.66	1.91	2.54
369	3.16	2.29	3.76	2.66	1.54	2.52
371	2.77	3.65	3.46	2.52	2.11	2.36
372	3.87	2.70	1.74	1.74	1.62	1.64
381	3.07	4.01	3.58	2.58	2.17	2.23
383	12.17	4.66	2.26	1.51	1.11	1.13
384	4.52	4.67	3.41	2.50	2.56	2.30

n.a., not available.

Source: as for table 3.1

Table 3.3 Fiscal deficit as a percentage of gross domestic product, 1974–1982 (percent)

Year	*Ratio of income to GDP*	*Ratio of revenue to GDP*	*Ratio of deficit to GDP*	*Ratio of indirect deficit to GDP*
1974	12.9	17.3	– 4.4	n.a.
1975	12.1	16.5	– 4.4	n.a.
1976	13.6	16.1	– 2.5	n.a.
1977	14.8	15.9	– 1.1	n.a.
1978	14.1	15.3	– 1.2	– 1.3
1979	14.6	14.3	0.3	– 1.9
1980	16.2	16.1	0.1	– 0.6
1981	17.6	17.7	– 0.1	2.3
1982	15.2	23.9	– 8.7	18.2

n.a., not available.

The fourth column shows the usual revenue minus expenditure definition of deficit. The last column shows an indirect measure of deficit estimated through the variation of the outstanding government debt.

Source: García, 1985

rate close to the difference between domestic and international inflation rates, avoiding an appreciation of the real exchange rate (table 3.4).

The rate of inflation, which averaged 77.2 percent in 1974, declined over the period. Although the fiscal deficit declined as well, inflation remained above 40 percent as of 1978. In October 1978 the Central Bank abandoned active monetary policy and relied exclusively upon exchange rate management for stabilization purposes. The monetary authorities started announcing the schedule of mini-devaluations in advance and reduced the pace of depreciation.

Table 3.4 Real exchange rate, 1974–1982 (base 1974 = 100)

Year	*United States*	*Germany*	*Argentina*	*Brazil*
1974	100.0	100.0	100.0	100.0
1975	113.8	116.2	71.6	112.2
1976	118.0	115.1	99.7	119.0
1977	111.2	115.4	83.5	114.2
1978	106.7	122.9	105.2	110.6
1979	92.0	107.9	127.2	87.7
1980	73.9	81.3	130.4	57.9
1981	83.1	70.5	114.4	64.2
1982	101.0	79.6	62.0	53.8

The real exchange rate is defined as the constant price index (CPI) of each trade partner divided by the Uruguayan CPI multiplied by the nominal exchange rate.

Sources: Banco Central del Uruguay, *Boletín Estadístico*, various issues; IMF, *International Financial Statistics*, various issues

Since domestic nominal interest rates were well above the yield on foreign-currency-denominated deposits (*ex post*), the lower announced rate of devaluation induced a high capital inflow and a fast build-up of the Central Bank's international reserves. The immediate effect following the implementation of the new stabilization policy was an accelerated rate of growth of money and prices, as well as negative real interest rates. As the path of devaluation was kept independent of the pattern of domestic price behavior, the real exchange rate appreciated and the export-oriented and import-competing sectors experienced a recession.

The lower rate of devaluation coupled with regional as well as international events[6] resulted in a fall in the rate of inflation after early 1981;

6 In February 1981 Argentina abandoned the announced exchange commitment. Since late 1980 the US dollar started appreciating against most European currencies.

however, as nominal interest rates did not fall accordingly, the economy faced extremely high real interest rates during the period.

Finally, capital outflow developed in 1981 and 1982. In 1981 the fiscal deficit reached 2.3 percent of GDP, and expectations of a change in the exchange rate policy became prevalent. In 1982 the fiscal deficit grew to 18 percent of GDP and the Central Bank exhausted its international reserves trying to maintain its exchange rate commitment. In November 1982, the announced exchange regime was abandoned and a floating exchange rate regime was adopted by the Central Bank.

Commercial Policy Reforms

From 1974 to 1982 major changes in the tariff and exchange regimes were adopted. The reform initiated evolved in two stages. From 1974 to 1978 the main commercial policy changes were the elimination of quotas, the reduction in the maximum level of *recargos*,[7] the simplification of the tariff regime, and the expansion of the export subsidization program. The second stage of the commercial policy reform spanned the years 1978–82 and consisted of a simplification of the tariff system, and its gradual and announced reduction. In the next two sections we discuss tariff reform and the export subsidization program.

Tariff Reforms

The First Stage

During the last quarter of 1974 there was a relaxation in the license assignment administration, including a more liberal treatment of capital goods imports.[8] Following the License Allowance Resolutions in the last quarter of 1974 and early 1975 there were decisions widening the original margins. In April 1975 the license regime was discontinued and the Central Bank established an advance deposit in pesos for the equivalent of 35 percent of the c.i.f. value of imports, which was gradually substituted over time for a minimum 7 percent tariff.

In addition, there was a declining trend in the level of *recargos* from 1974 to 1979 which brought the maximum rate from 300 percent in 1976 to

7 As will be discussed below, import duties are composed of different components, with *recargos* (surcharges) being the most important.

8 Capital good imports were subject to a cumbersome and bureaucratic procedure. Those interested in importing capital goods had to apply for a permit to two regulatory commissions. The treatment of imports outside the Executive Power Resolution of 1965 depended upon the financing conditions of the transactions.

90 percent in 1979. The *recargo* reduction was presumably targeted towards eliminating water in the tariffs.

The consular tax (CT), which was collected by Uruguay's Consulate Officers in foreign countries, was set in May 1976 at 10 percent of the value of imports and from 1978 at 4 percent.

Finally, during the period the government unified all fees charged by the Border Authorities under a single heading called IMADUNI.[9] A basic rate of 25 percent was set and each commodity was taxed in multiples of this rate. In August 1979 the IMADUNI rate was brought to 20 percent and a fourth component of the new tariff system, the port border tax (TMB), was set at 1 percent of the c.i.f. value of imports.

As a result of these tariff changes, both the average level and the dispersion of nominal tariffs experienced significant contraction during the period 1974–8. This reduction is paralleled by the implicit tariff index which is defined as the ratio of the domestic price of importables to the domestic price of exportables divided by the ratio of the foreign price of importables to the foreign price of exportables (see table 2.7).

The Second Stage

The second stage of the commercial policy reform spanned the years 1978–82. The core of the trade liberalization program in this stage was an Executive Power Resolution adopted in December 1978. The main characteristics of the liberalization program were first a simplification of the tariff structure, including an attempt to unify its administration under a unique authority and second that the tariff reduction was to be gradual and announced so as to reduce private sector adjustment costs. The target level was to be a base tariff of 35 percent which included four components: the *recargo* (10 percent), the IMADUNI (20 percent), the TMB (1 percent) and the CT (4 percent).

The program was to be executed in six years starting in January 1980 and reaching its target in January 1985. In practice, since the Executive Power Resolution was adopted in late 1978, the program was developed in seven years, with the first year's tariff reduction being zero. All commodities with tariffs at levels higher than 35 percent had to undergo an annual reduction of 16 percent of the excess between the actual and the target level during the first five years and a reduction of 20 percent in the sixth year. However, the decree did not establish a procedure concerning those imports whose tariffs were below the 35 percent level. Although the authorities were concerned with the final effective protection level, in practice no step was adopted during the program execution to increase the level of tariffs below 35 percent to the target level.

9 IMADUNI stands for "unified custom duty."

In addition, the resolution established that those commodities which were not produced in the country and which had tariffs above 35 percent were to be subject to a one-step adjustment to the base rate. The import of capital goods had a tariff rate of 10 percent; at the same time the port service charge was reduced to 30 percent of its previous level, which accounted approximately for the cost of the service provided.

The first stage of the gradual tariff reduction program was implemented in January 1980.[10] The number of tariff brackets was kept at its previous level – 28 – and those tariffs above 35 percent had one sixth of the difference between the actual and the target level cut. Those tariffs below 35 percent were not subject to any change. The second stage of the program was implemented in January 1981 as announced: tariffs above the target level were again reduced by one sixth of the gap between the original and target levels, while those below 35 percent did not experience any change. This time, however, the number of tariff brackets was simplified and reduced from 28 to nine categories. The maximum tariff rate was set at 90 percent. The third stage was implemented in January 1982 as planned, although we observe some minor differences between the announced and executed reduction in the 55–65 percent range. The number of tariff brackets or categories was again reduced from 12 to nine. In June 1982 the tariff regime experienced further unplanned changes in the midst of a balance-of-payments crisis: first, a minimum tariff rate of 10 percent was established; second, tariffs above 10 percent were multiplied by a factor of 1.1. At the same time, a minimum export subsidy of 10 percent was established, while those products which already perceived the benefit had the subsidy rate increased by 1.1. Thus, the June 1982 tariff–subsidy measures were a proxy for an exchange rate devaluation of 10 percent. Finally, in December 1982 the tariff reduction program was abruptly accelerated and subsequently discontinued. A tariff regime based upon three broad commodity categories – final goods, intermediate goods, and raw materials – was introduced. However, the number of tariff brackets was kept at five levels. The December 1982 reform implied a tariff reduction beyond the target for 1984.

Although no significant differences appear between the original planned tariff levels and that resulting from the actual execution before 1983, the data conceal major departures experienced during 1979 and 1980 as a result of special tariff reductions in advance of the program which were determined on behalf of the domestic price stabilization purposes.

There were two types of departure from the originally planned tariff-cut path. In the first place we have those commodities which were not

10 See Favaro and Spiller (1988, appendix table 3.5) for the planned and actual tariff levels according to the announced program from 1979 to 1983.

domestically produced and for whose case the decree established a one-step reduction to the 35 percent level. According to this regime more than 500 items had their tariffs reduced during the second half of 1979 and 1980. During 1980 the Executive Power also established through Decree 602/80 that those commodities not produced in the country, but substitutes, would have a tariff reduction to the 35–50 percent level whenever it could be argued that domestic production was not sufficient to satisfy demand. During 1981 this procedure raised strong opposition and its application was stopped.

A second type of departure, which differs from the first in the sense that its use was not originally considered in the tariff reduction program, was developed under the umbrella of stabilization policy. During 1979, as inflation soared, the government established several tariff reductions in advance of the originally planned path. These cuts affected mostly tractors and agricultural machinery, wool, and textiles, as well as foodstuffs, and were intended to curb inflation by increasing competition with foreign products in those sectors where prices were rising faster than justified by cost increase. The logic underlying these reductions was that only redundant protection and monopoly practices associated with the economy enclosure could explain the behavior of domestic prices. Here the main concern behind tariff reduction was stabilization policy. According to the decree, those items affected by the abrupt tariff cut were later exempted from the general tariff reduction up to the moment that they achieved the level of protection which hypothetically they would have had under the original plan. Through the application of these decrees a tariff level of 35 percent was levied on several agricultural products and food items which under the previous regime had paid the maximum tariff. Other products had their tariff reduction program accelerated two or three stages in a blow, with rate cuts from 116 to 76 percent as in the case of clothing, to 66 percent as in the case of most textiles, or to 36 percent as in the case of leather goods and shoes. Those products affected by an accelerated tariff cut had, in addition, a tariff rate of 10 percent levied on raw materials and intermediate products used in production processes. Finally, during 1982 most exceptional tariff cuts were revised and protection was restored in the midst of a severe depression. The accelerated tariff reductions provoked a rapid accumulation of items in the 30–50 percent bracket during 1980 and 1981.

Decree 787/79 also established that the *recargos* – the main component of the tariff rate – were to be levied upon c.i.f. prices, thus discontinuing the use of BROU's administered prices (*aforos*), which implied a powerful source of disguised protection in the case of several manufactured products (for example textiles). Paralleling this resolution, the Administration authorized the Ministry of Economics and Finance to set new administered prices, based upon international true market values, in order to control tax evasion and dumping practices. In practice, the BROU kept levying the *recargo* rate on the old-fashioned administered prices up to the moment when a new set of prices was available. During 1982 several administered prices were determined well above the international price levels, thus reintroducing the former protection practice.

The gradual tariff reduction program made several exceptions, with the most important cases being the car assembly and the sugar industries. The car assembly industry was exempted from the program until 1980, and assembled car imports were prohibited. From 1980 on, the government authorized car imports of up to 1500 cc power. In addition to the maximum tariff rates which applied, these imports were subject to tied export-compensating restrictions for a percentage of the value of foreign exchange used from 1981 onwards.

The other privileged sector was the sugar industry. Sugar imports were prohibited during the period except when domestic supply was insufficient to satisfy demand. Under these circumstances imports of raw sugar by refining firms were authorized. Protection in this sector did not recognize written rules. Since the import bureaucratic process involved previous authorization by the BROU, import prohibition could be implemented through private intervention in the administrative procedure.[11]

In summary, we identified two stages in the process of tariff reform developed between 1974 and 1982. The first stage spans the years from 1974 to 1978 and implied the dismantling of quantity restrictions as well as the reduction of maximum tariff levels. The process involved both a reduction in the average and dispersion of nominal tariff levels.

The second stage was characterized by a planned gradual tariff reduction. The policy was pursued up to the third stage and stopped in 1982 in the midst of a dramatic economic depression. Departures from the main program were observed as a result of accelerated tariff reductions in several areas implemented as a part of the stabilization policy program pursued. The second stage of the trade liberalization process involved a reduction in the average with no substantial change in the dispersion of nominal tariffs.

Export Promotion Policy

Export promotion was a major area of government concern particularly during the period 1974–8. Export promotion included subsidies on exports, or *reintegros*, subsidies on loans directed to export-oriented activities, and fiscal exemptions, as well as administrative devices simplifying imports of raw materials and intermediate products for the manufacture of export goods. We will analyze these instruments separately.

11 Cases of virtual import prohibition through this procedure were also observed during the period in the car assembly industry.

The Export Subsidy Scheme

The main export incentive used in the period was the *reintegro*. The *reintegro* is a subsidy, expressed as a percentage of the free on board (f.o.b.) price of exports, although in principle it is related to value added in the activity. The origin of this instrument was Law 13268 in July 1964; however, it did not have a wide scope of application until the beginning of the 1970s. According to Law 13268 the Executive Power was allowed to introduce subsidies on industrialized exports whenever this was necessary to compete in foreign markets. Initially, the subsidy rate had a ceiling of 20 percent.

Those firms interested in receiving the benefit had to apply for it to the Ministry of Industry and Energy; once the benefit was approved every producer of the good was entitled to receive it. Although the word *reintegro* has the same meaning as drawback, in practice they were not set as a tax rebate for indirect fees paid along the production process. In pracrtice, the subsidy rate was determined according to the competitive needs of the industrial sectors.

Reintegros were paid through certificates which could be used to pay taxes to either the central government or the social security administration. Whenever the firm had a surplus above its own tax obligations it could sell the certificate to other firms. Traditional exports were not allowed to receive *reintegros*; furthermore, during most of the period its use overlapped with *detracciones*, that is, taxes on traditional exports.

From 1964 to the beginning of the 1970s the use of *reintegros* was frequently interrupted and the allocation of the benefit remained associated with the real value of the exchange rate, thus being suspended in the aftermath of a devaluation. In 1972 the subsidy regime was expanded to cover most nontraditional products, and the subsidy rate was increased and fixed during a period of three years after which they would be gradually reduced.

From 1974 on there is a widened scope of application of *reintegros*. Through Law 14214, from June 1971, the subsidy rate could be increased above the former 20 percent ceiling up to 50 percent, and even to 80 percent in some special cases where market penetration was considered crucial. Law 14214 extended the *reintegro* benefit to the freight service whenever a national flag transport was used, and to the insurance service when it was given by the public insurance company. According to Law 14214 the *reintegro*, although paid as a percentage of the f.o.b. value of exports, was to be estimated based on the value added in every manufacture stage until export completion. It is to be noted that some products benefited from special treatment above this regime. Wool products, for instance, received 22 percent extra benefit through the so-called Law Piñedo which has to be added to the *reintegro* rate.

During the period 1975–8 a program of subsidy reduction and eventually elimination was announced. In practice, the subsidy elimination was postponed, although a gradual reduction from the 1974 levels was developed during the next three years. In 1975 subsidies were reduced by 10 percent and in 1976 they were lowered again by 10 percent, followed by further reductions of 20 percent in 1977 and 15 percent in 1978. New reductions were postponed up to 1979.

In December 1979 Uruguay adhered to the new General Agreement on Tariffs and Trade (GATT) Code on Subsidies and Countervailing Duties. According to the new regime a country, in order to levy a compensating tax on imports from a trade partner, has to prove that a subsidy policy which causes economic damage is being applied.[12] In 1981 the government announced its intention of eliminating the *reintegros* and establishing as a counterpart a drawback to compensate for indirect taxes paid along the production process. The government's intention was to resume gradual reduction of the subsidy rate until they reached a target level of 5 percent, equivalent to the estimated burden of indirect taxes by the end of 1985. The simultaneous deterioration of the real exchange rate, which was creating problems for nontraditional export activities, made such an action undesirable, and the program implementation was postponed. Finally, in 1982 a complementary 10 percent subsidy, to be based on the effective exchange rate of each export, was given to all export activities including, for the first time, traditional exports.

The performance of the nontraditional export sector and the extent of subsidies is presented in table 3.5. This table shows first that from 1973 on there was a rapid increase in the value of nontraditional exports, second that the average *reintegro* was stable following the general subsidy reduction between 1975 and 1977, third that there was an increase in the value of nontraditional exports between 1979 and 1981, despite a sharp fall in the real exchange rate during the period and a drastic reduction in exports of leather garments and shoes shipped to the United States and finally that the weighted average *reintegro* rate for exports which perceived the benefit was close to the ratio of the aggregate value of *reintegros* to nontraditional exports, except for 1979 and 1981.

Although the rate of growth of nontraditional exports was high by all standards, it is useful to recognize part of it as explained by international inflation. In particular, once we allow for changes in the price level of exports, much of the growth observed from 1979 to 1981 disappears. Hence inflation explains much of the presumably abnormal behavior of nontraditional exports from 1979 to 1981.

12 During 1979 exports of leather products had a drastic decline largely as a result of the reduction of incentives to exports shipped to the United States. The US government proved damage and imposed a countervailing duty on imports of these items coming from Uruguay. As a result the Uruguayan government eliminated benefits on these exports.

Table 3.5 Subsidy rate and value of nontraditional exports, 1971–1982

Year	*Weighted average exports with reintegro (%)*	*Ratio of reintegro to nontraditional exports (%)*	*Nontraditional exports (million US$)*
1971	n.a.	13.0	51.0
1973	n.a.	17.0	58.0
1974	21.9	21.5	144.3
1975	n.a.	18.0	189.3
1976	n.a.	20.0	293.7
1977	20.0	18.6	346.3
1978	15.7	14.2	437.4
1979	14.0	11.6	565.5
1980	13.4	12.7	642.7
1981	14.5	12.2	702.3
1982	n.a.	13.2	587.5

n.a., not available.
Excluding nontraditional exports that do not receive *reintegro*.
Sources: own calculations; ratio of *reintegro* to nontraditional exports, Bension and Caumont, 1981; 1982 data, CINVE, 1984

The destination of exports changed dramatically during the period, with regional transactions (particularly to Argentina) increasing in importance in overall trade. This phenomenon is presumably also related to a change in the composition of nontraditional exports. As we will see below, there is some indirect evidence in this direction from the pattern of imported inputs for the manufacture of export goods during the period.

The difference between the *reintegro* divided by total nontraditional exports and the weighted average *reintegro* rate is presumably explained during 1979 by the fall in *reintegro* incentives to leather goods imported to the United States as a result of countervailing duties imposed by this country on this type of transaction. The 1981 phenomenon is related to windfall exports to Argentina promoted by Argentinian firms which pursued benefits from the exchange controls prevailing in that country. Owing to the nature of this trade Uruguayan firms did not benefit from export subsidies.

The export promotion policies generated a substantial change of exports toward those sectors and goods which benefited from higher rates. This can be seen from comparing the average *reintegro* on nontraditional exports with the hypothetical *reintegro* rate that should have prevailed had the composition of nontraditional exports remained unchanged during this period. Except for 1978 the hypothetical *reintegro* rate is well below the actual rate.

Although discriminated against, traditional exports also benefited, to some extent, from the economic policy following 1974. The real effective exchange rate for traditional exports shows a real depreciation during the first two years of the new policy (1975–6) and appreciated slowly up to 1978. From 1978 on, the real effective exchange rate shows the same pattern for nontraditional exports. The real effective exchange rate for traditional exports was kept constant until 1979. This pattern differs from that observed in the real effective exchange rate for nontraditional exports during the same period, which depreciated. From 1979 on both the real effective exchange rate for traditional and nontraditional exports showed a drastic appreciation (table 3.6).

Table 3.6 Real exchange rate for nontraditional exports, 1974–1982 (1974 new pesos)

Year	*RECPI*	*REGDP*	*REWI*
1974	1.43	1.43	1.43
1975	1.91	2.04	2.04
1976	1.64	1.76	1.88
1977	1.43	1.57	1.88
1978	1.42	1.52	1.92
1979	1.28	1.32	1.92
1980	1.04	1.23	1.54
1981	0.94	1.01	1.29
1982	0.85	1.00	1.28

RECPI is defined as the nominal effective exchange rate on nontraditional exports, deflated by the CPI times the international export price index. REGDP is defined as the nominal effective exchange rate on nontraditional exports deflated by the GDP price index times the international export price index. REWI is defined as the nominal effective exchange rate on nontraditional exports deflated by the average wage index times the international export price index. The international export price index was adjusted to the new base using the inflation rate for manufactured producer prices of the United States during 1975.

Sources: Banco Central del Uruguay, *Boletín Estadístico*, various issues; for exports at the eight-digit ISIC level, BROU, unpublished data

The Export Financing Regime

Between 1968 and 1969 credit regimes to finance export activities under preferential credit conditions were devised. Credit lines were usually directed toward financing working capital, and benefited mostly nontraditional exporters.

During 1976–9, export financing under subsidized terms assumed an increasing role in foreign trade promotion. The main credit regime, known as the *preventa*, covered the time period for both production and shipment of export goods. According to the terms of the loan, the exporter received in advance a portion of the export revenue and froze the exchange rate for its repayment at the level existing at the time of the operation. Although the loan was formally agreed in foreign currency and paid a nominal interest rate in US dollars, in fact the borrower benefited from the exchange rate depreciation during the period before repayment was due. Thus the nominal foreign currency interest rate under this regime could, in practice, be negative.

As a result of domestic credit policy changes from 1979 this type of credit subsidy was eliminated and, although eventually reinstated, never again had such preferential characteristics.

Fiscal Exemptions

Nontraditional export benefited from preferential treatment during most of the period under scrutiny. Among the instruments used to create incentives on these activities we observe the following.

1. According to Law 13782 of November 1969, firms' net revenue attributed to activities which directly or indirectly involved the manufacture of export goods was tax exempted. It is to be noted that over time the concept of indirect exports evolved toward a wider meaning, increasing the scope of application of this incentive. In 1979 the tax reform established a gradual elimination of this benefit in three steps from 1980 to 1982. The exception accorded was 70 percent, 30 percent, and zero during 1980, 1981, and 1982 respectively.
2. Since 1972, Uruguay has incorporated VAT which allows deduction of taxes paid at different stages of production when the final good is exported. This particular tax structure helped to avoid discrimination against export activities.
3. In 1974 the government approved an industrial promotion law whose main target was to promote and diversify exports. According to this law, investment projects considered of national priority could be entitled to fiscal exemptions as well as preferential tax treatment. The main benefit recovered by national priority projects was an exemption from all tariffs and port service charges due on import of capital goods with this purpose. From 1979 on the tax regime eliminated all tax incentives.
4. An important administrative device favoring nontraditional exports was the simplification of the procedure permitting duty-free import of intermediate goods and raw materials used in the manufacture of export goods. Although the regime was created in 1911 it did not have a wide scope of application before 1974. The regime was designed to provide exporters with access to intermediate goods at

prices and qualities comparable with those of their international competitors. This regime became more important during the second subperiod. In particular, the ratio of such imports under temporary admission to nontraditional exports increased over time. This phenomenon is presumably the result of a change in the structure of nontraditional exports during the period.

In summary, the export promotion policy included subsidies in exports, preferential financing, fiscal exemptions, and administrative devices favoring imports to be manufactured and reimported. The subsidy scheme focused on the nontraditional industrial sector. The real exchange rate depreciated after 1974 and up to 1978 for nontraditional export goods and remained stable for traditional export goods. From 1979 on, both rates experienced an appreciation.

The Nature of Accompanying Policies

Exchange Rate Policy

Since March 1972 the exchange rate regime consisted of a system of periodic mini-devaluation. The purpose was to manage the exchange rate through small discrete changes so as to keep the real exchange rate at a stable level. In practice, however, the rate of devaluation did not keep pace with the difference between domestic and international inflation. From March 1972 to September 1974 a severe dual exchange control regime with a commercial and financial rate was in place.

The commercial rate was used to settle import and export transactions as well as to satisfy public sector demand originating in public debt service. The financial rate was used to settle all other authorized transactions (see table 2.7 for a comparison of the financial and the commercial rates). In September 1974 the new economic team established absolute freedom to perform foreign exchange transactions, including international capital movements. However, a dual exchange market was kept with a managed commercial rate. Whenever the financial exchange rate was below the commercial rate, the Central Bank supplied less foreign currency to importers and the system worked as in a fixed exchange parity. If, however, the financial rate was above the commercial rate, the system was mixed with a fixed commercial and a floating financial peg. In practice, the monetary authorities managed the rate of devaluation, keeping both rates close to each other. The ratio of the financial rate to the commercial rate was 1.18 in 1975 and 1.10 in 1976; from then until October 1978 both rates were essentially identical.

In October 1978 the Central Bank unified the financial and commercial markets. In addition the authorities started announcing the schedule of mini-devaluations in advance, in the first instance for a nine-month period.

The announced exchange system represented a major change in exchange rate management, as the Central Bank focused mainly on a stabilization objective rather than upon the effect on the export- and import-competing sectors of the economy. The new system implied a lower average real exchange rate but a much higher variance over time.

Also, during the period 1974–8 the exchange rate depreciated at a higher rate of inflation within the first two quarters following the beginning of the policy and appreciated in real terms particularly during the third and fourth year of the application of this policy. Similarly, the exchange rate showed a sharp depreciation *vis-à-vis* nominal wages within the first year and a tendency toward stability afterwards. However, during the 1978–82 period there was an accelerating appreciation of the exchange rate up to the third year of application of the announced peg regime.

An additional problem concerning exchange rate management during the period 1978–82 was the difficulty of maintaining a stable real parity in a world where wide variations in purchasing power parity were observed both among industrialized countries and particularly in the region. The real exchange rate between Uruguay and the United States shows a stable level up to 1978 and a sharp deterioration up to the period 1979–81 in contrast, the real exchange rate between Uruguay and Germany deteriorated up to 1979 and appreciated in 1980–1. This behavior is the mirror image of the real depreciation of the US dollar *vis-à-vis* the German mark up to 1979 and its appreciation in 1980–1. Even more interesting is the pattern of the real exchange rate with Uruguay's neighbors Argentina and Brazil. The size of the Argentinian and Brazilian economies, and the existence of an extensive border and the deep economic integration with the Uruguayan economy, makes it impossible to keep the level of economic activity unaffected by the economic cycles suffered by the Uruguayan neighbors. The real parity with Argentina shows a real depreciation up to 1980 and a dramatic fall in 1982. The real exchange rate with Brazil shows a stable level up to 1978 and a drastic fall afterwards.

In summary, the exchange rate management policy had two stages: from 1974 to 1978 the target was to keep a high and stable real parity, thus providing an incentive for export activities; from 1978 on, the main target was domestic stabilization policy. The rate of devaluation was kept independent of the pattern of domestic price behavior. This exchange rate policy, within the context of high domestic interest rates and open capital markets, induced a high capital inflow and an enormous build-up of international reserves during the period, thus contributing to an accelerating rate of money growth and inflation and a deterioration in the real exchange rate.

Monetary Policy

The monetary and financial sectors underwent significant reforms during the second half of the 1970s. We will again distinguish two periods: 1974–8 when monetary policy made use of traditional instruments (open-market operations, reserve requirements) and the control of monetary aggregates was pursued, and 1978–82 when the Central Bank assumed a passive monetary policy and limited its role to managing the exchange rate.

The 1974–1978 Period

One of the main objectives of the economic team appointed in 1974 was to build up international reserves. The main instrument used in the aftermath of the oil crisis was the liberalization of foreign exchange transactions and capital movements. In addition, restrictions on the level of net foreign assets commercial banks could maintain were discounted and interest rate ceilings on both loans and deposits were raised.

During the period 1974–8 the rate of growth of credit to the private sector was positive and high, particularly in foreign-currency-denominated loans. Most money aggregates showed a positive rate of growth during the four-year period. There was a higher rate of growth of foreign currency loans and deposits than of its counterpart in domestic currency; in addition, the interest rate was positive on loans and negative on deposits during most of the period. In what follows we describe these developments in detail.

During 1974 and 1975 the increment in the Central Bank's domestic credit expressed as a percentage of GDP was high as a result of the public sector's deficit financing. In addition, the ratio of base money to GDP increased and reserves were lost. From 1976 to 1978 the ratio of the increment in domestic credit to GDP was reduced as the fiscal situation improved, the reserve-to-loss ratio changed its sign, and the money base continued growing (table 3.7).

From 1976 on, the monetary authorities relied increasingly on the role of the price system for the allocation of credit, eliminating credit-allocation guidelines and raising interest rate ceilings. In addition, the Central Bank encouraged savings in the banking system, increasing authorized interest rate limits on deposits and allowing foreign-currency-denominated deposits. In May 1976 the Central Bank freed interest rates and in June 1976 dismantled the commercial banks' restrictions on net foreign assets positions.

The main monetary policy instrument used during the period was reserve requirements, although open-market operations were performed as well. From 1974 to 1978 the Central Bank's control of the monetary aggregate was the main instrument for controlling inflation. During this

Table 3.7 Changes in domestic credit, reserves, and base money as a percentage of gross domestic product, 1974–1978

	International reserves		*Domestic credit*		*Base money*	
Year	Δ *(new pesos)*	Δ/GDP *(%)*	Δ *(new pesos)*	Δ/GDP *(%)*	Δ *(new pesos)*	Δ/GDP *(%)*
1974	−181.8	−3.9	314.4	6.8	132.6	2.9
1975	−309.5	−3.7	587.8	7.0	278.3	3.3
1976	−11.9	−0.1	584.4	4.5	572.5	4.4
1977	−313.7	−1.6	846.0	4.2	2.7
1978	974.0	3.2	393.2	1.3	3,197.5	10.5

Source: Banco Central del Uruguay, *Boletín Estadístico*, various issues

period the monetary authorities gradually eliminated expansionary sources, such as discounting the commercial banks' credit instruments, and tightened control of the public sector's credit in paralleling improved fiscal performance.

In March 1976 the government eliminated by law the *curzo forzoso*, or the obligatory new peso contract denomination, allowing contracts in all types of currency.

Within the first year of application of the new monetary policy and the implementation of the deregulatory process there was a drastic deceleration in the rate of growth of all monetary aggregates and credit concepts. The rate of growth of real money aggregates and the banking system's credit to the public sector was negative, but the rate of growth of credit to the private sector in both domestic and foreign currency was positive. Within the next three years, however, there was an acceleration in the rate of growth of money aggregates, particularly base money and M3, owing to the growth in foreign-currency-denominated deposits. On the credit side, the introduction of the 1974 reforms was followed by a deceleration in the rate of growth of net domestic credit while there was an acceleration in the rate of growth of credit to the public and private sectors; in particular, the rate of growth of private sector credit in foreign currency in particular exploded during the period. The rate of growth of real money aggregates (except for M1 and the banking system's credit to the private sector) was positive during the three-year period following September 1975; in particular the rate of growth of private sector credit in foreign currency measured in real terms was extremely high during these three years (Favaro and Spiller, 1988, appendix table 3.10).

Interest rates on foreign-currency-denominated loans were cheaper *ex post*, although more variable than those prevailing in domestic currency loans. Interest rates in foreign currency deposits were *ex post* higher and almost equally as variable as those obtained in domestic currency operations. These tendencies are consistent with the strong rate of growth for both foreign currency loans and deposits during this period.

The real rate of interest on domestic currency loans was positive and high up to early 1978; the rate of interest corresponding to foreign currency loans was positive up to the second half of 1977. The rate of interest on deposits measured in real terms was negative for both foreign and domestic currency loans during most of the period.

The 1978–1982 Period

The second stage in monetary and financial policy started in October 1978 when the Central Bank abandoned active monetary policy and relied exclusively on exchange rate management for stabilization purposes. Since domestic nominal interest rates were above the *ex post* domestic yield in foreign-currency-denominated deposits, this policy contributed to inducing a strong capital inflow and a build-up of Central Bank reserves coupled with an accelerating rate of money growth. In addition to the expansionary effect generated by the capital inflow, two other policy measures acted in this direction. First, reserve requirements (which had been strongly reduced in late 1978) were finally eliminated during 1979. Second, the Central Bank increased the authorized leverage of commercial banks. The ratio of debt to net worth in commercial banks had a ceiling of 16 times up to 1978; during 1979 the authorized ratio was raised to 20 times, and during 1980 it was raised to 30 times. The ratio was planned to be reduced to 25 times during the period July 1981 to June 1982, with further reductions in the next two years until a target level of 22 times net worth was reached in 1984.

The discounting of the commercial banks' credit documents was eliminated in 1979, and open-market operations were abandoned on the grounds that they were considered inefficient and ineffective in controlling the behavior of money aggregates. All official credit controls as well as subsidized export credits were eliminated in early 1979. Finally, a domestic market in precious metals was created in order to broaden the assets selection available to investors.

With the first year of application of the new monetary policy there was an acceleration in the rate of growth of money and credit aggregates (in particular M2 and domestic currency credit to the private sector), with the exception of net domestic credit to the public sector which fell in nominal terms. This pattern was unchanged during the second year of application of this policy request. During the last two years of this period, there was a dramatic fall in the rate of growth of money aggregates and credit, except for public sector credit which exploded in both nominal and real terms (Favaro and Spiller, 1988, appendix table 3.11).

Interest rates on domestic currency (for both loans and deposits) were *ex post* more expensive and less volatile than those observed in foreign currency operations. The average interest rate on domestic currency loans during the passive-money policy period is very close to that observed in the 1974–8 active-money experience. However, the spread between domestic and foreign currency loans and deposit interest rates widened during the period.

The immediate effect of the application of the new policy was to lower real interest rates, particularly on foreign currency loans. Initially, with stable nominal interest rates, the acceleration in the rate of growth of money translated into a higher inflation rate and negative real interest rates. After the first year of application of the exchange rate management monetary policy, the real rate of interest in domestic currency loans was positive and high by all standards. The real rate of interest in foreign currency loans was also positive after the third quarter of 1979. From June 1980 onward, the real rate of interest on both loans and deposits in domestic and foreign currency reached record levels as stable nominal interest rates combined with a remarkable slowdown in the inflation rate.

In summary, monetary policy during the 1978–82 stage was concerned exclusively with exchange rate management. A lower announced rate of devaluation generated high dollar yields in domestic currency operations, thus creating incentives for capital inflow. The immediate effect of the application of the new monetary policy was an accelerating rate of growth of money and prices, and negative real interest rates. The combined effect of a continuous application of this exchange rate policy and regional as well as international developments from early 1981 was a remarkable fall in the rate of inflation and extremely high real interest rates during the rest of the period. Finally, in November 1982 the exchange rate policy was abandoned and a floating exchange rate regime was established.

Fiscal Policy

During the 1970s we observed major developments in fiscal policy, affecting tax revenue as well as government expenditure. In this section we consider first those changes occurring in the tax structure and second those occurring on the expenditure side from 1974 to 1982.

Tax Reform

During the 1950s and 1960s the tax regime underwent several modifications. Direct taxes appeared for the first time, and ideas about pursuing economic targets other than tax collection became relevant in the design of tax regimes. A personal income tax and later a tax on minimum agricultural earnings (based on an estimation of average land productivity and independent of net income) were levied. However, indirect specific taxes remained as the main source of central government's income, and taxes on labor were the basic resource of social security financing. Indirect taxes already included an embryonic consumption-type VAT which had numerous exemptions. Taxes on traditional exports were heavy, and discriminated against the agricultural sector. The personal income tax was based on income source (for example, agriculture industry). On average it was never significant in terms of either its share of global tax collection or the number of taxpayers affected – the number of taxpayers during 1968 and 1969 was 7,308 and 12,803 respectively. The taxation of firms' net earnings differed according to its activity or legal structure. The taxation of capital ownership included a tax on individual property and a tax on the firm's net wealth; in addition there were municipal taxes and fees. Although tax rates were high, the criteria of property valuation usually underestimated the true market value of assets. Public debt property was tax exempt, thus discriminating against private sector financial instruments. Finally, taxes on wages collected by the Social Security Administration were the main source of revenue for the consolidated government sector. Tax rates were high, reaching levels of 38–49 percent for the employer and 20–5 percent on the employee's side.

Between 1974 and 1980, the tax regime was completely revised. Reforms were developed in two stages, the first starting in 1974 and the second in 1979. The main trend was toward simplifying the tax structure, eliminating taxes and exemptions, and trying to cure discrimination against labor use and export activities. The main issues in the 1974 tax reform were the elimination of personal income and inheritance taxes, the unification of firms' net earnings taxation under a single tax (although corporations still paid a higher tax rate), and the extension application of VAT combined with the elimination of numerous specific taxes. In addition, social security taxes on wages were reduced and a tax on estimated agricultural income was levied (IMPROME).[13] The second wave of tax reforms started in 1978 with the elimination of taxes on beef and wool exports, which formerly could reach rates of up to 50 percent of the value of exports. The IMPROME was substituted for the IMAGRO (a tax levied on estimated net income from land exploitation), and the new regime made allowances for intermediate inputs expense. Continuous reductions in taxes on wages were paralleled by an increase in the VAT rate and a reform in the social security regime. Taxes on wages were simplified and the treatment of wages in different activities was homogenized. As a result of these reforms, there was a significant drop in the resources of the Social Security

13 IMPROME stands for "average" productivity tax.

Administration which had to be substituted for Central Government's transfers. In 1981 the 2 percent tax on wages for the Housing Program Fund was eliminated; in addition, sources of discrimination, such as the exemption in the firms' income tax regime of net revenues obtained through export activities and the exemption of revenues devoted to reinvestment purposes, were discontinued.

Although the tax reform was significant in terms of both its scope and its effect upon government revenues, it did not imply a modified tax pressure, mainly because of the substitution of one source of tax revenue for another. This phenomenon is the result of the reduction of wage taxes coupled with a broader application of VAT. The share of taxes on foreign trade transactions increased up to 1980 and fell afterwards, but its composition changed dramatically – export tax collection diminished over the whole period while import duties increased their share. Taxes on wages and on personal income diminished their share, while firms' net revenue tax increased its participation. Finally, taxes on net wealth increased their share over the whole period – a remarkable phenomenon since we would not expect procyclical behavior of this type of tax collection, particularly up to 1981 (table 3.8).

Table 3.8 Government revenue by tax source for selected years between 1973 and 1982 (percent)

Source	*1973*	*1975*	*1978*	*1979*	*1980*	*1981*	*1982*
1 Expenditure	35.9	43.1	40.6	39.0	42.3	45.9	44.3
VAT	19.9	24.6	24.5	23.7	26.2	29.4	27.5
Other specific	16.0	18.5	16.1	15.3	16.1	16.5	16.8
2 Taxes on wages	32.0	30.4	29.3	27.4	21.8	21.3	24.7
3 Taxes on international trade	12.2	6.2	8.1	12.9	13.5	11.7	9.4
Imports	5.3	5.7	7.9	12.8	13.5	11.7	9.4
Exports	6.9	0.5	0.2	0.1	0.0	0.0	–
4 Taxes on property	7.6	8.0	9.0	8.5	8.0	9.5	10.5
On net wealth	4.7	4.9	6.1	5.1	6.3	7.4	9.2
On wealth transfer	2.9	3.1	2.9	3.4	1.7	2.1	1.3
5 Taxes on income	6.0	5.8	7.4	7.6	10.6	8.2	6.9
Personal	4.0	2.1	2.0	1.5	2.4	0.6	0.3
Corporations	2.0	3.7	5.4	6.1	8.2	7.6	6.6
6 Other sources	6.3	6.5	5.7	4.5	3.8	3.4	4.2
Total	100.0	100.0	100.0	100.0	100.0	100.0	100.0

–, negligible.
Source: Garcia, 1985

In summary, the tax reform reduced taxes on wages, eliminated taxes on the export of Uruguay's two main traditional products, reduced tariffs on imports, and widened the application of VAT. The tax reform was related to export promotion policy through the attempt to reduce the cost of labor, whose use is intensive in most nontraditional export activities.

The Expenditure Reform

During the 1970s the structure of central government expenditure underwent significant changes: social security transfers, investment expenditures, and, at the end of the decade, debt services increased their share of total expenses (table 3.9).

Until 1980 social security transfers averaged approximately 13 percent of total central government expenditure; from then on, the share of these transfers jumped to more than 20 percent, reaching 32 percent in 1982. The counterpart of the increasing social security deficit is double: first the reduction of social security taxes over the period implied a direct fall in the system's traditional revenue source; second there was a significant increase in government social security transfers, particularly in 1981 and 1982. This increment is associated with an increase in the number of people entitled to receive social security transfers over the period as well as an increase in the real value of the transfers. Some of the reforms developed in the social security system during the period 1974–80 were directed toward tightening conditions for eligibility (increase in minimum retirement age, elimination of special programs); however, the ratio of the retired to the economically active population continued to grow.

From 1975 on, government investment expenditure increased rapidly, and during 1978–81 reached almost double the level of the previous decade (table 3.10).

Finally, although a recent phenomenon, it is important to note the increasing significance of government interest payments in overall government expenditure. From 1973 to 1980, interest payments averaged 4.5 percent of central government's expenditure; later in 1981 and 1982 they fell to 2 percent of this aggregate. However, this information distorts the real significance of the issue. In order to make precise the transfers involved, we have to look at the consolidated balance sheet of the public sector, including the financial institutions. In particular it is important to consider that the Central Bank increased its debt during 1982, and that the service involved is not computed in central government data.

In summary, the country experienced remarkable changes both in the tax structure and significance of different revenue sources and in the composition of expenditure during the 1974–82 period.

Tax pressure remained unchanged; hence the tax reform had the effect of substituting some forms of tax revenue for alternative sources. Social security transfers became increasingly important as an item in overall

Table 3.9 Composition of central government expenditure, 1973–1982 (percent)

Components	*1973*	*1974*	*1975*	*1976*	*1977*	*1978*	*1979*	*1980*	*1981*	*1982*
Total expenditure	100.0	100.0	100.0	100.0	100.0	100.0	100.0	100.0	100.0	100.0
Wages and salaries	64.2	68.3	62.0	62.2	57.7	55.3	53.3	48.3	39.1	37.8
Interest payments	2.1	3.5	5.6	7.2	6.4	5.6	4.4	2.2	1.9	2.6
Social security transfers	9.6	13.0	16.7	14.4	11.8	13.2	13.7	18.5	24.9	32.3
Public enterprises transfers	2.7	3.0	2.4	2.8	1.8	1.9	2.6	2.5	2.0	2.5
Municipal government transfers	1.5	1.1	0.7	0.6	–	–	–	–	0.4	0.7
Capital expenditure	9.9	9.6	10.4	11.5	12.4	15.6	17.8	17.1	16.4	9.6
Other	10.0	6.5	2.2	1.3	9.8	8.3	8.2	11.5	15.3	14.5

–, negligible.

Sources: García, 1985; Banco Central del Uruguay, *Boletín Estadístico*, various issues

Table 3.10 Share of public investment in total investment, government expenditure, and gross domestic product, 1960–1983 (percent)

Period	*Ratio of public investment to total investment*	*Ratio of public investment to government expenditure*	*Ratio of public investment to GDP*
1960–4	18.9	17.9	3.1
1965–9	19.5	13.7	2.5
1970–4	24.7	14.2	3.2
1975–9	42.5	35.6	7.6
1980–3	38.1	28.0	2.3

Sources: Banco Central del Uruguay, *Producto e Ingreso Nacionales*, various issues; *Boletín Estadístico*, various issues; *Indicadores de la Actividad Económico–Financiera*, various years; *Formación Bruta de Capital*, various issues

government expenditure as the system generated a gap between its own falling sources of revenue and its ever growing expenditure.

Domestic Controls

In this section we describe those policies concerning price, wage and investment administrative controls or guidelines, and policies affecting capital inflow and outflow.

Restrictions on International Capital Movements

As of 1974, the country experienced a severe exchange control regime which prohibited individuals or firms from holding or trading foreign-currency-denominated assets. All financial transactions had to be settled through the banking system and were subject to Central Bank regulations.

In September 1974 the government eliminated all foreign currency restrictions including those involving short-term capital movements. Paralleling this move the government approved the Foreign Investment Law (FIL) which accorded foreign investment approximately the same treatment provided to domestic resident investors. The FIL included a quite liberal profit remittance provision. Foreign firms were not obliged to use the FIL umbrella and, in practice most did not make the provisions.

Investment Controls

Among those administrative devices which affected investment as of 1974, we need to stress the role of regulations concerning the import of capital goods. Bureaucratic procedures required authorization from a special government commission. During the second half of 1974 most bureaucratic restrictions were lifted, and from May 1975 imports of capital goods were subject to an import regime like any other commodity. In 1978 the government eliminated barriers to entry in the beef industry, and in 1982 it approved a new banking law authorizing the entry of new firms in the market.

In March 1974 the government approved an Industrial Promotion Law (IPL) offering special incentives for investment in national priority projects. In order to be entitled to the benefits authorized by the IPL the projects had to meet certain criteria based on the Economic Development Plan which included employment generation, development of technology, and improvements in domestic resource use; however, the primary emphasis was on the expansion and diversification of exports on nontraditional industries. Among the incentives offered through the IPL were exonerations from tariffs and port services charged on imports of machinery, equipment, and spare parts, partial exoneration from certain social security taxes, and access to medium- and long-term financial resources. A special advisory council within the Ministry of Industry and Energy reviewed the project applications and recommended approval, which was formally provided by the Executive Power. From 1974 to 1979, 289 investment project requests were received and 173 were approved, representing almost US$160 million in investment. More than 50 percent of the value of approved investment was directed toward the food, leather, and textile industries with emphasis on export potential. In the initial stage of policy formulation, the benefits available seem to have contributed to make investors less cautious about export undertakings.

An additional subsidy schedule which benefited investment was an exemption of up to 50 percent of net income for the firm's income tax provision when it was destined for reinvestment in industrial equipment, or up to 20 percent to cover construction costs. The fiscal reform of 1979 eliminated both the subsidy on income to be reinvested within the industry and most exonerations provided formerly within the IPL.

Price Controls

As of 1974 a gradual process of price liberalization was started and controls were lifted on most products; however, by March 1978, 46 percent of all items included in the consumer price index (CPI) basket were controlled. As of December 1979, 77 percent of all items in the CPI basket were decontrolled.

In August 1978 the government approved agricultural reforms which brought sweeping changes to the sector. To enhance export capacity and strengthen producer incentives, fixed livestock prices were eliminated. In addition, geographical barriers to the marketing of beef were removed, the state-owned meat-processing plants were sold to the private sector, government intervention in the financial operations of private sector slaughter firms was discontinued, the maximum level of tariffs on farm machinery was reduced to 10 percent, and grain prices were freed.

In July 1978 the government eliminated rent controls on commercial buildings and in July 1979 the same step was adopted for residential buildings.

Wage Controls

In 1968 a price and wage control system had been established by the government. Under this regime private firms had to apply for price increases, justifying the move through the registered trajectory of their production costs. In parallel with price controls the government determined wage increases (although movements beyond the minimum official levels were authorized). In the second half of 1974 the government established a "unique wage increase" regime: during this period firms were not allowed to provide wage increments beyond official guidelines. From 1975 to 1982 the government determined minimum wage guidelines and let private firms follow their own policies beyond this limit. Finally, in 1982 the government allowed wages to be governed by market forces, although it still determined minimum wage levels.

4

Inferences for the Timing and Sequencing of Trade Liberalization

Introduction

Trade liberalization in Uruguay has been stalled. The new democratic government that assumed power in March 1985 has not shown any intention of reviving the trade liberalization experiment that was suspended in 1982. The experiment, however, has not been reversed.

We have three main purposes in this section. First, we will consider whether the Uruguayan trade liberalization experiment has had a major effect on the allocation of resources. Second, we will analyze the performance of the different sectors to assess whether there were important industrial characteristics that may have impacted on the success of the liberalization experiment. Finally, based on the previous discussions, we will perform a detailed analysis of the policies that characterized the experiment as they relate to its timing and sequencing. This analysis will facilitate the assessment of whether the stalling of the trade liberalization process could have been predicted as a result of its own mismanagement.

The Resource-allocation Effects of the Trade Liberalization Process

To analyze whether the experiment was a success or failure we have to provide criteria to evaluate it. Since the impact of a trade liberalization program should mostly be felt in the allocation of resources, a first criterion to analyze is whether it succeeded in reallocating resources from import-competing sectors to export-oriented sectors (table 4.1). Tables 4.4 and 4.5 (later) show that the process of moving away from import-competing and marginal trade sectors toward exporting sectors was strong during the initial period of trade liberalization, which involved the dismantling of the quota system and a policy of export promotion. The share of exporting sectors in GDP, however, fell drastically in 1979, with

Table 4.1 Key to industrial classification

ISIC code	*Sector*	*Classification*
311	Foodstuffs	X
312	Other foodstuffs	X
313	Beverages	MT
314	Tobacco	MT
321	Textiles	X
322	Clothing	X
323	Leather products	X
324	Footwear	X
331	Wood products	MT
332	Furniture	MT
341	Paper products	IC
342	Printing	MT
351	Chemical products	IC
352	Other chemicals	IC
355	Rubber products	X
356	Plastic products	MT
361	Clay products	X
362	Glass products	X
369	Other nonmetallic mineral products	MT
371	Basic steel products	IC
372	Basic nonferrous products	IC
381	Metallic products	IC
382	Machinery, except electrical	IC
383	Electrical machinery and equipment	IC
384	Transport products	IC
385	Scientific and professional instruments	IC
390	Other	

X, exporting sector; MT, marginal trade sector; IC, import competing.
The classification is based on the statistic *T* (see footnote to table 2.8).

the introduction of the new stabilization policy. From 1979 on, their share increased steadily, reaching in 1982 the same value as that in 1974 (51 percent). By the end of 1982, most of the reallocation of resources took the form of moving away from import-competing sectors towards marginal trade sectors. That the success of the trade liberalization experiment in reallocating resources was small from 1978 on can be seen from the ratio of exports to GDP which is presented in table 4.2. The table shows that from 1974 to 1977 there was a marked increase in the exports-to-GDP ratio which reached 14 percent by 1977, only to fall back from 1978 to nearly its historical level of around 10 percent.[1] In contrast, the structure of imports

1 However, it is important to notice the large increase in the share of the nontraditional in total exports.

Table 4.2 Ratio of exports to gross domestic product, 1974–1982 (percent)

Year	*Ratio of exports to GDP*
1974	9.8
1975	10.5
1976	14.3
1977	14.2
1978	10.7
1979	10.7
1980	10.2
1981	10.4
1982	10.8

Sources: Banco Central del Uruguay, *Producto e Ingreso Nacionales*, various issues; *Boletín Estadístico*, various issues

(see table 2.9) shows an increasing liberalization of the import side. While the ratio of final goods to total imports was only 30 percent by 1974, it exceeded 50 percent by 1982.

A further measure of success involves the impact of the experiment on factor productivity. As discussed above, factor productivity during the post-war period was stagnant. However, from 1974 on, almost all sectors showed substantial productivity gains. In particular, the marginal trade and import substitution sectors showed the largest productivity gains (table 4.3).

To summarize, the success of the Uruguayan trade liberalization program in reallocating resources away from the import-competing sectors seems to have been stalled by 1978, the year when a new stabilization policy was introduced which implied a substantial appreciation of the real exchange rate. An appreciation of the real exchange rate should have a negative impact on both the export and import-competing sectors. However, as we will discuss below, exporting sectors are those with relatively more elastic supplies. An appreciation of the real exchange rate, then, will have a stronger impact on the more elastic sectors, that is, on the exporting sectors. Thus the lack of success in reallocating resources arises mostly from macroeconomic circumstances rather than from a mismanagement of the trade liberalization process. However, the experiment was successful in increasing labor productivity during the period.

Table 4.3 Evolution of labor productivity: ratio of value added to person hour

ISIC code	*1976 to 1975*	*1977 to 1975*	*1978 to 1975*	*1979 to 1978*	*1980 to 1978*	*1981 to 1978*
311	0.98	1.05	0.97	1.05	1.08	1.11
313	0.93	0.92	0.98	1.10	1.11	1.21
314	1.04	1.01	1.05	1.28	1.24	1.30
321	1.06	1.09	1.16	1.02	1.06	1.13
322	1.00	0.96	0.92	0.96	1.06	1.10
341	1.04	1.12	1.27	1.01	1.04	0.91
342	1.00	1.00	0.99	1.14	1.21	1.21
351	1.06	1.03	1.15	1.19	1.03	1.15
353	1.23	1.13	1.19	0.98	1.13	1.35
355	0.86	0.81	0.82	0.99	0.99	0.90
361	0.97	1.08	1.07	1.06	1.13	1.23
381	1.09	1.12	1.11	1.09	1.02	0.98
383	1.15	1.14	1.19	1.10	1.38	1.51

Sources: Dirección General de Estadística y Censos, *Encuesta Anual de Actividad Económica, Industrias Manufactureras*, various issues

An Analysis of Sectoral Responses to Trade Liberalization

Major Patterns

As discussed above, the aggregate performance of the major economic variables differs widely during the 1974–8 and 1978–82 phases of trade liberalization. There is also substantial cross-sectional variation within industries in each of these periods. In general, export sectors exhibit a larger degree of volatility than import-competing or marginal trade sectors, displaying faster and sharper changes when faced with relative price movements; however, export sectors based on natural resources, although following a similar time trend, show smoother changes than the rest. Import-competing and marginal trade activities show similar patterns of change although the latter behave more smoothly.

Export-oriented Sectors

The 1974–1978 Stage

During this period employment and output grew in most sectors. The only actual output or employment contractions are observed in the nonmetallic mineral products (362) and rubber (355) industries. The real exchange rate increased over the period, thus confronting the manufacturing industry with a relative price incentive towards export-oriented activities[2] (table 4.4). Some sectors experienced very large rates of growth of exports and imports. These rates of growth have to be understood as a movement from an initial "inward-looking" situation, where international trade transactions were almost nonexistent, to an outward-looking strategy which opened the economy to foreign competition. Thus the textile (321), clothing (322), leather (323), and footwear (324) industries underwent a major structural change during the period, developing from activities which produced for the domestic market to export orientation. As will be discussed below, the textile (321), clothing (322), leather (323), and footwear (324) industries appear as strong deviants from general patterns of behavior during this phase.

Table 4.4 Rate of growth of output, employment, exports, imports, and the real exchange rate: export sectors, 1974–1978 (percent)

ISIC code	*Output*	*Employment*	*RER*	*Exports*	*Imports*
311–2	7.4	4.7	2.0	– 23.8	23.3
321	33.1	5.4	8.9	99.6	– 37.5
322	62.0	24.0	7.0	566.3	44.5
323	61.1	45.8	18.1	2.5	18,834
324	0.5	24.0	23.3	156.3	12,750
355	10.2	– 5.7	11.4	11.6	212.3
361	17.9	7.3	28.7	53.9	907.8
362	– 2.1	7.3	25.8	211.5	252.3
369	18.2	7.3	23.2	32.4	– 31.7

The change in the real exchange rate (RER) corresponds to 1974–7. The change in employment and output for sectors 323 and 355 corresponds to 1975–8.
Sources: Banco Central del Uruguay, *Boletín Estadístico*, various issues; Dirección General de Estadística y Censos, *Encuesta Anual de Actividad Económica, Industrias Manufactureras*, various issues

The 1978–1982 Stage

During the second phase of the trade liberalization experiment, most export-oriented sectors experienced a steady downward trend in employment and output (table 4.5).[3] The real exchange rate experienced a steady

2 The sectors classified as export oriented (according to the ratio T of net trade to apparent consumption are food (311, 312), textiles (321), clothing (322), leather (323), footwear (324), rubber (355), and nonmetallic products (361, 362, 368).
3 Observe, however, that food (311, 312) and nonmetallic mineral products (361, 369), although experiencing a contraction, behaved more smoothly than the rest of the industries. This behavior could possibly be related to the natural resource base characteristic of these sectors.

Table 4.5 Rate of growth of output, employment, exports, imports, and the real exchange rate: export sectors, 1978–1982 (percent)

ISIC code	*Output*	*Employment*	*RER*	*Exports*	*Imports*
311–2	−8.8	−7.5	−40.1	62.5	10.6
321	−36.6	−31.3	−40.7	12.8	7.7
322	−57.0	−56.3	−41.7	−24.9	−21.2
323	−33.4	−46.5	−33.3	11.1	−88.4
324	−64.5	−65.2	−38.0	−75.8	−106.2
355	−57.6	−29.0	−39.2[a]	−65.2	24.8
361	−8.0	−27.0	−35.0	−48.5	92.7
362	−47.6	−29.6	−34.3	−72.1	−24.9

[a] Corresponds to the change in the real exchange rate from 1977 to 1982.
Sources: as for table 4.4

deterioration during the 1978–82 period, so that the nontraditional export sectors were faced with increasing difficulties in maintaining their competing ability in the international market. Export and import performance differed widely across sectors: most sectors experienced export and import growth until 1980–1 except for footwear (324) whose exports and imports started to decline in 1978 and 1979 respectively.

The 1974–1978 Stage

During this period employment and output exhibited an upward trend for most import-competing sectors (see table 4.4)[4] with the exception of chemical products (351, 352). However, most import-competing sectors faced a deterioration in the real exchange rate. It is very likely that, because of the high starting level of protection, trade liberalization during the first phase mostly absorbed the water in the tariffs. During the period, however, competing imports experienced a dramatic increase in metallic products (381, 382), electrical machinery and equipment (383), and to a lesser extent transportation equipment and machinery (384). Two factors may explain the growth of these sectors during this period. First, since they are relatively capital intensive, the dismantling of the import-licensing system may have allowed them to increase their efficiency. Second, exports from the import-competing sectors show remarkably high rates of growth during the 1974–8 period when they benefited from export subsidy policy – the only exception to this pattern is the transportation equipment and

4 The import-competing sectors are paper (341), chemical products (351, 352), basic metals (371, 372), metallic products (381, 382), electrical machinery and equipment (383), and transport products (384).

machinery sector (384). However, the absolute value of overall transactions remained very small.

The 1978–1982 Stage

Employment exhibited a downward trend in most sectors after reaching a peak in 1978–9, while output kept growing until 1980–1 and decreased during the rest of the period. Overall, we observe a severe output contraction between 1978 and 1982, varying from 20 to 60 percent. The real exchange rate suffered severe deterioration during the period, because of both the tariff reductions performed and the simultaneous appreciation of the Uruguayan peso against most currencies.

Competing imports reached a peak in 1979–80 within most sectors, and decreased dramatically during 1982. Electrical machinery and equipment (383) and transportation equipment and machinery (384) were those activities which experienced the sharpest increase in competing imports during the 1980–1 boom. Exports from import-competing sectors reached a peak in 1979–80 and experienced severe deterioration during the rest of the period.

Marginal Trade Sectors

The 1974–1978 Stage

Paralleling the performance of the other sectors, the marginal trade sectors[5] exhibit a pattern of steady increase in output and employment during the period (see table 4.4). The behavior of beverages (313) and tobacco (314) differs slightly from this rule, particularly with respect to employment.

In general, we observe an increase in the real exchange rate faced by marginal trade sectors; import and export flows are irrelevant for this sector. There is an increase, however, in the share of export transactions for the plastics (356) sector – again, much in the same line as observed in import-competing sectors, which benefited from high subsidies on exports during the period.

The 1978–1982 Stage

During this period marginal trade sectors is very similar to that of the import-competing sectors. Employment exhibits a downward trend in the beverages (313) and wood and furniture (331, 332) industries, while tobacco (314), printing (342), and plastics (356) reached a peak in 1980–1 and experienced a dramatic contraction afterwards. Output maintained an

5 The marginal trade sectors are beverages (313), tobacco (314), wood and furniture (331, 332), printing (342), and plastics (356).

upward trend and reached a peak in 1980–1, falling afterwards; the only exceptions were wood products (331) and furniture (332) which decreased during the whole period. The real exchange rate experienced a steady deterioration, because of both tariff reductions and the real appreciation of the Uruguayan currency during the period 1978–81. Although it recovered slightly in 1982, it kept a historically low level (see table 4.4).

The Determinants of Sectoral Response to Trade Liberalization

Wide differences in the pattern of sectoral responses to the trade liberalization experiment are documented in the previous section. In this section we assess the characteristics that affect the responses of sectors to trade liberalization. The differential sectoral responses to trade liberalization are useful for identifying the supply elasticities of different industries. Supply elasticities, however, are not random, but are related to both the specificity of the industries' assets and their technology. We adopt the industry's human and physical capital intensity as a proxy for the level of the specificity of assets. These factors, then, should explain the differential short-run responses to trade liberalization. Moreover, since it may be expected that Uruguay does not have comparative advantage in high-skilled capital intensive industries, these characteristics should also be important in assessing whether the industries that expanded were those with the highest comparative advantage, thus implying that the trade reforms may have substantially improved the allocation of resources in the economy.[6]

We analyzed the impact of those factors for the two stages of the trade liberalization period (1974–8 and 1978–82). During the first stage the real effective exchange rate for exports was being increased while water in the tariffs was being eliminated. During the second stage the real effective exchange rate for both imports and exports was being reduced, with some sectors experiencing a slighly more rapid cut in their protection levels (see discussion above).

The empirical model for assessing the effect of the sectors' characteristics on their response is

$$\%\Delta E = a + b\%\Delta \mathrm{XR} + \%\Delta\,\mathrm{XR}\,(c\mathrm{XR} + dK + eS) \qquad (4.1)$$

where $\%\Delta E$ is the percentage change in employment during a period, $\%\Delta\mathrm{XR}$ is the percentage change in exchange rate during that period, XR is the level of the real effective exchange rate at the end of the period, K is the capital intensity (measured as energy expenditure per manhour), and S

6 We also analyzed whether the degree of concentration affects the sectoral responsiveness and found its effect to be negligible. Since it does not have a clear theoretical effect, we do not discuss its role here.

is the skill level (measured as the ratio of the average salary to the minimum national wage).

The rationale for the specification of (4.1) is as follows. Let the basic relationship between employment and the real exchange rate be

$$\log E_t = A + B \log \mathrm{XR}_t + C \text{ trend} \quad (4.2)$$

Upon differentiating (4.2) between two time periods, t and t' we obtain

$$\%\Delta E = a + B\%\Delta \mathrm{XR} \quad (4.3)$$

We now let the coefficient of log XR_t in (4.2) be a function of the level of asset specificity of the industry (K and S) and also of the average level of the real exchange rate during the period (that is, in principle we would expect that, at increasingly high real effective exchange rates, a proportional increase in the exchange rate would have a smaller effect on employment); thus we let

$$B = b + c\mathrm{XR} + dK + eS \quad (4.4)$$

Substituting (4.4) into (4.3) gives (4.1).

The coefficient b in (4.1) and (4.4) represents the percentage change in employment that a percentage change in the real effective exchange rate would bring about if all industries had the same human and physical capital intensities. The coefficients d and e show the importance of the different measures of capital in determining the impact of changes in real effective exchange rate on employment. The predicted signs are then as follows: $b > 0$, $c < 0$, $d < 0$, and $e < 0$; a should be positive for the 1974–8 period but negative for the 1978–82 period. The rationale for the predicted signs of b and c is straightforward. If d and e are negative, then our conjecture that human and physical capital intensities are measures of asset specificity will not be rejected. Finally, since the 1974–8 period was one of rapid growth while during the 1978–82 period there was a severe recession, the constant a should capture part of those macroeconomic effects.

We estimated (4.1) using export and import real effective exchange rates. Since there may still be some water in the tariffs in the period 1974–8, the results using import real effective exchange rates for imports may not be as reliable. We also tested whether model (4.1) is stable across the two stages by estimating (jointly) an equation for 1974–8 and another for 1978–82, and contrasting these results with those obtained from pooling, that is, restricting all the coefficients to be the same across periods (except for the constant a which, as discussed above should have opposite signs in the two stages). We also estimated (4.1) using the percentage change in output as the dependent variable.

The results of estimating (4.1) using the export real effective exchange rate are presented in table 4.6. The "apparently by unrelated" estimation of the model for the two period is given in the second and third columns,

Table 4.6 Estimation of equation (4.1) with the percentage change in employment as the dependent variable

	Apparently unrelated[a]			*Pooled*[b]		
	1974–8		*1978–82*	*1974–8*		*1978–82*
Constant	0.16		0.06	0.16		– 0.31
	(2.76)		(0.14)	(3.01)		(– 3.03)
%ΔXR	5.62		8.63		5.44	
	(1.70)		(2.73)		(2.46)	
(%ΔXR)XR	– 2.37		0.80		0.12	
	(1.43)		(1.03)		(– 0.39)	
(%ΔXR)*K*	– 0.21		– 0.28		– 0.27	
	(– 1.44)		(– 1.97)		(– 2.68)	
(%ΔXR)*S*	– 0.64		– 1.23		– 0.81	
	(– 1.15)		(– 2.12)		(– 1.97)	
R^2	0.42		0.54	0.31		0.51
SSE		31.37			37.77	
Degrees of freedom					26	

%ΔXR, percentage change in the real effective exchange rate for exports; *K*, capital intensity measured as the expenditure in energy divided by manhours for 1978; *S* , skill level measured as the average wage as a proportion of the national minimum wage; SSE, system sum of squared errors.

[a] The estimation for the unrestricted model takes account of constancy across the residual for the two equations. *t* statistics are given in parentheses.

[b] The pooled estimation uses the variances–covariance matrix of the unrestricted estimation. *t* statistics are given in parentheses.

and the "pooled" estimation is presented in the fourth column. The restrictions implied in pooling are not rejected since the difference in the sum of squared errors fall short of the critical $\lambda^2(4)$ value.

The results presented in table 4.6 support the discussion presented above. The estimated coefficients of capital and skill intensity are both significant and negative. Therefore, industries characterized by high capital intensity or high skill use will not respond very strongly to changes in their real effective exchange rate. Moreover, this pattern of response was similar in the two stages.[7] Thus we find that an across-the-board increase in the export real effective exchange rate for exports would have generated both a short-term and a long-term increase in those sectors with low human and physical capital intensity. Since, as we discussed above, those are the export-oriented sectors, this may explain their dynamic performance during the first stage (1974–8) and their drastic contraction following the new macroeconomic stabilization policy pursued during 1978–82, which implied a substantial fall in the real effective exchange rate across most industries.

7 Except for the coefficient *c* of XR which appears to be insignificant and changes signs between the two periods.

An analysis of the residuals of equation (4.1) shows that two groups of industries could be classified as "deviant" in terms of their response. On the one hand there is a group whose responsiveness to changes in real effective exchange rates is below average – foodstuffs (311), tobacco (314), textiles (321), and other chemicals (352). These industries are either high skill or capital intensive. Foodstuffs, tobacco, and textiles are relatively intensive while "other chemicals" (mostly pharmaceuticals) and tobacco are relatively high skill industries. These industries, then, will tend to respond less to variations in their real effective exchange rate. On the other hand there is a group of industries whose responsiveness to changes in real effective exchange rates is much stronger than the average. Among those we find clothing (322), leather (323), and footwear (324); these are low skill, labor intensive industries.[8] Table 4.7 presents the estimation of equation (4.1) with changes in gross product as the dependent variable. We observe that the results of the pooled estimation are similar to those for employment. Again, industries characterized by high skill and capital use show a relatively low degree of responsiveness to changes in real effective exchange rates.

To summarize, we have found above that the exporting sectors (in particular the nontraditional sectors) exhibited a larger degree of volatility

Table 4.7 Estimation of equation (4.1) with the percentage change in gross product as the dependent variable

	Apparently unrelated		*Pooled*	
Variable	*1974–8*	*1978–82*	*1974–8*	*1978–82*
Constant	0.33	− 0.79	0.34	− 0.55
	(3.61)	(1.46)	(4.14)	(− 3.33)
%ΔXR	3.77	8.65	6.07	
	(0.69)	(2.25)	(2.24)	
(%ΔXR)XR	− 4.05	− 0.33	− 0.20	
	(− 1.43)	(− 0.32)	(− 0.52)	
(%ΔXR)*S*	− 0.34	− 1.53	− 1.02	
	(− 0.37)	(− 2.20)	(− 2.02)	
(%ΔXR)*K*	0.01	− 0.34	− 0.25	
	(0.05)	(− 1.82)	(− 1.90)	
R^2	0.29	0.50	0.10	0.45
SSE	35.99		42.59	
Degrees of freedom	13	13	30	

See table 4.6 for explanation of variables and methodology.

8 We performed a similar estimation of (4.1) using the real effective exchange rates for imports. The results were similar to those presented in table 4.11, except that the coefficient of capital intensity is positive. However, the estimation explains why changes in employment are much worse than when the export exchange rate is used, as expected in the presence of water in the tariffs.

than the import-competing or marginal trade sectors. In this section we showed that their responsiveness is related to their being less intensive in specific assets (in particular, human and physical capital) than is the case for the import-competing or marginal trade sectors.

The role of specificity in determining the responsiveness of the industrial sectors can also be derived from analyzing whether the reduction in employment that accompanied the second stage of trade liberalization was related to sectoral characteristics and changes in real effective exchange rates. To analyze this issue we use the same model as above. We define the logarithm of the maximum employment loss (MEL) to a sector as the logarithm of the ratio of its employment in 1982 to its peak employment during the second half of the 1970s. Table 4.8 shows the values of the MEL, the logarithm of the skill level, the capital intensity, and the

Table 4.8 Values of the maximum employment loss, capital intensity, skill level, and industrial concentration

ISIC code	*MEL*[a]	*Capital intensity*	*Skill*	*Herfindahl index*
311	– 0.08	4.38	5.38	1.52
313	– 0.15	4.03	5.46	3.56
314	– 0.27	4.21	6.25	5.37
321	– 0.37	4.04	5.36	2.58
322	– 0.83	2.08	5.25	1.90
323	– 0.83	3.69	5.39	3.11
324	– 1.06	2.04	5.21	1.90
331	– 0.33	3.14	5.12	2.47
341	– 0.27	4.56	5.44	4.49
342	– 0.23	2.43	5.63	3.71
351	– 0.40	4.96	5.66	2.35
352	– 0.00	3.35	5.69	2.35
353	– 0.34	5.91	5.58	6.88
356	– 0.21	3.33	5.25	2.12
361	– 0.41	3.70	5.22	3.37
362	– 0.35	5.43	5.55	3.37
369	– 0.25	5.12	5.59	3.37
371	– 0.81	4.59	5.48	4.06
372	– 0.71	4.05	5.49	4.06
381	– 0.26	3.06	5.42	2.85
383	– 0.42	3.00	5.40	2.98
384	0.08	2.92	5.61	3.46
390	– 0.93	2.33	5.17	2.22

[a] Logarithm of the ratio of employment in 1982 to peak employment in the period 1977–82.

Sources: Banco Central del Uruguay, *Boletín Estadístico*, various issues; Dirección General de Estadística y Censos, *Anuario Estadístico*, various issues

industrial concentration (Herfindahl index). We observe that the MEL is positively related to skills, with no clear pattern being discerned from the other variables. This result is further confirmed in table 4.9, where we present the results of regressing MEL of the percentage change in the real effective exchange rate from 1978 to 1982 and its cross products with skill level, capital intensity, and industrial concentration. As above, we find that, for constant reduction in the real effective exchange rate, the sectors that developed larger employment losses were those with low skilled and low capital intensity. This result is consistent with the finding that those sectors have a much more elastic supply than the sectors with high skill and high capital intensity.

The results presented in this section show that many of the most dynamic sectors (that is, with relatively elastic supplies) are export oriented. Thus the opening of the economy should have a strong expansive effect on export-oriented sectors, while the contraction of import-competing sectors would be less drastic.

Table 4.9 Estimation of equation (4.1) with the maximum employment loss as the dependent variable

Variable	*I*[a]	*II*[a]
%ΔXR[b]	7.33	6.04
	(1.57)	(1.68)
(%ΔXR)*S*	– 1:34	– 1.10
	(– 1.48)	(– 1.54)
(%ΔXR)*K*	– 0.20	– 0.13
	(– 1.0)	(– 0.85)
(%ΔXR)*H*	0.21	– 0.01
	(0.87)	(– 0.05)
Constant	– 0.43	– 0.62
	(– 1.34)	(– 4.85)
R^2	0.23	0.35

S, skill; *K*, capital intensity;*H*, Herfindahl index.

[a] column I, results using export real effective exchange rate; column II, results using import real effective exchange rate.

[a] %ΔDR, percentage change in real effective exchange rate from 1978 to 1982 for exports and from 1978 to 1981 for imports.

Tariff Reform and Policy Coordination

In this section we analyze some of the crucial aspects of the trade liberalization process as they relate to its timing and sequencing, and, with hindsight, try to assess whether it could have been improved upon.

There are five main sequencing aspects of the Uruguayan trade liberalization experiment. First, it was introduced following a drastic fall in the terms of trade as a consequence of the oil shock of 1973. Second, its first stage consisted of removal of the import-licensing system and of the introduction of an export promotion program. Third, it consisted of a relatively long process with a measured and gradual pace, starting with the introduction of the export promotion in 1974 which was followed by the staged tariff reduction plan of 1978. Fourth, it was introduced after the opening of the capital account. Finally, it was accompanied by the use of the exchange rate as an anti-inflationary instrument from 1978 to 1982.

In the next section we will perform a tentative evaluation of the above features of the Uruguayan experiment.

The Timing of the Introduction

In the absence of a policy to open the economy, the adverse terms of trade resulting from the oil shock of 1973 and the sharp reduction in agricultural products exports to Europe would have implied a substantial reduction in the level of domestic activity. Given that Uruguay had stagnated since the mid-1950s, such a reduction in the level of domestic activity would have implied substantial political risks. Instead, by choosing to open the economy the administration was able to generate a period of seven years of sustained growth and investment (see table 2.1). Thus, it seems that the timing of liberalization was right. It provided the opportunity to avoid a severe contraction in domestic activity and to start a period of sustained growth.

It has been claimed that only a military regime could have undertaken such a trade liberalization policy. However, the drastic fall in terms of trade made income redistribution through foreign trade restrictions a very expensive policy. If political systems choose their income redistribution policies taking into account their relative costs, then the political demands for foreign trade restrictions should have fallen and any politically sensitive government would have made some adjustments toward opening the economy.

An Assessment of the Quota Removal Process

One of the first measures taken by the new economic team of Vegh Villegas was to remove the import-licensing system. This measure was crucial in several respects. First, since by 1974 the capital stock of the economy was substantially depreciated, the opening of the economy required a substantial increase in investment. Further, since a successful trade liberalization policy required a change in the industrial output mix, this would also require a substantial increase in imports of machinery and new intermediate products. Thus maintaining the quota system would have limited the ability of the exporting firms to invest and to adjust to the new incentives, affecting the success of the trade liberalization program. Also, the elimination of the quota system allowed the import-competing sectors to become more efficient, which in turn was translated into an increase in output during the first phase of the trade liberalization equipment, even in the face of an increase in competing imports. Thus, we can conclude that relaxation of import quotas was a successful and timely measure.

An Assessment of the Export Promotion Policy and the Speed of Liberalization

Export promotion policies can be useful instruments in a trade liberalization experiment if they are structured so as to compensate for the export tax implicit in import tariffs. Since the implicit tax is of a general equilibrium nature, the estimation of the proper set of export subsidies is, to say the least, an extremely cumbersome task. The Uruguayan export promotion policy of 1974–8 was very discriminatory. On the one hand traditional exports were not allowed to receive direct *reintegros*.[9] Furthermore, during the period, traditional exports were actually taxed. On the other hand, the *reintegros* varied in their importance, reaching above 80 percent of the activity's value added for some selected sectors. In 1975 it was announced that the *reintegros* were to be phased out, initially by 1978. However, the final elimination of the *reintegro* was postponed, although by 1979 most of the substantial *reintegros* were already eliminated. Although discriminated against, the traditional exports faced a relatively stable real effective exchange rate until 1979. However, the nontraditional sector's real effective exchange rate increased from 1974 to 1975 but fell systematically from then on (see table 3.6).

Since it is difficult to evaluate how much each specific sector was affected by the discriminatory characteristics of the export subsidy program, we compare the program's effects with those of a hypothetical neutral program with export subsidies and taxes structured so that all sectors would have had the same real effective exchange rate as the average sector during the period 1974–8.

A uniform export subsidy program of this sort would increase the exports in those sectors that have a relatively elastic supply.[10] We found

9 *Reintegros* were paid through certificates which could be used to pay corporation taxes or social security taxes

10 A "uniform" export promotion policy means a uniform exchange rate insofar as purchasing power parity holds. If it does not, then to follow a "uniform" export promotion policy the government may have to discriminate to account for differences in domestic and international prices. In what follows we assume that purchasing parity holds.

evidence earlier in the chapter that, for the Uruguayan case, the industrial sectors with the lowest supply elasticity are among those that benefited from import substitution policies (that is, sectors intensive in physical and human capital). Thus, a uniform export promotion policy would produce a contraction in import substitution sectors but an expansion in sectors having relatively large supply elasticities which were driven out of export markets by the implicit export tax involved in import substitution.

This result is supported by analyzing the response of sectoral exports to changes in the sector's real effective exchange rate for both periods. Using the same equation as in table 4.6, we present in table 4.10 the regression of the percentage change in exports on the change in the real effective exchange rate for the sector and on the sector's characteristics. Again, we find that exports are more sensitive to changes in real effective exchange rates for those sectors that are not intensive in human capital.

Table 4.10 Estimation of equation (4.1) with the percentage change in exports as the dependent variable

	1974–8		*1978–82*	
Variable	*I*	*II*	*III*	*IV*
Constant	0.70	0.71	2.59	2.45
	(1.71)	(1.66)	(1.84)	(2.00)
%ΔXR[a]	17.00	13.40	12.34	23.70
	(0.73)	(0.52)	(1.20)	(2.29)
(%ΔXR)XR	27.20	26.80	4.89	4.62
	(2.23)	(2.10)	(1.86)	(2.02)
(%ΔXR)*S*	− 4.78	− 3.78	− 1.05	− 3.67
	(− 1.22)	(− 0.78)	(− 0.55)	(− 1.79)
(%ΔXR)*K*	− 1.78	− 1.79	0.04	− 0.10
	(− 1.74)	(− 1.69)	(0.09)	(− 0.26)
(%ΔXR)*H*[b]	—	− 0.52	—	1.08
	—	(− 0.39)	—	(2.14)
R^2	0.47	0.48	0.32	0.53
Degrees of freedom	11.00	10.00	11.00	10.00

—, not applicable.
[a] For definition of the variables see table 4.6.
[b] *H*, logarithm of the Herfindhal index.

Table 4.6 can also be used to estimate the effect on sectoral employment from following, during the 1974–8 period, an export subsidy program that would equalize each sector's real effective exchange rate to the actual average. This estimation is performed by substituting the average changes and levels of effective exchange rates for the values of the individual sectors. If we compare the estimated changes in employment with the actual changes, we find the effects on the different sectors from following a discriminatory export promotion policy. To assess whether the discriminatory policy was in effect worse than a neutral policy, two tests are proposed. First, we calculate the average (simple and weighted) change in total employment that could have been achieved from following a "neutral" policy. Second, we analyze the characteristics of the sectors most affected.

Table 4.11 presents the employment gain that could have been achieved in each sector in the period 1974–8 if the export promotion program had been "neutral." The industries are classified according to whether they are in the exporting, importing, or marginal trade sectors (as derived from the *T* value in 1982), and the average weighted gain in employment obtained from following a "neutral" policy is calculated. We find that, for the period 1974–8, while the import-competing sector would not have been benefited from following a "neutral" policy,[11] the exporting and the marginal trade sectors would have benefited substantially. In particular, on average both the exporting and the marginal trade sectors would have been able to increase their employment by 8 percent during the period if the export promotion program had been "neutral." Since these are the sectors that have to expand in a trade liberalization program, table 4.11 suggests that the actual export promotion policy of 1974–8 may have discriminated against those sectors that could have generated the largest increase in both employment and exports.

Therefore we can conclude that the export promotion policy, while not necessarily being a failure, could have been substantially improved upon.

Table 4.11 Percentage gain in employment from a "neutral" export promotion policy, 1974–1978

Exporting		*Marginal Trade*		*Import competing*	
Gain	*ISIC*	*Gain*	*ISIC*	*Gain*	*ISIC*
0.098	311	0.202	313	– 0.059	341
0.108	321	0.116	314	0.089	351
0.038	322	0.024	342	0.150	352
0.43	324	0.019	369	– 0.013	381
0.121	361			0.033	383
0.011	362			– 0.296	384
Weighted average	0.087	0.097		0.002	
Simple average	0.082	0.074		– 0.038	

The classification is based on the *t* values for 1982.

11 Actually, some of the sectors that seem to have experienced a large employment gain from the discriminatory policy are among the import-competing sectors, like transport products (384).

In particular, it would have increased the output of the exporting sectors, which in the long run are the sectors that should expand following a successful trade liberalization program.

The speed of implementing a trade liberalization policy is important insofar as there are costs in moving from one sector to another. The largest adjustment costs are for those industries with assets which are industry specific. Human and capital intensity have been identified above as proxies for the specificity of the assets of an industry, since the elasticity of supply of the Uruguayan industries seems to be negatively related to those factors (see table 4.6).

Trade liberalization implies that the sectors with the lowest comparative advantage are those that should contract. For the Uruguayan case, however, those are sectors with relatively low short-run supply elasticity. Consequently, the reduction in their employment should not be too large in the short run. Thus a faster process would have been adequate. In particular, if the policy of export promotion had been coupled with a tariff reduction program, the short-run reduction in employment may not have been substantial.[12]

An Assessment of the Opening of the Capital Account

In 1974, before the trade liberalization process started, the capital account was fully liberalized. This was performed while the fiscal deficit was 2.8 percent of GDP (its average for the period 1972–4). Many economists have argued that under those circumstances the opening of the capital account would have a negative effect on the eventual success of a subsequent trade liberalization. Their argument is as follows. Opening the capital account first would generate an inflow of foreign capital which would, in turn, appreciate the domestic currency, whereas a real depreciation is required for a successful trade liberalization.

The Uruguayan experience does not fit the "current account first" scenario. Following the opening of the capital account, the domestic currency experienced a real depreciation which lasted until 1978. There are two probable reasons for this phenomenon. First, the expansionary effect of the capital inflow was balanced by a reduction in the fiscal deficit. Second, as has been seen, export subsidies were extensively used during the period. Moreover, while capital inflow started from the beginning of the trade liberalization experiment, the large inflow did not start until 1978–9, four years after the capital account was liberalized (see table 2.6). During that same period real investment was at record levels (see table 2.1). Thus there is no strong evidence that the opening of the capital

12 However, the quantitative aspect of this statement cannot be answered without a more detailed analysis of the behavior of the different sectors.

account had a negative impact on the performance of the liberalization process during the period 1974–8. Furthermore, it has ameliorated the transition costs towards an open economy.

We can also ask what the performance of the economy would have been during the period 1974–8 if the capital account had been closed. While this question cannot be fully answered without a detailed macroeconomic analysis, we propose to analyze it in a very narrow way by looking at its effect on the real interest rate and the real exchange rate.

Since during the period government deficits were, on average, 1.3 percent of GDP while the current account deficit was of the order of 5.5 percent of GDP, domestic savings fell short of private investments plus government deficit by approximately 4 percent of GDP. Thus, in the absence of an inflow of foreign capital, the gap between investment and savings would have had to be closed by an increase in the domestic real interest rate or by a further depreciation of the exchange rate. De Melo and Tybout (1985) have estimated the equation for the supply of private savings for the period 1974–83. They showed that, while the effect of the real interest rate on savings is negative, it is very small and statistically insignificant. In contrast, the real exchange rate seems to have a positive impact on savings.

Thus, if savings have to be increased by 4 percent of GDP, domestic interest rates would have to increase substantially or the real exchange rate would have to undergo a dramatic depreciation. Both policies would have a negative impact on the prospects for a successful liberalization experiment.

To summarize, there is no evidence that opening the capital account first had a negative impact on the performance of the liberalization experiment, at least up to 1978. From 1979 on, the use of the exchange rate as an anti-inflationary instrument may, as we will discuss below, have had a negative impact on the liberalization experiment by substantially appreciating the real exchange rate.

An Assessment of the Use of the Exchange Rate as an Anti-inflationary Instrument

Starting in October 1978 the Central Bank pre-announced the future value of the exchange rate with the intention of reducing, over time, the rate of devaluation. This policy was carried out during a period of substantial inflow of foreign capital, much of which was in the form of direct investments. A real appreciation of the exchange rate followed. That the appreciation of the real exchange rate was an important factor in the subsequent reduction in exports that followed can be seen from table 4.12. This table uses the estimates of the employment equations as reported in table 4.6 to predict what the employment levels of each industrial sector

Table 4.12 Percentage gain in employment from a constant real exchange rate policy

Exporting		*Marginal trade*		*Import competing*	
ISIC	*Gain*	*ISIC*	*Gain*	*ISIC*	*Gain*
311	0.027	313	– 0.038	341	– 0.067
321	– 0.006	314	– 0.128	351	– 0.091
322	0.025	362	– 0.161	352	– 0.045
324	0.147	369	– 0.202	381	– 0.017
				383	0.179
				384	– 0.029

Source: derived from table 4.9, column II

would have been if, given the path of trade liberalization, the real exchange rates during the period 1978–82 had been maintained at their 1978 levels. That is, let $(1 + T_{it})\ E_tP^*/P_{it}$ be the real exchange rate for sector i in period t, where T represents the level of protection and EP^*/P is the ratio of foreign to domestic prices. Then, we stimulate the change in employment from 1978 to 1982 if the real effective rate for sector t in 1982 had been $(1 + T_{i82})\ E_{78}P^*_{i78}/P_{i78}$. We compare this simulated change in employment from 1978 to 1982 with that which is predicted from table 4.6 when the real effective exchange rate attains its true historical values.

We observe that, if the real exchange rate had not appreciated as much as it did during the period 1978–82, employment in most of the exporting sectors would have expanded while employment in most of the remaining industrial sectors would have contracted even further. Thus the drop in the real exchange rate during 1978–82 may have been responsible for a large part of the stagnation of nontraditional exports during this period.

A further test of this hypothesis can be performed by analyzing industrial layoffs. Since we lack information on sectoral layoffs, we use as a proxy the difference between the maximum and the actual level of employment for those years after employment reached a peak. However, this measure of sectoral layoffs does not make allowance for the fact that individuals laid off from one industry do not necessarily remain unemployed.

In table 4.13 we analyze the attributes of those industries which started contracting as early as 1979. As observed, they are predominantly export oriented, relatively low in capital intensity and in labor skill intensity, and they exhibit low degrees of concentration. In 1980 we have to add to the contracting sector the oil refining (353) and basic metals (371) industries, which are capital intensive and labor skill intensive industries with high concentration ratios, and are respectively marginal trade and import competing according to their t statistic classification.

Table 4.13 Attributes of sectors that experienced a contraction during 1979

ISIC	*T*	*K/L*	*S*	*H*
311–2	−17.5	18	8	4.6
313	1.1	14	13	35.4
321	−31.1	15	7	13.2
3222	−10.1	2	5	6.7
323	49.5	12	9	22.4
324	−41.1	1	3	6.7
331–2	−1.9	8	1	11.8
351	61.5	21	22	10.5
352	9.3	10	23	10.5
381–2	39.3	7	11	17.3
383	30.0	6	10	19.8

T, net trade divided by apparent consumption; *K/L*, capital labor ratio ordered by rank; *S*, labor skills index ordered by rank; *H*, Herfindahl concentration ratio index.
Source: Favaro and Spiller, 1988, appendix tables 2.13–2.15

While it is difficult to make a precise estimation of that proportion of layoffs which is attributable to trade liberalization policy with respect to that which can be explained as a result of the business cycle, in this section we attempt to elaborate on this point by making use of information on unemployment levels by sector (Favaro and Spiller, 1988, appendix table 4.18). In table 4.14 we compare the level of layoffs for the total industrial sector with the sum of individual sector layoffs estimated using the previous methodology. The table suggests that a significant part of the estimated sectoral layoffs does not show up as a net employment loss at the industry aggregate level; rather, it mirrors a reallocation of the labor force within the economy as a result of major changes in relative prices occurring during the period. The ratio SSL/TL is also a proxy for the incidence of macroeconomic versus trade liberalization policy measures in generating unemployment. When the index SSL/TL differs significantly from unity, although macroeconomic shocks may remain an important source of

Table 4.14 Total layoffs versus sum of sectoral layoffs, 1979–1982 (number of individuals)

Concept	*1979*	*1980*	*1981*	*1982*
Sum of sectoral layoffs (SSL)	10,423	13,033	20,198	49,067
Total layoffs (TL)	6,980	6,799	13,212	42,264
SSL/TL	1.49	1.92	1.53	1.16

Source: Favaro and Spiller, 1988, appendix table 4.18

explanation of the path of employment, relative price changes resulting from trade liberalization or other sectoral policy measures represent a major factor in explaining movements in sectoral employment. When the index SSL/TL approaches unity, there is evidence that all sectors are moving their employment levels in the same direction, and hence there is reason to presume that a common monetary or real shock rather than a sector-specific shock, is causing changes in employment.[13]

While the exchange rate policy of 1978–82 may have generated much of the period's real appreciation, regional developments may also have contributed substantially. In particular, because of Uruguay's small size and its bilateral trade agreements with Argentina and Brazil, trade in "nontradeables" and in "import-competing" goods may develop. Thus the price of nontradeables and labor in Uruguay is strongly affected by the price of nontradeables and the real exchange rate in Argentina and Brazil. Therefore the appreciation of the Argentinian currency following 1978 resulted in an increase in the demand for Uruguayan nontradeables, inducing a parallel appreciation of Uruguay's real exchange rates. This appreciation was further exacerbated by an open capital account and an exchange rate policy targeted towards reducing the level of domestic inflation.

To summarize, much of the economic downturn that developed by the end of the 1970s seems to have been generated by a common macroeconomic shock rather than by the trade liberalization policy. While part of this shock may have been imported, the remainder seems to have been the result of an exchange rate policy concerned more with domestic price stability than with exchange rate stability.

Final Comments

The trade liberalization experience initiated in 1974 has had major consequences on the country's economic performance. It provides a rich episode illustrating the relevance of trade policy in reallocating resources and promoting economic growth. It also shows the complexity associated with the policy coordination and timing aspects of a tariff reduction program.

While Uruguay's experience in the two decades before 1974 had been characterized by stagnation, the economy's reaction following the oil shock of 1973 and the policy reforms implemented in its aftermath was dramatic. A deep external crisis followed the increase in oil prices and the closure of the EEC beef market to Uruguayan exports. This crisis, and an increas-

13 A more precise statement should make allowance for changes in employment within other sectors of the economy, namely services and agriculture.

ingly critical view of the import substitution policies of the 1940s and 1950s, influenced a change in the military government's view. While it initially relied on exchange controls and quantity regulations, it now moved to open the economy.

The elimination of quantity restrictions on imports, price controls and administrative restrictions on capital goods imports, and price controls and administrative restrictions on capital goods imports, together with the change in relative prices following the new policies of tariff reductions, exchange rate management, and export subsidies, increased factor productivity across the board. This, in turn, resulted in an expansion of the country's exports and resumption of economic growth. As a result, the economy experienced sustained export-led growth from 1974 to 1978. It also diversified its exports from a few agricultural products to a highly spread base where industrial products played a dominant role.

From 1979 to 1982 major changes in both regional circumstances and domestic policies slowed down the process of trade liberalization. This brought a transitory reversion in the process of export-led growth. However, the economy never returned to the highly concentrated export base of 1973.

The success of the trade liberalization process in reallocating resources toward export-oriented activities shows the relevance of trade policies in increasing the efficiency of a small economy. However, the failure of the trade liberalization reforms in providing further aggregate structural changes to the economy testifies to the importance of policy coordination and external circumstances more than to the direct effect of the tariff reductions implemented from 1979 to 1982.

There are reasons for believing that a somewhat different combination of trade, fiscal, and exchange rate policy could have avoided, at least partially, the damaging effects of the post-1978 developments. An increase in the speed of trade liberalization before 1978 would not have substantially increased unemployment in the short run. At the same time, it would have accelerated the development of new exporting industries which, because of the implicit tax inherent in a system of protection, did not exist before. Both developments should have generated further support for trade liberalization and promoted its stability. Furthermore, by deepening the process for trade liberalization at its earlier stages, the economy would have opened further, increasing its links with the world economy and reducing the importance of the links with Brazil and Argentina. This could have reduced the negative effects of the erratic swings in the Argentine real exchange rate and ameliorated the economic downturn experienced in the early 1980s.

The recovery of 1986–7 and the most recent reduction in growth are examples of the significance of regional events on the performance of the local economy. During 1986 the economy benefited by two favorable externals shocks. First, the decline in the price of oil and the fall in interest rates increased national income. Second, an upsurge in regional demand increased trade with neighboring countries. This led to a rapid recovery from the recession that started in 1982 with an external and fiscal crisis. The increase in regional trade was associated with the implementation of stabilization programs in Argentina and Brazil. These reforms included a currency reform and implied an appreciation of both currencies *vis-à-vis* the Uruguayan peso.

Regional shocks parallel domestic aggregate demand in their effect on marginal trade and export-competing activities. An increase in domestic aggregate demand, however, usually has a current account deficit as a counterpart. In contrast, positive regional shocks improve the current account, although the peso tends to appreciate *vis-à-vis* the currencies of other trading partners.

The importance of regional trade and the instability of the Argentine and Brazilian economies in the last decade are the key to understanding the performance of trade liberalization experiment. In the short run Uruguay can hardly neglect regional circumstances when initiating a major policy reform. In the long run, the economy will parallel that of its neighbors unless it strengthens its links with the world economy.

The experience of the Uruguayan economy also shows the importance of policy coordination for the success of a trade liberalization experiment. Although trade liberalization attempted to improve the terms of trade in favor of export-oriented industries, the combination of exchange rate policy, regional events, and tariff reduction resulted in a move in exactly the opposite direction.

The effect of opening the capital account prior to the liberalization of current account transactions appears to have been of minor significance in the performance of the economy. Although the liberalization of capital movements dates back to 1974, the domestic currency did not experience a real appreciation up to 1979. The significant capital inflow received from 1979 to 1981 was more probably the consequence of the interplay of domestic expectations and exchange rate policies than a true exogenous shock favored by prevailing capital account conditions.

In summary, this trade liberalization experiment provides important lessons for both the timing of a tariff reform and the coordination with other policies. The assessment of the experiment is mixed: on the one hand, the reforms implemented in 1974–8 had important and lasting effects. They were introduced at an appropriate time, they substantially simplified an extremely complex trade regime, they helped to develop a whole new set of exporting industries and to increase the efficiency of the industrial sector, and they changed the structure of the export sector and promoted growth in the midst of a depressed world economy. However, the speed of implementation, the coordination of tariff reductions with the export subsidy policy, and its coordination with macroeconomic policies could have been substantially improved. Finally, the design of exchange rate policy from 1979 to 1982 under the prevailing regional and international circumstances seems to have had a major role in the reversion of some of the most important trends experienced during the initial years of the trade liberalization experiment.

Thus the Uruguayan case shows, perhaps in a dramatic way, how the success and failure of a trade liberalization experience depends crucially on its coordination with macroeconomic and exchange rate policies.

References

Banco Central del Uruguay, *Boletín Estadístico*, various issues. Montevideo: Banco Central.

Banco Central del Uruguay, *Formación Bruta de Capital*, various issues. Montevideo: Banco Central.

Bancro Central del Uruguay, *Indicadores de la Actividad Económica-Financiera*, various issues. Montevideo: Banco Central.

Banco Central del Uruguay, *Producto e Ingreso Nacionales*, various issues. Montevideo: Banco Central.

Bension, Alberto and Jorge Caumont (1981) "Uruguay: alternative trade strategies and employment implications." In Anne O. Krueger et al., eds, *Trade and Employment in Developing Countries*, vol. 1, *Individual Studies*. Chicago, IL: University of Chicago Press for National Bureau of Economic Research.

Cámara Nacional de Comercio (1986) *La Tasa de Retorno al Capital en el Uruguay*. Montevideo: Cámara Nacional de Comercio.

Centro de Investigaciones Económicas (CINVE) (1984) *Protección Efectiva en el Uruguay*. Montevideo: CINVE.

de Melo, Jaime and James Tybout (1985) "The effects of financial liberalization on savings and investment in Uruguay." Washington, DC: World Bank, Development Research Department.

DGEC, *Anuario Estadístico*, various issues. Montevideo: DGEC.

DGEC, *Encuesta Anual de Actividad Económica, Industrias Manufactureras*, various issues. Montevideo: DGEC.

Díaz, Ramón (1979) "Siglo y medio de economía uruguaya." *Busqueda*, 86, 3. Montevideo.

DREC Dirección General de Estadística y Censos) (1968, 1978) *Censos Económicos Nacionales, Industrias Manufactureras*. Montevideo: DGEC.

Favaro, E. and P. T. Spiller (1988) "The timing and sequencing of trade liberalization policies: Uruguay, statistical appendix." Available from the Brazil Department, World Bank, Washington, DC.

Finch, Henry (1980) *Historia Económica del Uruguay Moderno*. Montevideo: Ediciones Banda Oriental.

García, I. (1985) *Situación Financiera del Gobierno*. Montevideo: Comisión Económica para América Latina.

Harberger, Arnold and Daniel Wisecarver (1978) *Private and Social Rates of Return to Capital in Uruguay*. Montevideo: Banco Central del Uruguay.

IMF (International Monetary Fund) *International Financial Statistics*, various issues. Washington, DC: IMF

Instituto de Economía (1968) *Estadísticas Básicas*. Montevideo: Universidad de la República.

Stigler, George J. (1983) *The Organization of Industry*, 2nd edn. Chicago, IL: University of Chicago Press.

Index